Unification of Tort Law: Damages

Principles of European Tort Law **Volume 5**

Other titles in this series:

The Limits of Liability: Keeping the Floodgates Shut – Edited by J. Spier – 1996 – ISBN 90-411-0169-1

The Limits of Expanding Liability: Eight Fundamental Cases in a Comparative Perspective – Edited by J. Spier – 1998 – ISBN 90-411-0581-6

Unification of Tort Law: Wrongfulness – Edited by H. Koziol – 1998 – ISBN 90-411-1019-4

Unification of Tort Law: Causation – Edited by J. Spier – 2000 – ISBN 90-411-1325-8

Unification of Tort Law: Damages

U. Magnus (Editor)

F. D. Busnelli / G. Comandé
H. A. Cousy / A. Vanderspikken
S. Galand-Carval
K. Kerameus
H. Koziol
U. Magnus
J. Neethling
W. V. H. Rogers
G. Schwartz
M. H. Wissink / W. H. van Boom

KLUWER LAW INTERNATIONAL
THE HAGUE – LONDON – BOSTON

Published by Kluwer Law International
P.O. Box 85889
2508 CN The Hague, The Netherlands

Sold and distributed in North, Central and South America by
Kluwer Law International
675 Massachusetts Avenue
Cambridge, MA 02139, USA

Sold and distributed in all other countries by
Kluwer Law International
Distribution Centre
P.O. Box 322
3300 AH Dordrecht, The Netherlands

Library of Congress Cataloging-in-Publication Data is available

This book is published with the financial support of the Austrian Ministry of Science, the Austrian Ministry of Justice and the Swiss Ministry of Justice.

Printed on acid-free paper

ISBN: 90-411-1481-5

Kluwer Law International incorporates the publishing programmes of Graham & Trotman Ltd., Kluwer Law and Taxation Publishers and Martinus Nijhoff Publishers

Printed in Great Britain by Antony Rowe Limited.

Preface

This book is a further – now the fifth – volume of the series 'Unification of Tort Law' by which the European Group on Tort Law (the former Tilburg Group) continuously publishes the results of its work.[1] This is done with the financial support of the Austrian Ministry of Science, the Austrian Ministry of Justice and the Swiss Ministry of Justice.

The Group has been founded in 1993 by Prof. Jaap Spier (formerly Tilburg, now Advocate General at the Netherlands Supreme Court, the Hoge Raad).

In the last years the Group has been considerably enlarged. Its members now represent the EU member staates, other European countries and potential EU members states and countries with special experience to merge different legal cultures:

Francesco BUSNELLI (Pisa),
Suzanne CARVAL (Paris),
Giovanni COMANDÉ (Pisa),
Herman COUSY (Leuven),
Bill W. DUFWA (Stockholm),
Michael G. FAURE (Maastricht),
Israel GILEAD (Jerusalem),
Konstantinos KERAMEUS (Athens),
Helmut KOZIOL (Vienna),
Ulrich MAGNUS (Hamburg),
Miquel MARTIN-CASALS (Girona),
Jorge SINDE MONTEIRO (Coimbra),
Johann NEETHLING (Pretoria),
Mirosław NESTEROWICZ and Ewa BAGIŃSKA (Toruń),
W.V. Horton ROGERS (Nottingham),
Gary T. SCHWARTZ (Los Angeles),
Lubo TICHY (Prague),
Geneviève VINEY (Paris),
Pierre WIDMER (Lausanne),
Michael WILL (Geneva).

The aim of the European Group on Tort Law is to find, develop and formulate common European principles of tort law. The method of the Group's work is described in greater detail elsewhere.[2] Suffice it here to say that the Group decided to split up the general tort law into separate elements like wrongfulness, causation, damages etc. and to prepare at first

1 The former volumes are: Spier (Ed.), The Limits of Liability. Keeping the Floodgates Shut (1996); Spier (Ed.), The Limits of Expanding Liability (1998); Koziol (Ed.), Unification of Tort Law: Wrongfulness (1998); Koziol (Ed.), Unification of Tort Law: Causation (2000) (all volumes are published with Kluwer Law International, the Hague).

2 *See* Spier/Haazen, The European Group on Tort Law ('Tilburg Group') and the European Principles of Tort Law, Zeitschrift für Europäisches Privatrecht (ZeuP) 1999, 469.

a comparison for each. For damages this volume presents the outcome of this work. The starting point was a questionnaire (see below p. 3) which the Group had agreed upon and which formed the basis of the ten country reports (see below pp. 7 et seq.). As was the case with the preceding projects the questionnaire contained on the one hand questions of a general and abstract nature, on the other hand a number of concrete cases in order to combine both conceptual and practical considerations. On the basis of all country reports, then, a general comparative report had been prepared (see below p. 185) and after discussion agreed upon by the whole Group and even by those members who were not able to deliver themselves a country report. The comparative report then founded the basis of the formulation of a draft of common principles which will be published soon.

In an early stage it was thought that the damages project should fully include the topic of immaterial loss. But this aspect developed to a project of its own under the guidance of Prof. Horton Rogers. Its results will be published separately.

Ulrich Magnus
Hamburg, July 2000

Contents

Questionnaire on the Law of Damages **3**

Austria (Helmut Koziol, Vienna)

Part I – General questions on the law of damages

1. The aims of the law of damages 7
2. The general principles of the law of damages 8
   (a) Complete or limited compensation? 8
   (b) Restitution in kind and compensation in money 9
3. Different forms of damages 9
4. General or specific legislation on the law and/or measurement of damages 10
5. Notion of damage 10
6. Different types of damage 10
   (a) Damage in reality 11
   (b) Patrimonial damage by way of calculation 11
   (c) Non-patrimonial damage 11
   (d) Distinction between patrimonial and non-patrimonial damage 12
7. Assessment of non-patrimonial damage 13
   (a) Measure of non-patrimonial damage 13
   (b) Different heads of non-pecuniary loss 13
8. Calculation of the recoverable patrimonial damage 14
   (a) Objective-abstract calculation of actual loss 14
   (b) Subjective-concrete calculation of pecuniary interest 14
   (c) Expenses for restoration 15
9. Compensation of the following losses when no other actual damage is present .. 15
   (a) Pure loss of use 15
   (b) Pure loss of earning capacity 15
   (c) Pure loss of holiday or free time 16
   (d) Damage to things which remain unrepaired 16
   (e) Expenses which become frustrated by the tortious act 16
10. Compensation for emotional shock and loss of consortium 17
11. Compensation for illegitimate losses 17
12. Special rules for the compensation of collective damages 17
13. Special rules for the compensation of ecological damage 18
14. The harm done to the victim causes him an advantage as well 18
   (a) Objective-abstract calculation 18
   (b) Subjective-concrete calculation 18
15. Rules on certainty of damage 18
16. Compensation awarded as rent or as lump sum 19

Part II – Cases

1. Wrongful birth case 19
   (a) Maintenance for the child 19
   (b) Lost earnings 20

(c) Pain and suffering 20
2. Wrongful life case 20
(a) Claim of the mother 20
(b) Claim of the child 20
3. Eye injury 21
4. Costs for hospital visits and adaptation of house 21
(a) Hospital visits of the wife 21
(b) Adaptation of the house 21
5. Scar case 21
6. Continued payment of wages 22
7. Monk case 22
8. Lost earning capacity 22
9. Lost spouse/partner 23
10. Offending publication 23
11. Rosenkavalier case 23
12. Prostitute case 24
13. Mercedes case 24
14. Loss of use 24
15. Damaged, but unrepaired car 24
16. Additional car damage 25
17. Damaged railway wagon 25
18. Detective case 25
19. Death of parents 26

Belgium (H. A. Cousy and Anja Vanderspikken, Leuven)

Part I – General questions
1. Aims of the law of damages 27
(a) The law of torts 27
(b) The law of contracts 27
2. General principles of the law of damages 29
3. Different forms of damages 30
(a) With regard to punitive or exemplary damages 30
(b) With regard to 'nominal damages' 30
4. Legislation on damages 30
5. Definition of recoverable damage 31
6. Different types of damages 31
7. Monetary assessment of non-patrimonial damage 31
8. Calculation of patrimonial damage 32
(a) Subjective/objective, abstract/concrete method 32
(b) Main principles on the calculation of compensation 32
(c) The moment at which the amount of damage is assessed 32
(d) The capitalisation method 33
(e) Which factors play a role ? 33
9. Compensation for particular kinds of losses 33
10. Compensation for emotional shock and loss of consortium 34

11. Compensation of illegitimate losses . . . 34
12. Compensation of collective damage . . . 34
13. Special rules on compensation of ecological damage . . . 35
(a) The rule that damage must be personally incurred and certain . . . 35
(b) Calculation of the compensation for ecological damage . . . 36
(c) An application . . . 37
14. Harm causing also advantages . . . 37
(a) General conditions to be fulfilled for taking into account the advantages rendered to the victim . . . 37
(b) Classifcation . . . 37
15. Certainty of damage . . . 38
(a) Future damages . . . 38
(b) Hypothetical damage . . . 40
(c) Other aspects on certainty . . . 40

Part II – Cases
1. Wrongful birth case . . . 40
2. Wrongful life case . . . 40
(a) The wrongful life action of the child . . . 40
(b) The wrongful birth claim of the parents . . . 41
3. Eye injury . . . 41
4. Costs for hospital visits and of adaptation of house . . . 42
(a) Adaptation of the house . . . 42
(b) Costs for hospital visits . . . 42
5. Scar case . . . 42
6. Continued payment of wages . . . 42
7. Monk case . . . 43
8. Lost earning capacity . . . 43
(a) General remarks on the compensation for permanent invalidity . . . 43
(b) Specific remarks with regard to the permanent incapacity sustained by children and students . . . 44
(c) Basis of calculation if a were the 6 year old child of a family with a low income, a having shown quite normal abilities so far. . . . 45
(d) B's negligence leading to a's being rendered clinically dead . . . 45
9. Lost spouse / partner . . . 45
(a) General principles . . . 45
(b) Non-marital partner . . . 45
(c) A's husband who maintained the household is killed in an accident for which B is responsible . . . 46
10. Offending publication . . . 47
11. Rosenkavalier case . . . 47
12. Prostitute case . . . 47
13. Mercedes case . . . 47
14. Loss of use . . . 48
(a) The recoverability of damage resulting from a loss of use in general . . . 48

(b) Assessment of compensation for loss of use applied to cars 49
15. Damaged, but unrepaired car 50
16. Additional car damage 51
17. Damaged railway wagon 51
18. Detective case 51
19. Death of parents 51

England (W. V. Horton Rogers, Nottingham)

Part I – General questions on the law of damages
1. Aims of the law of damages 53
2. General principles of the law of damages 55
3. Different forms of damages 55
4. Legislation on damages 56
5. Definition of recoverable damage 57
6. Different types of damages 58
(a) Damage to person, property, economic loss 58
(b) Actual/future loss 58
(c) Direct/indirect losses 58
(d) Damnum emergens/lucrum cessans 58
(e) Patrimonial/non-patrimonial loss 59
(f) Contract and tort 59
7. Monetary assessment of non-patrimonial damage 61
8. Calculation of patrimonial damage 62
9. Compensation for particular kinds of losses 64
(a) Pure loss of use 64
(b) Pure loss of earning capacity 64
(c) Pure loss of holiday or free time 65
(d) Damage to things which remain unrepaired 65
10. Compensation for emotional shock and loss of consortium 65
11. Compensation of illegitimate losses 66
12. Compensation of collective damage 66
13. Special rules on compensation of ecological damage 66
14. Harm causing also advantages 66
15. Certainty of damage 67
16. Lump sum or rent 68

Part II – Cases
1. Wrongful birth case 68
2. Wrongful life case 69
3. Eye injury 69
4. Costs for hospital visits and of adaptation of house 69
5. Scar case 70
6. Continued payment of wages 70
7. Monk case 71
8. Lost earning capacity 71

9. Lost spouse/partner ... 72
10. Offending publication ... 72
11. Rosenkavalier case ... 73
12. Prostitute case ... 73
13. Mercedes case ... 74
14. Loss of use ... 74
(a) Immobilised car ... 74
(b) Lost use of house ... 74
15. Damaged, but unrepaired car ... 74
(a) Sale of unrepaired car ... 74
(b) and (c) cost of repair and worth of the car ... 75
6. Additional car damage ... 75
(a) Accident car ... 75
(b) New for old ... 75
(c) Rent of garage ... 75
17. Damaged railway wagon ... 75
18. Detective case ... 76
19. Death of parents ... 76

France (Suzanne Galand-Carval, Paris)

Part I – General questions
1. Aims of the law of damages/comparison with the aims of tort law ... 77
2. General principles of the law of damages ... 78
3. Different forms of damages ... 79
4. Legislation on damages ... 79
5. Definition of recoverable damage ... 79
6. Different types of damage ... 80
7. Monetary assessment of non-patrimonial damage ... 81
8. Calculation of patrimonial damage ... 81
9. Compensation for particular kinds of losses ... 82
10. Compensation for emotional shock and loss of consortium ... 83
11. Compensation of illegitimate losses ... 83
12. Compensation of collective damage ... 83
13. Special rules on compensation of ecological damage ... 83
14. Harm causing also advantages ... 84
15. Certainty of damage ... 84
16. Lump sum or rent ... 84

Part II – Cases
1/2. Wrongful birth and wrongful life ... 84
3. Eye injury ... 85
4. Costs for hospital visits and of adaptation of house ... 85
5. Scar case ... 85
6. Continued payment of wages ... 85
7. Monk case ... 85

8. Lost earning capacity ... 86
9. Lost spouse / partner ... 86
10. Offending publication ... 86
11. Rosenkavalier case ... 86
12. Prostitute case ... 86
13. Mercedes case ... 87
14. Loss of use ... 87
15. Damaged, but unrepaired car ... 87
16. Additional car damage ... 87
17. Damaged railway wagon ... 87
18. Detective case ... 88
19. Death of parents ... 88

Germany (Ulrich Magnus, Hamburg)

Part I – General questions on the law of damages
1. Aims of law of damages ... 89
2. General principles of the law of damages ... 91
   (a) Full compensation ... 91
   (b) Restitution in kind ... 91
   (c) Compensation for the lost worth ... 92
3. Different forms of damages ... 92
4. Legislation on damages ... 92
5. Definition of recoverable damage ... 93
6. Different types of damage ... 94
   (a) Patrimonial/pecuniary and non-patrimonial/non-pecuniary damage ... 94
   (b) Contractual and tortious damage ... 95
   (c) Damage to person or property and pure economic loss ... 95
   (d) Damnum emergens and lucrum cessans ... 95
7. Monetary assessment of non-patrimonial damage ... 95
8. Calculation of patrimonial damage ... 96
9. Compensation of particular kinds of losses ... 97
   (a) Pure loss of use ... 97
   (b) Pure loss of earning capacity ... 97
   (c) Pure loss of holiday or free time ... 98
   (d) Damage to things which remain unrepaired ... 98
   (e) Frustrated expenses ... 98
10. Compensation for emotional shock and loss of consortium ... 98
   (a) Emotional shock ... 98
   (b) Loss of consortium ... 99
11. Compensation of illegitimate losses ... 99
12. Compensation of collective damage ... 99
13. Special rules on compensation of ecological damage ... 99
14. Harm causing also advantages ... 100
15. Certainty of damage ... 100
16. Lump sum or rent ... 100

Part II – Cases

1. Wrongful birth case ... 101
   (a) Maintenance ... 101
   (b) Lost earning ... 101
   (c) 'Tort moral' ... 101
2. Wrongful life case ... 101
3. Eye injury ... 102
4. Costs for hospital visits and of adaptation of house ... 102
5. Scar case ... 102
6. Continued payment of wages ... 102
7. Monk case ... 102
8. Lost earning capacity ... 103
   (a) Chemistry student ... 103
   (b) Child of six years ... 103
   (c) Living death ... 103
9. Lost spouse/partner ... 103
   (a) Pretium doloris and maintenance ... 103
   (b) Lost services ... 103
10. Offending publication ... 104
11. Rosenkavalier case ... 104
12. Prostitute case ... 104
13. Mercedes case ... 104
14. Loss of use ... 105
   (a) Immobilised car ... 105
   (b) Lost use of house ... 105
15. Damaged, but unrepaired car ... 105
   (a) Sale of unrepaired car ... 105
   (b) Costs of repair higher than worth ... 105
   (c) Costs of repair higher than difference between worth of undamaged and damaged car ... 106
16. Additional car damage ... 106
   (a) Accident car ... 106
   (b) New for old ... 106
   (c) Rent of garage ... 106
17. Damaged railway wagon ... 106
18. Detective Case ... 107
19. Death of parents ... 107

Greece (Konstantinos D. Kerameus)

Part I – General Questions

1. Aims of the law of damages ... 109
2. General principles of the law of damages ... 109
3. Different forms of damages ... 110
4. Legislation on damages ... 110
5. Definition of recoverable damage ... 110

6. Different types of damages 110
7. Monetary assessment of non-patrimonial damage 111
8. Calculation of patrimonial damage 112
9. Compensation for particular kinds of losses 112
10. Compensation for emotional shock and loss of consortium 112
11. Compensation of illegitimate losses 113
12. Compensation of collective damage 113
13. Special rules on compensation of ecological damage 113
14. Harm causing also advantages 113
15. Certainty of damage 113
16. Lump sum or rent 113

Part II – Cases
1. Wrongful birth case 114
2. Wrongful life case 114
3. Eye injury 114
4. Costs for hospital visits and of adaptation of house 114
5. Scar case 114
6. Continued payment of wages 114
7. Monk case 114
8. Lost earning capacity 115
9. Lost spouse / partner 115
10. Offending publication 115
11. Rosenkavalier case 115
12. Prostitute case 115
13. Mercedes case 115
14. Loss of use 116
15. Damaged, but unrepaired car 116
16. Additional car damage 116
17. Damaged railway wagon 116
18. Detective case 116
19. Death of parents 116

Italy (F. D. Busnelli and G. Comandé, Pisa)

Part I – General questions on the law of damages
1. Aims of the law of damages 117
2. General principles of the law of damages 118
3. Different forms of damages 118
4. Legislation on damages 119
5. Definition of recoverable damage 120
6. Different types of damages 121
7. Monetary assessment of non-patrimonial damage 124
8. Calculation of patrimonial damage 125
9. Compensation for particular kinds of losses 127
10. Compensation for emotional shock and loss of consortium 128

11. Compensation of illegitimate losses ... 129
12. Compensation of collective damage ... 129
13. Special rules on compensation of ecological damage ... 129
14. Harm causing also advantages ... 129
15. Certainty of damage ... 129
16. Lump sum or rent ... 130

Part II – Cases
1. Wrongful birth case ... 130
2. Wrongful life case ... 131
3. Eye injury ... 132
4. Costs for hospital visits and of adaptation of house ... 132
5. Scar case ... 132
6. Continued payment of wages ... 133
7. Monk case ... 133
8. Lost earning capacity ... 134
9. Lost spouse / partner ... 134
10. Offending publication ... 136
11. Rosenkavalier case ... 137
12. Prostitute case ... 138
13. Mercedes case ... 138
14. Loss of use ... 138
    (a) Immobilised car ... 138
    (b) Lost use of house ... 138
15. Damaged, but unrepaired car ... 139
    (a) Sale of unrepaired car ... 139
    (b) and (c) unworthy car repairs ... 139
16. Additional car damage ... 140
    (a) Accident car ... 140
    (b) New for old ... 140
    (c) Rent of garage ... 140
17. Damaged railway wagon ... 140
18. Detective case ... 140
19. Death of parents ... 140

The Netherlands (Mark H. Wissink, Leiden and Willem H. van Boom, Tilburg)

Part I – General questions on the law of damages
General remarks ... 143
1. Aims of the law of damages ... 144
2. General principles of the law of damages ... 145
3. Different forms of damages ... 145
4. Legislation on damages ... 145
5. Definition of recoverable damage ... 146
6. Different types of damages ... 147
7. Monetary assessment of non-patrimonial damage ... 148

8. Calculation of patrimonial damage 149
9. Compensation for particular kinds of losses 150
10. Compensation for emotional shock and loss of consortium 151
11. Compensation of illegitimate losses 151
12. Compensation of collective damage 152
13. Special rules on compensation of ecological damage 152
14. Harm causing also advantages 152
15. Certainty of damage 153
16. Lump sum or rent 153

Part II – Cases
1. Wrongful birth case 154
2. Wrongful life case 154
3. Eye injury 154
4. Costs for hospital visits and of adaptation of house 154
5. Scar case 154
6. Continued payment of wages 155
7. Monk case 155
8. Lost earning capacity 155
9. Lost spouse/partner 155
10. Offending publication 155
11. Rosenkavalier case 156
12. Prostitute case 156
13. Mercedes case 156
14. Loss of use 156
15. Damaged, but unrepaired car 157
16. Additional car damage 157
17. Damaged railway wagon 157
18. Detective case 158
19. Death of parents 158

South Africa (Johann Neethling, Pretoria)

Part I General questions on law of damages
1. Aims of the law of damages 159
2. General principles of the law of damages 160
3. Different forms of damages 160
4. Legislation on damages 161
5. Definition of recoverable damage 161
6. Different types of damage 162
7. Monetary assessment of non-patrimonial damage 163
8. Calculation of patrimonial damage 164
9. Compensation for particular kinds of losses 165
10. Compensation for emotional shock and loss of consortium 166
11. Compensation of illegitimate losses 166
12. Compensation of collective damage 167

13. Special rules on compensation of ecological damage 167
14. Harm causing also advantages 167
15. Certainty of damage 167
16. Lump sum or rent 167

Part II – Cases
1. Wrongful birth case 168
2. Wrongful life case 168
3. Eye injury 168
4. Costs for hospital visits and of adaptation of house 168
5. Scar case 168
6. Continued payment of wages 169
7. Monk case 169
8. Lost earning capacity 169
9. Lost spouse / partner 170
10. Offending publication 170
11. Rosenkavalier case 171
12. Prostitute case 171
13. Mercedes case 171
14. Loss of use 171
(a) Immobilised car 171
(b) Lost use of house 172
15. Damaged, but unrepaired car 172
16. Additional car damage 172
(a) Accident car 172
(b) New for old 172
(c) Rent of garage 173
17. Damaged railway wagon 173
18. Detective case 173
19. Death of parents 173

United States (Gary Schwartz, Los Angeles)

Part I – General questions
1. Aims of the law of damages 175
2. General principles of the law of damages 175
3. Different forms of damages 175
4. Legislation on damages 176
5/6. Definition of recoverable damage/different types of damages 176
7. Monetary assessment of non-patrimonial damage 176
8. Calculation of patrimonial damage 177
9. Compensation for particular kinds of losses 177
10. Compensation for emotional shock and loss of consortium 178
11. Compensation of illegitimate losses 178
12/13. Compensation of collective damage 178
14. Harm causing also advantages 178

15. Certainty of damage ... 179
16. Lump sum or rent ... 179

Part II – Cases
1. Wrongful birth case ... 179
2. Wrongful life case ... 179
3. Eye injury ... 179
4. Costs for hospital visits and of adaptation of house ... 180
5. Scar case ... 180
6. Continued payment of wages ... 180
7. Monk case ... 180
8. Lost earning capacity ... 180
9. Lost spouse/partner ... 180
10. Offending publication ... 181
11. Rosenkavalier case ... 181
12. Prostitute case ... 181
13. Mercedes case ... 181
14. Loss of use ... 181
15. Damaged, but unrepaired car ... 181
16. Additional car damage ... 182
17. Damaged railway wagon ... 182
18. Detective case ... 182
19. Death of parents ... 182

Comparative Report on the Law of Damages

Part I – General questions on the law of damages
1. Aims of the law of damages ... 185
   (a) Compensation ... 185
   (b) Prevention ... 185
   (c) Sanction/punishment ... 186
   (d) Declaration of right/'Rechtsfortsetzungsfunktion' ... 187
   (e) Restitutionary damages/gain avoidance ... 187
   (f) Summing up ... 187
2. General principles of the law of damages ... 188
   (a) Full or limited compensation ... 188
   (b) Restitution in kind v. compensation in money ... 188
3. Different forms of damages ... 189
4. Legislation on damages ... 189
5. Definition of recoverable damage ... 190
6. Different types of damage ... 191
   (a) Pecuniary and non-pecuniary loss ... 192
   (b) Contractual and tortious damage ... 192
   (c) Direct and indirect damage ... 193
   (d) Actual and future damage; damnum emergens and lucrum cessans ... 193
   (e) Damage to person and property and pure economic loss ... 193

(f) Summary ... 193
7. Monetary assessment of non-pecuniary damage ... 194
(a) Distinction ... 194
(b) Assessment ... 194
(c) Summary ... 195
8. Calculation of pecuniary damage ... 195
(a) General method ... 195
(b) Abstract v. concrete calculation ... 196
(c) Assessing the value of the damaged position ... 197
(d) Standardisation ... 197
(e) Free disposal of awarded damages? ... 197
(f) Further factors governing the assessment ... 198
9. Losses on the borderline between pecuniary and non-pecuniary damage ... 198
(a) Pure loss of use ... 198
(b) Pure loss of earning capacity ... 198
(c) Pure loss of holiday or free time ... 199
(d) Damage to things which remain unrepaired ... 199
(e) Frustrated expenses ... 200
10. Compensation for emotional shock and loss of consortium ... 200
(a) Compensation for emotional shock ... 200
(b) Loss of consortium ... 201
11. Compensation of illegitimate losses ... 201
12. Compensation of collective damage ... 202
13. Special rules on compensation of ecological damage ... 202
14. Collateral benefits ... 203
15. Certainty of damage ... 204
16. Lump sum or rent ... 204

Part II – Cases
Damage to the person ... 205
1. Wrongful birth case ... 205
(a) Maintenance ... 205
(b) Lost earnings ... 205
(c) Pain and suffering ... 206
2. Wrongful life case ... 206
3. Eye injury ... 207
4. Costs for hospital visits and of adaptation of house ... 207
5. Cost of operation for scar ... 207
6. Continued payment of wages ... 208
7. Monk case ... 208
8. Future income losses; living dead ... 209
(a) The injured chemistry student ... 209
(b) Child of six years ... 210
(c) Living dead ... 210

9. Lost spouse or partner ... 210
   (a) Pretium doloris for death of spouse or partner ... 210
   (b) Maintenance ... 211
   (c) Loss of services ... 211
10. Offending publication ... 211
11. Rosenkavalier case ... 212
   (a) Compensation for paid fee ... 212
   (b) 'Tort moral' ... 212
12. Injured prostitute ... 213
   Damage to things ... 213
13. Mercedes case ... 213
14. Loss of use ... 213
   (a) Lost use of car ... 213
   (b) Lost use of house ... 214
15. Damaged, but unrepaired car ... 214
   (a) Cost of fictitious repair ... 214
   (b) Cost of repairs exceeding value of car ... 215
   (c) Cost of repairs exceeding diminution in value ... 215
   (d) Summary ... 215
16. Additional car damages ... 215
   (a) Accident car ... 215
   (b) New for old ... 216
   (c) Useless rent for garage ... 216
17. Damaged railway wagon ... 216
   Pure economic loss ... 217
18. Detective case ... 217
   Compensation of advantages and disadvantages; collateral benefits ... 217
19. Death of parents ... 217

Index ... 219

Questionnaire on the Law of Damages

Questionnaire on the Law of Damages

Part I – General questions on the law of damages

1. Which are the aims of the law of damages? (Please answer whether or not they are identical with those of the general tort law. Please take into consideration that the law of damages is also relevant in the field of contract law.)
2. Which are, if any, the general principles of the law of damages? (E.g., complete or adequate compensation, compensation in money or restitution in natura, etc.)
3. Do different forms of damages exist: compensatory damages; punitive or examplary damages; nominal damages; legal fees and judicial costs? If so, which are the reasons for and the consequences of the distinction(s)?
4. Does general or specific legislation on the law and/or measurement of damages exist? If so what do they provide?
5. How is the notion of damage defined (as a legal or natural term)? Is there a statutory or otherwise generally accepted definition of what a recoverable damage is?
6. Are different types of damage recognised? E.g. damage to person or property and pure economic loss; actual and future loss; direct and indirect loss; damnum emergens and loss of profit; patriomonial and non-patrimonial loss). If so, which are the reasons for the distinction(s); which are its consequences? Do different rules exist for the calculation and compensation of contractual and tortious loss?
7. How and according to which criteria is patrimonial and non-patrimonial damage (e.g. pain and suffering) distinguished? How is non-pecuniary loss assessed? Do different heads of non-pecuniary loss exist? (Damages for infringement of the right of personality may be touched on, but must not be dealt with intensively).
8. How is the recoverable damage calculated? Which is/are the method(s)? (Subjective/objective, abstract/concrete?) Which are the main principles? Which factors play a role? (Fault, social situation, freedom of disposition of the victim on the sum of compensation etc?) Does a standardisation of awards exist?
9. How are the following losses compensated when no other actual damage is present:
   - pure loss of use,
   - pure loss of earning capacity,
   - pure loss of holiday or free time,
   - damage to things which remain unrepaired,
   - expenses which become frustrated by the tortious act?
10. Under which conditions, if at all, is compensation for emotional shock (e.g. by watching, or hearing of, a very severe accident of relatives or other people) and loss of consortium awarded?
11. Are illegitimate losses (e.g. income of an injured prostitute) compensated? Which limits, if any, do exist?
12. Do special rules exist for the compensation of collective damages (regularly minimal damage to many people; mass torts)?
13. Do special rules for the compensation of ecological damage exist?

U. Magnus (ed.), Unification of Tort Law: Damages, 3–6.

14. How is the problem solved that the harm done to the victim causes him some advantage as well? Which are the decisive factors and considerations?
15. Which rules exist on certainty of damage? (E.g. in case of future income losses)
16. On which factors does it depend wether the compensation is awarded as rent or as lump sum?

Part II – Cases

Damage to the person

1. A married woman (30 years old) undergoes a sterilization which fails due to a mistake on the part of the surgeon. One year later the woman gives birth to a third child (her other children are 9 and 10). She sues compensation of the following heads of damage:
   - maintenance for the ('wrongfully' born) child (60,000 Euro, calculated on the basis of 250.–/month during 20 years being the normal maintenance of a child);
   - lost earnings for herself (78,000 Euro = 13 monthly wages of 1,000 Euro during 7 years until the child attends school);
   - 'tort moral' (pain & suffering) for herself as a consequence of the undesired third pregnancy and a second operation for sterilization (3,000 Euro).
2. Doctor A negligently overlooks an infection of the pregnant B so that she gives birth to a severely handicapped child. On correct information she would have aborted the child. B and her child each claim compensation for the living costs of the child.
3. A defective product harms V, a 25 year old woman. V's right eye is severely injured. She has incurred medical costs (1,000 Euro) and her sight with the injured eye is permanently reduced by 50 %. What kind and amount of damages is she entitled to?
4. A who has been injured by B's negligence claims costs for hospital visits of his wife and for the adaptation of his house to the use by wheel chair to which A is now confined.
5. A has been negligently injured by B. A scar of the wound remains. A claims the costs of cosmetic operation to remove the scar although A in fact does not intend to undergo the operation.
6. Employee P had been injured by D and, because of that, was unfit to work for two weeks. Nevertheless, by virtue of law, his employer E had to continue payment of wages. P sues D for loss of two weeks' wages.
7. A, a monk aged 45, is injured in an accident for which B is liable so that A is unable to work for 6 weeks. A used to work gratuitously for his monastery. Can he or the monastery claim compensation for the loss of earning capacity (or wages) for 6 weeks?
8. A, a 20 year old student of chemistry, suffers severe brain injuries by B's negligence thus reducing A in future to temporary inferior jobs. A claims full compensation of his damage. On which basis is his damage calculated?

   Which is the basis of calculation if A were the 6 year old child of a family with small income, A having shown quite normal abilities so far?

   If B's negligence reduced A to the status of a living dead what could A then get as compensation?

   (Please neglect in these cases medical costs which are borne by the social system).

9. (a) A's husband (non-marital partner) is killed in an accident for which B is liable. A claims from B a pretium doloris and the maintenance which her husband (partner) had her provided.
(b) A's husband who had maintained the household is killed in an accident for which B is answerable. A claims compensation for loss of services.
10. A, a publisher, publishes an article which contains many untrue and offending statements of B's life (drug consum, sexual perversities etc.). B, a rockstar (a politician, an unknown citizen) sues A for compensation.
11. A person who is slightly injured in a traffic accident misses a concert-and-opera-tour to Vienna which he had booked twelve months ago (without taking the inability-insurance offered by the tour operator). – He sues the owner (or holder) of the car by which he was hurt, asking for compensation of the fee paid for the tour (6,000 francs) and 5,000 francs as 'tort moral' (for having missed a performance of the 'Rosenkavalier' with his favourite actress in the role of the 'Marschallin').
12. A, a prostitute, who earns 5,000 Euro/month is injured by B's negligence so that she can't work for a month. To what amount, if at all, is she entitled to?

Damage to things

13. P owns an old Mercedes convertible. As X has made him an offer to buy the car for 23,000 Euro, P is on the way to X to talk out some minor details of the deal. Near X's house D negligently collides with P and slightly damages the Mercedes. Therefore, X rejects to buy the car and the dealer Y, who had offered 20,000 Euro for the car the other day, now is willing to pay no more than 18,000. The cost of repairs would come to 4,000 Euro. How much has D to compensate?
14. (a) A has negligently damaged B's car. During repair B cannot use his car and claims
   - either the cost of a substitute (are there any limits?);
   - or an amount for loss of use (if this is awarded how is it calculated?).

   (b) A has negligently damaged B's house. During repair (6 months) B lives in a caravan. He claims an amount for loss of use of the house.
15. (a) A's car has been damaged by B's negligence. A sells the car unrepaired to C and claims the fictitious costs of repair from B.
(b) Same as (a). Costs of repair would be higher than worth of damaged (alternatively of repaired) car.
(c) Same case as (a). Costs of repair would be higher than difference between worth of undamaged and damaged car.
16. P's car is damaged by D's negligence.
(a) After repair the car is an accident car. Can P claim some compensation for that fact?
(b) After repair some parts of P's car are new (tires etc.). Can P claim full costs of repair or only reduced an amount ('new for old')?
(c) The repair takes two weeks. Therefore, for two weeks the garage rented by P is useless. D is only prepared to pay the cost of repairs. P sues D for the cost of the two weeks rent.
17. A, a railway line, sues B, who is liable for damaging a wagon. Besides costs of repair

A claims costs for maintaining a wagon which A had held reserve and had used during the time of repair.

Pure economic loss

18. A, a department store, employs a detective who catches B, a thief. A claims part of the salary of the detective from B.

Compensation of advantages and disadvantages; collateral benefits

19. A's parents are killed in an accident for which B is liable. A claims compensation for the loss of those who maintained him. Can B set off that A succeeded to his parents' property?

Austria

Damages under Austrian Law

Helmut Koziol

Part I – General questions on the law of damages

1. The aims of the law of damages

[1] The primary aim of the law of damages is to obtain *compensation* of the damage for the injured person.[1] As, in principle, the Austrian General Civil Code (ABGB) does not distinguish between tortious and contractual liability, it is common opinion that this is true in tort law as well as in contract law. Furthermore, this aim does not depend on whether liability is based on fault or is regardless of fault. Finally, the opinion is held that this aim is also important if immaterial damage is at stake.[2]

[2] In addition, the law of damages aims at *prevention*:[3] The liability to pay damages has a deterrent effect on a particular offender and also leads to general prevention. This is true in tort law as well as contract law and, furthermore, not only for liability based on fault, but also for strict liability.[4] The obligation to render compensation when damage is caused encourages steps to prevent damage as long as this is cheaper than compensation.[5]

[3] The idea of *sanction*, however, is relevant only for that part of liability which is based on fault.[6] § 1324 ABGB shows that the idea of sanction is important under Austrian law: The extent of compensation depends on the gravity of fault.[7]

---

1 F. Bydlinski, *System und Prinzipien des Privatrechts* (1996), pp. 187–188; Oberster Gerichtshof (Supreme Court, OGH) in Entscheidungen in Zivilrechtssachen (SZ) [1980] 53/173; [1999] *Zeitschrift für Verkehrsrecht* (ZVR) nr. 56.

2 F. Bydlinski, Der Ersatz ideellen Schadens als sachliches und methodisches Problem, [1965] *Juristische Blätter* (JBl), 253–254.

3 W. Wilburg, *Die Elemente des Schadensrechts* (1941), pp. 50–51; F. Bydlinski (supra note 1) pp. 190 et seq.

4 H. Stoll, *Das Handeln auf eigene Gefahr* (1961), pp. 347 et seq.; H. Koziol, Erlaubte Risiken und Gefährdungshaftung, in: F. Nicklisch, *Prävention im Umweltrecht* (1988), pp. 143–144; S. Panther, *Haftung als Instrument einer präventiven Umweltpolitik* (1992).

5 *Cf.* M. Adams, *Ökonomische Analyse der Gefährdungs- und Verschuldenshaftung* (1985), pp. 36 et seq.

6 *Cf.* W. Wilburg (supra note 3) pp. 50–51; E. Deutsch, *Fahrlässigkeit und erforderliche Sorgfalt* (2nd edn. 1995), pp. 20 et seq.

7 *Cf.* The Austrian Report, in: J. Spier (ed.), *The Limits of Liability* (1996), p. 56.

U. Magnus (ed.), Unification of Tort Law: Damages, 7–26.

[4] Neuner[8] and Wilburg[9] have worked out another function of the law of damages[10] which is based on the principle of prevention:[11] the '*Rechtsfortsetzungsfunktion*'. This expresses the idea that the infringed right of the injured party or its object of legal protection continues to exist in the offended party's claim for compensation. As the legal system protects rights and objects because of their common appreciation, the idea of continuation leads to a claim for compensation to the extent of the ordinary market value. For this reason, § 1332 ABGB rules that the tortfeasor has to compensate at least the trade value even if the loss of the injured person is less (objective-abstract adjustment).[12]

2. The general principles of the law of damages

(a) Complete or limited compensation?

[5] As mentioned above, the extent of compensation depends on the degree of fault (§ 1324 ABGB). If the injurer acted with slight negligence, he has to pay only the 'eigentliche Schadloshaltung', which means the 'actual loss', but neither the lost profits nor the immaterial damage. Moreover, damage has to be assessed in an objective way according to the market value (§ 1332 ABGB). Only if the injurer behaved with gross negligence or intent is he liable for full compensation, even for non-pecuniary damage. It should be mentioned that the importance of the distinction made by § 1324 ABGB in regard to the extent of compensation is minimised by the Supreme Court in holding the opinion that the loss of profits is an actual loss in those cases in which the plaintiff definitely would have made the profit.[13]

[6] The general rule of § 1324 ABGB is applicable not only in tort law, but also in the area of contractual liability. But there are exceptions: In the area of commercial transactions according to the Commercial Code, which is of German origin, the injurer is liable for full compensation even if he acted with slight negligence. As to immaterial damage,[14] on the one hand, the wrongdoer has to pay damages for pain and suffering irrespective of the degree of fault (§ 1325 ABGB); on the other hand, if property is damaged the injurer only has to pay for the sentimental value if he intentionally violated criminal law or inflicted wanton damage or acted with malicious intent (§ 1331 ABGB).

[7] § 1324 ABGB solely concerns liability based on fault. Because no parallel rule exists in the area of strict liability, the extent of compensation is doubtful if strict liability is at stake.

---

8 R. Neuner, Interesse und Vermögensschaden, [1931] *Archiv für die civilistische Praxis* (AcP) 133, 277.

9 W. Wilburg, Zur Lehre von der Vorteilsausgleichung, [1932] *Jherings Jahrbücher* (JherJB) 82, 51.

10 It is also relevant in the area of unjust enrichment; *cf.* W. Wilburg, *Die Lehre von der ungerechtfertigten Bereicherung nach österreichischem und deutschem Recht* (1934), pp. 27 et seq.; W. Wilburg, Zusammenspiel der Kräfte im Aufbau des Schuldrechts, [1964] AcP 163, 347 et seq.

11 F. Bydlinski (supra note 1) pp. 191–192.

12 *Cf.* The Austrian Report, in: J. Spier (ed.) (supra note 7) p. 56.

13 *Cf.* OGH in [1998] JBl, 312 = [1999] *Österreichisches Bankarchiv* (ÖBA), 488 with commentary by R. Rebhahn, Zinsen als Verzugsschaden, [1999] ÖBA, 441 et seq.; also *cf.* the decision 6 Ob 167/98x from 24th September 1998.

14 *Cf.* for further details The Austrian Report, in: J. Spier (ed.) (supra note 7) pp. 56 et seq.

Some[15] hold the opinion that, according to § 1324 ABGB, only the actual loss has to be indemnified, because the liability of the defendant is not based on gross negligence. But I believe that § 1324 ABGB can only be applied mutatis mutandis in the area of strict liability and, therefore, the extent of compensation depends on the weight of the reason for attributing the damage, especially the degree of dangerousness of the object.[16]

[8] It has to be stressed that in the area of strict liability the principle of full compensation is not upheld under Austrian law even if liability is based on dangerousness in the highest degree: Most of the rules which provide for strict liability limit the responsibility by setting maximum amounts. But, fortunately, the legislator has changed its attitude recently.[17]

(b) Restitution in kind and compensation in money

[9] According to § 1323 ABGB, damage has to be compensated primarily by restitution in kind. This means that the defendant must create a similar and equal situation to that which would have existed if the action causing the damage had not occurred.[18]

[10] The priority of restitution in kind stems from the idea that it best serves the function of compensation. Therefore, compensation in money is only then permissible if restitution in kind is impossible or impractical. As § 1323 ABGB provides for restitution in kind in the interest of the injured person, impracticality is already given if the plaintiff prefers compensation in money and this is not in conflict with the higher interests of the defendant.[19]

3. Different forms of damages

[11] Punitive and nominal damages are unknown under Austrian law. According to Austrian tort law, damages always aim at compensation.[20] This is true even if immaterial damage is at stake.[21]

[12] Legal fees and judicial costs receive special treatment: Normally their compensation complies with special rules of procedural law and not with the general rules of tort law.[22]

---

15 K. Wolff in H. Klang (Wolff in Klang), *Kommentar zum ABGB* VI (2nd edn. 1951), p. 127; R. Reischauer in P. Rummel (Reischauer in Rummel), *ABGB* II (2nd edn. 1992), § 1324 no. 9; B. A. Oberhofer, Der Ersatzanspruch bei Schäden wegen Tätigkeit in fremdem Interesse, [1994] *Österreichische Juristenzeitung* (ÖJZ), 734 et seq.

16 H. Koziol, *Österreichisches Haftpflichtrecht* I (3rd edn. 1997), no. 10/2. Espousing F. Bydlinski, *Die Risikohaftung des Arbeitgebers* (1986), pp. 91 et seq.; F. Kerschner, Die Reichweite der Arbeitgeberhaftung nach § 1014 ABGB, in: T. Tomandl (ed.), *Haftungsprobleme im Arbeitsverhältnis* (1991), pp. 66 et seq.

17 *Cf.* the Atomhaftpflichtgesetz (Nuclear Liability Act, AtomHG) 1999.

18 *Cf.* OGH in [1970] SZ 43/49 and [1990] SZ 63/53.

19 OGH in [1996] JBl, 392.

20 An exception is § 87 Urheberrechtsgesetz (Copyright Act, UrhG), which provides claims for damages even if no damage exists. *Cf.* H. Koziol, Zu schadenersatzrechtlichen Problemen des § 87 UrhG, in: R. Dittrich (ed.), *Beiträge zum Urheberrecht* IV (1996), pp. 51 et seq.

21 F. Bydlinski, [1965] JBl, 253–254; OGH in [1976] JBl, 315. Dissenting opinion R. Strasser, *Der immaterielle Schaden im österreichischen Recht* (1964), pp. 16 et seq.

22 *Cf.* M. Bydlinski, *Kostenersatz im Zivilprozeß* (1992); M. Bydlinski, Der Anspruch auf Ersatz 'vorprozessualer Kosten", [1998] JBl, 69 et seq., 143 et seq.

4. General or specific legislation on the law and/or measurement of damages

[13] As already mentioned, § 1323 ABGB provides that restitution in kind ranks prior to compensation in money. Furthermore, §§ 1323 and 1324 ABGB make a distinction between actual loss, loss of profit and immaterial damage, and rule that if the tortfeasor only acted with slight negligence, solely actual loss has to be compensated, and according to § 1332 ABGB this loss has to be measured by the 'gemeinen Wert', i.e. the market value. The discrepancy provided for commercial transactions has also been mentioned above.
[14] The special acts providing for strict liability usually contain rules on damages. Very often they set maximum amounts.
[15] As to the measurement of damages, § 1293 ABGB rules that loss of profit has to be assessed according to the 'gewöhnlichen Lauf der Dinge' (usual course of events). § 273 ZPO, moreover, stipulates that the judge is allowed to assess damages 'nach freier Überzeugung' (according to his free conviction) in case proof of a certain amount of harm is unreasonably difficult (see under no. 62.).

5. Notion of damage

[16] § 1293 first sentence ABGB gives a legal definition of the notion of damage: 'Damage is called every detriment which was inflicted on someone's property, rights or person.' In this broad definition, the ABGB covers real damage as well as damage assessed by way of calculation and, on the other hand, patrimonial as well as non-patrimonial damage.
[17] However, the second sentence of § 1293 ABGB restricts the meaning of 'damage' by saying: 'This is distinguished from the loss of profit which someone has to expect in the usual course of events.' Thus, § 1293 ABGB makes a distinction between damage (damnum emergens) and lost profit (lucrum cessans). But in other sections the ABGB uses the term damage in a broader sense that includes lost profit as well (cf. §§ 1294, 1295, 1324 ABGB) and calls damage in the sense of the first sentence of § 1293 'erlittener Schaden' (§§ 1323, 1324 ABGB) or 'wirklicher Schaden' (§ 1330 ABGB). Today, the term 'damage' is normally understood in the broad sense as the whole harm including lost profit. If solely damage in the narrow sense is meant, it is called 'actual loss' ('wirklicher' or 'positiver Schaden').
[18] It is under discussion whether damage is a legal or a natural term. The prevailing opinion held by Austrian scholars is that 'damage' is a legal term as defined by the civil code.[23]

6. Different types of damage

[19] Under Austrian law quite a number of different types of damage are recognised. First of all, the ABGB makes a distinction between patrimonial and non-patrimonial loss. Patrimonial damage can, in turn, be divided into different types. But it has to be stressed that in principle the ABGB treats tortious and contractual loss in the same way. Nevertheless, some types of damage are relevant, above all, in the area of legal transactions, e.g. damage by non-performance and damage caused by relying on a declaration.

---

23 T. Mayer-Maly, Schadenersatz für Gebrauchsentbehrung?, [1967] ZVR, 282–283; espoused by H. Koziol (supra note 16) no. 2/8.

(a) Damage in reality

[20] The negative consequences in reality are called 'real damage' ('realer Schaden'). This type of damage is decisive if compensation in kind is at stake: The defendant has to restore the situation which would have existed if the act which established liability of the defendant had not occurred. As already mentioned, § 1323 ABGB primarily foresees this sort of compensation. Monetary compensation for the damage by way of calculation requires that restitution in kind be impossible or impractical.

(b) Patrimonial damage by way of calculation

[21] Patrimonial damage by way of calculation is the diminution of a person's patrimony or patrimonial element measured in money. This damage always has to be determined by calculating a difference, as the negative consequences can only be ascertained by comparison of two quantities.

[22] As mentioned above, the ABGB (§§ 1293, 1323) distinguishes between two forms of patrimonial damage, namely actual loss (damnum emergens) and loss of profit (lucrum cessans); the latter term includes all forms of prospective loss. This distinction is important, as the tortfeasor must only compensate actual loss if he did not behave with gross negligence or with intent. To some extent, the borderline between actual damage and loss of profit is controversial:[24] There is no doubt that decrease in value of an existing right is actual loss; the same is true if expenses or obligations are increased. But the classification of patrimonial prospects is difficult, as even the chance of profit can be seen as an existing asset. Therefore, the Supreme Court recently held the opinion that loss of profit is actual damage if the attainment of the profit was almost certain.[25] But I think that this is true only if, in addition, a right to make the profit already existed.[26]

[23] The distinction between 'primary' (direct) damage and consequential loss is only decisive if limitation of liability is at stake.

[24] Some importance is, however, attached to the distinction between damage to personality, property or another right, on the one hand, and pure economic loss, on the other hand. The protection against pure economic loss is much less.[27]

(c) Non-patrimonial damage

[25] A disadvantage which does not lead to diminution of the patrimony measurable in money is called 'ideeller Schaden' (non-patrimonial or immaterial damage). Above all, such damage is caused by violation of rights of personality.

[26] Compensation in money for immaterial damage runs into difficulties:[28] Immaterial interests have to be assessed in monetary terms. Furthermore, non-patrimonial damage de-

---

24 *Cf.* W. Fröhlich, Schadensbemessung und Schadensüberwälzung, [1931] *Zentralblatt für die juristische Praxis* (ZBl), 536; H. Mayrhofer, *Schuldrecht I: Allgemeiner Teil* (1986), pp. 316 et seq.; H. Koziol (supra note 7) nos. 2/34 et seq.

25 *Cf.* OGH in [1992] SZ 65/94; [1998] JBl, 312.

26 H. Koziol (supra note 7) no. 2/38; espoused by OGH in [1995] JBl, 248; [1996] ÖBA, 213.

27 *Cf.* H. Koziol (ed.), *Unification of Tort Law: Wrongfulness* (1998), pp. 15 et seq.

28 *Cf.* F. Bydlinski (supra note 1) pp. 222 et seq.

pends on individual conditions and, therefore, is hardly measurable unless some objective clues are given. This is why compensation in money for non-patrimonial damage is more restricted than for patrimonial damage:[29] In principle, liability for non-patrimonial damage is established only if the tortfeasor acted with gross negligence or intent (cf. § 1324 ABGB).[30]

[27] But there are some exceptions to this principle: In the case of bodily injury, the plaintiff may claim compensation for pain and suffering even if the injurer only behaved slightly negligently or if strict liability is given; cf. § 1325 ABGB, § 13 no. 4 Eisenbahn- und Kraftfahrzeughaftpflichtgesetz (EKHG, Railway and Motor Car Liability Act).[31]

[28] Furthermore, there exist some special rules concerning rights of personality, for example in the case of infringement of reputation: According to § 1330 ABGB, compensation is restricted to patrimonial harm, e.g. loss of earnings. But if the defamation is published in mass media, the Mediengesetz (Media Act) provides a claim against the owner of the medium to compensate immaterial loss (see case 10.). In this context attention should be drawn furthermore to the new § 1328 ABGB: Any person who by punishable behaviour, malice, threat or by taking advantage of dependent condition induces another person to engage in sexual intercourse or other sexual acts has to compensate non-pecuniary damage.[32]

[29] If property is damaged, however, the injurer only has to pay for the sentimental value and only if he intentionally violated criminal law or inflicted wanton damage or acted with malicious intent (§ 1331 ABGB). As to breach of contract, in principle § 1331 ABGB is applicable and consequently immaterial loss only seldom has to be indemnified. But it is held that the defendant has to compensate non-pecuniary loss beyond the constraints of this rule if the contract aims at the protection of immaterial interests (cf. no. 49)

[30] Therefore it turns out that compensation in money for non-patrimonial loss depends on the rank of the legal interest and on the existence of objective clues to indicate the extent of the harm (see under no. 38).

[31] As the difficulties in assessing non-patrimonial loss do not exist if compensation in kind is at stake, there are no special restrictions on liability for immaterial harm if restoration is possible.

(d) Distinction between patrimonial and non-patrimonial damage

[32] Frequently, the question of whether the harm is patrimonial or immaterial causes considerable difficulties. In principle, the classification depends on whether the patrimony which is measurable in money was reduced or not.[33] For example, if property is destroyed, the patrimony is reduced by the market value of the property and the lost profit caused by the loss of the object, but not as far as affection value is concerned. The affection value is solely based on pure personal feelings.

---

29 *Cf.* F. Bydlinski (supra note 1) pp. 221 et seq.

30 The Supreme Court (OGH) is even more restrictive, *cf.* [1990] Evidenzblatt der Rechtsmittelentscheidungen (EvBl) nr. 135 and H. Koziol (supra note 16) no. 11/18.

31 In addition, I should mention that the claim on compensation for pain and suffering is hereditary: OGH in [1996] SZ 69/217 = [1997] JBl, 40; *cf.* also § 12 sec. 1 no. 4 EKHG.

32 *Cf.* E. Karner, Die Neuregelung des Ersatzes ideeller Schäden bei geschlechtlichem Mißbrauch, [1997] JBl, 685 et seq.; E. Karner, *Der Ersatz ideeller Schäden bei Körperverletzungen* (1999), pp. 161 et seq.

33 F. Bydlinski (supra note 1) pp. 221 et seq.

[33] Some further problems will be discussed under no. 9.

7. Assessment of non-patrimonial damage

(a) Measure of non-patrimonial damage

[34] Immaterial damage cannot be calculated in money. But money payment is apt to redress an immaterial injury, as it enables the claimant to procure amenities.
[35] As compensation is at stake, the nature, intensity, seriousness and duration of the harm have to be considered. Therefore, it is common opinion that the extent of compensation (e.g. for pain and suffering) depends on the significance of the injury, the consequences for the state of health and duration as well as the intensity of physical pain.[34] Furthermore, the emotional strain (e.g. owing to deformation) has to be taken into consideration.[35]
[36] There is discussion as to whether individual circumstances are relevant in assessing non-patrimonial loss. The Austrian Supreme Court holds the opinion that social position, cultural requirements and financial situation are of no relevance.[36] On the other hand, Steininger[37] rightly points out that in the area of patrimonial damage §§ 1323, 1324 ABGB provide that the extent of compensation depends on the seriousness of fault and that this has to apply mutatis mutandis in the area of non-patrimonial harm. Therefore, I hold the opinion that non-patrimonial damage, too, has to be assessed in an objective way if the tortfeasor acted with slight negligence, but that subjective circumstances must be taken into consideration in the case of gross negligence or intent.[38]
[37] In addition, I should mention that there are no fixed statutory sums, but one could say that there are 'judicial tariffs' for bodily injuries:[39] In assessing damages for pain and suffering, very often day rates defined according to the different levels of pain are used. But the Supreme Court disapproves of this method and insists on an overall assessment.[40] Nevertheless, the day rates are very helpful in calculating the overall amount.[41]

(b) Different heads of non-pecuniary loss

[38] As to different heads of non-pecuniary loss, it should be pointed out that § 1323 ABGB makes no distinction between various categories of immaterial damage, as this article refers in a general way to 'Tilgung der verursachten Beleidigung'[42] and provides that non-pecuniary harm has to be indemnified if the defendant behaved with gross negligence

34 *Cf.* OGH in [1992] ZVR nr. 99; [1994] ZVR nr. 111; [1997] ZVR nr. 82.
35 OGH in [1992] ZVR nr. 81; [1995] ZVR nrs. 44 and 73; E. Karner (supra note 32) pp. 88 et seq.
36 *Cf.* [1989] SZ 62/176; [1990] SZ 63/223.
37 V. Steininger, Minderung der Erwerbsfähigkeit ohne Verdienstentgang, *Wilburg-Festschrift* (1965) p. 202.
38 *Cf.* H. Koziol (supra note 16) nos. 11/23 and 24.
39 *Cf.* K.-H. Danzl/K. Guttiérez-Lobos/O. F. Müller, *Das Schmerzengeld in medizinischer und juristischer Sicht* (7th edn. 1998), pp. 108 et seq.
40 OGH in [1981] ZVR nr. 122; [1982] ZVR nr. 273; [1988] ZVR nr. 98; [1989] ZVR nr. 130.
41 *Cf.* K.-H. Danzl/K. Guttiérez-Lobos/O. F. Müller (supra note 39) pp. 112 et seq.
42 As F. Bydlinski, [1965] JBl, 179–180, 182, 240, 247 convincingly explains that this term means 'immaterial damage".

or intent. But in the end the Code does make a distinction: In the case of bodily injury (§ 1325 ABGB), the tortfeasor has to compensate for pain and suffering even if he only acted slightly negligently. The reasons is that the right of personality is of very high rank and, furthermore, we have objective clues about the seriousness of harm.[43] On the other hand, if property is damaged (§ 1331 ABGB), sentimental value only has to be compensated if the tortfeasor acted with special intent. One has to attribute this to the low rank of such immaterial interest and to the absence of objective evidence to indicate the extent of the harm.

8. Calculation of the recoverable patrimonial damage

[39] As mentioned above, the extent of compensation depends on whether the defendant acted with slight negligence or with serious fault. But the method of calculation varies as well:

(a) Objective-abstract calculation of actual loss

[40] If, in the case of slight negligence, the tortfeasor only has to indemnify the actual loss (§ 1324 ABGB), the assessment has to be carried out in an objective-abstract way.[44] This principle can be derived from § 1332 ABGB, as this article provides that property damage has to be valued at the market price at the time the damage occurred; thus, the value for the actual owner must not be taken into consideration. In keeping with this rule, the market value must generally be considered decisive if damage to an existing asset is to be calculated. However, if no asset is damaged, but the harm is solely caused by the creation of a monetary debt or expense, an objective-abstract calculation is not possible.[45]

[41] As mentioned above (see under no. 4), Austrian scholars justify the objective-abstract calculation by referring to the 'Rechtsfortwirkungsfunktion'.

[42] Some of the difficult problems we are up against if damage is calculated in a subjective-concrete way are easily solved if objective-abstract calculation is used. This is true, for instance, in cases of transferred loss (see case 6), adjustment of damages by benefits received (see question 14 and case 19) and reduced mercantile value (see case 16a).

(b) Subjective-concrete calculation of pecuniary interest

[43] If the damage was caused by grossly negligent behaviour or by intent, then the tortfeasor has to compensate the whole subjective loss of the plaintiff. This damage is assessed using the 'Differenzmethode':[46] One has to compare the injured party's hypothetical patrimony that would exist if the damaging act had not occurred, on the one hand, and the

---

43 To the importance of such objective clues *see* F. Bydlinski (supra note 1) pp. 222 et seq.; H. Koziol (supra note 16) nos. 11/7 et seq.; E. Karner (supra note 32) pp. 81 et seq., 84 et seq. and OGH in [1998] *Medien und Recht* (MR), 345 with commentary by M. Walter.

44 Prevailing opinion, *cf.* F. Bydlinski, *Probleme der Schadensverursachung* (1964) p. 28; W. Fröhlich, [1931] ZBl, 541–542; H. Koziol (supra note 16) nos. 2/56 et seq.; H. Mayrhofer (supra note 24) pp. 126 et seq.; W. Wilburg, JherJB 82, 126 et seq.; OGH in [1990] JBl, 718; [1996] ÖBA, 221. Dissenting opinion: Reischauer in Rummel (supra note 15) § 1332 no. 12.

45 *Cf.* H. Koziol (supra note 16) no. 2/66.

46 *Cf.* OGH in [1992] SZ 65/117; [1995] SZ 68/101.

plaintiff's actual patrimony, on the other hand. The difference is the subjective-concrete loss of the plaintiff. As all adverse effects have to be considered, the calculation of compensation has to take place as late as possible. Therefore, the judge has to take into account all events up to the last hearing in court.

(c) Expenses for restoration

[44] If restitution in kind is possible and practical, the plaintiff is entitled to claim it. This form of restitution is the best possible way to take into consideration the interests of the injured party: He not only receives compensation in money for the diminution of his patrimony, but his interest in the integrity of his belongings ('Integritätsinteresse') is also covered by restoration of the previous situation. This is the reason why § 1323 ABGB primarily provides for restitution in kind.

[45] Apathy[47] rightly pointed out that the protection of the interests of the plaintiff should not depend on whether realisation of the restitution in kind by the tortfeasor is practical or not. Therefore, if restoration by the tortfeasor is impractical, but the plaintiff is arranging it by himself, the defendant has to make the funds available that are needed by the plaintiff. Such compensation of the expenses is not limited by the market value of the destroyed object, even if the tortfeasor's behaviour was only slightly negligent.

9. Compensation of the following losses when no other actual damage is present:

(a) Pure loss of use

[46] The loss of use may lead to harm which is doubtless patrimonial damage, e.g. loss of profit or expenses for hiring an object for the time of repair.[48] But the possibility to use an object is no asset in and of itself and is covered by the value of material asset.[49] Therefore, if the owner only loses the amenities of the use, e.g. he has to go by bus instead of his comfortable car, then he suffers solely immaterial damage. As no sentimental value is at stake, this non-patrimonial loss does not have to be compensated by the tortfeasor in the case of damage of property (§ 1331 ABGB).

(b) Pure loss of earning capacity

[47] In the case of reduced earning capacity, the injured person can claim compensation even if he suffers no loss of earnings. This results from the possibility to calculate the damage in an objective-abstract way. Although it is true that § 1331 ABGB mentions this way of calcu-

---

47 P. Apathy, *Aufwendungen zur Schadensbeseitigung* (1979), pp. 46 et seq.; *cf.* also Ch. Huber, *Fragen der Schadensberechnung* (2nd edn. 1995), pp. 137 et seq.; H. Koziol (supra note 16) no. 2/74 and nos. 9/10 et seq.

48 The compensation of the expenses of hiring a car requires that the plaintiff actually hires the car; 'fictitious expenses' cannot be claimed. *Cf.* H. Koziol (supra note 16) no. 9/11.

49 F. Bydlinski, Der unbekannte objektive Schaden, [1966] JBl, 440; T. Mayer-Maly, [1967] ZVR, 286–287; OGH in [1994] JBl, 121.

lation only in the case of damage to property, prevailing opinion holds that this applies mutatis mutandis in the area of personal injury as well.[50]

(c) Pure loss of holiday or free time

[48] According to prevailing opinion, pure loss of holiday or free time is non-patrimonial damage.[51] As no sentimental value is involved, this damage does not have to be compensated even if the tortfeasor acted with special intent (§ 1331 ABGB). But sometimes patrimonial damage may be caused, e.g. if the plaintiff had repeated travel-expenses or if he lost earnings because of going on holiday again.

[49] It should be mentioned that in the case of breach of contract even non-patrimonial loss has to be compensated if the contract aims at the protection of immaterial interests.[52] This is usually true of tourist travel contracts.

(d) Damage to things which remain unrepaired

[50] If property is damaged, the owner can claim compensation of the market price and, in case the tortfeasor acted with gross fault, the lost profit as well. But, as mentioned above, the plaintiff cannot ask for compensation of the expenses of repair if he does not restore the object (cf. Case 15).

(e) Expenses which become frustrated by the tortious act

[51] If a commodity cannot be used as a consequence of the damage, there is no clear opinion as to whether the owner may claim compensation of the expenses which became frustrated. I would argue against such a claim, as the tortfeasor did not cause the expenses,[53] but rather frustrated the use. Of course, as a consequence of this, the owner may suffer patrimonial damage and the tortfeasor has to compensate it. But if this is not the case, only immaterial harm is involved, as the owner loses the amenities. According to § 1331 ABGB, the owner of the damaged property cannot ask for compensation of this non-patrimonial damage, as only loss of sentimental value is covered.

[52] It turns out, therefore, that the compensation of frustrated expenses would lead in the end to a compensation of immaterial damage contrary to § 1331 ABGB. Nevertheless, this seems justifiable, as the opportunity to use the good was gained by ascertainable expenses and, therefore, the decisive argument that assessment of non-patrimonial damage is extremely difficult does not apply. This is the reason why some hold the opinion that, within narrow limits, compensation of frustrated expenses can be accepted.[54] This is espoused by

---

50 F. Bydlinski (supra note 44) pp. 50 et seq.; V. Steininger (supra note 37) pp. 186 et seq.; R. Welser, Aktuelle Fragen der zivilrechtlichen Haftung aus Verkehrsunfällen, [1978] ZVR, 34; H. Koziol, *Österreichisches Haftpflichtrecht* II (2nd edn. 1984), pp. 134 et seq.; OGH in [1975] ZVR nr. 220; [1993] ZVR nr. 165. Dissenting Reischauer in Rummel (supra note 15) § 1325 no. 36.

51 OGH in SZ 62/77 = [1989] JBl, 792 with commentary by M. Siegl; H. Koziol (supra note 16) no. 2/16.

52 *Cf.* OGH in [1989] SZ 62/77; H. Koziol (supra note 16) no. 2/118, nos. 11/14 et seq.

53 *Cf.* OGH in [1987] SZ 60/102.

54 *Cf.* H. Koziol (supra note 16) no. 2/123.

the Supreme Court,[55] which holds the opinion that the tortfeasor has to compensate those expenses which the owner typically has to spend to be able to use the property, e.g. in the case of damage to a car, the motor vehicle tax as well as the motor insurance for the time of repair.

10. Compensation for emotional shock and loss of consortium

[53] If a person suffers an emotional shock, e.g. by watching or hearing of a very severe accident involving relatives or other people, he may have a personal claim in the case of bodily injury and – regarding immaterial loss – only for compensation of pain and suffering caused by this injury.[56] But according to the prevailing opinion in Austria, there is no claim for indemnity in the case of pure emotional harm caused by watching an accident or by the loss of consortium.[57]

11. Compensation for illegitimate losses

[54] No legal provision exists under Austrian law on this topic, but it is common opinion that, in principle, a tortfeasor does not have to compensate illegitimate losses.[58] The reason given for this is that such harm is not covered by the 'Normzweck' (scope of the rule):[59] Tort law does not aim to protect benefits which the legal system bans.

[55] But the scope of this rule is being debated. The Supreme Court[60] holds the view that the plaintiff may ask for compensation of lost illegitimate profits if he could have obtained a licence for his activity. Furthermore, it is the prevailing opinion that the injured prostitute can claim compensation for loss of income.[61] The argument put forward is that law only opposes the validity of the contract between the prostitute and her client, but does not demand repayment of the remuneration.

[56] Moreover, under Austrian law one has to bear in mind that the plaintiff can claim compensation of the damage assessed in an objective-abstract way. Therefore, the injured prostitute undoubtedly has a claim if her earning capacity has been reduced.

12. Special rules for the compensation of collective damages

[57] In Austria special rules for the compensation of collective damage do not exist. The

55 OGH in [1978] ZVR nr. 264.

56 *See* OGH in [1995] ZVR nr. 46; [1997] ZVR nr. 75; E. Karner, Rechtsprechungswende bei Schock- und Fernwirkungsschäden Dritter?, [1998] ZVR, 182 et seq.

57 *See* F. Bydlinski, [1965] JBl, 246 and 251; Reischauer in Rummel (supra note 15) § 1325 no. 1; *cf.* also OGH in [1987] ZVR nr. 23 and [1995] ZVR nr. 46. Dissenting opinion H. Koziol (supra note 16) no. 11/11.

58 OGH in [1985] SZ 58/101; [1990] SZ 63/106; [1999] Recht der Wirtschaft (RdW), 400; Reischauer in Rummel (supra note 15) § 1293 no. 12; H. Koziol (supra note 16) no. 8/36; F. Bydlinski, Unerlaubte Vorteile als Schaden, *Festschrift Deutsch* (1999), pp. 63 et seq.

59 *See* H. Koziol (supra note 16) no. 8/36; F. Bydlinski (supra note 58) p. 76.

60 [1990] SZ 63/106; espoused by F. Bydlinski (supra note 58) pp. 81–82.

61 OGH in [1981] SZ 54/70; H. Koziol (supra note 16) no. 8/37; F. Bydlinski (supra note 58) pp. 64–65, 75, 80–81.

present concept of tort law is individualistic: Every injured party has to claim compensation for itself.

13. Special rules for the compensation of ecological damage

[58] So far, no special rules for the compensation of ecological damage exist, but there is an 'Umwelthaftungsgesetz' (Environmental Liability Act) under discussion.

14. The harm done to the victim causes him an advantage as well

[59] The answer to the question depends on which type of calculation is used.

(a) Objective-abstract calculation

[60] According to the 'Rechtsfortwirkungsgedanken' (see question 1), in using the objective-abstract calculation one has to value the infringed asset in isolation, and not the whole patrimony. Therefore, advantages to the patrimony of the plaintiff caused by the tortfeasor do not have to be taken into consideration.[62]

(b) Subjective-concrete calculation

[61] On contrast, the subjective-concrete calculation by the 'Differenzmethode' (cf. 8.b) includes the whole patrimony of the injured person: One has to compare the injured party's hypothetical patrimony that would exist if the damaging act had not occurred and the plaintiff's actual patrimony. As a result, the advantages caused by the tortfeasor reduce the difference.[63] But it is common opinion that it would be unreasonable to take into account all advantages caused by the tortfeasor and thus ease his burden of compensation. If the advantage is a benefit provided by a third party, Austrian doctrine as well as the Supreme Court come to the conclusion that whether or not compensation is reduced depends on the purpose of the benefit.[64] For example, the insurance benefits or payments made by the employer to an injured person do not have the purpose of favouring the tortfeasor, but solely the injured person.

15. Rules on certainty of damage

[62] As to lost profit, § 1293 ABGB does not demand full evidence that the plaintiff would have netted the profit; on the contrary, it is sufficient that he would have netted it according to the usual course of events.[65] Furthermore, § 273 ZPO provides that the judge is allowed to assess damages according to his own conviction if proving a certain amount of harm is

62 W. Wilburg, JherJB 82, 125 et seq.; H. Mayrhofer (supra note 24) pp. 333–334.

63 *Cf.* OGH in [1977] SZ 50/50; H. Koziol (supra note 16) no. 10/33.

64 W. Wilburg, JherJB 82, 76 et seq.; H. Koziol (supra note 16) no. 10/38; H. Mayrhofer (supra note 24) p. 335; OGH in [1975] ZVR nr. 19; [1994] SZ 67/52; [1996] JBl, 583.

65 *Cf.* P. Rummel, Zur Verbesserung des schadenersatzrechtlichen Schutzes gegen unlauteren Wettbewerb, [1971] JBl, 393–394.

unreasonably difficult.[66] The prevailing opinion is that § 273 ZPO is only applicable if the plaintiff is able to make evident that damage, however small, was incurred[67] and solely the extent is dubious.[68]

16. Compensation awarded as rent or as lump sum

[63] The question of how the compensation has to be awarded if the injured person claims compensation for loss of earnings is not settled by the ABGB. According to the prevailing opinion, in principle damages have to be awarded in the form of rent, and are only rewarded as a lump sum if there are grave and weighty arguments.[69] The reason is that rent can be adjusted to the real development and does not have to be based on presumptions, as is the case with lump sums. The same is true in regard to claims in case of loss of maintenance. **[64]** More recent statutes than the ABGB, e.g., § 14 Eisenbahn- und Kraftfahrzeughaftpflichtgesetz (Railway and Motor Car Liability Act, EKHG), regulate the question in a manner corresponding to the prevailing opinion.

Part II – Cases

1. Wrongful birth case

(a) Maintenance for the child

[65] Up until now, the Austrian Supreme Court has not ruled on the question of whether the mother has a claim for compensation of the maintenance for the 'wrongfully' born child in the case of a failed sterilisation.[70] Nor have Austrian scholars discussed the topic in depth.[71] **[66]** One cannot deny that the mother suffers patrimonial harm, as she is obliged to pay maintenance. Nevertheless, I take the view[72] that the mother has, in principle, no claim: The obligation to maintain must not be viewed in isolation, as the relationship between mother and child is made up of several patrimonial and immaterial elements which form a unified whole. Advantages and disadvantages of such relations usually counterbalance one another.

---

66 *See* H. Fasching, Die richterliche Betragsfestsetzung gemäß § 273 ZPO, [1981] JBl, 225; K. Hofmann, Zur Auslegung des § 273 ZPO, [1996] *Österreichische Richterzeitung* (ÖRZ), 9.

67 It is sufficient to prove harm in the extent of one schilling.

68 OGH in [1950] SZ 23/224; [1956] JBl, 180; H. Fasching, [1981] JBl, 231; W. Rechberger/D. Simotta, *Grundriß des österreichischen Zivilprozeßrechts* (5th edn. 2000), no. 604. Dissenting opinion P. Rummel in H. Koziol (supra note 50) p. 303; H. Koziol (supra note 20) pp. 59–60.

69 *Cf.* E. Kunst, Der Kapital- und Rentenschaden in der Haftpflicht und Haftpflichtversicherung, [1978] ZVR, 65; OGH in [1961] SZ 34/27; [1973] SZ 46/45; [1975] ZVR nr. 198; [1990] ZVR nr. 121.

70 But it mentioned the problem in [1994] SZ 67/17. Furthermore the Supreme Court recently had to decide a case, in which a mother had not been informed about the severe handicap of her unborn child; *see* case 2.

71 One can only refer to shorter articles, *cf.* A. Mirecki, Bemerkungen zum Ersatz des Unterhaltsschadens, [1990] ÖJZ, 755 and 793.

72 *See* H. Koziol (supra note 16) nos. 2/22 et seq.

Only if providing maintenance is a very extraordinary burden to the mother could one say that, on the whole, patrimonial harm is caused.

(b) Lost earnings

[67] In my opinion the mother has a claim. The loss of earnings is a patrimonial harm caused by the surgeon and the arguments against a claim mentioned under (a) do not apply,[73] as solely the earning capacity of the mother is at stake.

(c) Pain and suffering

[68] Under tort law, § 1325 ABGB only provides a claim for compensation of pain and suffering if the plaintiff sustained injury. As pregnancy is no bodily harm, I tend to doubt that such a claim exists. No such difficulties crop up in regard to pain and suffering by the second operation, because as far as that is concerned bodily harm is involved.
[69] In addition, one has to take into consideration that the surgeon and the woman are parties to a contract and that – we have to assume – the woman also concluded the contract to avoid pregnancy and all the pain connected with it. Thus, even this pain may be in the scope of the protective purpose of the contract and, therefore, the surgeon has to compensate such pain and suffering as well.

2. Wrongful life case

(a) Claim of the mother

[70] Under the circumstances referred to in the hypothetical, causing an abortion would not have been illegal (see § 97 sec 2 Austrian Criminal Code). Nevertheless, the mother has no claim for compensation of the child's living costs:[74] The granting of permission to kill the unborn child does not aim at protecting the parents against patrimonial burdens. Therefore, one has to assume that patrimonial harm is not covered by the protective purpose of the duty neglected by the surgeon.
[71] Recently the Supreme Court[75] decided in a different way: If the doctor omits negligently to inform about a severe handicap of the unborn child, the parents may claim compensation for the additional financial loss caused by the severe handicap of the child, which would have been aborted on correct information.

(b) Claim of the child

[72] First of all, as the parents have to provide maintenance, the child itself does not suffer patrimonial harm. Apart from that argument, one has to consider that nobody, not even an unborn child, has a claim to be killed and, therefore, the surgeon did not violate a duty to the child.[76]

---

73 Dissenting W. Selb, Eltern wider Willen, [1971] *Juristenzeitung* (JZ), 208.
74 *Cf.* H. Koziol (supra note 16) no. 2/26.
75 *See* the decision OGH in [1999] JBl, 593.
76 *Cf.* H. Koziol (supra note 16) no. 2/31 and the decision OGH in [1999] JBl, 593.

3. Eye injury

[73] Firstly, persuant to § 1325 ABGB, V is entitled to demand indemnification for the medical costs, i.e. 1,000 euro.
[74] Secondly, if she suffers loss of earnings, she has a claim for compensation of this harm. But even if she achieves the same income she would have had without injury, she has a claim because of her decreased earning capacity. The so called 'abstrakte Rente' is a consequence of the objective-abstract calculation of damage (cf. Part I, under nos. 41 and 47). The Supreme Court justifies the 'abstrakte Rente' by pointing out that the injured person has to make greater efforts to avoid loss of income and that handicapped persons are more likely to lose their job.[77]
[75] Thirdly, V may claim compensation of pain and suffering, i.e. for immaterial damage. In assessing damages, the judge has to consider not only the physical, but also the emotional pains caused by the reduced eyesight.[78]
[76] In cases of bodily injury, all these claims are given even if the tortfeasor acted with slight negligence and the same is true if strict liability is involved.

4. Costs for hospital visits and adaptation of house

(a) Hospital visits of the wife

[77] The Supreme Court[79] holds the view that the injured person can claim compensation of the visiting expenses of his close relatives. The court thinks that the visits to the hospital are necessary or at least useful for the recovery and that, therefore, the expenses are part of the costs of convalescence.

(b) Adaptation of the house

[78] Besides loss of earnings and pain and suffering, § 1325 ABGB only mentions costs of cure. But it is common opinion that the tortfeasor also has to compensate all costs caused by the increase in needs,[80] thus also the expenses for adapting the house to the use of a wheelchair.[81]

5. Scar case

[79] Recently, the Supreme Court changed its practice and is now of the opinion that the injured person only has a claim on the costs of an operation if he actually intends to undergo the operation. If the injured person changes his mind and does not undergo the operation, he has to refund the money.[82]

---

77 OGH in [1975] ZVR nr. 167; [1993] ZVR nr. 165.
78 *See* OGH in [1995] ZVR nr. 44; Reischauer in Rummel (supra note 15) § 1325 no. 44.
79 [1989] SZ 62/116. Espoused by R. Welser, Der OGH und der Rechtswidrigkeitszusammenhang, [1975] ÖJZ, 39; *cf.* also Ch. Huber (supra note 47) pp. 291 et seq.
80 *Cf.* OGH in [1991] ZVR nr. 109; Ch. Huber (supra note 47) pp. 309 et seq.
81 *Cf.* OGH in [1977] ZVR nr. 9.
82 OGH in [1998] JBl, 109. This practice is in accordance with the prevailing doctrine, *cf.* P. Apathy

6. Continued payment of wages

[80] As the payments by the employer do not have the purpose of relieving the tortfeasor of his obligation, but rather to favour the employee, it is common opinion that these benefits must not be taken into consideration and, thus, do not reduce the damage suffered by the employee (see Part I, no. 61). Therefore, the employee has a claim. But one has to consider that, firstly, the loss is simply transferred to the employer. Secondly, the law that provides for payment of the employee, even if he is not able to do his work due to illness, does not aim at a betterment of the employee, but solely avoiding a loss in case of illness. As a result, doctrine as well as the Supreme Court are of the opinion that – by analogy to § 1358 ABGB, § 332 General Social Insurance Act and § 67 Insurance Act – an assignment by operation of law takes place so that the employer acquires the claim.[83]

7. Monk case

[81] Firstly, the loss is merely shifted from the monk to the monastery and, secondly, the gratuity of the monk's work does not have the purpose of relieving the tortfeasor of his liability. Therefore, the monk has a claim for compensation which has to be assessed according to the usual value of his services.

[82] One can reach the same result by using the objective-abstract method of calculation.

8. Lost earning capacity

[83] (a) A can claim compensation for the emotional suffering.[84] In addition, the tortfeasor has to indemnify A for loss of earnings. This loss is calculated on the basis that A would have earned more as a chemist than he does now; the loss has to be assessed on probability according to the usual course of events.[85] It has to be considered that A does not have a claim until that point from which time on he would have had earnings, i.e. after having finished his studies.[86]

[84] (b) The damage can only be calculated on the basis of probability judgement. In doing so, the Supreme Court takes into consideration the professions and the earnings of the parents.[87]

[85] (c) Aside from the lost earnings, A has a claim for compensation of immaterial harm: The Austrian Supreme Court recently[88] ruled that the injured person may recover damages

---

(supra note 47) p. 82; P. Apathy, Fiktive Operationskosten, [1986] ÖRZ, 265; Ch. Huber (supra note 47) pp. 275 et seq.

83 OGH in [1994] SZ 67/52; [1995] ZVR nr. 62; [1996] JBl, 583; V. Steininger, Schadenersatz bei Lohnfortzahlung, [1959] JBl, 475 et seq.; H. Koziol (supra note 16) no. 13/29.

84 *Cf.* OGH in [1957] ZVR nr. 181; [1971] ZVR nr. 255; [1988] ZVR nr. 56; [1989] ZVR nr. 135.

85 Loss of profits (lucrum cessans) is only compensable if the tortfeasor acted with gross negligence. *Cf.* OGH in [1957] EvBl nr. 219 and in [1999] JBl, 183.

86 *Cf.* Reischauer in Rummel (supra note 15) § 1325 nos. 22 and 23.

87 *See* [1966] EvBl nr. 354.

88 OGH in [1993] ZVR nr. 150; [1995] *Recht der Medizin* (RdM), 116. *Cf.* E. Karner (supra note 32) pp. 123 et seq.

for non-pecuniary loss even if he is comatose. The court's argument is that although the claimant is not sensitive to pain, he is entitled to claim compensation because of the severe impairment of his personality. Damages would be nearly the same as those for a sentient plaintiff with the same physical injuries. In the cases decided by the Supreme Court the amounts were ATS 1,400,000 and 1,500,000.

9. Lost spouse/partner

[86] (a) Austrian law does not provide claims on pretium doloris if a husband is killed (see Part I, no. 53).

[87] According to § 1327 ABGB, the tortfeasor must compensate the maintenance which the killed husband provided for A. But this only applies as far as statutory maintenance is concerned.[89] Therefore, if A is a non-marital partner she has no claim, because the killed partner had no legal obligation to furnish maintenance.

[88] (b) The legal obligation of a husband to run the household (§ 94 ABGB) is equal to the obligation to provide maintenance.[90] Therefore, according to § 1327 ABGB, A is entitled to compensation for loss of services.

10. Offending publication

[89] In cases of defamation, § 1330 ABGB expressly restricts the claim to compensation for patrimonial harm, e.g. loss of earnings. But if the defamation is published in mass media, the Mediengesetz (Media Act) provides a claim against the owner of the medium to compensate immaterial loss.

[90] The Media Act restricts compensation for non-pecuniary damage to ATS 200,000. Only in the case of defamation or exceptional consequences of a defamatory statement is the ceiling higher, namely ATS 500,000.

[91] In assessing damages, the court has to take into consideration not only the dissemination of the media and the consequences of publication, but also the financial situation of the media enterprise (§ 6 sec 1 Media Act).

11. Rosenkavalier case

[92] In the case of bodily injury, the whole non-patrimonial loss is covered by the 'Schmerzengeld' (compensation for pain and suffering, § 1325 ABGB), which has to be assessed as one sum. Therefore, A has no extra claim for having missed the performance of the 'Rosenkavalier'.

[93] As to the fee paid for the tour, one has to consider that the defendant did not cause the expenses and, thus, did not cause any patrimonial harm. Therefore, compensation of the frustrated expenses would ultimately lead to compensation of immaterial loss (cf. Part I, no. 52). As he has a claim for compensation of pain and suffering caused by the bodily in-

---

89 *See* OGH in [1992] JBl, 44; Reischauer in Rummel (supra note 15) § 1327 no. 16.

90 OGH in [1978] ZVR nr. 22; [1982] SZ 55/167; Reischauer in Rummel (supra note 15) § 1327 no. 27.

jury, the plaintiff would be compensated twice for the same damage if the defendant had to indemnify expenses which became frustrated.[91] Therefore, A has no claim for compensation of the fee paid for the tour.[92]

12. Prostitute case

[94] The Austrian Supreme Court ruled that the prostitute is entitled to full compensation (see Part I, nos. 55 and 56).

13. Mercedes case

[95] In any case, P can claim compensation in kind, i.e. the repair of the car or the costs of repair, i.e. 4,000 Euro, if he has the car repaired.
[96] As to compensation in money, one has to make a distinction: If D acted with slight negligence, he only has to compensate the actual loss calculated according to the market value. Therefore, assuming that the dealer is willing to pay the market value, D must pay 2,000 Euro.
[97] If D's behaviour was grossly negligent, he is liable for full compensation. This means that P has a claim for 5,000 Euro, as he had the possibility to sell the car to X for 23,000 Euro[93] and now can only gain 18,000 Euro.

14. Loss of use

[98] (a) Regardless of the degree of negligence given, B is entitled to claim the costs of a substitute car.[94] But if B's car is a luxury model, the costs for renting such a car are not included unless B has a special reason for doing so.[95] This is a consequence of the obligation of the injured party to lessen the damage as far as is reasonable ('Schadensminderungs-pflicht').
[99] B has no claim for pure loss of use (cf. Part I, no. 46).
[100] (b) B is entitled to claim compensation for renting the caravan, but again has no claim for pure loss of use.

15. Damaged, but unrepaired car

[101] As mentioned above (see Part I, nos. 44 and 50). A cannot claim fictitious costs of repair, because as A did not have the car repaired, B only has to compensate the decrease in value of the car.[96]

---

91 This sets the cases of bodily injury apart from cases of damage to a commodity, *cf.* Part I, no. 51.
92 *See* OGH in [1987] SZ 60/102; H. Koziol (supra note 16) no. 2/122.
93 If P and X had already entered the contract, the Supreme Court ([1957] EvBl no. 62; [1993] ecolex, 452) holds the view that the loss of this opportunity to sell at a high price has to be considered an actual loss. Dissenting opinion H. Koziol (supra note 16) no. 2/54.
94 OGH in [1956] SZ 29/43; [1985] ZVR nr. 131.
95 [1966] EvBl nr. 400; [1975] JBl, 92 with commentary by F. Bydlinski.
96 *Cf.* H. Koziol (supra note 16) no. 9/11.

[102] At first sight, it seems that the Supreme Court[97] takes a different view, but in the end it arrives at the same result: Although it does award the fictitious costs of repair, they do not exceed the decrease in value.

[103] If repair is much more expensive than the difference between the costs of purchasing a similar car and the value of the damaged car, the repair would be impractical and the tortfeasor would, therefore, on no account have an obligation to indemnify the costs of the restoration.[98]

16. Additional car damage

[104] (a) As the market value depends on whether the car is an accident car, the owner is entitled to claim the decrease in value ('merkantiler Minderwert').[99] This is a consequence of the objective-abstract calculation of damage which is permitted under Austrian law (cf. Part I, no. 40).

[105] (b) As to restitution in kind, the injured party can claim restoration of the previous situation, but not a better one. Therefore the defendant does not have to pay the full costs of new tires, but rather the use value of the old ones. But one has to consider that the injured party would have continued to use the old tires for some time and the costs of purchasing new tires would have accrued later; therefore, the defendant also has to pay for the expenses caused by the earlier acquisition.[100]

[106] Only if parts of the car are renewed which would have been usable for the whole lifespan of the car does the tortfeasor have to compensate the full costs: The owner would never have had to purchase such parts.

17. Damaged railway wagon

[107] According to the prevailing opinion,[101] B is not liable under tort law, as he did not cause the costs of buying and upkeeping the reserve wagon; but A is entitled to the costs under the law of negotiorum gestio. However, Huber[102] holds that the injured party has a claim under tort law to compensation for the incurred expenses if he used his own resources to repair the damage.

18. Detective case

[108] B did not cause the employment of the detective and of A's paying the salary. Therefore, B is not liable under tort law.[103]

---

97 [1990] SZ 63/46; [1995] ZVR nr. 7; [1995] SZ 68/101.

98 *Cf.* OGH in [1995] SZ 68/101.

99 P. Apathy, Merkantile Wertminderung unter besonderer Berücksichtigung der Bagatellschäden, [1988] ZVR, 289; OGH in [1990] ZVR nr. 49; [1993] ZVR nr. 164.

100 *Cf.* H. Koziol, Naturalersatz und Schadensberechnung beim Problem 'neu für alt', [1965] JBl, 337; espoused by the OGH in [1983] SZ 56/126.

101 OGH in [1973] JBl, 476 with commentary by H. Koziol; [1986] SZ 59/95; [1987] SZ 60/65; S. Meissel, *Geschäftsführung ohne Auftrag* (1993), pp. 88–89.

102 Ch. Huber (supra note 47) pp. 194 et seq., 392 et seq.

103 R. Welser, Zur Ersetzbarkeit von Detektivkosten beim Warenhausdiebstahl, [1977] ÖJZ, 646.

19. Death of parents

[109] One has to make a distinction: If A had succeeded to his parents' property in the case of their natural death as well, then B has not caused an advantage as far as the property is concerned. Therefore, the property does not have to be taken into account in calculating compensation[104] (see also Part I, no. 61). But A gained an advantage, as he has the use of the property.[105] However, this benefit only reduces A's loss if his parents had spent the profits of the property and, therefore, A would not have gained them if his parents had died a natural death.

[110] If, on the other hand, A had succeeded to his parents' property, B caused an advantage which reduces the damage.[106]

104 OGH in [1956] JBl, 472; [1977] ZVR nr. 172; R. Welser, Schadenersatzrechtliche Grundfragen bei Berechnung des entgangenen Unterhalts, [1968] JBl, 346.

105 *Cf.* OGH in [1968] JBl, 367; [1977] ZVR nr. 172.

106 *Cf.* H. Koziol (supra note 16) no. 10/49.

Belgium

Damages under Belgian Law

H. A. Cousy and Anja Vanderspikken

Special thanks to Bart De Temmerman for his useful comments and corrections

Part I – General questions

1. Aims of the law of damages

(a) The law of torts

[1] The law of civil liability is traditionally recognized to serve a double purpose: compensation and prevention (through deterrence). At the time of the Napoleonic codification, when the general principles of articles 1382 and 1383 of theCivil Code were introduced, the accent undoubtedly lay on the second aspect. The legal obligation to repair the damages inflicted onto a third person was indeed seen as a way to deter people from faulty behaviour (in the sense of unlawful behaviour and lack of due care). It may be fairly stated that at that time the general rule was that loss must lie where it falls. The law of torts was typically called the law of civil liability. Stronger yet, the French language does not speak so much about the law of civil liability but about the law of civil responsibility (le droit de la responsabilité civile). The accent clearly and strongly lay on the deterring effects which the law should have on the tortfeasor.
[2] The goal and function of the law of civil liability has changed. The law of civil liability (le droit de la responsabilité) has become the law of compensation. The accent indeed has turned toward the protection of the victim. Whereas the rule used to be that loss should only be shifted if the victim can identify a tortfeasor having committed a fault, the unwritten general rule now seems to have turned around. The main way to bring this change about has been the introduction in many a situation of some rule of strict liability.

(b) The law of contracts

(i) Remedies for breach of contract: the main aims
[3] In principle, breach of contract is sanctioned by specific performance (under some circumstances accompanied by the grant of additional compensation in money for extra damage). If specific enforcement of the contract is not possible, however, the party who did not fulfil his contractual obligations will be condemned to pay compensation in money. If the

U. Magnus (ed.), Unification of Tort Law: Damages, 27–51.

contractual obligation consists of the payment of a sum of money, the late payment will be compensated by the obligation to pay the legal interest.

[4] In thc case of a synallagmatic agreement, the aggrieved party can also ask for the rescission of the agreement, inc1uding possibly a claim for additional compensation for damage caused by the breach of contract. To succeed in this claim the party must prove that the other party negligently violated the terms of the agreement. It is up to the judge's discretion to decide whether the fault of the opposite party is serious enough to justify the rescission of the contract. If granted, this rescission has a retroactive effect (unless this is impossible or leads to unfair results), i.e. beginning at the starting point of the legal procedure.

[5] Again with regard to synallagmatic contracts, the party whose compliance with his contractual obligations is claimed, can in turn wait to perform said obligations if the claimant himself is negligently not complying with his obligations (exceptio non adimpleti contractus). In this case, there is no rescission of the agreement. The contract is only suspended until the opposite party fulfils his obligation.

(ii) Remedies for breach of contract: some peculiarities

[6] The principles concerning causation and damages applicable to contractual liability are similar to those of the law of torts. Therefore, it may be sufficient to briefly point out the few peculiarities with regard to the remedies in the event of breach of contract.[1]

[7] With regard to the *recoverable damages* some differences can be pointed out. While there is no specific legislation on this matter regarding tort law, the Civil Code holds several dispositions on the compensation one is entitled to in the case of breach of contract (art. 1146 – 1155 Civil Code).

[8] First, compensation can only be claimed for damage which was foreseen or foreseeable at the moment the contract was concluded. In order to be recoverable, however, it is sufficient that the occurrence of the damage, but not the amount, was foreseeable. This principle does not apply in the case of intentional breach of contract.

[9] Secondly, compensation should only be given with regard to the immediate and direct consequences of the non-compliance with the contractual obligations (art. 1151 Civil Code). This rule even applies to a case of intentional breach of contract. The Cour de Cassation has made it clear that this concept of 'immediate and direct consequences' refers to all damage which is the necessary consequence of the breach of contract: even indirect or circumstantial damage will be compensated, if this damage would not have occurred if there had been no breach of contract.[2] This ruling implies that with regard to contractual liability, as well as to liability in tort, the theory of the equivalence of causes is applied.

[10] Thirdly, the fact that the origin of the obligation to pay compensation is fundamentally different (breach of contract, unlawful act, breach of duty of care or wrongful omission) leads to differences. In both cases, specific performance (under some circumstances accompanied by the grant of additional compensation for extra damage) is preferred to compensation in money. In that case no proof has to be given of the existence of damage or its causal relation with the breach of contract. The amount of the compensation in money or of the

1 J. Ronse, *Schade en schadeloosstelling Deel 1* (1984) p. 411; W. van Gerven, *Verbintenisrecht Deel 1* (1988) pp. 109–142.

2 Cass. 24 June 1977, [1977–78] *Rechtskundig Weekblad* 775.

additional compensation can be agreed upon between the parties in advance in a 'clause pénal' (stipulation for a lump sum of damages).

2. General principles of the law of damages

[11] Compensation must be *full*, but should not exceed the actual damage. To assess compensation, the damage as it actually (*in concreto*) was incurred, is taken into account. According to the Cour de Cassation the legal term 'damage' in its meaning under Art. 1382 and following of the Civil Code, is purely based on facts. The Cour de Cassation may only control the legality of the interpretation given to the term 'damage' by the lower courts. A judge can, therefore, sovereignly establish the existence and the amount of the damage as well as the adequate form of compensation. 'The view that the assessment of damage is (essentially) *a matter of fact* also results in the Belgian supreme court, the Cour de Cassation, being extremely reluctant to review an assessment of damage (albeit there may be a tendency towards a more scrutinized review).[3]

[12] Compensation must be assessed as accurately as possible. An ex aequo et bono estimation should be the exception.

[13] The tortfeasor must compensate the victim either by 'specific performance' or in money. In general, preference is given to compensation by specific performance especially in cases where measures can be taken to end a wrongful situation. The victim is entitled to claim this kind of compensation, but is also obliged to accept it if offered by the tortfeasor.

[14] A judge may of course decide that specific performance is inadequate. In some circumstances e.g. the victim may abuse his right to claim specific performance by exercising this right in a way which does not correspond to the normal exercise of it by a careful and prudent man or if the advantage to the victim of specific performance is disproportionate compared to the disadvantages for the tortfeasor. The victim cannot claim the most expensive form of compensation in money if different forms are available, unless specific circumstances impose upon another solution (e.g. when a unique piece was damaged). The general rule remains that if the worth of the damaged good is smaller than the costs of repair or reconstruction, the victim cannot claim more than the worth of the damaged good.[4]

[15] It follows from the principle of the right to full compensation that the victim is not obliged to mitigate the damage as much as possible. The victim must only take every reasonable measure to limit the scope of the damages on pain of the possibility to a partly reduced claim for compensation. It is generally accepted that the reasonable costs made by the victim in this respect, can be recovered from the tortfeasor, even if they were not successful. The victim can no longer claim compensation for the avoided damages. However, advantages gained by the victim thanks to measures or efforts exceeding what could reasonably be demanded of him, are not taken into account.[5]

---

3 B. De Temmerman, Case note below BGH 7 May 1996, *European Review of Private Law*, 1999, 76–92 (77).

4 L. Schuermans/A. van Oevelen/C. Persyn/P. Ernst/J.L. Schuermans, Onrechtmatige daad. Schade en schadeloosstelling (1983–1992) [1994] Tijdschrift voor Privaatrecht 858–859, further referred to as [1994] *Case law review*.

5 [1994] *Case law review* 877–883.

3. Different forms of damages

(a) With regard to punitive or exemplary damages

[16] Damage is generally described as the difference between the actual situation of the victim and the hypothetical situation in which this person would have been, had he not been victimised.[6]

[17] It is up to the judge to decide how the victim will be indemnified in order to make compensation as accurately as possible. He may, however, not set this compensation on such a level as to turn the compensation into 'punitive damages'. Damages should not amount to punishment.[7] The actual damage is the judge's only standard. (i.e. the objective method to calculate the recoverable damages).

[18] It cannot be denied, however, that other factors may possibly influence the assessment of the damage, especially when no accurate data are available and an ex aequo et bono estimation is required. A judge may for example take into account how much profit the wrongdoer has made (or will make in continuing the tortious act) in a case of harmful publicity. This kind of reasoning will hardly ever appear from the motivation of the judgement, let alone be explicitly pronounced. The Cour de Cassation did acknowledge that compensatory damages may amount to restitution of benefits gained by the defendant in breach of a plaintiff's right. In the judgement 'a quo' the damage, suffered by a tenant who lost benefits from the application of a publicity board on his house (the subtenant made such a publicity contract on his own behalf in breach of the tenant's exclusive right to conclude such contracts), was assessed on the basis of the amount of benefits wrongfully gained by the subtenant. The Cour de Cassation upheld this judgement although it did not enter into a discussion on the question to which extent 'restitutionary' damages may be compensatory.[8]

(b) With regard to 'nominal damages'

[19] Comparable to 'nominal damages' is the symbolic compensation of 1 Bef which is often awarded with regard to pain and suffering, in cases concerning the infringement of personality rights or in environmental tort cases when an ecological group claims compensation.[9] This symbolic compensation is considered to be compensatory (for more comments, see the answer to general question nr. 7).

4. Legislation on damages

[20] To our knowledge no such legislation exists. The Product Liability Act of 25 February 1991 does not provide a limit on the liability for the serial damages to persons, as was made possible in the EC directive of 25 July 1985 on Product Liability.

---

6 L. Schuermans/A. van Oevelen/C. Persyn/P. Ernst/J. L. Schuermans, Onrechtmatige daad. Schade en Schadeloosstelling (1983–1992), [1994] *Tijdschrift voor Privaatrecht* 856, nr. 1.1, further referred to as 'Case law review 1994'.

7 Cass. 10 October 1972, [1973] *Arresten van het Hof van Cassatie* 146.

8 Cass. 29 October 1981, [1981–82] *Arresten van het Hof van Cassatie* 315.

9 For some critical notes on this: A. Carette, *Herstel van en vergoeding voor aantastingen aan niet-toegeëigende milieubestanddelen* (1997) p. 99.

5. Definition of recoverable damage

[21] See the answer to question 3.

6. Different types of damages

[22] These distinctions are made but only for academic and didactic purposes. The rules of liability and of compensation are the same irrespective of the nature of the fault. Some practical results may however follow from the specific features of each of the above mentioned types of damage. See e.g. with regard to the application of the 'splitting up method', the starting point of the period to be taken into account for the award of legal interest, etc. (see also the answer to question nr. 15).
[23] With regard to differences in the compensation for contractual or tortious loss, see question 1.

7. Monetary assessment of non-patrimonial damage

[24] The Cour de Cassation has always and explicitly considered 'moral damage' to be a recoverable damage. In the case concerning the pain and suffering of parents as a consequence of harm to their child, the Cour de Cassation gave the following description of the claim for 'moral damages': the claim for compensation for moral damages aims to compensate the pain, the grief and any other moral suffering.[10] Not only the direct victim can claim compensation for moral damages, but also other persons who suffered damage 'through repercussion', e.g. his or her relatives. The victim's own fault will affect the claim of the heirs exercising their rights ex haerede as well as their claim for their personal damages (Case law review 1994, 928). From time to time the following heads of non-pecuniary loss are mentioned: pretium doloris, invalidity, loss of affection, pretium voluptatis, prejudice d'agrément.
[25] The main principles explained in the answers to questions 1–3 apply to both patrimonial and non-patrimonial damage. No exact calculation standards are available and one must acknowledge that the compensation that will be awarded will never cover the pain and suffering. This can only be symbolic and is quite often limited to one 'symbolic' franc. On this issue the Cour de Cassation explicitly stated that plaintiffs are entitled to full compensation and that the award of more than one franc does not offend against public decency.[11] Capitalisation is seldomly applied in the case of the compensation for moral damages, but if so, the time span taken into account will be the total life expectancy of the plaintiff.[12]
[26] With regard to the claim of very young children and persons with a mental illness or deficiency, the Cour de Cassation ruled that the right to full compensation for pain and suffering is not affected by the fact that the victim is not able to understand that the sum which will be awarded is meant to compensate that damage.[13]

---

10 Cass. 3 February 1987, [1986–87] *Arresten van het Hof van Cassatie* 724.
11 Cass. 7 December 1970, [1971] *Arresten van het Hof van Cassatie* 339.
12 Case law review 1994, 1119.
13 Case law review 1994, 899–900.

8. Calculation of patrimonial damage

(a) Subjective/objective, abstract/concrete method

[27] The answers to these questions mainly follow from the definition of 'damage' (see question 3). Damage is generally described as the difference between the actual situation of the victim and the hypothetical situation in which this person would have been, had he not been victimised.

[28] Elements external to the damage which would increase or decrease compensation, may not be taken into account (i.e. the *objective method* to calculate the recoverable damages). To calculate the recoverable damage, the damage as it actually (*in concreto*) was incurred, is taken into account. With regard to events taking place after the wrongful act, the Cour de Cassation's ruling is capable of a dual interpretation.[14] According to the first doctrine, no account may be taken of events taking place after the wrongful act and which have nothing to do with the fault or the damage. According to the other point of view, account has to be taken of events — even if they took place after the wrongful act — as long as they are not connected with the fault but related to the damage. This ambiguity in the rulings of the Cour de Cassation leads to different outcomes in the jurisdiction of the lower courts and is criticised by legal doctrine.

(b) Main principles on the calculation of compensation[15]

[29] In principle, the recoverable damages are calculated as accurately as possible on a mathematical basis starting from the elements brought forward by the victim. To assess the pecuniary damages following incapacity for work e.g. the judge will use the capitalisation method based on the victim's earnings, unless there are insufficient criteria to establish the earnings accurately enough or unless the actual loss of income caused by the incapacity to work is considered to be very minor. It is said that in these two circumstances damages will be evaluated ex aequo et bono. The ex aequo et bono method is also applied if the capitalisation method leads to an underestimation or an overvaluation of the damages. The application of the ex aequo et bono method requires the judge to motivate why the mathematical calculation proposed by the victim cannot be applied and to assess that it is impossible to establish the recoverable damages otherwise because of lack of sufficient criteria.

[30] It also occurs that capitalisation is applied starting from an ex aequo et bono assessed calculationbase, e.g. for the assessment of compensation for a young child for the loss of expected earnings, had he not been victimised.[16]

(c) The moment at which the amount of damage is assessed

[31] The calculation of the amount of damages starts out from the situation at a moment, close to the moment of the actual compensation, i.e. at the time of the judgement.[17] In order to be able to assess future damage at that moment, capitalisation coefficients are usually

---

14 Case law review 1994, 1038–1042.
15 [1994] *Case law review* 1019–1025.
16 [1994] *Case law review* 1026.
17 [1994] *Case law review* 980 and 1036–1043.

applied. These coefficients take the following elements into account: the capitalisation interest rate, the foreseeable time the damage will endure and the risk of decease. This mathematical 'actualisation' of future damages is an application of the principle of full compensation in concreto. The aggrieved party, however, can claim the granting of 'une rente' (in the sense of periodical payments at equidistant intervals), if this seems the most adequate form of full compensation.[18]

(d) The capitalisation method[19]

[32] Three different tables are applied. The table with fixed annuities is less applied than the so-called 'table Levie' which, in addition to the table with fixed annuities, also takes into account the chances of death of the victim. The so-called 'table Jaumain' does not only take into account the victim's chances of death but also those of the entitled parties. This table is also frequently applied.

(e) Which factors play a role ?

[33] In principle only the actual damage (as proven by the victim) is taken into account to calculate the amount of compensation.[20] Although the judge must assess the existence and the amount of the damage in an unambiguous way, there will always be a certain margin in a way that he is able to take various factors into account. This is illustrated by the answers to the cases commented on further in the text. Concerning the victim's freedom of disposition with regard to the sum of compensation, we refer to the answers given to the questions on damage to things.

[34] It can be stated however, that the existence of regularly published tariffs and case law reviews leads, to some extent, to a standardisation of awards.

9. Compensation for particular kinds of losses

[35/36] (a) Pure loss of use

See further question 14 with regard to damage to things.

[37] (b) Pure loss of earning capacity

See further question 8 with regard to damage to the person.

[38] (c) Pure loss of holiday or free time

To our knowledge there has been no extensive legal discussion about this head of damage. This kind of damage may be compensated under the head of 'moral damages'.[21]

[39] (d) Damage to things which remain unrepaired

This issue raises the question of the victim's free disposition of the sum of compensation. See further question 14 concerning damage to things.

---

18 [1994] *Case law review* 1051- 1052.

19 [1994] *Case law review* 1109–1122.

20 [1994] *Case law review* 859.

21 For a case in which loss of holidays of two consecutive years was compensated see Corr. Charleroi 24 April 1986, *Revue générale des assurances et des responsabilités* 1988, nr. 11382.

[40] (e) Expenses which become frustrated by the tortious act
In principle, this kind of damage will be compensated. This is illustrated by the follwing cases: compensation for the loss of the season ticket for the school bus;[22] loss of expenses for cancelled planned holidays[23] and the costs for sporting gear which became useless due to the accident.[24]

10. Compensation for emotional shock and loss of consortium

[41] In the case of the 'Heyseldrama', the Brussels Court of Appeal decided that the emotional shock suffered by the relatives of the injured or dead football fans cannot be considered to be an autonomous head of damage and must therefore be assessed in light of the severity of the injuries sustained by the relatives. The tragic character of the events and the fact that they could be watched by millions of television viewers are only elements in the calculation of the compensation and are not the only criterium, since the damage (emotional shock) in fact follows from the existence of the injuries sustained by the victims.[25]

11. Compensation of illegitimate losses

[42] In order to be admissible in court, a tort claim must be based on the infringement of a legitimate interest which does not necessarily coincide with the infringement of a legitimate legal right. No compensation is awarded with regard to illegal losses. It is, however, important to stress that not every infringed interest becomes illegal just because the victim finds himself in a wrongful situation. E.g., the injuries and other material damages of a smuggler caused by an accident will be compensated, his loss of earnings (gained through smuggling) will not.[26]

12. Compensation of collective damage

[43] The answer to this question is based on the following text: DALCQ. R.O., 'Problèmes actuels en matière de causalité', *Revue générale des assurances et des responsabilités* 1996, nr. 12656.
[44] *The problem of the admissibility of class actions*

Apart from certain legal provisions allowing consumer organisations to bring legal actions (e.g. the action for a cease and desist order) on behalf of their members, no class actions or collective actions are admitted by the courts. This distrust toward class actions is based on the general principle: 'nul ne plaide par procureur'. This consumer protection legislation providing the possibility of collective action by consumer organisations can be found in the

---

22 Gent 24 December 1990, [1991] *Bulletin des Assurances* 666.
23 Corr. Charleroi 24 April 1986, [1988] *Revue générale des assurances et des responsabilités* nr. 11382.
24 Rb. Brussel 24 January 1986, [1988] *Revue générale des assurances et des responsabilités* nr. 11339.
25 Brussel 26 June 1990, [1991] *Revue générale des assurances et des responsabilités* nr. 11774.
26 [1994] *Case law review* 918–922.

following Acts: The Act on Commercial Practices and on Consumer Protection of 14 July 1991, The Financial Services Act of 4 December 1990, The Act on Consumer Credit of 12 June 1991, Act on Misleading Publicity with regard to Liberal Professions of 21 October 1992 and the Act on the Legal Actions concerning the Protection of the Environment of 12 January 1993.

With regard to ecological damage, see also question 13.

13. Special rules on compensation of ecological damage

[45] The structure and most elements of the following answer are borrowed from CARETTE, A., *Herstel van en vergoeding voor aantastingen aan niet-toegeëigende milieubestanddelen*, Antwerpen, Intersentia, 1997, 63–198.[27]

(a) The rule that damage must be personally incurred and certain

(i) Damage must be personally incurred

[46] In order to be recoverable from the negligent party, general tort law requires the damage to be *personally incurred* by the plaintiff. This principle causes major problems when claiming compensation for damage to the environment. Under Belgian law a claim with regard to non-owned elements of the environment is usually found inadmissible in court. Articles 17 and 18 of the Code of Procedure state that a claim is inadmissible in court if the claimant has no interest. Case law interpreted this legal requirement so that the claimant must have a *personal* interest in order for his claim to be admissible. In a civil tort law procedure this implies the proof of the infringement of a subjective right or of a personal legitimate interest. This means that a mere factual advantage for the claimant is not sufficient (the Council of State, which is an administrative court, rules on objective rights so that claims brought before this court by ecological groups are more easily accepted). For the admissibility of a tort claim, the application of these principles requires the proof of a *personal* damage. Applied to environmental tort cases it is a matter of translating harm to the environment to a personally suffered (individual) damage. E.g. one can bring charges for air pollution because this pollution harms the claimant's personal health or his garden. On the same basis non-patrimonial damage could be claimed. It is very doubtful, however, whether compensation for moral damage due to harm to the environment will be awarded, considering the difficulties already encountered when trying to receive moral damages for the death of a pet. Certain case law however awards moral damages to an organisation defending ecological interests (an ecological group).

[47] It goes without saying that ecological groups will encounter great difficulties to prove their personal interest in cases where environment protection is concerned. As for the individual claimants, they will only succeed to bring an admissible action, if they can prove their own existence, their physical or 'moral' goods (including their property, honour and good reputation) were harmed. This is the reason why some ecological groups buy or manage nature reserves in order to have a kind of contractual basis on which they will be able to protect wildlife, water, etc. in this area. The fact that the protection of the environment is the

27 *See* also Case law review 1994, 913–917.

statutory purpose of the group would not be sufficient to prove the infringement of the group's own interest. With regard to the chances of success of a claim brought by an ecological group for the recovery of costs made for prevention or cleaning up ecological damage, we refer to the possibility of denial of this claim on the basis of the theory of breach of causality.[28]

[48] The protection of the environment as such remains a possible side-effect of a claim in order to restore someone's personal damage, provided that specific performance or cessation of the harmful activity will be imposed or that the awarded sum of money is used for the recovery of the environment.

[49] The Act of 12 January 1993 on Claims concerning Environment Protection[29] *a*uthorizes the Public Prosecutor (Procureur du Roi), a public authority or a non-profit-organisation complying with certain conditions, to bring an action for a cease and desist order ('action en cessation') in order to protect the environment. This legal right concerns only the violation of legislation with regard to the protection of the environment (objective criterium). Only a clear and certain violation of this legislation will be taken into consideration. This claim can only lead to a court order of cessation of the harmful activities and/or to judicially imposed measures to prevent this activity or the ensuing damage.[30]

(ii) Damage must be certain

[50] Furthermore, Belgian law requires the damage to be *certain*. Future damage will be compensated provided the origin of the damage will unquestionably follow from an actual situation. The claim with regard to the prevention of a future personal damage can indirectly favour the recovery of the harmed environment.

(b) Calculation of the compensation for ecological damage

[51] If the plaintiff, bringing a claim based on general tort law, successfully proves that the damage is personal and certain, he will be compensated according to the general principle that the damage is the only standard for the establishment of the compensation. There is no specific legislation with regard to the calculation of the compensation for ecological damage.

[52] Compensation takes the form of specific performance or of compensation in money. Preference is given to specific performance unless this would be impossible or believed to be an abuse of right. This is often the case with regard to harm to the environment, in which case a sum of money is due by the tortfeasor. If this sum can not be assessed on a mathematically accurate basis, compensation will be assessed ex aequo et bono. In the end, compensation for damage to non-owned environmental elements is often merely symbolic because of a lack of an economic market for the harmed environmental elements.

[53] If money is awarded, the plaintiff is not obliged to disburse it on the recovery of the environment.

[54] Since the ruling of the Cour de Cassation of 26 June 1980, it is no longer questioned that the civil courts can prohibit an activity even if the government forwarded a licence for this

28 *See* our general remarks in the Belgian report on causality in Belgian tort law, and for a more comprehensive study: A. Carette (supra note 9).

29 Belgisch Staatsblad 19 February 1993.

30 Cass. 8 November 1996, [1996–97] *Rechtskundig Weekblad* 1256.

activity or set additional (safety) measures. The civil courts may, however, never intrude on the discretionary powers of the public authorities.

(c) An application

[55] To the extent that an ecological group can prove damage which is personal to the association, this group can claim compensation. A group of neighbouring citizens claimed the prohibition for certain companies to dump industrial waste on a waste site in their village. Their claim was successful because the group was held to be the 'representative of each member to defend each citizen's personal interest.[31]

14. Harm causing also advantages

(a) General conditions to be fulfilled for taking into account the advantages rendered to the victim

[56] The party incurring liability has the burden of proof of the prima facie existence and amount of the alleged advantage. There must be certainty not only about the reality of the advantage but also about its realisation. In addition it must be established that the advantage would not have been gained had the damage not occurred. Under certain circumstances an additional requirement must be met (in order to avoid unjust rulings), i.e. the legal ground on the basis of which the victim can hold on to the advantage.

(b) Classifcation

[57] According to Prof. J. RONSE, a well-known authority in the field, there is no general criterium applicable in Belgian case law in order to establish the advantages attributable to the compensation. This author distinguishes four kinds of advantages.[32]

(i) Advantages caused by the tortious act
[58] An event bringing some kind of advantage to the victim, which took place after the wrongful act but was caused by this act, reduces the amount of damage caused by the negligent party. His duty to pay compensation will be proportionally reduced provided it is sufficiently certain that the advantage would not have occurred had the damage not been caused.
[59] On the basis of this reasoning a judge will refuse to take into account the advantages of the heirs following from the succession of the deceased, whose death resulted from the wrongful act.
[60] With regard to advantages consisting in savings, Ronse states that forced and unwished-for savings are not deducted from the wrongdoer's debt. It follows that no account will be taken of the fact that a person could not make or continue a trip because his car was damaged.

---

31 Brussel 2 November 1989, A. Lebrun, *Aménagement, environnement, urbanisme et droit foncier* (1990) p. 42.
32 J. Ronse (supra note 1) nos. 519 — 605.

(ii) Advantages attributable to the victim's behaviour
[61] We refer to the principles, set out in the answer to question 2, applicable on the limits of the victim's duty to mitigate the damages.
[62] All advantages following from the measures willingly taken by the victim and exceeding what can reasonably be required from him, are not attributable on the assessment of the compensation. The outcome of cases where this principle has to be applied, greatly depends upon the facts of each case.

(iii) Advantages following from the compensation
[63] If the damage does not amount to a 'total loss', compensation may easily exceed the true amount of the damage, e.g. if the victim retains a wrecked car or ruined clothes or if old and damaged parts are replaced by new parts.
[64] These questions are governed by the general principles of the right to full compensation established as accurately as possible.

(iv) Advantages resulting from payments with regard to the accident, be it by the negligent party or by third parties
[65] The payments to the victim are not attributable to the amount of his compensation if these payments had a proper legal basis clearly separate from the tortious act and the negligent party's duty to compensate the damages, unless there is a legal exception to this principle of cumulation of allowances or parties diverged from it in a contract. E.g. the benefits flowing from a life insurance contract can be cumulated with damages; the payments by an insurance company following a car insurance (liability insurance) cannot.
[66] If, however, the allowances aim to compensate the damage caused by the tortfeasor, cumulation is not accepted, unless (in general), the third party who paid the allowances has no recourse against the tortfeasor.

15. Certainty of damage

[67] In order to be recoverable, damage must be certain, which means that the likeli-hood of the damage must be such that a judge can not seriously consider the contrary, even if it remains theoretically possible that the expected damage may never actualize.[33]

(a) Future damages

(i) General remarks
[68] To be recoverable, future damage must be the normal outcome, development, consequence, completion or recurrence of an actual (certain) situation. The calculation of the amount of damages to be awarded will be done ex aequo et bono, starting from the situation at a moment as close as possible to the time of the actual compensation, i.e. at the time of the judgement.[34] See also the answer to question 8 with regard to the main principles of the calculation of recoverable damages.

33 [1994] *Case law* review 977.
34 [1994] *Case law review* 980.

[69] The mere apprehension of possible future damage cannot constitute a basis for recovery. This concern may however be accompanied with an actual (recoverable) disadvantage, especially if the threat of future damage is sufficiently severe.
[70] Additional compensation cannot be awarded after a definitive ruling, unless this judgement contains a proviso concerning future deterioration of a specific item of loss, so that the awarded damages are only provisional. According to the Cour de Cassation, a judge can sovereignly decide whether or not to grant such a reserve and to which extent. However, because a judge must take all necessary measures to guarantee full and sufficient compensation for all the certain consequences of the damage, reserve should always be made under the following circumstances: if it is certain that damage will be suffered although the amount of the damage cannot yet be calculated and if the occurrence of the damage is not certain but highly probable.[35]

(ii) Specific rules with regard to death and permanent invalidity[36]
[71] With regard to expected increases in earnings and opportunities of promotion in the case of a deceased victim, the authors of the caselaw review suggest that a distinction must be made between these opportunities in the past (i.e. between the death and the judgement or between the consolidation – in most of the cases of permanent invalidity – and the judgement) on the one hand and in the future on the other hand. This is the so called 'splitting up method' or division method. The lost opportunities during the first period are retrievable and provable while one must speculate as to the evaluation of the lost opportunities for the future. Since the end of the 1970's, this method has become a widespread tool in assessing damages not only in the event of death or permanent invalidity but also for the assessment of the economic value of a housewife, of the aid by others or of pain and suffering. The application of the splitting up method implies that capitalisation is only used for future damage (the second period) and that compensatory interest can only be awarded with regard to the damage in the past. In addition to the date of the judgement as the decisive moment for the division, other factors are accepted such as the maturation of the youngest child, the anticipated end of a professional career, the expected beginning of a (new) career, the possibility of early retirement, etc.
[72] The review of case law shows considerable diversity in the way a judge reaches his decision on the assesment of this kind of future damages. This is illustrated by the fact that the division method is not always applied, e.g. when the judge wants to grant a lump sum (the allowance of a lump sum is not at all irreconcilable with the division method). Other considerations may contribute to this diversity of case law on the assessment of future damages. The calculation base may be the employer's wage calculation notes or an ex aequo et bono set lump sum. The relevant factors taken into account vary according to the facts of each case: e.g. the economical context on the day of the judgement, increase in wages as a consequence of promotion or seniority according the professional scales, inflation, the normal living costs that the deceased would have spent, etc. The capitalisation method as such varies because of the different length of the time spans taken into consideration, the starting points of those time spans, varying interest rates, different calculation tables.[37]

---

35 [1994] *Case law review* 1001–1006.
36 [1994] *Case law review* 1123.
37 [1994] *Case law review* 1121–1123.

(b) Hypothetical damage

[73] Hypothetical damage is 'damage' which is funded only on assumptions, its existence depends on future events. This hypothetical 'damage' as such gives no right to compensation. Coincidence is never taken into account.[38]

(c) Other aspects on certainty

[74] The loss of an advantage which is gratuitously granted and therefore not legally enforceable, can be compensated if the gain of this advantage was sufficiently continuous and of course legitimate.[39]

Part II – Cases

1. Wrongful birth case

[75] The following case law is relevant for the answer to this question: [40]
[76] Because of lack of sufficient post operative care and counselling after a vasectomy, a surgeon was ordered to pay the costs of maintenance and education of the child born 324 days after the operation.[41]
[77] A claim against a surgeon after a negligently performed sterilization on a woman was accepted. Damages were awarded for the costs of the operation which was unsuccessful, the incapacity caused by that operation, the costs of the pregnancy and delivery, the costs of the enlargement of the house and the pecuniary costs of the child support and education of the child until the age of 21. 'Moral damages' were not awarded, neither were the costs of the vasectomy which the husband had undergone afterwards, the loss of opportunities on the labour market by the mother and the efforts to raise the child.[42]
[78] See also question 2 with regard to the unacceptability of a claim by the child in this case (wrongful life action).

2. Wrongful life case

(a) The wrongful life action of the child

[79] KRUITHOF. R., 'Schadevergoeding wegens de geboorte van een ongewenst kind?', *Rechtskundig Weekblad* 1986–87, 2737–2778; VANSWEEVELT, T., *Aids en Recht, Een aansprakelijkheids- en verzekeringsrechtelijk studie, in Reeks Aansprakelijkheidsrecht*, Antwerpen, Maklu en Brussel, Ced.Samson, 1989, 108.
[80] It is accepted by the majority of Belgian legal doctrine and case law that a child can claim damages for wrongful acts which took place after its conception, provided they are

38 [1994] *Case law review* 1000.
39 Cass. 4 September 1972, [1973] *Arresten van het Hof van Cassatie* 1.
40 [1994] *Case law review* 886–889.
41 Rb. Antwerpen 17 January 1980, [1981] *Bulletin des Assurances* 183.
42 Rb. Kortrijk 3 February 1989, [1988–89] *Rechtskundig Weekblad* 1171.

born alive and viable. This means that a child has no right to claim damages for negligent acts dating from before the conception. Kruithof gives the following examples of such cases: negligent genetic advice by the doctor to the parents, defective contraceptives, negligent medical failures regarding sterilization, etc.

[81] Kruithof however, gives some serious arguments based on Belgian law on damages to deny such a claim for wrongful acts which took place after the child's conception. One of these arguments is that in these wrongful life cases it appears impossible to establish the existence of the damage. It is indeed difficult, even almost impossible, to compare the actual situation of the victim (life as a handicapped) and the situation had the negligence not taken place (non-existence of the child).

(b) The wrongful birth claim of the parents

[82] Contrary to what is stated with regard to the wrongful life action by the child, it is possible to compare the situation of the parents after the negligent act or omission and their situation would this not have occurred. According to Kruithof, it has not yet been explicitly dealt with in Belgian case law which items of damage are recoverable. Belgian courts, however, frequently ackowledged claims of women who had an unwanted and illegitimate child due to a man's illegal behaviour (e.g. after being raped). To the knowledge of this author, the argument was so far never raised properly that the damage could not be compensated because it would correspond to the infringement of an illegitimate interest.

[83] If it is accepted that compensation will be awarded with regard to a wrongful birth claim, it must be ascertained whether the advantages gained by having the child should be taken into account in the assessment of the amount of the damages. The advantages gained directly through the wrongful act itself, most importantly the love and affection of the child for his parents, should be taken into account. With regard to allowances paid by third parties in relation to the wrongful act, Kruithof argues that the payments meant to alleviate the parents' maintenance and educational duties should also be taken into account. All this leads to a very delicate exercise for the judge who must assess the damages in concreto and as accurately as possible. Another delicate issue concerns the question whether there is a breach of causality between the wrongful behaviour of the liable party and the legal duty of maintenance of the parents. As was explained in the Belgian report on causality, the Cour de Cassation accepts a departure from the theory of equivalence of causes if the causality is broken by a separate legal requirement by the 'victim' to make certain expenses. This argument has not yet been raised in Belgian case law. The claim of a surgeon for the operation costs for his own son against the person liable for the accident was denied because the father-surgeon only fulfilled his own legal and moral obligations.[43]

3. Eye injury

[84] The victim will be awarded the full recovery of her medical costs (1.000 Euro). The invalidity will be compensated taking into account the principles established in the answer to question 8.

43 Corr. Tongeren 30 January 1968, [1968] *Revue générale des assurances et des responsabilités* nr. 8346.

[85] According to the Product Liability Act of 25 February 1991, the moral damage for pain and suffering can be compensated. Belgian legislation does not provide a limit on the liability for the serial damages to persons as was made possible in the EC directive of 25 July 1985 on Product Liability.

4. Costs for hospital visits and of adaptation of house

(a) Adaptation of the house[44]

[86] According to the principle of full compensation, the costs for adaptation of the house are recoverable damages. It is not certain that the adaptation of the house to the need of a handicapped person objectively and necessarily gives a surplus value to the building. On the contrary, the adaptation could discourage future buyers.[45]

(b) Costs for hospital visits

[87] Applying the same principle of full compensation, these costs will be compensated. It is not clear, however, whether this claim for the costs of hospital visits belongs to the victim[46] or to the visiting relatives.[47] Some courts even accept the claim for the costs of presents for the nursing staff to the extent that this gesture is customary.[48]

5. Scar case

[88] A cannot be forced to undergo the operation, but A is held by the duty to mitigate the damages (see also general question 2). In a similar case the Court of Appeal of Antwerp ruled that, unless there is proof of exceptional pain resulting from the operation and/or of the likelihood of the realisation of certain risks, the refusal to undergo surgery is not justified. The Court assessed damages ex aequo et bono and granted a proviso with regard to a possible deterioration of the damage or for the possibility that the costs of the operation would exceed the compensation or in the event that the operation would increase the damage.[49]

6. Continued payment of wages

[89] P cannot sue D for loss of wages because his damage is fully compensated. The right of the employer to recover the wages and legally imposed social security contributions from the tortfeasor is explicitly recognised by the Act on Employment Contracts of 1978.[50]

---

44 [1994] *Case law review* 889.

45 Liège 6 December 1984, [1985] *Revue générale des assurances et des responsabilies* nr. 10964.

46 Brussels 31 May 1985, [1988] *Revue générale des assurances et des responsabilités* nr. 11359.

47 Corr. Liège 8 November 1983, [1986] *Revue générale des assurances et des responsabilités* nr. 11049.

48 Bergen 18 February 1982, [1986] *Revue générale des assurances et des responsabilités* nr. 11026.

49 Antwerp 21 June 1991, [1992] *Bulletin des Assurances* 146; see also Brussel 12 March 1997, [1997] *Tijdschrift voor aansprakelijkheid en verzekering in het wegverkeer* 216.

50 Liège 18 February 1987, [1987] *Revue Régionale de Droit* 264; [1994] *Case law review* 929.

7. Monk case

[90] The loss of an advantage which is gratuitously granted and therefore not legally enforceable can be compensated if the gain of this advantage was legitimate and sufficiently continuous.[51]

[91] A person held responsible for the death of a prioress was condemned to pay the pecuniary loss of the monastic community because this community benefited from the continuous advantage of the gratuitous work of the prioress.[52]

8. Lost earning capacity

(a) General remarks on the compensation for permanent invalidity[53]

[92] According to normal case law, permanent invalidity is usually divided into four categories:

1. permanent invalidity involving real loss of income
2. permanent invalidity involving decrease of economic value on the labour market without immediate loss of income
3. permanent invalidity involving additional efforts for the victim but no loss of economic value
4. permanent invalidity involving no additional efforts for the victim.

[93] Only the first two categories imply incapacity for work. The difference between invalidity (a mere medical term) and incapacity (which refers to an economic concept) is a major feature of the law of damages. According to well established Belgian case law, the victim must prove that the invalidity leads to a loss of income in order to claim damages for incapacity to work. Indeed, the level of invalidity does not necessarily coincide with the level of incapacity for work.

(i) Permanent invalidity involving real loss of income

[94] The facts presented in the question appear to fall under this category. Usually only a severe level of invalidity will lead to a loss of income. In principle, this damage will be compensated on the basis of capitalisation, by annuities (rente) or by a combination of both. Only under rare circumstances will severe incapacity for work be compensated on an ex aequo et bono basis. A fictitious calculation base can be taken into account. In the case of a university student, damages were assessed commencing from the income of a starting educator (600,000 Bf).[54]

[95] An employee sustained a permanent invalidity of 60 %. The court did not only consider this medical factor, but also the victim's professional skills and his adaptability on the labour market. On the basis of these elements a.o., the court held that, despite the 40 % theoretically

---

51 Cass. 4 September 1972, [1973] *Arresten van het Hof van Cassatie* 1.

52 Gent, 26 May 1986, [1988] *Revue générale des assurances et des responsabilités* nr. 11367.

53 [1994] *Case law review* 1184–1197.

54 Antwerpen 22 April 1988, [1990] *Bulletin des Assurances* 791.

remaining capacity to work, the employee in fact no longer had any prospect of earning his own income.[55]

(ii) Permanent invalidity involving loss of economic value without loss of earnings

[96] E.g. The decrease of the economical value of a student in medicine whose permanent invalidity of 25% could be reduced to 15% by operation, was established taking into account the loss of the opportunity to practice medicine as a specialist. The capitalisation is applied on the basis of available statistics on his expected starting wages.[56]

(iii) Permanent invalidity involving no loss of income, only extra efforts

[97] The assessment of this kind of damage will be done ex aequo et bono.

(iv) Permanent invalidity involving no loss of economic value

[98] This kind of invalidity refers to cases such as e.g. loss of teeth, loss of sexual or reproductive capacity, very small invalidity level ranging from 1 to 10 %, etc. According to the authors of the case law review these kinds of damages are merely moral damage.

(v) Conclusion

[99] The case law review contains multiple examples of the significant diversity in damages awarded in the case of permanent invalidity. This diversity is primarily caused by the fundamental choice to be made between the assessment by capitalisation or ex aequo et bono.[57]

(b) Specific remarks with regard to the permanent incapacity sustained by children and students

[100] In the legislation on industrial accidents, application is made of a reference wage which can be used to assess the calculation basis in combination with the valuation of other factors such as the social environment of the victim, his discipline and study results. The court of appeal of Brussels ruled that it would be arbitrary to estimate the personal injuries sustained by a candidate student pilot on the basis of the earnings of a complete career as a pilot. The victim only lost the opportunity to build on such a career. Therefore the court took into account his income which he would have earned entering into the labour market ex aequo et bono.[58]

[101] A judge refused to increase the permanent invalidity of a 19 year old boy from 65 % to 100 % because in view of his moderate school results it was unlikely that — had the accident not occurred — he would have been immediately hired as an assistant accountant.[59]

[102] The loss of a school year can cause damage to future professional prospects. The victim must prove that this damage is sufficiently certain on the basis of his skills, talent and ambition. Past school results play an important role. Damages awarded by the courts for the loss of a school year vary considerably.

55 [1994] *Case law review* 1010.

56 Brussels 21 December 1988, [1990] *Revue générale des assurances et des responsabilités* nr. 11609.

57 [1994] *Case law review* 1197–1207.

58 Brussels 1 March 1985, [1987] *Revue générale des assurances et des responsabilités* nr. 11173.

59 Corr. Brussels 16 April 1986, [1986] *Bulletin des Assurances* 431.

(c) Basis of calculation if A were the 6 year old child of a family with a low income, A having shown quite normal abilities so far.

[103] A six year old girl sustained a total incapacity for future employment. Although the child was psychologically still healthy, she fell behind considerably in school. A compensation worth 950,000 BF was awarded.[60]

(d) B's negligence leading to A's being rendered clinically dead

[104] In two recent cases the material damage of the victim in this situation was assessed on the basis of his living costs, without taking into account the loss of economic value.[61] There appears to be no consensus on the award of moral damages to the victim.

9. Lost spouse / partner

(a) General principles

[105] The general principles on the compensation for *loss of income* in the case of death of the sole family income earner are the following.[62] The basis is the net income of the deceased after deduction of a lump sum representing the personal living costs of the deceased. The authors of the case law review conclude that even for identical family situations very different percentages for the deduction for personal living costs of the deceased are withheld, ranging from 20 to50%.
[106] With regard to the *moral damage*, distinction must be made between the moral damage by repercussion (i.e. damage related to the attachment to the deceased) on the one hand and the moral damage ex haerede suffered by the victim prior to his death on the other hand.[63]
[107] A rightful claim for *moral damage by repercussion* requires the infringement of a legitimate interest and the existence of true bonds of affection. To prove this, it is no longer necessary to be next of kin or to have lived in the same house as the deceased. The average awarded sum for the moral damage suffered by repercussion in the case of death of the husband is 250,000 Bef. For the claim *ex haerede* a legal bond must exist. The proof of the infringement of a legitimate interest or the existence of the bond of affection is not required for this point of damage.

(b) Non-marital partner[64]

[108] A concubine is entitled to compensation if the partner dies, provided two conditions are fulfilled.
[109] The first condition concerns the admissibility of the claim, i.e. the question whether the infringed interest is a legitimate one. Before adultery was depenalised in 1987, the loss

60 Brussels 1 December 1987, [1991] *Revue générale des assurances et des responsabilités* nr. 11862; [1994] *Case law review* 992–993.

61 Bergen 7 May 1992, [1995] *Revue générale des assurances et des responsabilités* nr.12509 and Corr. Huy 21 December 1984, [1989] *Bulletin des Assurances* 533.

62 [1994] *Case law review* 1131–1152.

63 [1994] *Case law review* 1162–1184.

64 [1994] *Case law review* 945–956.

of the adulterous relationship was considered to be not susceptible to compensation because it was illegitimate.[65] The Cour de Cassation ruled in 1990 in rather general terms, that the adulterous character of a relationship does not make the interest of the concubine illegitimate. This ruling however is subject to criticism and is not unanimously applied by the lower courts.[66]

[110] The second condition concerns the validity of the claim, i.e. the requirement of certainty of the damage for the assessment of which the endurance of the relationship will be an important factor.

[111] A concubine who lived with her partner for 12 years and with whom she shared the parenthood of a child, was not compensated for the loss of the income of the partner and for his help in the housekeeping because she settled for a precarious relationship without any certainty of its stability. She was compensated only for pain and suffering because the breach of the ties of affection could be considered as the infringement of a legitimate interest.[67] In another case, however, although taking place in the same time period, pecuniary as well as non-pecuniary damages were awarded to the concubine because she could prove with sufficient certainty that the deceased would have been her partner for life.[68]

[112] In conclusion it can be stated that if damages are awarded with regard to the death of a concubine, these damages are usually smaller than those awarded to the marital partner. Caselaw on this remains divergent.[69]

(c) A's husband who maintained the household is killed in an accident for which B is responsible

[113] The annual loss of the economic value of a househusband/wife is generally calculated on the basis of capitalisation of fixed daily or monthly values or recently also on annual sums. These vary according to the family situation and whether or not the deceased was a full-time househusband/wife or not. The age and life expectancy of the surviving spouse are usually also taken into account. Generally, the full life expectancy of the deceased is taken into account, unless the dependency of the entitled parties to the deceased is limited in time.[70] In some cases the capitalisation period is limited to the pensionable age and for the remaining period a fixed sum is awarded. The capitalisation must be preceeded by the deduction of the personal living costs of the deceased (whether or not he or she had an income). The application of this general principle to the case of the death of the househusband/wife frequently leads to inequitable results because the judge must not only deduct the living costs of the deceased househusband/wife from the sum of compensation equivalent to the pecuniary value of his or her work in the household. In addition (and this element especially may lead to the unfair result) this economic value should not be added to the income of the surviving spouse in order to calculate the contribution of the deductable living costs. Consider-

---

65 Cass. 19 December 1978, [1978–79] *Arresten van het Hof van Cassatie* 489.

66 [1994] *Case law review* 949.

67 Brussels 2 October 1986, [1987–88] *Rechtskundig Weekblad* 1438–1439; [1994] *Case law review* 953.

68 Liège 12 November 1986, [1987] *Revue de jurisprudence de Liège, Mons et Bruxelles* 408–409.

69 [1994] *Case law review* 954 and 1169–1170.

70 [1994] *Case law review* 1118–1119.

ing the outcome of this calculation method as unfair, some judges deviate from it and do prefer to assess the lost economic value ex aequo et bono.[71] In the case law review three examples are given of a lump sum awarded in the case of the death of a housewife: 60 years old – full time: 750,000 Bf; 54 years old – part time: 1,400,000 Bf; 43 years old — full time: 1,000,000 Bf. These judgements date respectively from 1983, 1984 and 1986.[72]

10. Offending publication

[114] Not many case law was found on this subject. In any event, we reiterate the fact that the Belgian law of damages does not allow punitive damages. It is, however, possible that in the assessment of the damages the profit made by a negligent publisher is taken into account in order to grant some deterring effect to the judgement. We did not find a judgement where such a reasoning was explicitely formulated, most likely in apprehension of being overruled by the scrutiny of the Cour de Cassation with regard to the adherence to the principle of the compensatory character of the Belgian law of damages.
[115] The following case law may provide an idea of how a Belgian court would render a judgement in a similar case.
[116] The pecuniary and moral damage suffered by a doctor whose photo was published in a popular newspaper as an illustration for two articles on the actual problems of the doctors, were set ex aequo et bono on 300,000 Bef.[73]

11. Rosenkavalier case

[117] Applying the principles of tort law which are in general very favourable for the victim, a Belgian court will probably order the compensation of the fee paid for the tour and might even be inclined to order the payment of a (symbolic) sum of money for the moral damage. The fact that the victim did not subscribe an inability insurance will not be held against him (cfr. the rather restricted application of the duty of the victim to mitigate the extent of the damage).

12. Prostitute case

[118] In the line of the answer to general question 11, we are inclined to state, she will be fully compensated for all legitimate losses she can prove to have suffered (e.g. personal injuries, material damages), but not for the loss of income insofar as prostitution is esteemed to violate the public order.

13. Mercedes case

[119] We recapitulate the principles on damages applicable to this case.

---

71 [1994] *Case law review* 1141–1142.
72 [1994] *Case law review* 1147–1152.
73 Brussels 8 November 1989, [1992] *Revue générale des assurances et des responsabilités* nr. 11906.

[120] 1. Damage is generally described as the difference between the actual situation of the victim and the hypothetical situation in which this person would have been, had he not been victimised. Elements external to the damage which would increase or decrease compensation, may not be taken into account (i.e. the objective method to calculate the recoverable damages).
[121] 2. Hypothetical damage, funded only on assumptions gives no right to compensation. Coincidence is never taken into account.
[122] 3. A victim cannot claim the most expensive form of compensation in money if different forms are available. If the worth of the damaged good is smaller than the costs of repair or reconstruction, the victim cannot claim more than the worth of the damaged good – unless the specific circumstances of the case dictate otherwise, e.g. if replacement is not possible and repair is.[74]
[123] Following these principles D owes P 4,000 Euro. P can still try to sell his car to dealer Y, this will not affect D's obligation to compensate P.

14. Loss of use

[124] The following answer is based on the text of an annotation by B. DE TEMMERMAN, under BGH, 7 May 1996 due to appear soon in the European Review of Private Law and on the Case law review 1994.
[125] B. De Temmerman examines Belgian case law with regard to this point of damage comparing it with German case law. His research led a.o. to the conclusion that issues with regard to damage resulting from loss of use are rarely raised before the court and if so, trial judges rule on them without falling back on underlying principles. The following framework can however be given with regard to (the majority of) Belgian case law on this subject.

(a) The recoverability of damage resulting from a loss of use in general

[126] The loss of use must be fully compensated separate from the compensation for the loss of the good in itself.[75]
[127] On this issue we quote B. De Temmerman: 'At first sight, the question of whether a recoverable loss may be acknowledged irrespective of the concrete circumstances of the case should be answered, under Belgian law, in the negative, bearing in mind that damage must be assessed in concreto.' There is, however, another principle that more and more often is invoked, i.e. the principle of the plaintiff's freedom to decide whether to use the awarded damages for reparation or not. Thus it is considered that the plaintiff should also be entitled to compensation for loss of use during the (hypothetical) repairs. The case law of the trial judges is not unanimous on this issue. B. De Temmerman rephrases the ruling of the Cour de Cassation in a judgement of 18 October 1995 as follows: 'the immobilization of a damaged car as such is not equated with damage.' 'It remains to be seen whether there may be damage without immobilization, e.g. when the plaintiff continues to drive his damaged car.

---

74 Brussels 12 March 1985, [1985, II] *Pasicrisie* 82–85; [1994] *Case law review* 858–859 and 1066–1067.
75 [1994] *Case law review* 1409.

In principle, if the Cour de Cassation upholds the rule of assessment in concreto, this question should be addressed in the negative. But, as has been noted, case law tends to abandon this rule to some extent, invoking the principle of the plaintiff's freedom of use.' 'In the case-law of the Cour de Cassation (this) principle is only invoked in the case of the assessment of damage resulting from the loss of or damage to property: the plaintiff is entitled to the cost of replacement or repairs including VAT, without regard to the question of whether or not the plaintiff allocates the funds to the reparation of damage.'

(b) Assessment of compensation for loss of use applied to cars

[128] Again we quote B. De Temmerman. 'For decades Belgian case-law is characterized by a rather inconsiderate use of a tariff, elaborated by judicial practice, which assesses the damages on a daily basis. Thus, the assessment of damages amounts to a multiplication of a daily allowance with the number of days for which the car could not be used. The tariff itself is unchallenged. There is only an abundant (and reported) body of case law concerning the determination of the duration of the period of immobilization. Damages, however, are not always assessed ex aequo et bono. While earlier case law seems to have been very reticent towards the reimbursement of the cost of hire if the plaintiff actually hired a substitute car, it is now generally considered that damages may not be assessed ex aequo et bono in such a case and that, subject to certain conditions, the plaintiff is entitled to the reimbursement of the cost of hire.'

(i) Duration of loss of use for cars

[129] The relevant time period for the calculation of the compensation for the loss of use for cars, is usually divided into two periods.

[130] The first period, the so-called waiting period, is the time span between the accident and the end of the appraiser's examination. The second period is either the time needed for repairs, which is usually indicated in the insurance appraiser's report after consent between the appraiser and the garage owner/repairman as a mandate of the aggrieved car owner, or either, in the case of a total loss, the time needed for the aggrieved party to acquire another car and to fulfill the required formalities with regard to legally operating this car on the road.

[131] To the extent that a car is immobilised after an accident, the loss of use is a separate item of damage, irrespective of the use which was made of the car or the profession or usual activity of the owner of said car. The type of use made of a car, however, can play a role in the assessment of the duration of the period of loss of use.[76]

[132] (a) The waiting period. In principle, the waiting period begins the day of the accident. There is recent case law which establishes the end of this period on the date of the insurance appraiser's investigation or the date of the first appraiser's assessment, but generally the day on which the total loss is certain and therefore also the day that the aggrieved party must take steps to acquire another car. This certainty usually follows from the result of the appraiser's report or from a statement of the appraiser. If it is clear in the immediate aftermath of the accident that the car is completely destroyed, occasionally no compensation for loss of use for a 'waiting period' is awarded. More and more courts are departing from the assessment

76 [1994] *Case law review* 1409–1410.

of the waiting period on a fixed basis (one day or three days) and tend to establish its duration in concreto.[77]

[133] (b) Duration of repairs. In practice, very few disputes arise with regard to this matter because the duration of repairs is agreed upon between the appraiser and the garage owner-repairman as a mandate of the aggrieved car owner. In some judgements, account is taken of the actual period needed for the repairs by a sufficiently careful and prudent garage owner, if this period exceeds the time span stipulated in the agreement, provided that this is not due to the aggrieved party's fault.[78]

[134] (c) Period of replacement. Although some case law still assesses this period automatically to six days, more and more judgements take the actual period of replacement into account provided the victim (sufficiently careful and prudent), ordered a substitute car similar to the damaged car and he personally declared his non-approval of the short period formulated in the appraiser's report.

(ii) Assessment of the amount of damages to be compensated

[135] Every four years a non-binding, illustrative list of daily allowances for loss of use (including the period of replacement) is published by the Royal Federation of the Justices of the Peace and the Police Court Judges.

[136] (a) On the basis of a lump sum. According to B. De Temmerman: 'The unquestioned use of the assessment ex aequo et bono, (. . .) may possibly explain why, (. . .) the question as to whether the plaintiff is entitled to damages assessed on the basis of the cost of hire, even if he does not hire a substitute car, has not yet been addressed in case-law, however surprising this may be.'

[137] (b) Reimbursement of cost for hiring a replacement car. Earlier case law was basically opposed to the reimbursement of the cost of hire and always assessed the damages ex aequo et bono. B. De Temmerman states: 'This position has since been renounced. There is however some disagreement on the question as to whether the plaintiff is entitled to reimbursement irrespective of the type of use to which the car is put. A minority line of authority requires that the plaintiff needs the replacement car in the exercise of his business or profession, for travelling to and from work or similarly compelling reasons; the hire of a replacement car by an unemployed plaintiff has been considered to be a failure to mitigate the damage. The majority case law, however, does not draw any differences between private use on the one hand and professional or business use on the other.'

[138] The owner of a damaged car, who uses a replacement car, saves costs on his own vehicle. These savings are often deducted in the assessment of the damage (usually a lump sum).

15. Damaged, but unrepaired car

[139] (a) A will be awarded the restitution of the fictitious costs of repair (free disposition of the vicitim of the sum of the compensation).

[140] (b) and (c) If these conditions are fulfilled the car is said to be an 'economical total loss'. In principle the costs of repair will not be restituted, unless no replacement car with

---

77 [1994] *Case law review* 1411–1412.

78 [1994] *Case law review* 1413–1414.

the same features as the damaged car can be found. The Cour de Cassation ruled that the duty to compensate the costs of repair only exists to the extent of the replacement value of the car.[79] Case law on this issue is abundant and not always in the same vein.

16. Additional car damage

[141] (a) Certain case law grants compensation for the loss of the value of the car because it has become an accident car.
[142] (b) It is very likely that the advantage gained because of the replacement of new parts for old will be taken into account in the assessment of the damage. See also the answer to the general question nr. 14.
[143] (c) A judge may be inclined to award some compensation for this item of damage in light of his duty to provide the victim full compensation. It remains to be seen, however, under which circumstances and to what extent the judge will find the garage to have become useless.

17. Damaged railway wagon

[144] The Belgian railway line (N.M.B.S.) has a transport duty to the extent that this transport is not impeded by circumstances which the N.M.B.S. could not avoid, e.g. caused by the negligence of a third party. Therefore, the causality was not broken by the legal obligation to build up a reserve. The court also accepted that the compensation for the damage for the loss of use could be calculated on the basis of the formula used by the N.M.B.S. (which differentiates between different engines, the value of replacement, the residual value as a percentage of the replacement value, the interest rate and the annuity according to the life of the material.[80]

18. Detective case

[145] In a case described in the case law review, it was found to be justified that an insurance company paid tip-off money in order to gain information on a thief and to establish the deceit in court, so that the thief was convicted to reimburse the tip-off money.[81]
Recently the Cour de Cassation ruled otherwise in a case corresponding exactly to the facts given in this question. The fact that a theft was committed in a department store which employed security agents, does not prove the causal relationship between the theft and the obligation of the owner of the stolen goods to pay the fee of these agents. The owner has no right to recover this fee from the thief.[82]

19. Death of parents

[146] See the answer to the general question nr. 14.

---

79 Cass. 23 October 1986, [1987–88] *Rechtskundig Weekblad* 54.
80 [1994] *Case law review* 1007.
81 [1994] *Case law review* 889–890.
82 Cass. 15 November 1995, [1995] *Arresten van het Hof van Cassatie* 1016.

England

DAMAGES UNDER ENGLISH LAW[1]

W. V. Horton Rogers

Part I – General questions on the law of damages

1. Aims of the law of damages

[1] Undoubtedly the principal purpose of damages for tort is to compensate the plaintiff[2] for the loss he has suffered thereby. The classic statement is that of Lord Blackburn in *Livingstone v Rawyards Coal Co.*[3] (a case of misappropriation of property): damages are 'that sum of money which will put the party who has been injured, or who has suffered, in the same position as he would have been in if he had not sustained the wrong for which he is now getting compensation or reparation'. Note, however, that in some cases (e.g. the non-pecuniary aspects of personal injury claims, defamation, false imprisonment) substantial damages may be awarded as 'compensation' for a 'loss' which is not in fact measurable in money terms (see I.6 below).

[2] In addition to compensation there are at least two other aims of the law of damages in certain cases.

[3] (1) Exemplary or punitive damages may be awarded in two classes of case where the tort is intentional: [4]

[4] (a) Where there is oppressive, unconstitutional or arbitrary behaviour by a servant of the state (including for this purpose a police officer). See *Thompson v Metropolitan Police Commissioner,*[5] which attempts to control awards of such damages against the police, subjecting them to a limit of £50,000.

---

1 For comparative purposes at the time of writing (summer 1998) very rough currency convertors for the figures quoted are: ATS 20; BFr 60; FFr 10; GrDr 5; Dm 3; ItL 3,000; NLGld 3.2; PrtEsc 300; SwFr 2.4; SARnd 8.5; SwKr 13; US$ 1.7; Euro 1.6.

2 This material was prepared before the advent of the new Civil Procedure Rules, which means that henceforth we shall use 'claimant", despite the fact that the old terminology is used all over the common law world and is familiar to civilian comparative lawyers.

3 (1880) 5 App Cas 25 at 39.

4 In theory there is a third class – where legislation specifically allows it, but there do not appear to be any examples of this. Exemplary damages are more restricted in England than in most common law jurisdictions. For a comparative review see Law Commission Consultation Paper No. 132 (1993).

5 [1997] 3 W.L.R. 403.

U. Magnus (ed.), Unification of Tort Law: Damages, 53–76.

[5] (b) Where the defendant has calculated that the gain to be made by committing the wrong is likely to exceed any compensatory damages payable to the plaintiff or that the plaintiff is likely to be unwilling to take the risk of suing – e.g. a knowing or reckless libel published to boost circulation. See *John v Mirror Group Newspapers*.[6] These awards are also controlled more tightly than in the past but, unlike the previous category, it is not possible to specify a particular maximum. However, it is thought that the Court of Appeal would be likely to take a sceptical view of any award of more than £100,000, even in a bad case. The aim of the law here is deterrence,[7] to teach the defendant and others like him that tort does not pay; but the *effect* of an award may be to strip the defendant of the profit he has made by his wrongdoing, though in some cases this may be done more directly by the next category.
[6] Though the existence of exemplary damages has often been criticised as anomalous they are a distinctive feature of common law systems and the Law Commission has recommended that they should be retained and that the present restrictions should be removed so that they would be generally available for wilful wrongdoing[8] displaying a deliberate disregard of the plaintiff's rights.[9]
[7] (2) Restitutionary damages. These are currently controversial (still more so in cases of contract[10]) and their availability may be limited by their historical connection ('waiver of tort') with quasi procedural issues which have now disappeared. However, they are generally regarded as available where the defendant profits by the wrongful appropriation (or probably use) of the plaintiff's property. Thus if D misappropriates P's jewels and manages to sell them for more than they are worth, P may sue D for the price received ('money had and received') rather than for their value in an action for conversion. In practice the modern cases have concerned matters like detaining goods beyond the permitted period, dumping waste on land without permission or failing to remove material left on the plaintiff's property and the cases have awarded the plaintiff a 'fair rental' as damages rather than inquiring into the gain actually made by the defendant, which rather 'fudges' the line between compensation and disgorgement. On the other hand, it seems clear in principle that there is no requirement that the plaintiff should have lost a real opportunity to use his property in other ways.[11]
[8] *Role of judge*. Differences in outcomes between legal systems are often attributable to differences in the power accorded to the trial judge. Damages are primarily a matter for the trial judge but they must be awarded in accordance with settled principles of law and the judge must give his reasons in the normal way. On a matter of quantification the Court of

6 [1997] QB 586.

7 In both categories (a) and b) there is a further requirement that the tort committed must be one for which exemplary damages had been awarded before 1964. This is an anomalous and irrational requirement which has arisen for historical reasons which there is no space to explain here. See AB v. South West Water Services [1993] QB 507 and LCCP No 132 (above).

8 But not for breach of contract.

9 Law Com No. 247 (1997) (available at http: //www.gtnet.gov.uk/lawcomm).

10 Contrast Surrey CC v. Bredero Homes [1993] 1 WLR 1361 with Att Gen v Blake [1998] 1 All ER 833.

11 It should be noted that the disgorgement principle is very firmly established in two areas: an account of profits is a standard remedy for infringement of intellectual property rights (copyright, patents, trade marks, passing off) and a person who owes a fiduciary duty to another must account for profits made by him by breach of that duty.

Appeal is likely to give the trial judge some 'margin of appreciation' but even here it will interfere with an award which is 'plainly' too high (or too low). My impression is that the trial court is more tightly controlled than, say, under the French system. In recent years the Court of Appeal has shown itself more ready to interfere with awards of damages for non-material loss in matters like reputation or liberty (see below).

2. General principles of the law of damages

[9] Damages are always money. A mandatory injunction orders the defendant to undo the wrong *in natura* but the remedy is of limited practical importance. For example, a defendant who has removed support from his neighbour's land by excavation *might* be ordered to restore the support[12] but it is inconceivable that if D damaged P's car in a collision that D would be ordered to have the car repaired. The underlying principle is that specific relief will be refused where damages would be an adequate remedy and in the case of mandatory injunctions the instinct of the common law is to take a rather optimistic view of the adequacy of damages.

[10] The quotation above from the *Livingstone* case is consistent with 'complete' compensation. However, this is limited by general principles of law (e.g. legal causation and remoteness, contributory negligence) and by the law of damages itself (e.g. the principle that the plaintiff must mitigate his loss and cannot recover compensation for damage which he could have avoided by taking reasonable steps). The general law and the law of damages are of course linked in a way which makes the division more one of convenience of exposition than of substance. To illustrate from the law of contract, the prima facie measure of damages for non delivery in a contract of sale of goods is the difference between the contract price and the (higher) market price when the goods should have been delivered. That might be regarded as the prima facie rule of remoteness in such cases. Equally, however, it might be regarded as reflecting the fundamental duty to mitigate by seeking a 'cover' purchase. So also in tort: suppose D is in breach of a duty of care to P to value a property upon the security of which P proposes to lend money. The loan is £500,000, the reported value is £700,000 and the true value is £550,000. By the time the borrower defaults on the loan there has been a collapse in property values and the value has fallen to £400,000. Is D liable to P for the shortfall in the security? No. Although P's loss is factually caused by D's negligence and although market movements are certainly foreseeable one must ask what was D's duty and it was to take care to provide accurate information and he is therefore liable only for losses which are attributable to the information being wrong.[13]

3. Different forms of damages

[11] As to *compensatory*, *exemplary* and *restitutionary* damages see I.1. above. *Nominal*

12 But for such a claim which failed see Morris v Redland Bricks [1970] AC 652, principally on the ground that the cost of the work would have been disproportionate to the value of the plaintiff's land.

13 Banque Bruxelles Lambert SA v Eagle Star Insurance Co. [1997] AC 191.

damages[14] are available where the tort is actionable per se,[15] though in the great majority of cases the plaintiff's object in bringing the proceedings is to obtain substantial damages for what, for want of a better word, may be called 'non-material' loss (see I.7 below). The award of nominal damages is an indication that the plaintiff has suffered an infringement of a legal right but has suffered no loss (or has proved no loss). It *may* further indicate that he had no good reason for bringing the suit, which may lead the court to exercise its discretion in refusing him costs.[16] However, there are some cases in which the plaintiff will be regarded as having a legitimate reason for bringing the case even though no loss has at present been suffered, for example in a case of trespass to land where there is a dispute as to the relative rights of the parties or to prevent the establishment of a right by prescription. In these cases nowadays it is doubtful if it is *necessary* to bring an action for nominal damages since alternative remedies will be available in the form of a declaration or an injunction.

[12] *Legal fees and judicial costs* are generally covered by the 'costs' which are normally awarded against the unsuccessful party in a civil action in favour of the successful party. Any shortfall between these and actual expenditure[17] is not recoverable as damages. Where as a result of the defendant's wrong the plaintiff has been successfully sued by a third party, the damages and reasonably incurred costs of the plaintiff in that action are recoverable. Almost all the cases are claims for breach of contract and the most obvious example is that of a suit brought against a (now) plaintiff buyer by a sub-buyer as a result of defects in the goods attributable to the (now) defendant seller.[18] If the plaintiff has been successful in the proceedings brought by the third party the only amount in issue will be the shortfall in the costs actually incurred and those recovered from the third party. Traditionally, in contrast with the situation on costs in the suit between plaintiff and defendant, this shortfall was recoverable, but some doubt has now been cast on this.[19]

4. Legislation on damages

[13] In tort there is no general legislation on damages, though that reflects the generally non-codified nature of tort. Statutes imposing liability commonly leave the issue of damages to common law principles,[20] though statutes implementing international conventions (e.g. air accidents, collisions at sea) inevitably deal with damages since limitation of liability is commonly a core purpose of these conventions. Section 1 of the Damages Act 1996 provides that

---

14 There seems to be no particular figure. For many years the norm was £2, nowadays it seems generally to be £5 or £10.

15 Breaches of contract are always actionable per se.

16 Derisory awards like 1p, which one sometimes finds in libel cases, are commonly called 'contemptuous damages' and are even more likely to lead to this result.

17 In the past this was likely to be very substantial. The gap has now narrowed and all costs 'reasonably incurred' are prima facie awardable, but in the majority of cases there is still likely to be some shortfall. Furthermore, the new Civil Procedure Rules will introduce the idea of proportionality into the recovery of costs.

18 In one of the few tort cases, The Wallsend [1907] P 302 (P's ship sunk by D; P sued by river authority for costs of removing wreck) the claim for damages in respect of costs failed because the plaintiff had been unreasonable in contesting a clear-cut claim against him.

19 Lonrho v Fayed (No. 5) [1993] 1 WLR 1489.

20 *See*, e.g. the Animals Act 1971; Part I of the Consumer Protection Act 1987.

in calculating lump sum damages for personal injury the court is to take account of such assumed rates of return on capital as may be prescribed by the Lord Chancellor, but this is not at present in force (see I.8). There are various particular statutory provisions dealing with, e.g., collateral benefits,[21] fatal accidents,[22] misappropriation of property[23] but the general picture is a case law based system.

5. Definition of recoverable damage

[14] There is no general statutory definition of damage (see I.4) though statute may of course make actionable in a particular situation that which does not generally amount to damage[24] – or vice versa. I am not sure that damage as a 'natural term' is very meaningful, save perhaps in the most obvious sense of physical injury to person or property.[25] 'Damage' seems to me to be a legal concept, the meaning of which will vary from one category of liability to another. Thus 'pure' loss of reputation is remediable only by an action for defamation (or malicious prosecution); where, however, actual pecuniary loss can be shown it is no bar to its recovery under some other head that the injury may also be said to affect the plaintiff's reputation. For example, if D writes a carelessly inaccurate reference on P which is not actionable as defamation[26] but which causes P to lose a job with X, P may sue D for negligence.[27] Some torts (e.g. libel, assault, false imprisonment) are actionable per se, that is to say no actual financial or physical damage need be shown. In these cases the 'general damages' may properly include damages for mental distress. Negligence is never actionable per se[28] and, standing alone, mental distress is not damage unless it amounts to a recognizable psychiatric illness, in which case it is treated like any ordinary physical injury or disease. Thus if P is killed in a crowd disaster at a football stadium the feeling of terror which he suffers because of his knowledge of impending death (which, when it comes, is virtually instantaneous) does not give his estate[29] a claim for damages for that sensation.[30] Where, however, there is a long term injury the 'tariff' figures for pain and suffering and loss of

---

21 *See* II.6.

22 *See* II.9.

23 Torts (Interference with Goods) Act 1977.

24 *See*, e.g. Protection from Harassment Act 1997 (anxiety and distress).

25 Note, however, that the Oxford English Dictionary gives meanings in the following order: (1) 'loss or detriment caused by hurt or injury affecting estate, condition or circumstances"; (2) 'injury, harm, esp. physical injury to a thing such as impairs its value or usefulness"; (3) ' disadvantage, inconvenience, trouble, a matter for regret, a misfortune' [the sense of the modern French exclamation 'dommage!"]; (4) '(law) the value, estimated in money, of something lost or withheld".

26 E.g. because, the occasion being one of qualified privilege, D is not malicious; or because the statement, though damaging, does not reflect on P's character.

27 Spring v. Guardian Assurance [1995] 2 AC 296.

28 Historically, negligence is an 'action on the case", a category which always required proof of actual damage. Note, however, that some modern statutory torts dealing with sex and race discrimination and harassment allow recovery of damages for matters like anxiety and distress.

29 His dependants of course have a cause of action under the Fatal Accidents Act for the financial consequences of his death and some of them have a claim for 'bereavement' (see below).

30 Hicks v Chief Constable of S Yorkshire [1992] 2 All ER 65.

amenity[31] may be increased somewhat to allow for mental distress suffered by the victim.[32]
[15] One may say that personal injury or physical damage to property always amounts to damage in the eyes of the law. But economic loss (i.e. financial loss which is not consequent on personal injury or property damage) caused by negligence is not generally recoverable unless there is a 'special relationship' between the parties.[33] There is no such restriction in respect of fraud, intentional interference with contract or other expectations, malicious falsehood or passing off. Alternatively, one might say that because these torts require the plaintiff to be in some sense the 'target' of the defendant's wrongdoing, the requisite relationship is already built in. Economic loss is also of course compensable in the statutory torts relating to trade marks, copyrights and patents, though these are generally regarded as areas of law in their own right. The statement that 'economic loss is not damage recognized by law' is therefore plainly wrong. But so is the reverse statement. Sometimes it is, sometimes it is not. Typically we decide the question by reference to concepts (e.g. the duty of care) other than damages.

6. Different types of damages

(a) Damage to person, property, economic loss

[16] See I.5. above.

(b) Actual/future loss

[17] Pre-trial losses are 'special damage'.[34] Future losses are 'general damages'. The former are generally capable of being proved and calculated with a precision absent from the latter.

(c) Direct/indirect losses

[18] I think in English terminology this would be the distinction between direct and *consequential* losses. One could not say that there were 'different rules' for the latter, save that they are perhaps more likely to be cut down on grounds of remoteness or mitigation. Thus in a case of damage to goods the direct loss would be diminution in value/cost of repair and the consequential loss would be loss of income from the use of the goods until a substitute could reasonably be hired. On this basis in a personal injury case the direct loss would be loss of amenity and loss of earnings would be 'consequential'. However, the latter are so important in these cases that I think most lawyers would regard them as part of the 'basic' or 'direct' damage. Nothing really turns on the classification.

(d) Damnum emergens/lucrum cessans

[19] Under this terminology the distinction is completely unknown to the common law.

---

31 *See* I.6.
32 The former conventional award to the estate of a deceased person for 'loss of expectation of life' was abolished by the Administration of Justice Act 1982.
33 *See* 'England' in Spier (ed) *The Limits of Expanding Liability* (1998).
34 This phrase has, unfortunately, different meanings according to its context.

Insofar as it means the distinction between 'positive damage' and 'loss of expectation' it roughly mirrors the common law distinction between damages in tort and contract (see below). However, I suspect the resemblance is not exact. Thus, as I understand it, if a French seller fails to deliver and the buyer has to pay a higher price for a substitute, that would be damnum emergens, whereas if the buyer lost a valuable sub sale that would be lucrum cessans. However, in English law both losses would be remediable only in contract and both would be regarded as falling within the 'expectation' measure of damages.[35]

(e) Patrimonial/non-patrimonial loss

[20] Again the terminology is not used. The usual terminology is 'pecuniary/non-pecuniary' rather than patrimonial/non-patrimonial or material/immaterial.
[21] Though I know of no comprehensive judicial definition, the concept of 'pecuniary loss' in the law of damages covers those losses which are concerned with a person's wealth, whether money (whether he has it or merely expects to have it, as in the case of loss of future earnings), intangible property such as shares or copyrights,[36] or tangible property such as land and goods. Hence all other losses are 'non-pecuniary'. The latter category covers, for example, pain and suffering and loss of amenity in a case of personal injury; loss of reputation in a case of libel; social discredit in a case of malicious prosecution; mental distress; or physical inconvenience and discomfort.
[22] The common characteristic of such losses is that while they must be given a monetary value in damages that figure must in the nature of things be a 'conventional' or even artificial one, not based on any market value. As it has been put in the context of personal injuries, such losses are:

"not susceptible of measurement in money. Any figure at which the assessor of damages arrives cannot be other than artificial and, if the aim is that justice meted out to all litigants should be even-handed instead of depending on idiosyncracies of the assessor . . . The figure must be 'basically a conventional figure derived from experience and from awards in comparable cases'."[37]

(f) Contract and tort

[23] English law generally accepts that there may be concurrent liability in contract and tort.[38] Where the damage is a of a type recoverable in an action of tort it will generally also be recoverable in any parallel claim for breach of contract. If a bus is driven negligently and crashes causing injury to passengers their damages would be the same whether the claim was framed as contract or tort. Generally speaking the principles of remoteness of damage in contract are more restrictive for the plaintiff than those in tort[39] and the implications of this

35 As opposed to the 'reliance' measure, which covers wasted expenditure.
36 Hence the phrase does not have the same meaning as 'economic loss' in the substantive law of liability.
37 Lord Diplock in Wright v BRB [1983] 2 AC 773 at 777. One may note that the comparability exercise is much harder outside the field of personal injuries.
38 Henderson v Merrett Syndicates [1995] 2 AC 145.
39 Czarnikow v Koufos, The Heron II [1969] 1 AC 350.

where the claim lies concurrently in contract and tort have not been fully worked out.[40]

[24] The fundamental distinction that contract is about the enforcement (albeit generally via a substitute money payment) of promises and torts about the repairing of harm is reflected in the approach to damages. The statement that in both contract and tort damages serve to put the plaintiff in the position he would have been in if the wrong had not been committed is entirely correct but apt to mislead as concealing the distinction between the wrongs of tort and breach of contract. The basic contract rule is that the plaintiff is entitled to be put in the position he would have been in *if the contract had been performed* ; in tort he is to be put in the position he would have been in *if the tort had not been committed.* Thus suppose S sells to B for £100,000 a picture which he fraudulently represents to be an early work of van Ruisdael. Such a picture would have an open market value of £120,000. The picture is in fact by an apprentice and is worth only £10,000. Assume that there is no contractual warranty or undertaking as to the provenance of the painting. Assume also that B is not in a position to rescind by returning the picture. B's damages for deceit are £90,000 (money paid less value received). If on the other hand there was a warranty that the picture was by van Ruisdael the contract damages would be £110,000 (value lost less value received).[41]

[25] Two qualifications complicate this distinction. First, even in a tort case the plaintiff may recover damages for loss of opportunity. Thus in *East v Maurer*[42] B bought one of S's two hair salons in a town as a result of a fraudulent misrepresentation by S that he intended[43] to go abroad and not to work in the other salon. There was no covenant not to compete in the contract of sale. When S in fact remained in town running the other salon most of the customers of B's salon followed S. B could not claim the profit he would have made if S had gone abroad for that would have been to give him the benefit of a contract which had not been made; but B was entitled to recover damages representing what he would have made from laying out his money on another salon. The second qualification is that the plaintiff in an action for breach of contract who is unable to prove that he would have made a profit may in the alternative fall back on claiming his reliance[44] loss (i.e. expenditure) subject to the liberty of the defendant to reduce or extinguish this, if he can, by proving the amount of any loss that the plaintiff would have made had the contract been performed. One (Australian) view is that this is not really a different approach to damages but merely a rule of practice that in the absence of evidence the law presumes that the plaintiff would have made enough on the deal to cover his costs.[45]

---

40 *See* Parsons v Uttley Ingham [1978] QB 791. In the context of time limits on claims the plaintiff is free to rely on whichever claim is to his advantage: see Henderson v Merrett Syndicates above. However, such 'tactical' behaviour has been restricted in the context of contributory negligence: Barclays Bank v Fairclough Building [1995] QB 214.

41 It will be observed that if B had made a bad bargain (i.e. paid more than the going rate for a genuine van Ruisdael) the tort damages would be higher than the contract damages.

42 [1991] 1 WLR 461.

43 Deliberate breach of a promise is not fraud; but it is fraud to make a promise that you do not at the time of making intend to perform.

44 *See* Restatement 2d Contracts, § 370 – 'the reliance interest".

45 Commonwealth v Amann Aviation (1991) 104 ALR 1.

7. Monetary assessment of non-patrimonial damage

[26] As pointed out above (I.6.e), awards for non-patrimonial losses are not susceptible to scientific calculation. What the courts have done in cases of personal injury is to set a figure for the worst case (currently about 220,000 Euro) and then construct a 'tariff' working down from that, making assumptions about the relative seriousness of different injuries. Even where an injury has a comparatively uniform physical effect (e.g. loss of a leg) the tariff cannot be regarded as absolutely fixed because of the effect on different plaintiffs. Thus a person who had a passion for playing football might get rather more for that injury than one whose habits were sedentary. In some cases (e.g. scarring and sterility) the brackets are so wide that it is almost meaningless to speak of a tariff.

[27] The plaintiff's age is a relevant factor but in the majority of cases will not figure in the calculation unless the plaintiff is very old,[46] the tendency being to focus on the injury.

[28] If we take a case of personal injury, damages are recoverable for both non-pecuniary and pecuniary loss. Under the first head damages cover pain and suffering and loss of amenity (i.e. loss of enjoyment and loss of faculty) on a judicial 'tariff' up to about £150,000 for the worst case. In practice in nearly all cases the two elements of non-pecuniary loss will be awarded in a single, undivided sum; together they are the *dommage moral*. The tariff figures are not precisely fixed and some modest adjustment may be made if the effect on the plaintiff of the injury departs from the norm. In some cases the very variable nature of the effects of the injury is reflected in the fact that the tariff figure is a very broad band (e.g. scarring). There is no a priori reason why the top figure should not be 10% or 1,000% of what it actually is, but the theory is that the other figures should be broadly justifiable on a comparative basis.[47] However, the Law Commission has recently recommended a substantial rise in damages for non-pecuniary loss, of between 150 and 200 % in all but comparatively minor cases.[48] The larger element of personal injury awards in serious cases represents loss of earnings and expenses. See I.8.

[29] Where the tort consists of interference with reputation or liberty substantial pecuniary loss is rarely provable but awards may still be large- awards are not merely symbolic. Damages in these cases are said to be 'at large' and they clearly represent vindication rather than compensation in the strict sense,[49] even if there is no element of exemplary damages involved. In some such cases there is still trial by jury, which sets the damages, subject to guidance by the judge and the Court of Appeal's power to control excessive verdicts. In libel cases both counsel and judge may suggest appropriate figures to the jury, which should also be told in a general way of the level of damages for non-pecuniary loss in personal injury

---

46 *See* e.g. Nutbrown v Sheffield HA (1993) 4 med LR 188 (72 year old man awarded one half what judge would have given a 30 year old).

47 *See* generally the Judicial Studies Board's Guidelines for Assessment of Damages (4th ed. 1998).

48 Law Com No 257 (1999) (available at http://www.open.gov.uk/lawcomm/). Since the time of writing, the courts have countenanced more modest increases of up to 30 per cent: Heil v. Rankin [2000] 3 All E.R. 138.

49 There was a series of cases in the late 18th century in which the government claimed power to issue general warrants to search for evidence of sedition. In Huckle v Money (1763) 2 Wils. 205 the plaintiff recovered £300 (£30,000 today?) for having been detained under one of these warrants for six hours, during which time he admitted the defendant had 'used him very civilly by treating him with beef-steaks and beer'.

cases, though the two areas are not directly commensurable. The Court of Appeal has indicated[50] that for wrongful arrest the correct starting point is about £500 for the arrest simpliciter, £3,000 for 24 hours wrongful detention and on a declining daily scale thereafter. This assumes that the case does not attract exemplary damages (see above). The picture is complicated by the fact that even where exemplary damages are not awarded, the damages may be 'aggravated' by the defendant's bad behaviour. In theory these are still compensatory for they are awarded in respect of the increased psychological hurt to the plaintiff which stems from the defendant's conduct. Thus a humiliating assault causing no injury or a weak defence of truth in a libel case persisted in by merciless cross-examination of the plaintiff would justify larger awards than in cases where such elements were absent.

8. Calculation of patrimonial damage

[30] The assessment of damages is a large subject and only a bare outline can be given here.[51]

[31] *Personal Injury Cases*. The 'tariff' approach for non-pecuniary loss has been outlined above and this represents a 'standardisation' of awards. Damages for future loss of earnings are awarded in a lump sum arrived at by the multiplier/multiplicand method. The multiplicand is the plaintiff's net annual loss,[52] the multiplier is geared to the length of time for which the loss is likely to last and takes account of the general vicissitudes of life and the income earning capacity of the lump sum. Until recently the multipliers in general use have reflected an assumed return on capital (or discount rate) of about 4.5% per annum net, though the multiplier may be increased or decreased if the evidence shows that the plaintiff's claim presents special features, e.g. high prospects of promotion or some pre-existing propensity to early death. On this basis a typical 30 year old plaintiff suffering permanent disability and presenting no unusual features could expect to receive about 18 times his net annual loss. The same general approach was taken to the recovery of expenses.[53]

[32] Now, however, the House of Lords has held (by reference to the return on Index Linked Government Stocks, which may be regarded as approximating to the 'true' rate of interest since the capital debt is increased in line with inflation) that the discount rate should be 3%.[54] This has of course led to a substantial rise in the multipliers in use.

[33] *Damage to and destruction of property*. Damage to goods is fundamentally based on diminution in value, though in most cases this is arrived at by taking the cost of repair. Similarly, where goods are destroyed the measure is prima facie their value, normally arrived at by the cost of a substitute of the same age and condition, or, where that would be impracticable or unreasonable, a reasonable equivalent. The 'sentimental' value of the goods to the plaintiff does not generally justify expenditure on repairs in excess of the value of the goods,

---

50 In Thompson v Metropolitan Police Commissioner [1997] 3 W.L.R. 403.

51 *See* McGregor, *Damages*, 16th ed. (1997) § 1324 – 2022.

52 I.e. net of income and social security taxes and other direct outgoings, such as pension contributions, which will no longer occur. The lump sum of damages is not taxable, though its income is. But as to structured settlements see I.16 below.

53 The plaintiff is entitled to recover the cost of reasonable private treatment and is not required to use the National Health Service.

54 Wells v Wells [1998] 1 WLR 329.

though no doubt there is some leeway for the court here. For example, the market value of a pet cat might be 5p but I imagine it would not be too difficult to convince a court that, say, a £50 veterinary bill to 'repair' it would be recoverable.

[34] Permanent misappropriation of goods would again lead to an award of their value, together with (as in the case of damage or destruction) consequential loss.

[35] At one time the courts tended to speak in terms of a hard and fast rule that value had to be taken as at the time of the wrong. However, while this may still be the starting point, the 'rule' now seems to have broken down and damages have frequently been based on the value (or cost of repairs) at the time of the trial or some intermediate date between the wrong and the trial. Even if the damages are assessed as at the date of the wrong the plaintiff is entitled to interest from then until judgement,[55] but interest is a general market rate and this may not be enough to give full compensation if, say, repair costs have gone up faster than the general rate of inflation[56] or property of the type misappropriated has increased in value. Generally the courts now seem more inclined to inquire whether the plaintiff has acted reasonably or, in a case of misappropriation, what he would have done with the property had it been returned. This may render the outcome of cases less certain than a mechanical or abstract rule and also sits rather uneasily with the principle stated by the House of Lords in *Edison SS Co v Liesbosch Dredger*[57] that losses caused by the plaintiff's impecuniosity are too remote. The assumption underlying the *Edison*, that the plaintiff is to be deemed to be a person of sufficient means to repair his losses in advance of recovering damages from the defendant, may be criticised as unrealistic and judging by the reported cases it seems regularly to be distinguished on tenuous grounds or even ignored. On the other hand, like the former 'breach date rule' it is arguably an efficient rule for the settlement of disputes.

[36] *Other wrongs.* The nature of the exercise when damages are 'at large' has been outlined above. When proof of actual damage is required the items and sums recoverable will reflect the nature of the interest protected. Thus the law of nuisance protects the occupier in the 'quiet enjoyment' of his property, which means that he recovers damages based upon the diminution in value of his interest caused by the interference. This may be permanent or temporary. Thus if the neighbouring pig farm is a nuisance the plaintiff does not recover damages for the effect of the smell upon his comfort but for the diminution in the letting value of the property caused by the smell. In the case of malicious falsehood and interference with contract or business relations damages will typically represent diminution in trade.

[37] *Strict/fault liability.* There is certainly no general common law principle that the quantum of compensatory damages is affected by the strictness of the liability under which they are incurred. Nor, as far as I am aware, are there any statutory examples of this (save in so

---

55 Interest on personal injury damages is governed by different rules. The plaintiff is entitled to interest on pre-trial loss of earnings in the normal way, but not to interest on future loss of earnings. Interest is awarded on damages for non-pecuniary loss but at a lower rate because the 'tariff' roughly keeps pace with inflation and the award will be made on the scale prevailing at the time of the trial, not the wrong.

56 As in Dodd Properties v Canterbury CC [1980] 1 WLR 433.

57 [1933] AC 449 (dredger sunk; plaintiffs could recover cost of reasonable substitute but not extra cost of buying one on credit)

far as legislation implementing international conventions may impose limits on damages).[58] Thus the calculation of damages under the Animals Act 1971, which imposes strict liability for dangerous animals would be exactly the same as for a comparable injury caused by negligence. Of course, certain heads of liability may not cover a particular type of loss, which is a rather different point. Thus liability for misappropriation of goods (conversion) is basically strict but a conversion is rather unlikely to cause, say, personal injury.[59] So also there is a quasi-strict liability at common law for damage caused by keeping 'dangerous things' under the 'rule in *Rylands v Fletcher*' and the better view nowadays would seem to be that this is confined to damage done to neighbouring property and does not cover personal injury.[60]
[38] What is said above relates only to compensatory damages. The availability of exemplary damages does turn on the mental state of the defendant.
[39] *Social situation of parties and destination of damages*. Generally the social situation of the parties is irrelevant (though one category of exemplary damages can only be awarded in respect of 'governmental' action- see I.1). What the plaintiff intends to do with the damages is also generally irrelevant, as is shown by the fact that substantial damages for loss of amenities may be awarded to a person who is in a permanent coma and is unable to spend the money.

9. Compensation for particular kinds of losses

(a) Pure loss of use

[40] When profit earning goods are damaged, damages for loss of use will be reflected in damages for consequential loss. In the case of non-profit earning goods the cost of hiring a reasonable substitute is plainly recoverable. However, in principle damages are recoverable for loss of use even if no substitute is hired. In *The Mediana,*[61] which concerned damage to a lightship for which the plaintiff kept a substitute, Lord Halsbury said: 'Supposing a person took away a chair out of my room and kept it for 12 months, could anybody say you had a right to diminish the damages by showing that I did not usually sit on that chair or that there were plenty of other chairs in the room?' There seems, however, to be some reluctance to apply this nowadays in the case of 'private' property such as cars (see II.14 below).

(b) Pure loss of earning capacity

[41] I take it that this refers to what is here commonly called 'handicap in the labour market'.[62] P is injured but suffers no (or limited) current loss of earnings (e.g. because he is

58 The threshold requirement for property damage under the Product Liability Directive seems too trivial to rate a mention.
59 Though cf. Dobson v. N. Tyneside HA [1997] 1 WLR 596, where the plaintiffs' bizarre and unsuccessful claim for conversion of the brain of the deceased seems to have been connected with the fact that its loss produced evidential problems for their claim for medical negligence in respect of his death.
60 *See* Hunter v Canary Wharf [1997] AC 655.
61 [1900] AC 113.
62 Our terminology is not consistent. Sometimes 'loss of earning capacity' is used to denote 'actual' loss of earnings.

unemployed or because his disability does not prevent him following his current job). However, his ability to obtain a new job will be diminished by his disability. Damages for this are recoverable,[63] though their assessment is necessarily somewhat speculative and the multiplier/multiplicand method is rarely suitable. In the usual pragmatic, unsystematic way of the common law the theoretical basis of this has not been fully thought through. Thus it is not wholly clear whether the loss represents an 'asset' which is to be given an objective value, though it has been said that a plaintiff is 'not entitled to damages for loss of capacity to earn money unless it is established that he would, but for his injuries, have exercised that capacity in order to earn money.'[64] On this view an entrepreneur who retired at 55, having accumulated enough capital to satisfy all his needs, would recover nothing under this head.

(c) Pure loss of holiday or free time

[42] In practice such losses will generally be subsumed into the general damages for loss of amenity but increases have been made to reflect such losses.[65] This is perhaps particularly likely where the injury is short term (e.g. a broken leg).

(d) Damage to things which remain unrepaired

[43] Because the cost of repairs is used as a practical measure of diminution in value, it is in general irrelevant that P has not had the repairs done or even that he will never do so (see II.15(a) below).

10. Compensation for emotional shock and loss of consortium

[44] Damages for loss of consortium existed at common law, though in modern times the 'domestic services' (servitium as opposed to consortium) element predominated. They have been abolished. The 'services' element is covered by the injured spouse's own claim or, in a fatal case, by the claim of the dependants under the Fatal Accidents Act. In a fatal accident case a spouse may recover a statutory sum of £7,500 for bereavement (non-pecuniary loss) (see II.9(a)).

[45] Emotional trauma amounting to a psychiatric illness is 'damage' but the rules on its recovery are (unless suffered from fear for the plaintiff's own safety) rather more restrictive than in respect of ordinary physical injury. However, these rules are plainly matters of substantive law rather than of the law of damages.[66]

---

63 Smith v Manchester Corporation (1974) 17 KIR 1.

64 Browning v War Office [1963] 1 QB 750 at 766.

65 Ichard v Frangoulis [1977] 1 WLR 536; Hoffman v Sofaer [1982] 1 WLR 1350.

66 *See* generally Alcock v Chief Constable of South Yorkshire [1992] 1 AC 310. Briefly, there must be a sufficient relationship of love and affection between the plaintiff and the direct victim and the trauma must be suffered by direct perception of the event (what an American writer has called the requirements of 'nearness, hearness and dearness"). For a full review and a proposal to drop the direct perception requirement see Law Com No 249 (1998) (available at http: //www.gtnet.gov.uk/lawcomm).

11. Compensation of illegitimate losses

[46] While a criminal is not an outlaw and is not barred from suing even though he is engaged in criminal activity at the time of the injury,[67] he may not recover as damages for lost earnings the proceeds of crime of which he has been deprived (on this see further II.12).[68]

12. Compensation of collective damage

[47] There are no special rules for the 'mass tort' situation, though in practice such cases, if successful, are likely to be settled out of court, perhaps after determination of liability in selected 'lead actions'.

13. Special rules on compensation of ecological damage

[48] Nor are there any special rules of a general nature for ecological damage. 'The environment' is not a legal person and claims must therefore be brought by persons with proprietary or possessory interests in the property affected[69] or under special statutory provisions.[70]

14. Harm causing also advantages

[49] As we have seen, the plaintiff cannot recover damages for loss which is attributable to his failure to mitigate. Logically anterior to this is the proposition that he may not recover damages in respect of loss which has in fact been reduced by benefits which have come to him as a result of the wrong. The fundamental principle is stated by Viscount Haldane LC in *British Westinghouse Co v Underground Railway*[71] (a case of contract, but the underlying principle is the same): 'When in the course of his business [the plaintiff] has taken action arising out of the transaction, which action has diminished his loss, the effect in actual diminution of the loss he has suffered may be taken into account even though there was no duty on him to act.' Thus in *Bellingham v Dillon*[72] injuries received by a driving instructor prevented him from buying on credit an expensive driving simulator. However, some three and a half years later he managed to buy one as bankrupt stock at a fraction of the original price.

---

67 Revill v Newbery [1996] QB 567. Rather different considerations apply if criminal A sues criminal B (e.g. for mishandling the gelignite).

68 Burns v Edman [1970] 2 QB 541 (a strong case because it was a fatal accident and the claim of the dependants, who were not involved in the criminality, is a quasi-independent claim. However, despite criticism, the decision seems plainly correct – if the earnings were the proceeds of crime the law cannot countenance a suit based on their loss).

69 Which would normally be based upon diminution in the value of the property or the cost of removal of the pollution. Blue Circle Industries Plc v. M.o.D., The Times, December 11, 1996 (contamination requiring removal of large quantities of soil – damage). But compare Merlin v. British Nuclear Fuels plc [1990] 2 Q.B. 557 (radiation contamination of building ; air space could not be regarded as damaged, nor did the risk of developing cancer amount to personal injury).

70 Thus the Merchant Shipping Act 1995 imposes liability upon tanker owners for 'clean up' costs or the cost of measures to avert or minimize damage.

71 [1912] AC 673 at 689.

72 [1973] QB 304.

The profits made by him with this before his claim was tried more than outweighed the profits lost in the period before he bought it. It may, however, be difficult to determine whether there is an adequate causal link between the injury and the action taken by the plaintiff. In *Hussey v Eels*[73] P bought a bungalow after a negligent misrepresentation as to its condition. He elected not to do the repairs and remained in the house for two years until he acquired planning permission to build two houses on the site and then sold the site along with the planning permission to a developer for a sum which, mathematically, extinguished the loss. The Court of Appeal held that the unlocking of the development potential could not be regarded as part of one continuous transaction beginning with the acquisition of the house from D and that the money made from the sale to the developer did not go to reduce D's liability.

[50] A very large quantity of case law concerns 'collateral benefits' in personal injury cases. This is dealt with in II.6. below. However, the basic principles in that area are also applicable in other cases: (1) the receipt by P of insurance money is res inter alios acta and does not go to reduce D's liability (whether or not the insurer is subrogated to P's claim); (2) similarly, benevolent payments by a third party do not reduce D's liability.

15. Certainty of damage

[51] The plaintiff must show on a balance of probability that he has suffered a loss caused by the defendant's tort. Thus where the plaintiff's injury was caused either by event A (which is D's responsibility) or event B and the judge concludes that there is, say, a 30% chance that it was caused by A, P's claim against D fails. If, on the other hand, the judge decides that it is marginally more likely than not that the cause was A, then this is treated as a matter of historical fact and the damages are not discounted for the, say, 49% chance that it might have been caused by B alone.[74] The position is, however, different where the plaintiff's case depends upon some act or decision that would, hypothetically, have been taken by a third party.[75] In such a case, provided there is more than a speculative chance that the third party would have behaved differently had the defendant performed his duty then the plaintiff has proved a loss and damages are awarded suitably discounted for the possibility that the third party would have behaved in the same way, even if it is more likely than not that he would have behaved differently. Thus if D writes a negligent reference to X on P's application for employment it may be uncertain whether if X had received an accurate reference he would have employed P. But 'once a duty is held to exist and the defendant's negligence is proved, the plaintiff only has to show that by reason of that negligence he has lost a reasonable chance of employment (which would have to be evaluated) . . .. He does not have to show that, but for the negligence reference, [X] *would* have employed him.'[76]

---

73 [1990] 2 QB 227.

74 Hotson v E Berkshire HA [1987] AC 750. In the majority of cases percentages are of course almost meaningless – they are symbols for points along a spectrum of inference from 'weak' to 'irresistible".

75 Allied Maples v Simmons & Simmons [1995] 1 WLR 1602.

76 Spring v Guardian Assurance [1995] 2 AC 296 at 327, per Lord Lowry.

[52] The above is concerned with whether the plaintiff has proved actionable damage. A distinction must be taken with regard to contingencies in assessing *damages* for that damage. There are uncertainties as to both the future (e.g. will the plaintiff's need for nursing assistance be cut short by premature death?) and the 'hypothetical future' (if the plaintiff had not been disabled from work by the defendant would he have lost his job anyway for some other reason?).[77] Here again there is no question of 'all or nothing' – the plaintiff receives as damages the value of his loss, suitably discounted for the contingencies. In most cases the contingencies are built into the discount rate upon which the standard multipliers are based[78] but where the case presents some special feature the court must do the best it can to value the chance. A limited qualification is that where the evidence shows that there is a chance that the plaintiff's condition may deteriorate at some time in the future it may award provisional damages and reopen the case if the deterioration occurs. However, this has been interpreted as requiring the chance of some 'clear and severable event' and not merely, say, the risk of arthritis which commonly follows joint injuries.

16. Lump sum or rent

[53] With one exception damages[79] are always awarded by a court as a lump sum, whatever the nature of the claim. It is, however, always open to the parties to settle an action on the basis of periodical payments. Provided the settlement is based upon the periodical payment of portions of a notional lump sum of damages[80] this offers fiscal advantages to both sides and such 'structured settlements' are not uncommonly made in more serious cases. The exception to the general rule about the powers of the court is that under section 6 of the Damages Act 1996 the court may give judgement by way of periodical payments with the consent of both parties. This is to preserve the possibility of a 'structure' where the case has to go to trial on an issue of liability.

Part II – Cases

1. Wrongful birth case

[54] The courts once regularly awarded damages for 'all such expenses as may be reasonably incurred for the education and upkeep for the unplanned child, having regard to all the circumstances of the case and, in particular, to his condition in life and his reasonable require-

77 Unless, that is, events between the injury and the trial inform make the hypothetical actual, as in Jobling v Associated Dairies [1982] AC 794 (independently operative disease obliterating effect of injury). Compare Baker v Willoughby [1970] AC 467.

78 It is open to courts to refer to actuarial tables which, depending upon their basis, may take account of matters other than general population mortality.

79 It is possible to make an order for specific performance of a contract to pay periodical sums but this can obviously have no application to a case of tort.

80 Though this may be satisfied by D purchasing an annuity in favour of P.

ments at the time the expenditure is incurred.'[81] These cases have now been overruled on grounds of public policy.[82] The mother may, however, recover damages for lost earnings and for non-pecuniary loss in respect of the pregnancy and the second operation.[83]

2. Wrongful life case

[55] It is assumed that the child is irretrievably damaged by the infection before there is any breach of duty by the doctor.[84] The child cannot sue for 'wrongful life' for the court has no means of comparing the condition of handicapped existence with non-existence.[85] However, the mother may recover damages[86] for the extra cost of raising a disabled child. Though this situation was not in issue in *McFarlane's* case[87] the policy considerations are not the same as with a healthy child.[88]

3. Eye injury

[56] The medical costs are recoverable if they are reasonable in quantum (the plaintiff is under no obligation to use the public health service). As to non-pecuniary loss, a case of serious but incomplete loss of vision in one eye without significant risk of future impairment of the sight of the other eye would attract between about £11,000 and £18,000, depending on seriousness).[89] There is insufficient data to comment on loss of earnings, if any.

4. Costs for hospital visits and of adaptation of house

[57] I know of no case which actually *decides* that the cost of visits is recoverable but such claims are often conceded, correctly so on the basis of what is said in *Hunt v Severs.*[90] The rationale would seem to be that the visits serve a therapeutic purpose so, logically, the cost might be irrecoverable if the plaintiff were in a coma.

[58] Reasonably necessary costs of special accommodation are recoverable.[91] Such cases

---

81 Allen v Bloomsbury HA [1993] 1 All ER 651 at 662, containing a useful summary of the other case law. The hypothetical is somewhat unrealistic in assuming 'straight line' costs.

82 McFarlane v Tayside Health Board [2000]2 AC 59.

83 These non-pecuniary losses were also allowed in the earlier cases.

84 Were this not the case, the child might have a claim on the basis of the Congenital Disabilities (Civil Liability) Act 1976, though after the passing of the Act it was decided that a claim lay at common law: Burton v Islington HA [1993] QB 204.

85 One must distinguish the case of the child who would have been born healthy but for the disability caused by the negligence of the defendant. He may sue: Burton v Islington HA [1993] QB 204 and the Congenital Disabilities (Civil Liability) Act 1976.

86 The problem of quantification of damages does not apply to a claim by the child for medical and nursing expenses attached to the disability, but such claims will in practice be brought by parents.

87 See above.

88 The defendants in McFarlane conceded this.

89 Total blindness about £105,000; total loss of sight in one eye, about £30,000.

90 [1994] 2 AC 350.

91 George v Pinnock [1973] 1 WLR 118.

may in practice be complex because the adaptation may increase the value of the property and leave the increased value in the hands of his successors after the plaintiff has ceased to have need for it. The practice is to award interest upon the difference between the value of the original and adapted home for the period of the plaintiff's disability, though even this has given rise to difficulty.[92]

5. Scar case

[59] Though this presents some analogy with the case of the unrepaired property, where the cost of cure measures the diminution in value, it is not quite the same. The plaintiff is entitled to damages for the non-pecuniary loss inherent in having the scar and these are set by comparison with other injuries rather than by reference to the cost of medical treatment.[93] However, these tariff figures assume a condition which cannot be cured by treatment. The plaintiff is entitled to the cost of reasonable treatment necessitated by the injury. Can the plaintiff claim the cost of treatment which will cure the condition but which will exceed the tariff figure for the uncured condition, or is he like the property owner who cannot recover repair costs exceeding the value of the goods? I reserve my opinion on this one. But I am clear that he cannot recover the cost of treatment he does not propose to have.

6. Continued payment of wages

[60] Whether or not the defendant and the employer are different persons, if the payment can be regarded as 'sick pay' (which assumes a continuing contractual relationship) it diminishes the loss of earnings and therefore reduces the defendant's liability for that,[94] unless (where employer and defendant are different persons) it is paid on terms that it is to be repayable in the event of recovery of damages. If, on the other hand, an employment is terminated and the payment is made as a contractual pension it is not offset against the damages for loss of earnings[95]- a pension and 'salary' are two conceptually different things. So also if the employer terminates the contract and pays the pension ex gratia it would be ignored as a charitable payment by a third party.[96]

[61] Though rather outside the scope of the hypothetical, it may be helpful to note that the whole question of collateral benefits in personal injury cases[97] is currently controversial. Social security benefits are governed by the Social Security (Recovery of Benefits) Act 1997, reenacting with modifications, a system which has existed since 1989. The detail is

---

92 Where there is a high multiplier the award of interest at actual market rates may result in a sum in excess of the full capital cost of the work, as in Roberts v Johnstone [1989] QB 878. But the 2% fixed on in that case may be too low: see McGregor, *Damages* (16th ed.) § 1664.

93 The tariff figures in this area are necessarily a broad band. The current range for serious facial scarring for males is about £8,500 to £30,000.

94 The employer has no claim by way of subrogation or otherwise against the tortfeasor.

95 Parry v Cleaver [1970] AC 1.

96 Though the law is not wholly clear it is probable that any payment by the defendant is to be deducted in determining the loss.

97 For the present regime in fatal accident cases see II.19 below. Though they differ in detail, Scots and Irish law are broadly similar to English law.

complex but, broadly speaking, there is full deduction of relevant social security benefits against damages for loss of earnings and expenses in respect of benefits received during the five years after the injury or the date of judgement/settlement, whichever is sooner (there is no deduction in respect of damages for non-pecuniary loss).[98] However, the defendant is required to account to the social security authorities for the amount of benefits received during this period.[99]

[62] Insurance receipts by the plaintiff are irrelevant to the defendant's liability and are ignored, at least where the premiums are paid by the plaintiff.[100] This is so whether the policy is one of indemnity or not,[101] though in the former case there is no 'double recovery' because if the plaintiff sues having received the insurance money he will hold the damages on trust for his insurer. In practice most cases covered by indemnity policies will lead to litigation by the insurer in the insured's name via the doctrine of subrogation.[102] The general position on insurance payments is also taken by nearly all common law systems[103] and, as I understand it, by some civil law systems.[104]

7. Monk case

[63] It is clear that the monastery cannot recover damages for the loss of the monk's services. The case falls within the general principle that (statute aside) an injury by D to P which causes economic loss to X is not actionable by X.[105] On balance the monk, too, has no claim for pecuniary loss since there is no chance that he would have turned his earning capacity into money: see I.9 above.

8. Lost earning capacity

[64] Cases like these are on the borderline of 'loss of earnings' and 'loss of earning capacity' but this one would be solved by the standard multiplier/multiplicand approach. In the case of the student, given evidence of the general earning patterns of such graduates I do not think

---

98 Note that the scheme applies to out of court settlements. Under the original version of the present scheme, the deduction took place against all damages and it was perfectly possible for the damages to be wiped out altogether. However, deduction was inapplicable where the loss did not exceed £2,500 and in suitable cases there could be advantage for both parties in settling at this figure. There is no longer any 'small claims' exemption.

99 Even if this exceeds his liability to the plaintiff, e.g. because of contibutory negligence.

100 The position is rather uncertain where they are paid by a third party.

101 Thus property damage insurance is generally on an indemnity basis, personal accident insurance is not.

102 Except in marine cases, claims by subrogated loss insurers are probably not common, though note that the 'knock for knock' agreement, whereby most motor insurers agreed inter se not to pursue subrogation claims, has lapsed.

103 There is contrary legislation in a few of the United States.

104 For a full discussion of the present law and possible change see LCCP No 147 (available at http://www.gtnet.gov.uk/lawcomm).

105 This is so even if X has made a payment to P which is deducted in arriving at D's liability to P: there is no restitutionary claim based upon X having by compulsion of law discharged D's liability: Metropolitan Police District Receiver v Croydon Corp [1957] 2 QB 154. Contrast the right of an indemnity insurer to take over P's claim by subrogation.

this would be a particularly difficult case, for some have been solved on less promising material. Thus in *Cassel v Riverside HA*[106] the Court of Appeal upheld a multiplicand of two and a half times the national average wage for a child injured at birth in view of his propitious home and family environment. The earnings from the inferior jobs are of course brought into account against this.

[65] In the case where the plaintiff is reduced to a state of living death, this would not affect the damages for loss of earnings (assuming no reduction in life expectancy).[107] Such a plaintiff is, however, entitled to recover substantial damages for non-pecuniary loss, which may therefore be regarded as an 'objective' determination of damages.[108] The current tariff range for very severe brain damage is roughly the same as for quadriplegia.

9. Lost spouse/partner

[66] (a) Where the plaintiff is the wife she has a claim for loss of financial support under the Fatal Accidents Act 1976. If there are no dependent children this would, in a typical 'middle income' case, be likely to be about two thirds of the husband's net income. There is also a statutory claim for £7,500 for 'bereavement'. Where the plaintiff is a non-marital partner (of the opposite sex[109]) there is a similar claim for loss of support under the Act provided that the parties lived together as husband and wife for two years prior to the death. In this case there is, however, no bereavement claim.

[67] (b) The wife would be regarded under the Fatal Accidents Act as suffering a financial loss equivalent to that in the wife's claim in (a). Damages would prima facie be the reasonable cost of providing equivalent domestic services. The bereavement claim for £7,500 also lies. The common law action for 'loss of services' has been abolished (see I.10 above).

10. Offending publication

[68] Since damages awards for libel have almost always been made by jury, they are not reasoned and proof of actual loss is rarely available. I doubt if the judge would be entitled to direct the jury that the 'value' of these allegations could vary according to the types of plaintiff listed, though no doubt a clergyman or a judge might credibly testify that he suffered more distress from, say, an accusation of sexual impropriety than a rock star. For what it is worth, the Court of Appeal's assessment of the general damages recoverable by Elton

---

106 [1992] PIQR Q168.

107 Where life expectancy is reduced a living plaintiff may recover damages for lost earnings during the 'lost years": Pickett v British Rail Engineering [1980] AC 136. In the period after the assumed death these will be broadly comparable in practice to dependants' damages under the Fatal Accidents Act, since they will reflect the reduction in the plaintiff's expenditure in not having to support himself. In the case of a young child, however, lost years damages are so speculative that no award should probably be made: Croke v Wiseman [1982] 1 WLR 71. Although tort claims generally survive for the benefit of the plaintiff's estate, a dead person cannot claim loss of earnings during the lost years. This is to prevent duplication of the damages awarded to the dependants under the Fatal Accidents Act.

108 West v Shephard [1964] AC 326.

109 There is no claim of any description in respect of a stable homosexual relationship.

John in respect of a newspaper story that he had bizarre eating habits was £25,000,[110] though the story was more than usually hurtful because of his successful battle with various forms of addiction. Where juries award modest or derisory sums for libel it may be hard to be sure whether they are taking a conservative view of what is necessary to vindicate a reputation or implying that the claim should never have been brought (see I.3 above).

11. Rosenkavalier case

[69] Recovery of expenditure rendered futile by the breach is a well-recognized alternative basis for the assessment of damages for breach of contract, but in cases of tort the plaintiff does not generally incur expenditure 'in reliance on' any conduct of the defendant's.[111] Nor, here, is the expenditure caused by the breach (compare e.g. repair costs or medical expenses). However, plaintiffs whose ships have been damaged have recovered in respect of wages of crew during the repair period, so it is hard to see why the plaintiff here should not recover the cost of his wasted holiday.[112] Since insurance arrangements made by the plaintiff are res inter alios acta as far as the defendant is concerned, it logically follows that the plaintiff's failure to take out cancellation insurance is not a failure to mitigate.

[70] In the case of a temporary injury of this nature damages for non-pecuniary loss are very much a matter for the trial judge. In *Ichard v Frangoulis*[113] a sum (in today's money) of about £3,000 was regarded as proper compensation for the combination of a moderate shoulder injury and its effect on a month's holiday in Greece, so perhaps the Sw Fr 5,000 is not wholly out of court. Plainly, however, it is much too high for the Rosenkavalier element alone.

[71] In a case like this the defendant would no doubt contend that the loss was unforeseeable and therefore too remote. This should fail – all that is necessary is that the broad nature of the loss should be foreseeable. It is hardly far-fetched to contemplate that the plaintiff's holiday may be spoiled by an injury and then it should be irrelevant whether it is attendance at Rosenkavalier or a week in Benidorm.

12. Prostitute case

[72] *Burns v Edman* (see I.11 above)[114] concerned a professional burglar. However, it cannot be the law that merely because the plaintiff commits incidental illegalities in the course of his work that he is then debarred from recovery, in whole or in part. In New Zealand in *Le Bagge v Buses*[115] it was no bar to recovery for lost earnings that the plaintiff regularly infringed driving hours regulations and in Australia in *Mills v Baitis*[116] the fact that the plaintiff was operating his car repair business in premises without planning permission was ignored.

---

110 John v Mirror Group Newspapers. [1997] QB 586.

111 I put on one side those cases where tort liability is based upon 'assumption of responsibility".

112 The Inflexible (1857) Swab 200.

113 [1977] 1 WLR 536.

114 *See* also Meadows v Ferguson [1961] VR 594 (no recovery for earnings from illegal street betting business).

115 [1958] NZLR 374.

116 [1968] VR 583.

In the hypothetical of the prostitute there is a further factor. Prostitution as such is not criminal (though there are various offences associated with the trade) though it may be 'unlawful' in a broader sense (for example, for the purpose of enforcing contracts) and I believe that the tax authorities collect tax from prostitutes where they are able to do so. Though there is no case in point, I think it unlikely that there would be a bar to this claim.

[73] Although in *Burns v Edman* the judge made a reduction in the (now abolished) conventional sum for 'loss of expectation of life' this is questionable and I doubt whether nowadays the non-pecuniary element in the plaintiff's claim would be affected by her profession, even if I am wrong about the lost earnings.

13. Mercedes case

[74] Putting aside the somewhat far fetched possibility that D has reason to know of P's circumstances, the damages would plainly be the diminution in value of the Mercedes, prima facie measured by the cost of repairs (see II.15(a) below).

14. Loss of use

(a) Immobilised car

[75] The plaintiff is entitled to the cost of hire of a reasonable substitute.[117] If he is unable to do this it seems that he may recover something for inconvenience in having to walk or use public transport but the Court of Appeal has recently denied that the owner of a private car may recover damages for 'pure' loss of use.[118]

(b) Lost use of house

[76] Essentially the same as (a). The plaintiff would be entitled to the cost of renting a substitute *house*, so if we assume this to be £X and the inconvenience of living in a substitute house to be £Y, those together should be the overall limit on damages – i.e. if the cost of renting a caravan is 0.5 X and the inconvenience of living in a caravan is 2 x Y, the plaintiff should not recover the extra.

15. Damaged, but unrepaired car

(a) Sale of unrepaired car

[77] In *The London Corporation*[119] the plaintiff recovered the cost of repair of his damaged ship even though he had disposed of it unrepaired before trial and in *The Glenfinlas*[120] the cost of repairs which were never done to a vessel which was torpedoed before the trial was

---

117 This would not, it seems, be so if the plaintiff owned more cars than were necessary to meet his transport needs or was unable to use a car during the relevant period: Giles v Thompson [1994] 1 AC 142. See also Dimond v Lovell [1999] 3 All ER 1.

118 Alexander v Rolls Royce Motors [1996] RTR 95. Compare The Mediana under I.9 above.

119 [1935] P 70.

120 [1918] P 363n. However, there is arguably a causation problem in this situation.

admitted by the defendant. This is perfectly rational so long as it is remembered that the cost of repair is being used as a practical measure of diminution in value.[121]

(b) and (c) cost of repair and worth of the car

[78] Generally the plaintiff cannot recover repair costs which will exceed the pre-accident value of the car.[122] Case (c) seems to me only another way of saying this. In case (b) I cannot see that it is an objection that the cost of repair will exceed the value of the *damaged* car. All of this must be read with the caveat that a higher cost of repair (or a cost of replacement at more than pre-accident value) may be recoverable if it is a method of avoiding greater consequential loss. This is more likely in relation to land and buildings than goods.[123]

6. Additional car damage

(a) Accident car

[79] In principle there can be damages for residual devaluation of the repaired car,[124] though I suspect the practical answer is that there would be a reluctance by the average district judge to accept the fact if the car had been repaired by an accredited repairer.

(b) New for old

[80] Plaintiff may claim full cost of repair. Unlike insurance law, tort law makes no deduction for 'betterment'.[125]

(c) Rent of garage

[81] This would seem to be covered by the principle of *The Inflexible* (see II.11).

17. Damaged railway wagon

[82] The plaintiff is entitled to damages for loss of use of the wagon (see I.9) and in such a case as this the calculation is likely to be on the basis of the running cost of the substitute or

---

121 Indeed, generally the only practical measure. There is a meaningful market price for Mercedes 230s in average condition. There is no 'market' in Mercedes 230s with dented right wings or broken rear lamp clusters but it is rational to assume that a buyer will diminish his price by at least the cost of repair. The conclusion is perhaps questionable in The London Corporation, where the disposal was to a shipbreaker.

122 Darbishire v Warren [1963] 1 WLR 1067. O'Grady v Westminster Scaffolding [1962] 2 Lloyd's Rep 238 (old MG, lovingly tended, the apple of its owner's eye) has been explained as a case of a 'unique article' but seems better viewed as showing that sometimes even judicial hearts may rule heads.

123 *See* generally Dominion Mosaic and Tile v Trafalgar Trucking [1990] 2 All ER 246.

124 Payton v Brooks [1974] RTR 169 at 176.

125 Bacon v Cooper (Metals) Ltd. [1982] 1 All ER 397; Harbutt's 'Plasticine' v Wayne Tank & Pump Co [1970] 1 QB 447.

of interest on the capital locked up in it. Most of the cases are about ships[126] but the principle has been applied to a bus.[127]

18. Detective case

[83] I can see no basis upon which the store can recover this cost. The expenditure on the detective is not caused by the theft, though it is incurred to prevent events of that kind. Nor is it 'rendered futile' by the tort, as in the holiday case above. I can of course see an intutive policy argument for recovery. However, if there were such a principle it is difficult to see any basis on which the attributed expense could be allocated – or apportioned if, over a period of time, there were more than one defendant.

19. Death of parents

[84] The claim for loss of financial support on death is, and always has been (since 1846) entirely statutory. Until 1982 benefits received from the estate of the deceased were deductible from the fatal accident claim of dependants, though since in most cases the dependants would have inherited the estate on natural death it was only the value of the accelerated receipt which was deductible. The current provision of the Fatal Accidents Act 1976 (inserted by the Administration of Justice Act 1982) is, on the face of it, disarmingly simple:

'4. In assessing damages in respect of a person's death in an action under this Act, benefits which have accrued or will or may accrue to any person from his [i.e. the deceased's] estate or otherwise as a result of his death shall be disregarded.'

[85] It is plain that this is much more generous to claimants than the equivalent law in relation to personal injury cases, where there is a patchwork of rules, requiring deductions in respect of some benefits but not in respect of others. However, the limits of it are not easy to state, particularly since it has been interpreted to cover benefits other than direct receipts of money.[128] However, it plainly precludes any setting off of the inheritance in the hypothetical. Hence B recovers in full for the loss of financial support during his upbringing. The only possible qualification is that if the parents were so wealthy that before death the family lived off income and capital the claimant has on one view suffered no loss (putting aside any issues of inheritance tax) because he now has the capital and income, and the suffering of loss is a logical preliminary to offsetting sums against it. This was accepted as arguable by the Court of Appeal in *Wood v Bentall Simplex*[129] but it is questionable whether that is consistent with assumptions made in other cases.[130]

---

126 *See* e.g. The Mediana [1900] AC 113; Admiralty Comrs. v SS Suquehanna [1926] AC 655.

127 Birmingham Corpn v Sowsbery (1969) 113 SJ 877.

128 For a full discussion see LCCP No. 148 (1997) (available at http: //www.gtnet.gov.uk/lawcomm). Why this distinction should be drawn is not obvious, but there are not likely to be votes in worsening the position of widows and orphans.

129 [1992] PIQR P332.

130 E.g. Pidduck v Eastern Scottish Omnibuses [1990] 1 WLR 993 (before death husband in receipt of retirement pension of £X, wife had no income of her own; on death wife become entitled to pension from same source of £0.5X; on wife's claim for loss of support from husband's pension, her receipt of her pension to be ignored under s.4).

France

Damages under French Law

Suzanne Galand-Carval

Part I – General questions

1. Aims of the law of damages/comparison with the aims of tort law

[1] The main function of an award of damages is to compensate the victim for the loss he suffered at the result of the defendant's wrong. Whatever the nature of that loss (personal injury, economic loss, *dommage moral*) the sum of money he receives is deemed, according to the *Cour de cassation*, 'to restore the equilibrium which has been broken by the damage' (*rétablir l'équilibre détruit par le dommage*).

[2] Compensation is also the principal purpose of the other remedies available to the victim of a tort. If the so-called *procédés de réparation en nature* are so widely accepted in the modern law of torts, it is precisely because they very often appear as the most efficient way to put the victim in the position he would have been in, had the tort not been committed.

[3] Officially, damages cannot fulfill a punitive function. There are no punitive or exemplary damages in the French law of torts and the *Cour de cassation* regularly recalls that the amount of damages cannot vary according to factors such as the gravity of the fault or the profits made by the wrongdoer.

[4] This is the general rule which must, of course, be set aside whenever a statutory provision imposes another measure of damages. For instance, article 1152 of the Civil Code states that penalty clauses are valid, although the judge might reduce those which are obviously excessive in amount. This means that damages for breach of contract may be punitive, and it is worth noting that judges, when exercising their mitigating power under article 1152 al.2, amost never reduce the amount of excessive penalties to that of the loss, so as to keep them some penal function.

[5] It must also be borne in mind that, although damages must be awarded according to the principles laid down by the *Cour de cassation*, this Court does not exercise a tight control over the awards of the trial judges. The assessment of damages (*l'évaluation du dommage*) is abandoned to the 'sovereign appreciation' of the trial Courts. This gives them quite an important margin of decision and it clearly appears from the case-law that the awards (especially those for *dommage moral*) quite often incorporate a punitive element. Infringement of privacy, for instance, frequently gives rise to substantial damages which, although allegedly compensatory, are obviously intended to punish the wrongdoer.

U. Magnus (ed.), Unification of Tort Law: Damages, 77–88.

[6] There is, of course, a considerable overlap between the aims of the law of damages and those of the law of torts : both are primarily governed by the compensation principle and, subsidiarily, by the aim of punishment. Tort law, however, is not strictly confined to those two purposes. It also performs a function of prevention, which is particularly useful when the tort is a continuing one. When such a tort is being committed, the victim may ask the judge to take such measures as appropriate to restrain its continuation, and thus, to prevent future harm to occur. For instance, when the plaintiff is the owner of a business and sues the defendant for unfair competition, he is not only entitled to damages for the loss already suffered : he can also ask for more drastic measures, such as an injunction to cease the unlawful activity or even the closure of the defendant's business. Obviously, this is a function that damages cannot perform. Although they are in the discretion of the court, such remedies are far more frequently granted than they used to be in the past.

2. General principles of the law of damages

[7] The predominant principle is the so-called *principe de réparation intégrale* ('complete compensation principle') which commands that the victim be compensated for his whole loss, but for no more than that (*tout le préjudice mais rien que le préjudice*).

[8] Several important rules are drawn from this general principle.

[9] First, damages must be awarded for all kinds of losses, irrespective of their nature. As will be seen below, the French law of torts does not make any discrimination in this respect : the pure economic loss, for instance, is not less easily remediable than damage to property.

[10] Secondly, the damages must be calculated on the basis of the extent of the loss at the date of the trial. This is obviously the only sensible way to assess damages for personal injuries : it would be unconceivable to disregard the evolution of the victim's injuries between the accident and the trial. But the rule also applies to property damage. Here, the purpose of the rule is to make sure that neither inflation, nor the variations in value of the good damaged, will prevent the plaintiff from acquiring a substitute. Thus, if the replacement cost of a damaged property car was 1,000 euros at the date of the accident and has gone up to 2,000 euros at the date of the trial, the victim is entitled to the latter sum.

[11] Thirdly, the victim cannot be compensated twice. Full compensation does not mean overcompensation. An important outcome of the rule is the offsetting of almost all the benefits received by the victim at the result of the accident against the damages. Although the law in this area is quite complex, it may be described as governed by the general idea that all payments made to the victim must be deducted from the damages if they are compensatory in nature. This is true of all social security benefits (medical expenses, pensions, various annuities), of the wages paid by the employer when the victim was off-work and of some private insurance benefits. Offsetting benefits obviously avoids overcompensating the victim. But it does not mean that the wrongdoer (or his insurer) pays less. In order to avoid what would be an undesirable effect of the system, various statutory provisions give the employer, the insurer and the Social security a subrogation claim against the wrongdoer.

[12] As regards the modes of compensation, it is now widely accepted that damages are not the only remedy available to the victim. The judge may perfectly decide that compensation will take place *in natura*, if this is possible and appropriate. This kind of remedy is of growing importance in the present law and this is partly due to the fact that the civil judge may resort to the coercive technique of *astreinte*. Compensation *in natura* is rather frequent in the field of nuisance (*troubles du voisinage*) : today, judges do not hesitate to order the defendant to repair or replace a damaged property or to demolish a building.

[13] Until now, the *Cour de cassation* has decided that the victim has no right to the compensation *in natura*, which is in the discretion of the court. Things might well change, however, in a near future, since it clearly appears from the case-law that the *Cour de cassation* is very favourable to this type of remedies.

3. Different forms of damages

[14] As explained above (§ 3), there are no punitive or exemplary damages in French law.

[15] Judges can award *'un franc de dommages et intérêts'*, which can probably be equated with the English nominal damages. Although this a well-established judicial practice, it is rather ambiguous because the *Cour de cassation* does not officially admit that damages may be awarded when no loss has been suffered. When resorting to this award, judges therefore take care not to use words such as 'symbolic award' (*condamnation de principe* or *dédommagement symbolique*) and merely say that, in their opinion, 'the loss suffered by the victim is exactly compensated by one franc'.

4. Legislation on damages

[16] There are very few provisions dealing with the assessment of damages in the Civil Code. All of them are to be found in Section IV, Title III, Book III, relating to damages for breach of contract.

[17] According to art. 1149, damages must be awarded not only for *damnum emergens*, but also for *lucrum cessans*. This is only so, however, in so far as the loss is the direct and foreseeable consequence of the breach (art. 1150 and 1151).

[18] Article 1152 rules that penalty clauses are valid, but subject to a judicial mitigating power.

[19] Finally, article 1153 provides that compensation for the loss arising out of the late payment of a sum of money may only consists in the award of interest, calculated on the basis of the legal interest rate (*le taux de l'intérêt légal*).

[20] Outside the Civil Code, some statutes provide for various limitations of liability. This is so, for instance, in the field of nuclear accidents or air-transport accidents.

5. Definition of recoverable damage

[21] There is no statutory definition of what is a remediable loss in articles 1382 to 1386 of the French Civil Code. Those provisions only mention *le dommage* among the three conditions for tortious liability, the other two being causation and *le fait générateur* (fault / 'act of a thing' etc). The provisions dealing with contractual liability are a little more precise : article 1149, for instance, specifies that damages must be awarded both in respect of *damnum emergens* and *lucrum cessans*. Still, they do not provide for a general definition and it was therefore for the *Cour de cassation* to fill this gap.

[22] It has done so in a broad and liberal way : as a general rule, every loss is recoverable, provided it is *certain, personal, direct and legitimate.*
[23] The condition of certainty is linked to the question of proof : the victim must establish both the existence and the extent of his loss.
[24] The requirement of a 'personal' loss is intended to prevent a plaintiff to ask damages for a loss sustained by another person. The rule is *prima facie* a sensible one, but it has proved to have negative side-effects : it prevents private bodies such as *associations* (*associations de défense des consommateurs*, for instance) or trade unions, to sue wrongdoers on behalf of their members or even of the whole community they are aiming to represent. It is now subject to numerous statutory exceptions.
[25] The condition of directness is a mere reference to the general requirement of causation.
[26] As far as the last requirement is concerned, that of 'legitimacy', it was originally imposed by the *Cour de cassation* in order to prevent a non-marital partner (*une concubine*) to bring an action in damages for loss of financial support. The formal basis for this solution was a provision of the *Code de procédure civile* (now, article 30 of the *Nouveau code de procédure civile*), which provides that 'the right to bring an action is open to those who have a legitimate interest in the success or failure of a claim' (*un intérêt légitime au succès ou au rejet d'une prétention*). It was construed by the Court as prohibiting compensation for a loss which stemed from an unlawful or immoral cohabitation. This harsh and conservative solution was given up in the seventies. Today, the condition of a legitimate interest has little practical outcome. It is sometimes used to deny compensation to a victim who was injured while taking part in a prohibited activity (generally a criminal offence). It could also be used as a bar to the claim of a victim whose loss arises from an immoral occupation, such as a prostitute (see below, case 12).
[27] To sum up, it may be said that all these conditions are not stringent ones.
[28] In some circumstances however, the law imposes additional requirements.
[29] This is so, in theory, when the victim sues in damages for breach of contract. According to article 1150, damages for breach of contract are only recoverable in respect of the loss which was foreseeable at the time of the contract. This is subject, however, to the *exception de dol* : if the breach was deliberate, damages must be awarded even in respect of unforeseeable loss. The scope of this exception has been considerably widened by the use of the rule *culpa lata dolo aequiparatur* which enables the judge to equate gross negligence (*faute lourde*) with intentional breach. Gross negligence being itself widely defined, it clearly appears that, in practice, the condition of foreseeability has almost vanished.
[30] In the field of nuisance, the victim may bring his action for damages on the basis of article 1382 (liability for fault) or of article 1384 al.1 (damage caused by things). But he may also claim damages for *troubles anormaux du voisinage*, a case of strict liability which was created by the *Cour de cassation* at the end of the nineteenth century. If he chooses to do so, he only has to show that he was exposed to an 'abnormal trouble'. As a counterpart, he only recovers damages for the abnormal loss, i.e. that loss which exceeds, according to a well-established formula, 'the normal inconveniences of the neighbourhood'.

6. Different types of damage

[31] Obviously, different types of losses are distinguished, according to their nature (property damage/personal injury/injured feelings/economic loss . . .), or to other distinctive features (pecuniary/non-pecuniary ; past/future, etc.). But all these distinctions are merely descriptive. As explained above (see question no. 5), the French law of torts has not established different rules for the various kinds of losses: damages are recoverable for any kind of loss, provided the four general conditions mentioned above are met.

7. Monetary assessment of non-patrimonial damage

[32] The French terminology is *dommage patrimonial ou extra-patrimonial*, the last one being also frequently called *le dommage moral*. The first category includes property damage and economic loss. The second encompasses all those losses which merely consist in a diminution of the victim's well-being. This last word is understood in a very broad way. It covers both the physical well-being of the victim (in this sub-category, we find for instance the so-called '*préjudice physiologique*', which may probably be equated with the English 'pain and suffering', the aesthetical loss, sexual loss etc) and his mental or moral well-being (this category includes, for example, hurt feelings, distress and sorrow).

[33] There is no specific rule governing the assessment of non-pecuniary losses. Obviously, this is generally a somehow irrational process and it has long been thought that the best solution was to leave this question to the 'wisdom of the Court'. Today, however, the prevailing opinion is that there should be some rationalisation, especially in personal injury cases. Courts have already worked in this direction, by establishing internal 'judicial tariffs' (in French, *barèmes d'indemnisation*).

[34] Several publications of datas are available to the courts, some of which are internal to a court of appeal's jurisdiction, the others being established at national level by private editors (see for instance the '*tableaux de jurisprudence des cours d'appel*', periodically published by the Jurisclasseur, or the special publication of the Gazette du Palais, called '*Indemnités*'). The *Cour de cassation* does not forbid the reference to tariffs but regularly points out that they can be no more than a mere help to assessment. In its opinion, the only acceptable method is to take previous awards as a starting point for assessment and then, to adjust the figures to the 'personal, individual and concrete situation of the victim'.

[35] Damages awarded for infringement of personality rights or other *dommages moraux*, are probably also calculated with reference to previous awards, though I have not heard of *barèmes* being established for these matters.

8. Calculation of patrimonial damage

[36] As a general principle, damages must be calculated *in concreto*, having regard to every characteristics of the victim's loss. But obviously, it is sometimes necessary (and wishable) to introduce some degree of abstraction in the assessment of damages. I have already stressed that damages for non-pecuniary losses are, to some extent, standardised. It is generally easier to concretely assess damages for pecuniary losses but even in this field, abstraction is not completely absent. Future loss of earnings, for example, is calculated on the basis of the plaintiff's annual income (which is a concrete element) and life expectancy (which is statistically determined and therefore abstract).

[37] The social situation of the victim is irrelevant (though not his income !), and so is the basis of the defendant's liability (fault or strict liability).

[38] There is no control whatsoever on the way the victim uses the damages he has recovered.

9. Compensation for particular kinds of losses

[39] *Pure loss of use*. I am not sure of what is meant by the word 'pure'. When a property is damaged, which was of some use to the victim, he can obviously claim damages for loss of use (*perte de jouissance*). Their amount depends on whether the victim hired a substitute or not.
[40] If he did so, he can recover the cost of hiring, provided it was reasonable.
[41] If he did not do so, then it seems unlikely that he may recover an expense he did not incur. In some cases, it was decided that in such a situation, damages could be awarded for some of the expenses which were uselessly incurred while the good was being repaired, although they did not derive from the tort itself : for example, when the damaged property is a car, the cost of hiring a garage or the insurance premiums. On the whole, the question is not a very debated one and it is difficult to find information on this topic. It is very likely that the judges consider this loss as a kind of *dommage moral* which they very freely assess. And after all, it seems rather logical to pay attention to the *consequences* of the loss of use which, if no substitute is hired, are essentially non-pecuniary (inconveniences etc).
[42] If the good was used for professional purposes (a profit-earning good), damages must be awarded for all the profits lost before it could be repaired or replaced. But I doubt whether one can speak of 'pure loss of use' in such a case ; the loss is plainly actual.
[43] *Pure loss of earning capacity*. As a principle, no damages can be awarded for a pure loss of earning capacity. Compensation is possible only for actual loss of income. Thus, if the victim is a tramp, or a child, or a retired person, he recovers nothing under this head.
[44] The rule is subject to one exception only. When the victim did not work at the time of the accident, but was very likely to work in a near future (for example, a student or a woman who had temporarily stopped working to look after her young children), then he can recover damages for loss of a chance to earn money. Damages are assessed on the basis of a percentage (representing the lost chance) of the average earnings in the job the victim would probably have had. This does not work, however, when the victim is a child or a young person who has not yet sufficient prospects of career (e.g., a 18 year old who has just completed his 'baccalauréat' and has not yet engaged in specialised studies). This is an area in which many scholars would approve the introduction of an 'abstract calculation', so as to allow a permanently disabled child to recover 'something' in respect of loss of earnings.
[45] As regards the disabled housewife, who is unable to perform the housework she used to do, she is not seen as having lost an 'earning capacity' (whether actual or 'pure') but a 'working capacity' which plainly has a pecuniary value. She is entitled to recover the cost of replacement services.
[46] *Damages to things which remains unrepaired*. The general idea which governs compensation for property damage is that the victim must recover enough money to get back a good which is identical to the damaged one. Thus, damages are assessed on the basis of the cost of repairs or replacement, and not on the basis of the diminution in value, which is generally lower.
[47] The fact that the good remains unrepaired is irrelevant. The justification for this is that

the victim should not be asked to have the repairs done before trial (since he would have to advance the money for it). As to what happens after trial, it is up to the victim to spend his money as he wishes, there is no judicial control over the use of damages.

10. Compensation for emotional shock and loss of consortium

[48] The question of compensation for nervous shock has never been debated as such in France. This is probably so because the relatives of an injured person are entitled to damages for their feeling of distress and sorrow. This specie of *dommage moral* is called *le préjudice d'affection*. It is recoverable by the close relatives of the victim (spouse, children, parents, grandparents) but also by all those who had special relationships with him (for instance a *fiancée* or a godchild who lived with him).

11. Compensation of illegitimate losses

[49] See above, § 26, and below, case 12.

12. Compensation of collective damage

[50] It depends on what is meant by 'collective damages'. These words may first refer to an addition of individual losses, such as the economic loss suffered by fishermen because of a sea-pollution, or the loss suffered by the users of a defective drug. They may also refer to the *dommage moral* suffered by a community as a whole at the result of a wrongful act. For instance, the marketing of a defective drug does not only make individual victims, it also infringes on the legitimate expectations of the community of consumers.
[51] As regards the first side of the question (the range of individual losses), it is doubtful whether special tort rules are needed. The main issue is a procedural one : should not the victims be authorized to join together, so as to bring a single action against the tortfeasor? Although the 'class actions' do not belong to the French legal tradition, some statutory provisions have recently been adopted, which make it possible for a private body (usually *une association*) to act on behalf of a group of identified victims.
[52] The other side of the question (compensation for the loss suffered by a community as a whole) is dealt with by numerous statutes which enable private bodies (again, *associations* or trade unions) to sue in damages the authors of criminal offenses which have directly or indirectly infringed on the collective interests of a community (the community of workers, of consumers, of road users etc). The action, called *l'action civile*, is brought before a criminal Court. It is an action in damages but it has a very important collateral effect since it automatically activates the criminal proceedings against the defendant. The assessment of damages is particularly difficult : the amounts awarded vary from one franc (*le franc symbolique*) to quite substantial sums of money. It is a widely shared opinion that such awards are punitive in nature.

13. Special rules on compensation of ecological damage

[53] There is no special rule governing compensation for ecological loss. Damages may be awarded for property damage or economic loss deriving from a wrongful pollution but only in so far as they are sustained by individuals (private landowners, fishermen etc). Private associations can recover damages for *dommage moral* if they act for environmental purposes. Today, it is widely felt that preventive and restoration measures would be the most appropriate way to deal with environmental damage. But still, there remains the crucial issue of locus standi. Therefore, it is not only tort law but also procedural law which has to adapt to this specific problem.

14. Harm causing also advantages

[54] For a very general outline of the solution adopted in respect of collateral benefits, see above, § 11.

15. Certainty of damage

[55] As explained in § 23 above, the victim cannot recover damages for a loss which is not established with certainty (*certitude*). For instance, if he claims compensation for lost profits without bringing convincing evidence of both their existence and extent, he gets nothing.
[56] Certainty, however, is obviously understood as a relative requirement. This is particularly true of future losses, since a condition of absolute certainty would prevent all compensation in their respect. According to the *Cour de cassation, 's'il n'est pas possible d'allouer des dommages et intérêts en réparation d'un préjudice purement éventuel, il en est autrement lorsque le préjudice, bien que futur, apparaît aux juges du fait comme la prolongation certaine et directe d'un état des choses actuel et comme étant susceptible d'estimation certaine'*. French law even seems to be more lenient in this respect than English law since future loss of income, for instance, is compensated without any 'discount for contingencies'.

16. Lump sum or rent

[57] There is no hard and fast rule on this topic. Damages may be awarded as a lump sum or on the basis of periodical payments. The choice within these two devices is in the discretion of the court.

Part II – Cases

1./2. Wrongful birth and wrongful life

[58] In recent cases, the *Cour de cassation* has decided that the parents of a healthy child could not recover damages in an action for wrongful birth. According to the Supreme Court, 'a birth is not, on its own, a recoverable loss'.
[59] The same solution has been adopted by the *Conseil d'Etat*.
[60] This general rule is subject to a limited exception : according to the *Cour de cassation*, damages can be awarded in respect of a 'special loss' (un *préjudice particulier*) suffered by the mother at the result of the birth. This could be the case when the mother is in a very

difficult financial position or when she suffers a psychological trouble at the result of the birth.
[61] The opposite solution prevails when the mother gives birth to a disabled child. In such a case, both the child and his parents can recover damages. The child is entitled to compensation for his handicap and his parents, for the financial and moral losses they suffer thereby.

3. Eye injury

[62] V can recover damages for:
- the medical costs ;
- the lost earnings if any (passed and future) ;
- the 'physiological loss' (*dommage physiologique*), ie, the impairment itself, which must be compensated even if it has no consequences on the professional activities of the victim;
- the *pretium doloris* (ie : the physical suffering) ;
- the loss of amenities if any (*préjudice d'agrément*) ;
- and, presumably, the aesthetical loss.

4. Costs for hospital visits and of adaptation of house

[63] The victim's relatives may recover the cost of their visits if these visits were necessary. This is probably the case here, so the answer is yes.
[64] As to the cost of adapting the house, it is plainly recoverable.

5. Scar case

[65] It is difficult to imagine a victim claiming damages for the cost of an operation and saying he does not want to undergo it ! All I can say is that, as a general rule, the victim may recover the cost of an appropriate treatment without having to pay for it first.
[66] The same rule applies in the field of property damage. The victim can recover the cost of repairs even if he has not had the good repaired yet.

6. Continued payment of wages

[67] Having suffered no loss, P cannot claim damages for lost earnings. But P's employer has a subrogation claim againts D, for the whole amount of the sums paid to P as well as for the social security contributions.

7. Monk case

[68] The monk cannot recover damages for lost earnings since he is not paid for his work. Nor can he recover damages for the loss of an 'abstract earning capacity' : the French law of torts only deals with actual losses and ignores abstract ones.
[69] The monastery is in a different position. If it appears that A's accident caused it an economic loss (for example, the monastery had to replace A by an outside worker), then, in principle, it can recover damages in this respect.

8. Lost earning capacity

[70] A can first recover damages for the non-pecuniary losses described in case 3 above (physiological loss, pretium doloris, loss of amenities . . .).
[71] As to the loss of earnings, the solution varies according to the victim's age. If A is a 20 years old chemistry student, he may argue that he has been deprived of a substantial chance to have a well-paid job. If the argument is convincing (the Court will have regard to his previous results), then he will recover a percentage of the difference between the wages he gets and those he would probably have got. If A is six years old, he recovers nothing. This harsh solution is justified by the fact that the young age of the victim makes it impossible to assess his prospects of career. It is a general opinion that in such a case, the rule of 'concrete assessment' should leave the way to a standardized assessment of damages but until now, the *Cour de cassation* has not accepted this solution.
[72] The *Cour de cassation* has recently ruled that the loss of a comatose victim is to be assessed *objectively*. This means that he must be compensated as if he were conscious and that he is entitled (this was the disputed question) to damages for loss of amenities and physical pain.

9. Lost spouse / partner

[73] (a) A may recover damages for loss of financial support, notwithstanding her status, wife or non-marital partner.
[74] She also has a claim for her *préjudice d'affection* (distress and sorrow).
[75] (b) Yes, this is a recoverable loss.

10. Offending publication

[76] B can recover damages for 'dommage moral'. The amount will depend on the facts of the case and on the judge's opinion of what his reputation is worth.
[77] The court can also order the publication of a corrective notice or of the judgement itself.

11. Rosenkavalier case

[78] The price paid by B to the travel agency (6,000 francs) is recoverable. As to the 5,000 francs for 'dommage moral', I have some serious doubts. First, I am not sure that B could convince the judge of the *existence* of such a loss : the requirement of 'certainty' would thus be lacking. Secondly, even if B brings convincing evidence of his loss, an award of 5,000 francs (ie almost equal to the price of the tour itself) seems unlikely.

12. Prostitute case

[79] This is a case where the requirement of a 'legitimate' loss could well be a bar to the prostitute's claim. Although her profession is not, strictly speaking, illegal, it is undoubtedly still seen as immoral by a majority of judges. Thus, it can be said that the prostitute has no 'legitimate interest in the success of her claim' (Code de procédure civile, article 30, see above §9).

NB : The questions of deciding what is moral or not and whether it is legitimate for the law of torts to punish immorality are more controversial today than they used to be in the 19th century and first half of the 20th. Therefore, it is not unlikely that this kind of case will be decided differently in a near future.

13. Mercedes case

[80] P can undoubtedly recover the cost of repairs (4,000 euros). If it is established that, in spite of the repairs, the value of the car has decreased, he must also be compensated for this loss.

14. Loss of use

[81] (a) P has a claim for loss of use (*perte de jouissance*). It is not easy to know how judges assess damages for such a loss but if P has hired a substitute, then he can recover the hiring cost, provided it is reasonable.
[82] (b) The answer is the same : P can recover damages for loss of use. If the caravan is his, he incurs no expenses but can still recover damages for something which probably amounts to a 'dommage moral' (inconveniences and so on).

15. Damaged, but unrepaired car

[83] (a) Since he is no longer the owner of the car, A cannot recover the cost of repairs. However, as he has probably sold the car for an inferior price, he can claim damages for the diminution in value.
[84] (b) If A has sold the car, the answer is the same as in (a). If A keeps the car, he can recover the cost of repairs only if it is lower than the cost of replacement. If the car cannot be replaced (it is a 'unique' car), then A is entitled to damages for the cost of repairs, whatever its amount.

16. Additional car damage

[85] (a) Yes, P can recover damages for the diminution in value.
[86] (b) The *Cour de cassation* has repeatedly ruled that the victim is entitled to the full cost of repairs and that there can be no deduction for betterment (*abattement pour vétusté*).
[87] (c) It is difficult to argue that the two weeks rent is a loss suffered because of D's negligence. And after all, if P hires a substitute, he will be able to park it in his garage. Nevertheless, if P does not hire a substitute, this cost could possibly be taken into account by the judge to assess damages for 'pure loss of use' or 'inconveniences'.

17. Damaged railway wagon

[88] If this 'replacement solution' is not more expensive than another one, then the cost of maintening the wagon is recoverable.

18. Detective case

[89] In French law, there is no restriction on the compensation for pure economic loss. As seen in case 7 (claim of the monastery), the victim who paid wages to a third party because of the defendant's negligence can recover damages in this respect. If A cannot get damages in this case, it is not because of the economic nature of his loss but merely because the payment of the wages is not a consequence of D's tort.

19. Death of parents

[90] According to the Cour de cassation, the inheritance must not be deducted from the damages for loss of financial support.

Germany

DAMAGES UNDER GERMAN LAW

Ulrich Magnus

Part I – General questions on the law of damages

1. Aims of law of damages

[1] It is common ground that it is the central aim of the law of damages to fully indemnify the victim for the loss.[1] That means that the debtor has to make good no more and no less than the damage which he has caused to the creditor. This compensation principle (*Ausgleichsprinzip*) applies wherever in private law – and even in public law – a person is liable for damage unless special rules provide otherwise.[2] Compensation is not only regarded as the fundamental purpose of the law of damages but as well of the law of tortious or contractual liability in general.[3]

[2] According to the clear majority of opinions **prevention** of damage is no separate aim of the law of damages, but is welcomed as a 'desirable side effect' of the compensation principle.[4] However, a growing number of authors points to the importance of the preventive purpose of the law of damages,[5] especially under aspects of the economic analysis of law.[6] Even the courts base their judgements in certain cases on the preventive purpose: where, e.g., insurance companies withhold payment despite of their clear liability victims are awarded

---

1 Esser/Schmidt, *Schuldrecht I/2* (7th ed. 1993), p. 158; Lange, *Schadensersatz* (2nd ed. 1990); *Münchener Kommentar*/Grunsky (MünchKomm/Grunsky), Bürgerliches Gesetzbuch II (3rd ed. 1994), Vor § 249 no. 3; *Palandt*/Heinrichs, Bürgerliches Gesetzbuch (58th ed. 1999), Vorbem. vor § 249 no. 4.

2 *See* Palandt/Heinrichs, Vorbem. vor § 249 no. 2 with numerous references; *Staudinger*/Medicus, Kommentar zum Bürgerlichen Gesetzbuch mit Einführungsgesetz und Nebengesetzen (12th ed. 1980), Vorbem. zu §§ 249–254 no. 13 et seq.

3 Especially clear Esser/Schmidt (supra note 1) p.158.

4 Esser/Schmidt (supra note 1) p. 161; Lange (supra note 1) p. 10; Larenz, *Lehrbuch des Schuldrechts I* (14th ed. 1987) § 27 I; MünchKomm/Grunsky Vor § 249 no. 3; Palandt/Heinrichs Vorbem. vor § 249 no. 4.

5 Compare Magnus, *Schaden und Ersatz* (1987), p. 282; Schäfer/Ott, *Lehrbuch der ökonomischen Analyse des Zivilrechts* (2nd ed. 1995), p. 100; Hager [1990] *Juristen-Zeitung* (JZ), 400 et seq.; Wagner [1991] JZ, 175. Even more farreaching Kötz, *Deliktsrecht* (8th ed. 1998) no. 36 et seq.

6 *See* Schäfer/Ott *ibid.*; also Kötz *ibid.*

U. Magnus (ed.), Unification of Tort Law: Damages, 89–107.

higher sums than would be necessary to compensate them for their actual loss.[7] And even more openly the courts recognise prevention as a justification for awarding high damages where mass media have wrongfully and intentionally invaded the victim's right of privacy and personality.[8]

[3] In the field of damages for pain and suffering, which can be recovered only in tort, also a further function of damages has gained wide acceptance: here damages shall also serve to satisfy the victim's injured feelings and his wishes for revenge and punishment (so called 'Genugtuungsfunktion des Schmerzensgeldes').[9] Although the idea of satisfaction resembles to some extent the consideration that damages serve as penalty or sanction for civil wrong this latter idea is nearly unanimously rejected.[10] Punishment is no aim of civil suits under German law. Therefore, damages are generally awarded irrespective of fault or of the gravity of fault.[11] In particular, punitive damages are unknown to German law.[12]

[4] Another function that can be attributed to the law of damages is that of continuing and realizing the infringed right of the victim by means of damages (Rechtsfortsetzungsgedanke).[13] But it is disputed whether this idea has some bearing on the calculation of damages.[14] The English concept of nominal damages appears to be based on similar considerations as the *Rechtsfortsetzungsgedanke*: to show by damages that the infringement of rights is not accepted even if no actual loss occurred.[15] Under German law the same aim is pursued by procedural means (*Feststellungsklage*) whereas within the area of damages neither the idea of prolonging the infringed right[16] nor nominal damages are generally accepted.[17] Without damage there can be no damages.

[5] Finally the law of damages can function as instrument to retransfer gains which the wrongdoer made or had due to his wrongful conduct. Under German law that function is primarily fulfilled by the law of unjust enrichment. The law of damages looks at the victim's loss, not at the wrongdoer's profit.[18] Only on rare occasions damages can be calculated according to the gain the person liable had.[19]

---

7 BGH VersR 1964, 1103; BGH VersR 1967, 256; Compare, e.g., OLG Karlsruhe NJW 1973, 851.

8 BGH NJW 1996, 984; BGHZ 128, 1; BGHZ 132, 13.

9 The leading case is BGHZ 18, 149; further BGHZ 120, 1.

10 BGH NJW 1993, 781; Esser/Schmidt (supra note 1) et seq.; Lange (supra note 1) pp. 12 et seq.; but contra Gottwald, *Schadenszurechnung und Schadensschätzung* (1979), p. 160.

11 For details compare Lange (supra note 1), pp. 13 et seq. But an evident exception applies in employment law: there the employee is liable – towards his employer – according to the degree of fault.

12 BGHZ 118, 312 (refusing the recognition of a US-judgement on punitive damages).

13 Developed by the Austrian scholars Neuner – [1931] *Archiv für die civilistische Praxis* (AcP) 133 at 277 – and Wilburg – [1932] *Jherings Jahrbücher der Dogmatik und des bürgerlichen Rechts* (JherJB) 82 at 51 -; see also the Austrian Report by Helmut Koziol p. 2; for a full comparative discussion see Stoll, *Haftungsfolgen im bürgerlichen Recht* (1993), pp. 190 et seq.

14 Pro: Larenz (supra note 4) § 27 I; Palandt/Heinrichs Vorbem. vor § 249 no. 5; contra: Lange (supra note 1) pp. 11 et seq.

15 Compare the English Report by Rogers p. 5.

16 Esser/Schmidt (supra note 1) p. 165; Lange (supra note 1) pp. 11 et seq; Staudinger/Medicus § 249 no. 136.

17 Stoll (supra note 13) pp. 188 et seq.

18 Lange (supra note 1) p. 9.

19 Particulary in case of infringement of intellectual property rights: here the victim can claim as

[6] In summary, German law of damages serves the main aim of full compensation but in specific situations also preventive, sanctioning, satisfactioning, gain-avoiding purposes are taken into consideration.

2. General principles of the law of damages

(a) Full compensation

[7] The leading principle is that the victim is entitled to indemnification of the whole loss. As a rule the wrongdoer has to indemnify in full for any loss which he has caused and which is not due to the victim's contributory negligence (principle of complete reparation – *Totalreparation*).[20] As mentioned above, the amount of damages does, thus, not depend on the degree of fault on the part of the wrongdoer but on the extent of the loss only.[21] The judge has no discretion either to reduce or to increase damages on grounds of slight or grave fault or no-fault, poverty or richness of the parties, adequacy, social fairness or the like.[22] Under constitutional aspects it is doubted, however, whether children should be fully liable for disastrous losses they have responsibly caused so that they are financially ruined for the rest of their lives.[23]

[8] In the field of strict liability the principle of full compensation is subject to an exception of almost general application: Most acts on strict liability set maximum limits for damages and exclude compensation for non-pecuniary damage (pain and suffering).[24]

(b) Restitution in kind

[9] The primary method of compensation is restitution in kind. According to § 249 sent. 1 BGB the wrongdoer has to restore the state of affairs that would have existed had the damaging event not occurred. Restitution in natura (*Naturalrestitution*) is thought to protect best the victim's rights (integrity interest) and to reflect what the wrongdoer is obliged to achieve: a state as near as possible to the undamaged situation.[25] But despite the restitution in natura-principle damages are regularly awarded in terms of money. The reason for this is that in case of damage to person or things the creditor can – and mostly will – choose money instead of restitution in kind (§ 249 sent. 2 BGB). He can claim that sum of money that would be necessary for restitution in kind.

---

damages the profit of the infringor, compare § 97 par. 1 s. 2 UrheberrechtsG and the court practice: BGH GRUR 1963, 640; BGHZ 34, 320.

20 Lange (supra note 1) p. 13; Palandt/Heinrichs Vorbem. vor § 249 no. 6; Staudinger/Medicus § 249 no. 2.

21 But there are exceptions, compare n. 11.

22 The introduction of such a reduction rule ("Reduktionsklausel") into the Civil Code was proposed but did not pass the parliamentary hurdles, compare § 255 a BGB Referentenentwurf 1967 and thereto Lange (supra note 1), p. 19 et seq.; Staudinger/Medicus Vorbem. zu §§ 249–254 no. 29.

23 Doubting constitutionality of full liability: Canaris [1987] JZ 1002. The majority view accepts full liability: Palandt/Heinrichs Vorbem. vor § 249 no. 6.

24 E.g., §§ 8, 10 ProdukthaftungsG, §§ 6, 9, 10 HaftpflichtG; §§ 13, 15 UmwelthaftungsG; §§ 11, 12 StraßenverkehrsG; §§ 29, 31 AtomG.

25 BGH NJW 1985, 793; Esser/Schmidt (supra note 1) p. 187; Lange (supra note 1) pp. 211 et seq., Palandt/Heinrichs § 249 no. 1.

(c) Compensation for the lost worth

[10] If restitution in natura is either impossible or insufficient the debtor must compensate the creditor in money (§ 251 par. 1 BGB). If restitution is possible with unreasonable expenditures only, the debtor may also compensate in money (§ 251 par. 2 BGB). 'Unreasonable' here means that – as a thumb rule – expenditures surmount the worth of the undamaged thing by more than 30 %.[26] In alle three cases of infeasible restitution the debtor must only compensate for the lost or reduced worth of the damaged thing or right. Thus, between restitution in kind and compensation in money there is a sharp distinction in German law.[27] As long as restitution is owed the creditor can claim the costs of adequate measures for restoring the undamaged state, even if these costs are considerably higher than the thing's worth.[28] If only compensation is owed because restitution is either impossible, insufficient or disproportionate, damages are calculated on the basis of the reduction in worth (worth compensation principle, Prinzip des Wertersatzes).[29] There may ensue considerable differences in the sums of damages calculated the one way or the other.[30] The difference is justified by the argument that the integrity of the victim's rights, his indemnity interest deserves that better protection.[31]

3. Different forms of damages

[11] As mentioned above (sub. I.1) German law does not recognise punitive, exemplary, aggravated or nominal damages as such. Damages are compensatory in nature; only in particular situations additional purposes – prevention, sanction, satifaction – play a role.[32]
[12] Legal fees and judicial costs for court procedings are regulated by provisions of the Civil Procedure Code.[33] The loosing party has to bear the costs (§ 91 par. 1 sent. 1 ZPO). Costs for solicitors outside court proceedings can be awarded as damages as long as they are reasonable to pursue a justified damages claim or to defend against an unjustified claim.[34]

4. Legislation on damages

[13] The BGB contains only few and rather general provisions on the extent and

---

26 BGHZ 115, 371; Palandt/Heinrichs § 251 no. 7, 25; in case of injured animals the limit of unreasonable expenditures for healing is extended to much higher percentages than 130 % of the animal's worth: see § 251 par. 2 sent. 2 BGB and the court practice: LG Lüneburg [1984] NJW 1243; LG Karlsruhe [1986] NJW 542.

27 BGHZ 5, 109; BGHZ 102, 325; Palandt/Heinrichs § 249 no. 3 et seq. with further references.

28 BGHZ 54, 85; BGHZ 61; 349; BGH [1992] NJW 1619; Palandt/Heinrichs § 249 no. 6.

29 BGH [1984] NJW 2571; BGH [1985] NJW 2414; Palandt/Heinrichs § 251 no. 10; Staudinger/Medicus § 251 no. 2.

30 If the victim can claim restitution costs regularly he can get about 30 % more than if he can claim compensation of worth only, compare n. 26.

31 BGHZ 115, 371; BGH [1992] NJW 1618; Lange (supra note 1) p. 236; Palandt/Heinrichs § 251 no. 25.

32 *See* above text at n. 4 et seq.

33 §§ 91 et seq. ZPO.

34 BGHZ 111, 171; BGH [1986] NJW 2244; Palandt/Heinrichs § 249 no. 20 et seq.; Staudinger/Medicus § 251 no. 84 et seq.

measurement of damages in general (§§ 249–253 BGB) and some slightly more specific provisions on damages in tort (§§ 842–845, 847 BGB). Moreover, special acts add modifying rules on ecological damage, namely § 32 par. 7 GentechnikG, § 16 UmwelthaftungsG.

[14] The general provisions prescribe the above mentioned restitution-principle basing damages on the restitution costs (§§ 249, 250 BGB). They are also thought to contain the principle of 'Totalreparation'.[35] They further provide for the case when restitution is impossible, insufficient or disproportionate basing damages then on the lost or reduced worth (§ 251 BGB). Moreover, § 252 BGB makes lost profits recoverable if the profits had accrued with probability; they must not be certain. Finally, non-pecuniary damage cannot be claimed unless provided for by statute (§ 253 BGB).

[15] The special provisions on damages in tort prescribe that also disadvantages in employment or otherwise which result from a tortious act against the person of the victim can be recovered (§ 842 BGB)[36] and that the victim can claim a rent instead of a lump sum (§ 843 BGB). In case a husband or wife is injured or killed who cared for the marital household damages for loss or reduction of these services are due (§§ 844, 845 BGB).[37] § 847 BGB provides for 'Schmerzensgeld'. It is an exception to § 253 BGB and allows expressly recovery of immaterial damage caused by bodily harm.

[16] The special provisions on ecological damage provide that the costs of measures for the restitution of nature and landscape are recoverable even if they – considerably – surmount the worth of the damaged thing thereby modifying § 251 par. 2 sent. 1 BGB.[38] The different calculation of damages under the restitution-principle and the worth-compensation-principle[39] is thereby avoided in order to better protect nature and environment. But it must be noted that ecological damage if someone's property is damaged or destroyed thereby also causing ecological damage.

5. Definition of recoverable damage

[17] The Civil Code does not contain a definition of the recoverable damage. The many provisions which presuppose damage as condition of liability as well as the specific rules on damages (§§ 249 et seq. BGB) use the term without defining it.

[18] The courts also avoid a general definition. In scholarly writing damage is defined as any loss that somebody suffered with respect to his legally protected rights, goods and interests.[40]

---

35 *See* above at n. 20.

36 § 842 BGB clarifies that actual financial consequences of lost or reduced earning capacity but also reduced opportunities to marry (BGH [1959] JZ 365) etc. have to be compensated. Under §§ 249, 253 BGB that could be doubtful; see Staudinger/Schäfer § 842 no. 1, 13 et seq.; also Palandt/Thomas § 842 no. 3.

37 The same is true if a family member is injured or killed who was obliged by statute to render services or pay maintenance (§§ 844, 845 BGB).

38 For a full discussion see Staudinger/Kohler § 16 UmweltHG no. 2 et seq.

39 *See* above at n. 26.

40 Deutsch, *Unerlaubte Handlungen, Schadensersatz und Schmerzensgeld* (3rd ed. 1995), no. 423; Fikentscher, *Schuldrecht* (9th ed. 1997), no. 452; MünchKomm/Grunsky Vor § 249 no. 6; Palandt/Heinrichs Vorbem. vor § 249 no. 7.

But there is nearly general agreement that this definition is to vague as to solve conrete problems of the law of damages.[41]

6. Different types of damage

(a) Patrimonial/pecuniary and non-patrimonial/non-pecuniary damage

[19] German law draws a distinct and decisive borderline between pecuniary damage ('Vermögensschaden') and non-pecuniary damage ('Nichtvermögensschaden'). Although statute uses the term 'Nichtvermögensschaden' (non-pecuniary loss)[42] it nowhere defines the expression and no generally accepted definition has evolved so far. The main distinguishing feature between pecuniary and non pecuniary damage is whether the lost position has some economic worth, which can rather easily and objectively be measured in terms of money or whether it concerns personal goods like feelings etc. which can be measured in a subjective way only.[43]

[20] Both kinds of losses are treated alike only as long as restitution in kind is sought.[44] With respect to monetary compensation – the remedy that really counts – it is but pecuniary damage that is fully recoverable. The Civil Code (§ 253 BGB) expressly orders that non-pecuniary damage cannot be compensated in money unless statute so provides. And statute allows it in three cases only: for pain and suffering from bodily injuries in tort law (§ 847 BGB), for ruined holidays under a package tour contract (§§ 651 f BGB) and for sex discrimination under an employment contract (§ 611 a par. 2 BGB) The courts further added – praeter legem – monetary compensation for grave infringements of the right of personality.[45]

[21] The reason given for the sharp distinction between 'Vermögensschaden' and 'Nichtvermögensschaden' is that non-pecuniary damage can only be estimated but cannot be measured objectively in terms of money.[46] Furthermore, the authors of the BGB expressed their dislike with money compensation for immaterial losses at all as well as with the wide discretion judges would necessarily exert while assessing non-pecuniary damage in money.[47] Thus, German statutory law disfavours monetary compensation of immaterial losses.

[22] The notion of 'Vermögensschaden' is therefore decisive in many cases in order to get redress at all. The courts conclude a pecuniary damage from the difference between two situations (so-called *Differenzhypothese*): the victim's fortune after damage and his fortune without damage; and in general all positions of economic or financial worth count as fortune.[48] Where it is doubtful if a position has some objective economic worth – e.g., in case of the mere loss of use – the courts look at the fact whether or not the victim really needed the lost position.[49] That was answered in the affirmative where the victim lost the use of his

41 Lange (supra note 1) p. 39 et seq.; Magnus (supra note 5) p. 21; Palandt/Heinrichs Vorbem. vor § 249 n. 7; Staudinger/Medicus Vorbem. zu §§ 249–254 no. 32 et seq.

42 E.g., §§ 253, 847 BGB (Civil Code), § 29 par 2 AtomG (Nuclear Liability Act).

43 *See* Lange (supra note 1) pp. 51 et seq.

44 Palandt/Heinrichs Vorbem. vor § 249 no. 7.

45 BGHZ 26, 349; affirmed by BVerfGE 34, 269.

46 Lange (supra note 1) pp. 51 et seq.; Stoll (supra note 13) no. 236.

47 Motive (zum BGB) II 22; *see* also Stoll, Gutachten, in: *Verhandlungen des 45. Deutschen Juristentages 1964 I* (1964), pp. 12 et seq.

48 *See* the leading case BGHZ 98, 212 (Großer Senat).

49 BGHZ 98, 212.

house for some months[50] but denied where the victim could not use his swimmingpool[51] or fur coat.[52]

(b) Contractual and tortious damage

[23] Contractual and tortious damage is measured and compensated according to the same principles. The only difference between both kinds of damage is that the parties of a contract may freely modify these principles before any damage occurred. Moreover, the scope and extent of protection a contract grants may militate for or against compensation of certain losses.[53]

(c) Damage to person or property and pure economic loss

[24] The distinction between damage to person or property and pure economic loss concerns the grounds of liability but does not matter in the field of damages. Under general tort law pure economic interests are protected in exceptional situations only.[54] But once liability is established both damage to the integrity interest of the victim (personal and property rights) as well as to the pure economic (expectation) interest is measured and compensated according to the same principles.

(d) Damnum emergens and lucrum cessans

[25] As just mentioned, German law does not distinguish in principle between loss to existing goods (damnum emergens) and loss of future profits (lucrum cessans). Both kinds of losses have to be compensated in full. The Civil Code provides that lost profits are recoverable if they had been made with probability (§ 252 BGB).[55]

7. Monetary assessment of non-patrimonial damage

[26] No hard and fast rules exist on the monetary assessment of non-pecuniary damage. Non-pecuniary damage is damage that cannot be measured in exact and objective, market-oriented terms of money but must be estimated (compare above under I.6.a).
[27] As to damages ('Schmerzensgeld') for pain and suffering for bodily harm, their assessment has to take into acount all relevant circumstances of the case.[56] The primary factors are the gravity and endurance of pains and the lasting consequences of injuries; but also age and personal situation of the victim, degree of fault on the part of the tortfeasor matter.[57] And even the economic situation of both parties or the fact that they are insured plays a role.[58]

---

50 BGHZ 98, 212.
51 BGH DB 1980, 1016.
52 BGHZ 63, 393.
53 Especially in sales law the extent of damages depends on how far special warranties reach, compare § 463 BGB.
54 Compare Kötz (supra note 5) nos. 252 et seq.
55 It is common ground that the provision reduces the procedurally necessary degree of certainty of damage; BGHZ 29, 399; BGHZ 74, 224.
56 Leading case BGHZ 18, 149 (Great Senate).
57 BGH *ibid.*
58 BGHZ 18, 149 (159 et seq.); BGH [1993] NJW 1531; Deutsch (supra note 40) no. 480;

Schmerzensgeld is also due where the victim does not suffer because he is reduced to the state of a 'living dead'.[59]

[28] The 'Schmerzensgeld' is one single sum which compensates for all pains suffered. The judge is not allowed to grant separate amounts for different 'heads' of suffering, for different purposes or different times.[60] Some guidance for the assessment is given by so-called 'Schmerzensgeldtabellen', tables which report the sums and circumstances of decided cases.[61] The highest sums the courts have awarded so far are in the range of 500,000 DM for quadriplegy.[62]

[29] Damages for infringements of the right of personality – especially through mass media – are calculated in a similar way. Again all relevant circumstances of the case have to be taken into account. But here the gravity of the infringement, fault on the part of the infringor and preventive considerations play the prominent role among the different factors.[63] As compared with damages for pain and suffering, the awards are relatively high.[64]

8. Calculation of patrimonial damage

[30] In general the recoverable patrimonial damage is calculated by way of the already mentioned 'Differenzhypothese': the difference between the present (damaged) state of the victim's sphere and that state that would have presently existed had the damage not occurred constitutes what the victim can claim as damages.

[31] The difference must be calculated objectively. Subjective estimation of worth ('Affektionsinteresse') does not matter unless it can be based on market-values.[65]

[32] Furthermore, in principle the damage has to be assessed on a concrete basis. It is not some abstract loss for which the victim should be indemnified but only his actual and concrete loss.[66] There are some exceptions to that rule, in particular the following:

- in sales on fixed term the difference between contract and marktet-price can be claimed as damages for non-performance (§ 376 par. 2 HGB [Commercial Code]);
- in case of infringement of intellectual property rights the infringed person can claim a licence fee;[67]
- according to a widespread but disputed opinion the victim can always claim the

Palandt/Thomas § 847 no. 11.

59 BGHZ 120, 1.

60 BGHZ 128, 117; Palandt/Thomas § 847 no. 11.

61 Hacks/Ring/Böhm, *Schmerzensgeldbeträge* (16th ed. 1994); Hempfing, *Ärztliche Fehler-Schmerzensgeld-Tabellen* (1989); Slizyk, *Beck'sche Schmerzensgeldtabelle* (2 ed. 1994).

62 Deutsch (supra note 40) no. 497 et seq. with references.

63 BGH [1996] NJW 984.

64 100.000 DM for the publication of an interview that never took place (BGH [1996] NJW 984); 100.000 DM for numerous injuries and rapes with utmost cruelty and brutality over a period of six months (LG Frankfurt [1998] NJW 2294).

65 BGHZ 92, 85: The plaintiff himself had made a modell-ship which the defendant destroyed. The plaintiff was only awarded the market-value of similar ships but no additional sum for injured affection or the like. See further Palandt/Heinrichs § 251 no. 11; Staudinger/Medicus § 253 no. 17.

66 Lange (supra note 1) pp. 353 et seq.; Palandt/Heinrichs Vorbem. vor § 249 no. 50.

67 Lange (supra note 1) pp. 354 et seq.; Palandt/Heinrichs Vorbem. vor § 249 no. 52; Staudinger/Medicus § 249 no. 178, § 252 no. 23 et seq.; see also above n. 19.

objective worth of a thing even if it had no meaning nor worth for the victim;[68]
• future losses of income can and often must be calculated on an abstract hypothetical basis.
[33] The assessment of patrimonial damage does neither take account of fault on the side of the debtor nor of the social or economic situation of the parties. And regularly it has no bearing on the recoverability or amount of damages how the creditor will dispose of the awarded sum.[69] Thus, the creditor can claim the necessary costs of repair even if he leaves the damaged thing, e.g., his car unrepaired.[70] But in case of bodily injuries he cannot claim the – abstract – costs of a medical operation which he does not intend to undergo.[71]
[34] Standardisation of assessment is only partly used, namely in the field of compensation for loss of use of cars and motorbikes. There, a detailed table exists producing the immobilisation loss per day for each type of motorvehicle.[72]

9. Compensation of particular kinds of losses

(a) Pure loss of use

[35] The pure loss of use is indemnified in certain cases only: the courts award compensation for mere loss of use – where no costs for hiring a substitute accrued – of houses or flats,[73] cars[74] and ships[75] or other things which a person really needs for daily life.[76] In all others cases of lost use – e.g., of swimming-pool,[77] fur-coat,[78] tv-set[79] – monetary compensation has been denied.[80]
[36] As far as lost use is indemnified, the claimant is awarded a sum above the costs of wear and tear but below the rental value.[81]

(b) Pure loss of earning capacity

[37] German law does not recognize as recoverable the mere loss of the abstract capacity to earn money.[82] An exception applies in cases where a husband or wife who cares for the

---

68 Larenz (supra note 4) § 29 I b; Palandt/Heinrichs Vorbem. vor § 249 no. 53; expressing doubts: Lange (supra note 1) pp. 246 et seq.
69 Freedom of disposition of the victim (*Dispositionsfreiheit*); BGHZ 66, 239; Magnus (supra note 5) pp. 61 et seq.
70 BGH *ibid.*
71 BGHZ 97, 14.
72 Latest version: [1998] NJW 2106 (the table is prepared under the auspices of the ADAC, the biggest German motor club).
73 BGHZ 98, 212.
74 BGHZ 40, 345; BGHZ 45, 212.
75 BGH [1978] VersR 418.
76 *See* already above under I.6.a).
77 BGH [1980] DB 1016.
78 BGHZ 63, 393.
79 LG Berlin [1980] VersR 830.
80 For further discussion see Magnus (supra note 5) pp. 141 et seq.; Palandt/Heinrichs Vorbem. vor § 249 no. 25 et seq.
81 To the methods of calculation see BGHZ 98, 212.
82 BGHZ 38, 58; BGHZ 54, 50; BGH [1995] NJW 1023; Lange (supra note 1) pp. 380 et seq.; Palandt/Heinrichs Vorbem. vor § 249 no. 37.

marital household is injured. He or she can claim the costs of hiring a person for that job even if in fact nobody is hired and although the injured spouse does not earn money by his or her housekeeping.[83]

(c) Pure loss of holiday or free time

[38] In general loss of holiday or free time is no separately recoverable damage.[84] But as mentioned above, under package tour contracts ruined holidays for which the debtor is liable justify a reasonable indemnification.[85] Moreover, the fact that holidays were ruined may be taken into account when assessing the 'Schmerzensgeld' for bodily harm.[86]

(d) Damage to things which remain unrepaired

[39] The creditor can claim the sum necessary for repair even if he keeps the thing unrepaired.[87] The creditor is free in his disposition on the awarded sum of damages.

(e) Frustrated expenses

[40] This is a rather unsettled topic. In some cases the victim can claim compensation for expenses which have been frustrated through the damaging act, in most cases he cannot. The courts give redress when the victim was justified to trust that his expenses would not be rendered useless.[88] It is mainly in contract situations that the victim's expectations are protected this way.[89] But in general no compensation is due. The so called 'frustration doctrine' (*Frustrationslehre*) is rejected by the prevailing view.[90] But it is agreed that the victim may claim those costs which are spent in advance to avoid damage of the kind that occurred.[91]

10. Compensation for emotional shock and loss of consortium

(a) Emotional shock

[41] A person who observes, or hears of, a severe injury or even death of a near relative is entitled to compensation of his physical and psychic injuries if there is any medically recognizable illness.[92] Under these conditions he can also claim damages for pain and suffering.[93]

---

83 BGHZ 38, 59; BGHZ 50, 305 (Great Senate).
84 BGHZ 86, 212; BGHZ 106, 32.
85 § 651 f par. 2 BGB.
86 BGHZ 86, 212.
87 *See* above at n. 67.
88 BGHZ 57, 80.
89 *See* also Lange (supra note 1) pp. 254 et seq.; Palandt/Heinrichs Vorbem. vor § 249 no. 32 et seq.
90 BGHZ 55, 146; Lange *ibid.*; Palandt/Heinrichs *ibid.*; contra Esser/Schmidt (supra note 1) pp. 183 et seq.
91 BGHZ 32, 284; BGHZ 70, 201; BGHZ 75, 238; BGH [1986] VersR 1127; Deutsch (supra note 40) no. 463; Lange (supra note 1) pp. 293 et seq.; Palandt/Heinrichs Vorbem. vor § 249 no. 43 et seq.
92 BGHZ 56, 163; BGHZ 93, 351.
93 *See* the tragic case of OLG Nürnberg [1998] NJW 2293 where a boy of 15 and a girl of 12 saw how their mother was murdered. Each child got 10,000 DM Schmerzensgeld.

In all other situations compensation is denied. It is said to be the normal risk of life to become the observer of horrible scenes in traffic elsewhere.[94]

(b) Loss of consortium

[42] Under German law a person whose marital house-caring partner has been killed can claim the costs of hiring someone for the housework.[95] But no other damage can be claimed. In particular, the surviving partner is not entitled to any kind of pretium doloris unless the conditions mentioned under (a) are given and he himself has suffered a severe shock that constitutes a medically recognizable illness.[96] Apart from that situation however, one spouse can claim nothing if the other is 'only' injured.

11. Compensation of illegitimate losses

[43] As a rule nobody can claim compensation for lost profits to which he is not legally entitled.[97] In principle that rule is also applied in case of lost income earned by immoral activities or means. But the Federal Court awarded an injured prostitute the minimum income in order to avoid that she had to be maintained by the public.[98]

12. Compensation of collective damage

[44] So far, German law does not provide special rules on collective or mass damages. The subject has been discussed at the 62. Deutschen Juristentag 1998.[99] But no proposals for reform concerning the law of damages have been put forward then.

13. Special rules on compensation of ecological damage

[45] As already mentioned, the UmwelthaftungsG (Act on environmental liability) provides for some special rules on ecological damage. If tangible things are damaged in a way that also nature and environment are impaired, then the creditor can claim costs of restitutionary measures even if they would be unreasonably high – or disproportionate – as compared with the worth of the thing (§ 16 par. 1 UmwelthaftungsG). Under the general law of damages reasonableness up to which restitution is allowed normally ends when the costs of restitution of a thing exceed the limit of 130 % of the worth of the thing.[100] In case of ecological damage that limit does not apply. It is therefore argued that costs for restitution are nearly never

---

94 Compare Palandt/Heinrichs Vorbem. vor § 249 no. 71.
95 *See* BGH [1980] NJW 2196; BGHZ 104, 113; for the case that the spouse is not killed but injured compare above under I.9.b).
96 BGHZ 120, 1; Kadner [1996] *Zeitschrift für Europäisches Privatrecht* (ZEuP) 135 et seq.
97 BGHZ 75, 368; Lange (supra note 1) pp. 350 et seq.; Palandt/Heinrichs § 252 no. 3; Staudinger/Medicus no. 11 et seq.
98 BGHZ 67, 119; for further discussion see Staudinger/Medicus § 252 no. 16 et seq.
99 *See* the Gutachten of von Bar, *Empfehlen sich gesetzgeberische Maßnahmen zur rechtlichen Bewältigung der Haftung für Massenschäden?* (1998).
100 *See* above under I.2.b).

unreasonable may they be even much higher than the worth of the damaged thing.[101] In fact a similar rule applies here as in the case of an injured animal.[102]

14. Harm causing also advantages

[46] In German law the problem addressed here is treated under the heading of 'Vorteilsausgleichung' (balancing of advantages). It is a rather disputed part of the law of damages. According to common understanding, gains which the victim had through the damaging event can be set off against the victim's loss.[103] But it is disputed in which situations and under which conditions set-offs should be allowed.
[47] A minimum condition is a causal link between the damaging event and the advantage.[104] Moreover, the set-off of the advantage must correspond to the purpose of damages: the wrongdoer must not inequitably profit from the fact that the victim made also a gain.[105] The latter condition is for example given when the victim has been fraudulently induced to conclude a sales contract but had a profit from the resale of the good bought.[106] But in the end, which advantages count and which do not is decided on a case by case basis.[107]

15. Certainty of damage

[48] In general the courts award damages only if it is sufficiently certain – that means a degree of probability next to certainty[108] – that the victim had the loss in the claimed amount. If the victim cannot or does not produce facts which show the loss with that degree of certainty, the claim will be dismissed. But an exception applies where lost profits are claimed. Here § 252 BGB eases the victim's burden of proof: probability instead of certainty suffices that the profits would have ensued. Moreover, § 287 ZPO allows the court to estimate the existence and amount of damage if it would be too expensive or otherwise too difficult to show the exact amount.

16. Lump sum or rent

[49] As a rule damages are awarded as lump sum. But if the victim of a tort suffers from lasting impairments he can claim a rent (§ 843 BGB).

---

101 Staudinger/Kohler § 16 UmwelthaftungsG no. 17.
102 Above n. 26.
103 *See* Lange (supra note 1) pp. 483 et seq.; Palandt/Heinrichs Vorbem. vor § 249 no. 119 et seq.; Staudinger/Medicus § 249 no. 137 et seq.
104 BGHZ 49, 61; BGHZ 81, 275.
105 BGHZ 8, 329; BGHZ 30, 33; BGHZ 91, 210; BGHZ 91, 361.
106 BGH [1984] NJW 229.
107 Compare Palandt/Heinrichs Vorbem. vor § 249 no. 125 et seq. with extensive references.
108 The judge must be 'convinced' of a fact (§ 286 ZPO); he must be sure so that no reasonable doubts remain, see BGHZ 53, 245; BGHZ 61, 169; BGH [1993] NJW 935.

Part II – Cases

1. Wrongful birth case

(a) Maintenance

[50] The mother – or the parents, as the case may be – can claim maintenance for the unwanted child.[109] The Federal Court held on several occasions that not the child as such is a – pecuniary – damage but the – financial – obligation of the parents to maintain it.
[51] Maintenance is due as a rent, not in a lump sum. The amount is calculated according to the provisions of the RegelunterhaltsVO (Ordinance on the ordinary maintenance). The limits there – 349 DM [ca. 175 Euro] per month until the child is six; 424 DM [ca. 212 Euro] until the 12th year; 502 DM [ca. 251 Euro] until the 18th year – are normally applied. But they can be slightly increased or reduced due to special circumstances.[110]

(b) Lost earning

[52] The mother is not entitled to compensation of income she could have earned but for the care of the child.[111]

(c) 'Tort moral'

[53] Under German law the mother can claim compensation for her pain and suffering caused by the pregnancy and the birth.[112] The civil courts award amounts in the range of 6,000 DM [3,000 Euro].[113]
[54] Moreover, the mother can claim a sum for pain and suffering for the first useless operation which was a tort since she did not validly agree to a useless operation.[114]

2. Wrongful life case

[55] This case is decided on nearly the same footing as the preceding one although there are some factual differences: here the doctor was not contractually obliged to hinder the entry of pregnancy but only to give correct advice. It is not the existence but the handicapped existence that is complained of. Moreover, even on correct advice it would have needed a further free decision and independent act to abort the child.

---

109 Despite a controvery between the two Senates of the Federal Constitutional Court (contra liability BVerfGE 88, 203 [296], pro liability BVerfG [1998] VersR 190), the civil courts award the parents damages for the wrongful birth of a child: BGH 124, 136; BGH [1995] NJW 1609; BGH [1995] NJW 2409.
110 BGHZ 76, 265.
111 BGH [1981] NJW 630; BGH [1997] NJW 1638.
112 BGHZ 124, 128; OLG München [1992] VersR 1413.
113 That was the amount against the constitutionality of which the defendant sued before the Bundesverfassungsgericht, see BVerfG [1998] VersR 190.
114 BGH [1980] NJW 1452.

[56] Nevertheless it is settled that the mother can claim even the **full** maintenance for her child and also a sum for her pain and suffering.[115]
[57] On the other hand the child is entitled to nothing. It cannot argue that its handicapped existence constitutes a damage as compared with a state of non-existence.[116]

3. Eye injury

[58] V can claim compensation of her medical costs and an estimated amount of about 5,000 DM [2,500 Euro] for pain and suffering.[117]

4. Costs for hospital visits and of adaptation of house

[59] A can claim costs for reasonable visits of his wife or other near relatives.[118] As well he is entitled to compensation for the adaptation costs.[119]

5. Scar case

[60] Under German law A has no right to claim damages because his loss is thought to be an abstract one only which he cannot recover.[120]

6. Continued payment of wages

[61] Under German law P's claim is transferred to E by *cessio legis* (§ 6 Entgeltfortzahlungs G) who now can sue D for the loss of two weeks' wages.

7. Monk case

[62] Under German law A has no right to compensation because his loss of – abstract, financially not exploited – earning capacity is not regarded as a pecuniary damage.[121] The monastery does have a loss but that is not recoverable because it is the reflex only of A's injury. So-called 'Drittschäden' are not compensable unless statute so provides (see preceding case).

---

115 BGHZ 89, 104; BGHZ 124, 136; see also Lange (supra note 1) pp. 331 et seq.
116 BGHZ 86, 240; BGHZ 89, 95.
117 In 1977 3,000 DM (1,500 Euro) were awarded for a reduced sight (by 10 %) and wounds from hitting a bottle of beer on the head of a 17 year old girl; compare Hacks/Ring/Böhm (supra note 61) no. 210.
118 For similar cases see BGH [1985] NJW 2757; BGH [1989] NJW 766; BGH [1991] NJW 2341; compare also Lange (supra note 1) pp. 308 et seq.
119 For a similar case BGH [1982] NJW 757; see also Palandt/Heinrichs § 249 no. 11.
120 *See* the case BGHZ 97, 14.
121 OLG Celle [1988] NJW 2618 in a comparable case; also Palandt/Heinrichs Vorbem. vor § 249 no. 37, but contra LG Karlsruhe [1996] NJW-RR 1239.

8. Lost earning capacity

[63] Apart from costs for medical treatment (which A can claim as far as they are not borne by the social system), the calculation of damages for lost income is difficult in these cases. The courts have to estimate the earning prospects of the victim and therefore to take into account all relevant circumstances of the individual case.[122]

(a) Chemistry student

[64] The court must assess A's prospects to finish studies successfully and to find a job as chemist. Then it must be estimated how much A probably would have earned. The difference between the probable income as a chemist and the probable real income is A's damage. A therefore can claim a rent in the amount of that difference. But the rent only starts to run after the date A probably would have finished his studies. A is also entitled to compensation for pain and suffering depending on the gravity of his brain injuries.

(b) Child of six years

[65] The future loss of income of a young child is even more difficult to assess. The courts take the parents' situation, in particular the father's profession and income as a guideline on the assumption that the child would probably reach the same standard of income.[123] But a rent for lost income can only be awarded for the time after the probable end of education.

(c) Living death

[66] In these cases the debtor has to bear all costs of care for the victim. He also owes a considerable sum for pain and suffering even if the victim has lost all abilities and does not feel the pain any more.[124]

9. Lost spouse/partner

(a) Pretium doloris and maintenance

[67] Under German law the surviving husband can claim compensation of lost maintenance (§ 844 par. 2 sent. 1 BGB). The non-marital partner has no such right to sue.
[68] A pretium doloris is only due if the surviving spouse or non-marital partner him- or herself suffered an injury.[125]

(b) Lost services

[69] A is entitled to compensation for lost services.[126]

---

122 *See* for similar cases BGH [1965] VersR 489; BGH [1973] NJW 700; OLG Frankfurt [1983] VersR 1083 (20 year old man who could not study chemistry).
123 OLG Frankfurt [1989] VersR 48; OLG Karlsruhe [1989] DAR 104.
124 BGHZ 120, 1.
125 *See* above under I.10.b).
126 BGHZ 104, 113.

10. Offending publication

[70] On the assumption of A's evident or even gross negligence, A owes B in any case a considerable sum as compensation for infringed privacy and repute.[127] But the more famous a person is, the higher are the awards.

11. Rosenkavalier case

[71] Under German road traffic law, a person who is bodily injured without fault on the part of the car holder is only entitled to compensation for his costs of medical treatment and for the actual financial loss due to an impairment of his earning capacity or to an increase in his expenditures (§ 11 StraßenverkehrsG). Therefore here the victim would get nothing.
[72] In case of holder's negligence the outcome is different: The victim then can claim the costs of the concert-and-opera-tour.[128] This solution is generally agreed.[129] But the correct reasoning is disputed. The main argument is that the worth of the theatre visit etc is commercialised and reflected by its price.[130] Moreover, no distinction should be drawn between the destruction of a thing (bought for some money) which contains immaterial values, like a disc, a parfum or the like and the destruction of the opportunity (also bought for a certain price) to have an immaterial enjoyment, like a theatre visit.[131]
[73] But no separate pretium doloris could be awarded for the missed 'Rosenkavalier' performance. In assessing the pretium doloris for the bodily harm, the court could take into account that the performance was missed. This could – but need not – lead to a very moderate increase of the sum otherwise awarded for pain and suffering. But it must be noted that the courts tend to reject damages for pain and suffering at all in cases of very slight injuries.[132]

12. Prostitute case

[74] In a like case the Federal court awarded the prostitute a reduced compensation for lost earning: she could claim a standard minimum income only (about 1,700 DM or 850 Euro).[133]

13. Mercedes case

[75] The restitution principle (§ 249 BGB) would P entitle to the costs of repair only (4,000

127 Caroline of Monaco was awarded 100,000 DM for an invented interview, BGH [1996] NJW 984.
128 *See* Palandt/Heinrichs Vorbem. vor § 249 no. 36; in case of lost opportunity to attend the booked cruise: OLG München [1986] NJW-RR 964.
129 *See* Lange (*supra* n. 1) p. 252; Palandt/Heinrichs *ibid.*; Staudinger/Medicus § 253 no. 55.
130 *See* references in preceding no.
131 *See* Palandt/Heinrichs *ibid.*
132 BGH [1992] NJW 1043; KG [1973] OLGZ 327; Palandt/Thomas § 847 no. 7. A recent bill on a reform of the law of damages also proposed to exclude damages for pain and suffering in case of slight injuries.
133 BGHZ 67, 119; OLG Düsseldorf [1984] NJW 2474: 1,500 DM; Palandt/Heinrichs § 252 no. 4: today 1,700 DM; see also above under I.11.

Euro). But instead he can claim lost profits if they are sufficiently probable (§ 252 BGB). The difference between X's offer and Y's offer (5,000 Euro) may represent the lost profit, but only if the offers are reliable, market-oriented offers.

14. Loss of use

(a) Immobilised car

[76] In principle, A owes the costs which B has to spent for the rent of a comparable substitute because such a rent meets best the restitution principle.[134] But the German courts have developped detailed rules which restrict or modify the principle. Thus, B is entitled to rent a substitute only if he really needs one. His need has been denied when he drives so little that a taxi would be cheaper.[135] Moreover, the rental costs have to be reduced by B's savings for his own car – an amount normally set at 15 % of the rental costs.[136] And there are further restrictions mainly based on equity considerations.[137]
[77] If B does not rent a substitute, he can claim an abstract indemnity for the lost use.[138] It amounts regularly to 30–40 % of the rental costs.[139] Again, the courts have developed numerous subrules for this 'immobilisation fee'.[140]

(b) Lost use of house

[78] The same principles as under (a) apply here. B can claim a part of the rental value of the house.[141]

15. Damaged, but unrepaired car

(a) Sale of unrepaired car

[79] A can claim the fictitious costs of repair even if he sells the damaged car for a reasonable price. The principle of freedom of disposition allows the creditor to dispose of the sum due as damages as he pleases.[142]

(b) Costs of repair higher than worth

[80] As mentioned above, the creditor can demand the costs of repair as long as they do not

---

134 BGHZ 98, 212 (Great Senate).
135 *See*, e.g., OLG Frankfurt [1992] VersR 620; OLG München [1993] VersR 769.
136 BGH [1967] NJW 552; OLG Köln [1993] NJW-RR 913; OLG Hamm [1996] VersR 774.
137 *See* extensively: Palandt/Heinrichs § 249 no. 13 et seq. citing dozens of decisions including many of the Federal Court.
138 *See* above I.9.
139 Palandt/Heinrichs Anhang zu § 249 no. 1 and the table mentioned above in n. 70.
140 For further discussion *see* Magnus (supra note 5) pp. 131 et seq.; Stoll (supra note 13) pp. 306 et seq.
141 *See* the leading case BGHZ 98, 212 and above under I. 9.a).
142 BGHZ 66, 244; BGH [1985] NJW 2469; MünchKomm/Grunsky § 249 no. 15.

exceed the limit of 130 % of the worth of the car in its undamaged state.[143] The worth of the undamaged car is what had to be spent for a like car.[144]

(c) Costs of repair higher than difference between worth of undamaged and damaged car

[81] There would be no difference to the solution under (b). The difference of worth between a damaged and an undamaged car (which can be regarded as the victim's actual loss) does not set a limit on the costs which the victim can claim for repair. As long as repair is possible and sufficient, the debtor owes costs of repair up to 130 % of the undamaged car's worth.

16. Additional car damage

(a) Accident car

[82] Under German law the victim is entitled to so-called 'merkantiler Minderwert' if the car was badly damaged and even if it was completely repaired. The 'reduced commercial value' is a separate head of damages which can be estimated according to different methods.[145] These methods lead to sums between 10 % and 30 % of the costs of repair.[146]

(b) New for old

[83] In principle, the victim must accept a reduction in the sum of damages if the restitution leads to advantages the victim otherwise would not have had.[147] Therefore, if new parts which substitute the old ones have a longer 'life-expectancy', then the victim can claim only a reduced amount of restitution costs.

(c) Rent of garage

[84] The prevailing view is that expenses rendered futile by the tortfeasor's conduct cannot be compensated.[148] Therefore, P has no actionable right.

17. Damaged railway wagon

[85] The courts have awarded costs of preventive measures of the kind here described,[149] although it is difficult to establish a causal relation between the individual tortfeasor's act and the preventive measure that took place prior to the act.

---

143 BGHZ 115, 371.
144 BGHZ 115, 371; BGH [1992] NJW 1618.
145 BGH [1980] NJW 281; Palandt/Heinrichs § 251 no. 21 et seq.
146 *See* Staudinger/Medicus § 251 no. 35 with further references.
147 BGHZ 30, 33.
148 BGHZ 55, 151; Palandt/Heinrichs Vorbem. vor § 249 no. 32 et seq. with extensive references.
149 BGHZ 32, 284; BGHZ 70, 201.

18. Detective Case

[86] In a like case the Federal Court dismissed the store's claim for part compensation of its payment to the detective.[150] But the store can demand a reasonable sum (regularly 50 DM or 25 Euro) from the thief for being caught.[151]

19. Death of parents

[87] As mentioned, the so-called 'Vorteilsausgleichung' (balancing of advantages) is a disputed part of the law of damages. In cases of the described kind the outcome depends in the first line on the heriditary status of A. If A would have been his or her parents's heir, in any case B is not entitled to set-off A's 'advantage' that A inherited his or her parents' property as such because that had happened anyhow.[152] But the advantage that it happened earlier must be taken into account. Therefore, the freely disposable income from the property, if any, must be set off against the damage.[153]

[88] If A under normal circumstances would not have inherited from his or her parents, then the whole inherited property must be set off against his loss of maintenance.[154]

---

150 BGHZ 75, 230.

151 BGHZ *ibid.*

152 BGHZ 8, 328; BGH [1957] NJW 905.

153 BGH [1974] NJW 1236; BGH [1979] NJW 760.

154 For further discussion see Palandt/Heinrichs Vorbem. vor § 249 no. 139 et seq. with references.

Greece

DAMAGES UNDER GREEK LAW

Konstantinos D. Kerameus

Part I – General Questions

1. Aims of the law of damages

[1] General tort law is qualified in Greece mainly by two requirements that have to be met: namely the perpetrator's illegal behavior and his fault. The rules on damages as such (amount, extent, mitigating circumstances, adequate causation etc.) do not seem to assume a function specific to tort law; they are rather coined in contemplation of the loss suffered by the victim, whatever the source may have been, i.e. regardless whether in the area of contract or tort law. The general purpose of the law of damages is the satisfaction of the injured party for the injury he has suffered. In accordance, the Supreme Court has held that the upper limit of the protection of the injured party is the restitution of damage,[1] the surplus being considered as unjust enrichment.

2. General principles of the law of damages

[2] Pursuant to Article CC 297.1 compensation is, in principle, made in money and by way of exception *in natura*. Article CC 297.2 provides that the court may, after taking into consideration the specific circumstances of each case, order in lieu of compensation the restoration of the former state of affairs, if this is not against the interests of the injured party (the creditor). As a rule, compensation is complete. By way of exception, compensation may be only 'reasonable' or 'equitable', that is limited, if so allowed by any special provision. Such provisions deal with situations in which a requirement for liability may be missing but still the legislator thinks that some amount of compensation would be appropriate. For instance, Article CC 918, that applies also in case of contractual liability (Art. CC 331), provides that a person who has caused prejudice may, where he or she is not held liable because of lack of capacity for committing a tort, be ordered by the court, taking into account the respective situation of the parties, to pay a reasonable compensation if the prejudice cannot be satisfied in some other way.

---

1 AP 1006/1977, EEN 1978. 281 [282 I]; see also AP 6/1990 [Full Bench], NoB 1990. 1321 [1322 I – II].

U. Magnus (ed.), Unification of Tort Law: Damages, 109–116.

3. Different forms of damages

[3] Under Greek law, damages can be only compensatory. The imposition of a penalty and consequently the punishment of the culprit is not the purpose of compensation which only aims the protection of the injured party by restoring it to the *status quo ante*.[2] Thus the degree of fault is irrelevant for the extent of compensation. Any kind of fault is at the same time required and sufficient.

4. Legislation on damages

[4] Under Greek law, compensation may be due for impossibility of performance, default or improper performance of the contract due to fault by the other contracting party (contractual liability). Other legal grounds may be pre-contractual liability and delictual liability. The main rules on compensation are to be found in Articles 297–300 CC, which are located in the General Part of the law of obligations. As far as the assessment of damages is concerned, Greek courts[3] traditionally compare the plaintiff's actual financial situation to the level on which it would have stood, had the prejudicial event not taken place. Qther ways of measuring compensation may apply in specific cases. Thus the Athens Court of Appeal in case 1102/1983,[4] dealing with contractual liability, measured compensation based on the difference between the value of performance and counter-performance. More specifically, the buyer by refusing to accept delivery of the goods and pay the price and by declaring that he revokes his order came in default. The Court held that, in principle, the seller was entitled to freely choose between (a) fulfilling his own performance and seeking full damages for the non- performance of the debtor, or (b) not performing his own obligations and recovering as compensation the difference between full damages and the value of his performance.

5. Definition of recoverable damage

[5] There is no general or statutory definition under Greek law with respect to the notion of 'recoverable damage'. Non recoverable are, however, damages caused to the psychological world of a person during performance, or non-performance, of a contract. By contrast, such damages may be recovered in the area of delictual liability: Article 932 CC gives the court the right to award equitable compensation for non- patrimonial damage to the person whose health, honor or freedom has been harmed or restrained. The same right is granted to the family of the victim in case of fatal injury. The claim for such moral reparations is not assignable and does not pass to the heirs unless it has been acknowledged by contract or an action on it has been served on the defendant (Art. CC 933).

6. Different types of damages

[6] As a general principle under Greek law, the party concerned is compensated only for the

---

2 *See* Stathopoulos, in: Georgiadis-Stathopoulos, *Civil Code II* (1979) Arts 297–298 no. 3.
3 *See* AP 807/1973 [Full Bench], NoB 1974. 321, 1.
4 HellDni 1983.819, 820 II, majority opinion.

damage actually suffered.[5] The Greek Civil Code in Article 298.2 reckons also the compensation for loss of profit by providing that as loss of profit is considered what can be expected as probable profit in the usual course of events by reference to specific circumstances, and in particular to the preparatory measures taken. The assessment of damages may be abstract in the context of commercial transactions with regard to goods having a readily available market. In those instances, the creditor seeking damages is under no obligation to prove his individual loss due to the debtor's default; instead, he can claim the pecuniary difference between the contractual price of the goods and the market price of same on the date of the debtor's default.[6] The leading opinion of the Greek Supreme Court[7] fixed the date of the debtor's default as the point of reference for the abstract computation of damages. Under Greek legal doctrine and case law, the amount of recoverable damages does not depend on their qualification as *damnum emergens* or *lucrum cessans*. On the contrary, both items, if proven, are recoverable as damages on equal footing. The rules of proof are nevertheless different, since in the latter case (*lucrum cessans*) reasonable probability suffices.[8]

[7] As already stated, non-patrimonial loss is also recognized under Greek law under the term of 'moral loss' (Art. CC 932). Greek courts seem hesitant in awarding high compensations for moral loss.

[8] The Greek Civil Code provides also for delictual liability in case of a person's health or body being damaged (CC 929). It expressly states that in such a case the victim may claim all his future expenses because of the harm caused. In other words, according to the Greek Civil Code, in case of injury to the body or the health of a person, the obligation shall, in addition to medical expenses and the damage already accrued, extend to the detriment which the act brought to bear on future earnings, and to the additional expenses he will have to sustain because of an increase in his needs. The same Article gives also the right to third persons to ask for compensation if, because of the tortious act, they are deprived of the victim's services to them. Such third parties are being only indirectly affected, i.e. they are qualified as the indirect victims of tort.[9]

7. Monetary assessment of non-patrimonial damage

[9] The distinction between patrimonial and non-patrimonial damage goes back to the area in which the loss has been inflicted. If this area is the plaintiff's assets in the broad sense of the word, the damage is patrimonial, otherwise non-patrimonial. The assessment of non-patrimonial damage is left to the discretion of the court.

[10] Under Article C.C. 932 the satisfaction for moral damage has to be *reasonable* in the court's opinion. Reasonableness is taken here to correspond to all circumstances accompanying the particular case, therefore is, according to its very nature, hostile to generalization or

---

5 Ligeropoulos, in: *Commentary on the Civil Code* (ErmAK), Art. 298 nos 23, 83; Stathopoulos (supra note 2) nos 25–27: *damnum emergens*.

6 Ligeropoulos (supra note 5) 85–86; AP 790/1958, Full Bench, NoB 1959.422; Athens Court of Appeal 1294/1976, HellDni 1976.534.

7 AP 790/1958, supra.

8 AP 79/1966, NoB 1966.805 [806]; Ligeropoulos (supra note 5) Art. 298, no 16; Balis, *Law of Obligations* (3rded., reprint 1969), p. 88; Stathopoulos (supra note 2), p. 20.

9 Deliyannis- Kornilakis, *Special Law of Obligations III* (1992), pp. 242–244.

classification. Greek courts often enumerate the circumstances that as a rule influence their judgement when assessing damages. Among these circumstances the Court of Cassation[10] has recognized the financial situation and social position of the tortfeasor. An additional hint is offered by Article C.C. 59 which asks the court to take into account the kind of infringement' in order to decide whether, and obviously to what extent as well, to award moral damages.

[11] Two main different heads of non-patrimonial or non-pecuniary loss exist: (a) compensation for moral damage suffered because of a tortious act (Art. CC 932) (see supra, under 5, 6); (b) compensation due to infringement of the right of personality (Art. CC 57–59). Such articles provide that if someone infringes somebody else's right of personality or makes use of thelatter's name in an illegal manner, the person being harmed, e.g. the person having a right on that name or suffering in any way whatsoever a loss for that reason may ask for the suppression of the harmful act and the non-continuance of the same in the future. The victim may also ask for compensation under tort law. Article 59 goes on by providing that the restitution of moral damage suffered may also be granted.

8. Calculation of patrimonial damage

[12] There are no specific rules on computation of damages. As a matter of principle, the computation is concrete, that is it takes into account all relevant subjective circumstances of the victim. Only by way of exception the computation of damages is based on objective criteria (see supra under 6). Standardization of awards does not exist, even in fact not. The victim's own fault may play a role when assessing the extent of damage. More specifically, the principle of mitigation of loss that is enshrined in Art. 300 para. 1 sent. 2 CC constitutes the main reason for limiting compensation. According to the aforementioned Article, 'if a person having suffered loss omitted to prevent or mitigate the same . . . the Court may refrain from awarding compensation or reduce the amount thereof'.

9. Compensation for particular kinds of losses

[13] In principle, the losses enumerated under this question should be recoverable under Greek law pursuant to the rules already stated under question 6 above and particularly if the requirement of adequate causation is met; this may not be the case in no 5. As far as no 3 is concerned, it should be repeated (see supra, no 6) that a Greek court would be reluctant to award compensation in such cases, although under the Civil Code such claim would be provided for.

10. Compensation for emotional shock and loss of consortium

[14] As already stated, emotional shock is only recoverable under CC 932, that is in the area of delictual liability (see supra, under 6).

10 1349/1993, HellDni 1994.1272 [1273 I].

11. Compensation of illegitimate losses

[15] It is held that illegitimate losses can not be compensated as law should not support such illegal activities.[11]

12. Compensation of collective damage

[16] Under Article 926 of the Greek Civil Code, if several persons unlawfully and culpably caused harm, or if several persons are responsible for a certain harm, they are liable jointly and severally. The notion of class action does not exist in the Greek legal system, except in cases of consumers' protection. However, there may be a permissive joinder of parties under Art. 76 no. 2 of the Greek Code of Civil Procedure.

13. Special rules on compensation of ecological damage

[17] The Greek Civil Code contains no special provision with. respect to ecological damage. Some international conventions deal with the matter, such as the Lugano Convention of 22 June 1993 on civil liability for damage resulting from activities dangerous to the environment. But even here it is not clearly stated who is the responsible person or entity for remedying the damage caused by such activities, or who will have the right to collect the compensation to be awarded. Instead of doing so, the Convention leaves it to national courts to tackle the issues. In Greece, rules on ecological damage can also be found in national laws dealing with maritime accidents.

14. Harm causing also advantages

[18] If the harm inflicted to the victim causes him some advantage as well, the loss and benefit emanating from the same tortious act should be set off. The main reason for this is the existence of adequate causation between the harm and the advantage generated by the same event.[12] Other relevant circumstances may also play a significant role; such circumstances may be the victim's financial situation or the latter's degree of fault. [13]

15. Certainty of damage

[19] See above under 6.

16. Lump sum or rent

[20] Under Art. 930 CC, compensation may be awarded as a rent or as a lump sum. The rule is the former. A lump sum can be awarded only exceptionally if there is an important reason for that.

---

11 Ligeropoulos (supra note 5) Art. 298, no 22.
12 Ligeropoulos (supra note 5) Art. 298, nos 46–52a.
13 Ligeropoulos (supra note 5) Art. 298, no 52.

Part II – Cases

1. Wrongful birth case

[21] In general, actual damage (which should be concrete) and loss of profit (which could be probable) may be awarded under the proviso of adequate causation. However, this case would be contemplated as a contractual violation rather than delictual behaviour. Under such approach, the
answer to the case should be given, in principle, in the affirmative. Non-pecuniary damages cannot be claimed on the basis of non-performance of contractual obligations.

2. Wrongful life case

[22] The claim is legal pursuant to CC 914, 932, at least so far as the additional expenses because of the health defects are concerned. By contrast, it is doubtful whether the regular living expenses for a normal child are recoverable as well.

3. Eye injury

[23] The lady may claim her medical costs as well as all other expenses to be incurred in the future because of an increase of needs together with compensation for moral loss. Both items of damage would cover the whole expected period of life.

4. Costs for hospital visits and of adaptation of house

[24] Hospital visits can hardly be claimed, resulting as they are from the marital relationship. By contrast, the cost of adapting the house to the use of a wheel chair can be claimed.

5. Scar case

[25] The damage and the tortious event should be linked to each other by the factor of adequate causation, i.e. if no operation takes place there is no damage to pay. A scar does not imply *per* se a financial loss. However, the injured person could have asked for compensation for moral loss.

6. Continued payment of wages

[26] If such compensation is awarded to him, P would unlawfully get richer as he will get the same salary twice. In principle, no damage can be identified here.

7. Monk case

[27] A, working for nothing, does not have any claim for loss of earning capacity. The monastery, however, could recover the wages which would now have to be paid for a replacement.

8. Lost earning capacity

[28] Full compensation may be asked on the basis of Article CC 929. The special circumstances enumerated under this case would influence the judge when awarding compensation, i.e. the chemistry student would get a larger award than the normal 6-year old child. The 'living dead' would receive full compensation for the life which he would otherwise be expected to enjoy.

9. Lost spouse / partner

[29] (a) It is true that CC 928 refers only to the lawful spouse having by the law the right to receive the maintenance from her husband; nevertheless it cannot be excluded that the court treats also a non-marital partner that has lived with the fatally injured person for a long time with sympathy.
[30] (b) As the maintenance of the household can be considered an obligation connected to the spouses' common life, the corresponding compensation may be claimed under Art. CC 929.

10. Offending publication

[31] Under Article CC 920, pecuniary loss caused to a person as a result of untrue defamatory rumors circulated by another renders the latter liable to compensate the former, if their untruth was known or was culpably unknown to the party who circulated the rumors. So, the answer to the case should be in the affirmative. The amount of damages would depend on the degree to which the plaintiff participates in public life.

11. Rosenkavalier case

[32] If adequate causation can be established the fee for the tour can be claimed. Moral loss would presumably not cover the failure to attend a cultural event.

12. Prostitute case

[33] Illegal earnings cannot be claimed. However, the case of prostitution is not necessarily answered negatively, to the extent that social security and other social assistance is nowadays granted to prostitutes as well, so that prostitution has been probably 'legalized', although it may be said to remain immoral.

13. Mercedes case

[34] The full cost of the actual damage should be recovered together with loss of profit, if any, provided that adequate causation exists. Probably, P would not be entitled to more than 4,000 Euro.

14. Loss of use

[35] Loss of use of either the car or the house is recoverable. The cost of a substitute, which should be comparable to the frustrated use in all significant respects, may be considered as a method of assessing damages, regardless of whether the victim did have resort to a substitute (abstract computation of damages).

15. Damaged, but unrepaired car

[36] Fictitious damage, as already stated, (supra, no 5) can not be claimed. As far as hypotheticals (b) and (c) are concerned, the culprit should compensate the difference between the actual price and the one which would have been otherwise obtained.

16. Additional car damage

[37] The answer to case (a) should be given in the affirmative if the damage can be assessed in a concrete way ('merkantiler Minderwert'). So far as (b) is concerned, P can claim full costs of repair for the damage caused; any improvement of P's car ('new for old') can hardly be assessed and, for the rest, P did not ask for new parts. With respect to (c) the garage rent can not be claimed as the damage is not actual but fictitious and, in any event, hard to assess.

17. Damaged railway wagon

[38] All costs of repair may be claimed. The cost of maintaining the reserve wagon is not linked to B's behaviour. However, it is oriented towards the general eventuality of damages and, therefore, may be awarded if the computation of damages is abstract.

18. Detective case

[39] Pure economic loss is not recoverable under Greek law. However, the consideration set forth *supra*, under no. 17 might apply here as well.

19. Death of parents

[40] As already mentioned, advantages and disadvantages emanating from the same tortious event should be causally linked. Adequate causation is here doubtful. In addition, the collateral 'benefit' of receiving the parent's property is, from a value-oriented point of view, far away from the particular context of the parent's fatal injury and therefore, perhaps, hardly amenable to set-off.

Italy

Damages under Italian Law

F. D. Busnelli and G. Comandé

Part I – General questions on the law of damages

1. Aims of the law of damages

[1] The main goal of the law of damages is compensation. Art. 1223 c.c., enclosed in the contract section of the code but extended to tort liability by art. 2056 c.c., is the general rule. Art. 1223 c.c. expressly provides that damages must include both losses incurred by the creditor and lost profit.

[2] Original understanding of the civil code seems to show a mismatch between the goal of the law of damages and that of tort law, being the latter mainly to sanction the illicit fact intended *stricto sensu* as the willful or negligent fact (art. 2043 c.c.). The original frame of the code organizes tort liability as a special kind of liability, disciplined at the end of the fourth book devoted to the law of obligation. Contractual liability (that is: default/ breach of contract), instead is disciplined at the beginning of the fourth book devoted generally to obligations. This explains why art. 2056 c.c. on the evaluation of damages merely says that 'damages to the damaged person must be calculated according to articles 1223, 1226, 1227' all regulating damages for breach of contract. Nevertheless, this original framework has changed a lot by way of scholars' interpretation, case law, and special statutes introducing stricter criteria for imputing liability.

[3] On one hand, the system has experienced quick changes in the understanding of tort liability. Nowadays it is thought as a tool to redress wrongful damages. Therefore the aims of tort law are closer to the aims of the law of damages. However, it must be noted that their aims seem not to exactly coincide. In fact, the original punitive goal of tort law is still plainly kept alive by art. 2059 c.c. that limits moral damages awarding only to the hypos provided for by the law (mainly but not exclusively when the tort constitutes also a crime, pursuant to art. 185 criminal code). Moreover, tortious liability does not cover the whole field of the law of damages. It is covered also by compulsory insurance (car accidents for example) and social security system (work related injuries).

[4] On the other hand, we experienced a mutual exchange in the central role of contractual and tortious liability with regard to the law of damages. Tort law seems over and over to appear as the general type of liability, when contractual liability seems a special one.

U. Magnus (ed.), Unification of Tort Law: Damages, 117–141.

2. General principles of the law of damages

[5] It can be argued from art. 1223 c.c. that the main principle of the law of damages in tort liability is to make the victim whole. This idea still distinguishes compensation under tort law and indemnity under social security schemes.

[6] Of course both statutory or agreed upon limits on the amount (the kind) of damages can be admitted. However, broadly speaking, those limits cannot apply to damages to the person. For instance, dealing with conventional limits on liability, it is worthwhile to remember art. 1681 c.c. on the transport of people: it make void all clauses that limit carrier liability for damages to the traveler. Our Constitutional Court,[1] judging on the constitutionality of the law enforcing the Warsaw Convention on air transport, explained that statutory limits on liability are not constitutionally correct if there are not enough guarantees on certainty and adequacy of damages compensation ('adeguate garanzie di certezza e adeguatezza per il ristoro del danno'). On the contrary, limits on damages to things are fundamentally permissible upon the condition they respect the 'principle of reasonableness' and they take into account the balancing of contrasting interests at stake.[2]

[7] Normally compensation in money, once for all, deemed to be equivalent to the suffered losses ('risarcimento per equivalente') is the rule – as it can be easily grasped by art. 2058 c.c. However, the injured person can claim 'specific restitution when it is in whole or in part possible' (art. 2058 section 1 c.c.) and it is not 'too costly for the debtor' (art. 2058 section 2 c.c.). In fact, art. 2058 c.c. allows the judge to exclude specific redress only because it is too burdensome for the tortfeasor. However, art. 18 of Law no. 349, July 8, 1986 on environmental damages compensation provides for special type of specific redress. 'When a malicious or negligent deed, in violation of legal dispositions . . . involves the environment by damaging it', the Italian Government (or other official bodies with territorial jurisdiction) has the right to take action against the damager, claiming specific redress regardless of the excessive economic burden on the tortfeasor.

[8] Art. 2057 c.c. of the civil code provides that ' when damages to persons are permanent, damages awards can be made by the judge, taking into account conditions of the involved parties and the nature of the damages, as a life annuity'. This is the sole article dealing with tort liability in the civil code that expressly refers to personal injuries damages. Note, however, that the rule was constantly ignored by case law.

3. Different forms of damages

[9] We could define the Italian tort system as a 'bipolar' one in which a general rule of liability (art. 2043 c.c.), without general limits to damages awards for pecuniary losses ('danni patrimoniali' as they can be defined *a contrario* from art. 2059 c.c.), lives together with a special rule of 'limited reparability' for non pecuniary damages (art. 2059 c.c.). The former aims mainly to compensation goals. The latter is mainly directed to satisfactory-punitive functions.

[10] The Italian system differentiates itself from the French one, that joins together all

1 Corte Cost., 6 maggio 1985, n. 132, [1985] *Resp. civ. e prev.* 537.

2 Corte Cost., 22 novembre 1991, n. 420, [1991, II] *Cons. Stato* 1827.

damages under one extremely general rule (art. 1382 code civil), but goes closer to the German system that distinguishes between pecuniary and non pecuniary damages limiting the latter to hypotheses fixed by law (par. 253 BGB). Nevertheless, the BGB considers 'personal injuries or damages to health' or liberty deprivation (par. 847 BGB), associating under the same rule both the goal of compensation and the satisfactory-punitive function in a system at the same time 'mono-normative' and bipolar. Whereas the Italian system distinguishes more consistently between the two goals. It identifies non economic losses in those that can not be objectively evaluated economically (art. 2059 c.c.), while the general rule of art 2043 c.c. takes care of all damages that can be evaluated economically, according to compensation goals. However, art. 2059 c.c. typifies too strictly non economic damages – at least in the general scholar understanding of it – because it mainly links them to the existence of a crime (art. 185 criminal code).

[11] Scholars divide themselves in two groups. The first one wishes to repeal art 2059 c.c. (either by law or with a decision of our Constitutional Court), inclining to the French model of *globalisation*. The second group wants to retain the rule, inclining to its reform in order to make it more flexible likewise the Swiss system. In fact, the Swiss system demonstrates that it is possible to avoid too restrictive rules without quitting a bipolar system: the concept of 'seriousness of the offense' can limit recoverability of non economic damages understood *stricto sensu*.

[12] We prefer the last prong of the alternative. It seems also more coherent with insights coming from European community law. For example, the EC directive 85/374 on defective products liability distinguishes between personal injuries (together with damages in case of death), dealt under a general rule of liability, and moral damages to which each member State can set limits (art. 8). The *ratio* of this rule is clear enough: compensation for personal injuries fulfills mainly a compensatory goal, whereas restoration of moral damages aims mainly to satisfactory-punitive tasks and the legislator can limit it without any violation of constitutional principles.

[13] As we shall see, in Italy personal injury damages are mainly taken care awarding damages for 'danno alla salute' that has a compensatory goal and, considering the constitutional protection devoted to fundamental (sacred) individual rights, this interest 'cannot suffer limits to the compensation for its damage'.[3]

4. Legislation on damages

[14] Our civil code gives only some general principle on damages evaluation. It specifies some of them on the two main types of damages: loss suffered (*damnum emergens*) and lost profit (*lucrum cessans*).[4] The general proposition is that damages must be demonstrated in their exact amount. However, if it is not possible damages are 'awarded by the judge with its equitable evaluation' (art. 1226 c.c. recalled by art. 2056 c.c.). In any event, 'lost profit is appreciated by the judge with equitable consideration of the circumstances of the case' (art. 2056 c.c. section 2).

---

3 In these terms Corte Cost. 14 luglio 1986 n.184, [1986, I] *Foro it.* 2053, with comment of G. Ponzanelli, *La Corte Costituzionale, il danno non patrimoniale e il danno alla salute.*

4 It can be argued from art. 1223 c.c.

[15] On the contrary, there are special rules to award personal injury damages under social security law. The workers' compensation act (law n. 1124 of June 30 1965) imposes strict rules for awarding indemnities (art. 66ff) as a percentage of the wages. Our Constitutional Court stressed that this scheme does not cover entirely worker's 'danno alla salute' and invited the legislator – who has not yet answered – to reform it in order to give insurance protection to 'the risk of worker's infringement of psycho-physical integrity' *per se*, regardless of any incidence on his\her income.[5] The reform still has to come. Therefore our Corte di Cassazione decided that the injured worker can claim his 'danno alla salute' according to the general rules of liability.[6]
[16] Recently the Constitutional Court,[7] dealing with the constitutionality of law n. 210 of February 25, 1992 on indemnities for people damaged due to compulsory vaccinations, blood transfusion or inoculation of blood derivates, established the principle according to which 'indemnification' ('indennizzo'), even though different from full compensation ('risarcimento') under art. 2043 c.c., can 'never be trivial'. Moreover, 'it must take into account all element of the loss itself'. According to some scholars these elements make the law n. 210/1992 suspicious of unconstutionality. In fact, the Constitutional Court recently gave another decision clarifying the issue.[8]

5. Definition of recoverable damage

[17] Our civil code does not define the concept of damage. Therefore, its meaning, as received from economics, varies over time. The only constant is that it must be a detriment capable to be evaluated from an economic standpoint.
[18] The traditional wisdom on it goes back in time to the *Differenz Theorie*, interpreted as a reduction in the damaged person's 'patrimony'. Roman categories of *lucrum cessans* and *damnum emergens* sketched in art. 1223 c.c. testify the reach of this 'patrimonial and abstract' understanding of the concept of damage. However, the gradual growth of a 'personal and definite' conceiving of damage inspired a different understanding of it, that wants to protect the human being as such together with his\her interests having the individual being as a reference point. Those protective exigencies are clearly expressed by art. 1226 c.c.. and art. 2056 c.c. section 2 inserting in the system criteria for equitable evaluation of damages.
[19] In detail, the move from a static economy to a dynamic one and the growth of the occasions for personal injury damages in modern industrial societies increased both frequency and seriousness of this type of damages.
[20] Thus it can be registered a first 'revolution' in the conceiving of damage with an upsetting of the relationship between damages to the patrimony (intended as the resulting sum of properties) and damages to the persons. In 1962 for the first time an item of an Encyclopedia ('Encicplopedia del Diritto') was expressly devoted to 'damages to persons' (personal inju-

---

5 Corte Cost., 15 febbraio 1991, n. 87, [1991] *Resp. civ. e prev.* 245
6 Cass. civ., sez. lav., 20 gennaio 1993, n. 698, [1993] *Giust. civ. Mass.* 96.
7 Corte Cost. 18 aprile 1996 n. 118, [1996, n. 5] *Danno e Responsabilità* 576, with comment of G. Comandé, *Diritto alla salute tra sicurezza sociale e responsabilità civile.* For a discussion of all the decisions of the Constitutional Court on the issue see ID, *Il diritto alla salute, la trilogia costituzionale ed i limiti di bilancio: ancora sulla legge n. 210 del 1992 e sulla sua rilevanza sistematica*, [1998] *Danno e Responsabilità* 431.
8 Corte Cost., 26 febbraio 1998, n. 27, [1998] *Danno e Responsabilità* 429.

ries).[9] For a long time this was a topic neglected by Italian Scholars, even though personal injuries damages were already an issue with great interest for the practice of law and the real life of the people.

[21] We can register a second 'revolutionary' move, this time in the conceiving of damages to persons. In fact, the quoted item of the 'Encicplopedia del Diritto' maintained the thesis that 'earning is the parameter to award personal injury damages', therefore personal injury damages end up in 'the economic loss to the injured coming from a diminution of his/her ability to work'. With the beginning of the 19eighties both the Supreme Court (Corte di Cassazione) and the Constitutional Court (Corte Costituzionale) confirmed judicial trends started by the lower courts in Genova and Pisa. Judges in Pisa and Genova, working in tight connection with tort-scholars at their respective city universities, deeply changed Italian jurisprudence on personal injury damages. This new trend springs from a constitutional approach to personal injury damages: an individual right to health, constitutionally protected by art. 32 of the Constitution, belongs to everyone. According to the Supreme Court, the principle to which courts should be bound is that damages coming from the infringement of the right to health must be compensated even though it does not impair ability to generate earnings: indeed regardless of the earning capacity whose impairment should be independently compensated.[10] Hence, case law gave birth to a new kind of damage to the person ('danno alla salute' or 'danno biologico') that gained soon a primary and crucial role in personal injury losses. In fact, the Constitutional Court stated that 'danno alla salute' is 'a first, essential, prioritary compensation that conditions every other one'.[11] The Court also fostered the extension from tort liability to work related injuries of the 'constitutional principle of full and not limitable compensation of danno alla salute'.[12]

6. Different types of damages

[22] In order to go through different types of damages we need to distinguish those ones grounded in a legal rule and (pseudo)damages that scholars attempted to shape, transplanting institutions known in other legal experiences.[13]

[23] (a) Within this second category we find pure economic losses and future damages.

---

9 Gentile, *Danno alla persona*, *Enc. dir.*, vol. XVI (1962), pp. 634 et seq.

10 This way, almost literally, C. Cass., 6 giugno 1981, n. 3675 *Foro it.*, 1981, I, 1884. Most of the leading decisions on personal injury damages can be found, as an appendix, in M. Bargagna/ F. D. Busnelli (eds), *La valutazione del danno alla salute* (3rd ed. 1995). Here also other materials and comments from members of the Research Group on Danno alla Salute of Pisa under the auspices of the Italian National Researc Council. See also of the same Research Group M. Bargagna/F. D. Busnelli (eds), *Rapporto sullo stato della giurisprudenza in materia di danno alla salute*, CEDAM (1996), analysing over 1000 decisions.

11 Corte Cost. 14 luglio 1986 n.184, quoted.

12 Corte Cost., 27 dicembre 1991, n. 485, [1992] *Resp. civ. prev.* 63, with comment of E. Navarretta, *Capacità lavorativa generica, danno alla salute e nuovi rapporti tra responsabilità civile ed assicurazione sociale (In margine a Corte Costituzionale 485/1991)*. More details on 'danno alla salute' in work related and traffic accidents are in D. Poletti, *Danni alla persona negli accidenti da lavoro e da automobile* (1996).

13 On different criterias to choose legal rules and kind of damages in a comparative perspective see G. Comandé, *Alternative Istituzionali e Risarcimento del Danno alla Persona* (1998), forthcoming.

[24] A1) The distinction among, on one hand, damages to the person or to the property and, on the other hand, pure economic losses (among which, for example, damages for wrong informations) can be justified in the German legal system where it is important to shape a comprehensive category for all non-contractual damages linked to all enumerated rights in § 823, section 1, BGB (life, body, health, freedom, property, or other similar rights). It is also clear the reason why this legal system moves towards contract or quasi-contract kinds looking forward for something like *Selbstbindung ohne Vertrag*. However, the same justifications do not allow Italian scholars to introduce those categories in our legal system where non-contractual damage can be compensated always only if it can be qualified as wrongful. If damages are not wrongful they cannot be compensated through a forced expansion of contractual domain. At the same time it cannot be even asked – for those who think not to interpret the criterion of wrongful damage 'as Germans' do – the question whether or not a pure economic loss can be compensated under the general rule of liability provided for by art. 2043 c.c.

[25] The example of damages for wrong informations helps to explain how useless it would be in our system to introduce a general category of pure economic damages, that by the way has not any normative grounds in our country. Both the opinion of those scholars who think liability for wrong information can never be found and the opinion of those scholars who explain that kind of liability in contractual phrasing in order to protect the addressees of the information, can be questioned. Here the true problem is to select reparable losses, according to the criterion of wrongfulness provided by art. 2043 c.c., avoiding both the unfairness of undifferentiated refusal of legal protection and the risk of an unrepressible proliferation of compensation claims.

[26] A2) It is also ambiguous and without normative grounds the distinction between actual and future damages. Admitting equitable compensation for losses such as *lucrum cessans* does not allow us to extend *sic et simpliciter* compensation to future damages as such. Even though we find these words (future damages = 'danno futuro') in actual cases, this terminology is clearly improper. Indeed it is a firm principle in case law that damage, to be recoverable, must be actual. It must link itself to an actual infringement of the protected interest: the natural extension toward the future is a characteristic of all permanent losses – such as *lucrum cessans* – to which refers art 2057 c.c., but this does not exclude the actual nature of the those losses. Indeed, it weighs heavily on damages evaluation since it must be done according to equitative criteria to take into account future effects of the (actual) loss.

[27] Therefore, in our legal system damages – future in a strict meaning – linked to an hypothetical (even probable, but not actual) infringement of an interest of the injured party can not be recovered: loss of a chance can not be recovered. However, this type of losses insidiously penetrated in our case law where judges are not always aware of the difficulties – often flagged out by scholars – in transplanting solutions shaped both in another legal system and on its needs. Really, loss of chance finds its unique and not repeatable justification in the French legal system where there is only one broad general rule art. 1382 of the French code civil. When transplanted in our legal system, loss of chance reveals all its ambiguities both for heterogeneity of possible hypos to refer to (ranging from the mere possibility to win a contest to the well-grounded expectation to receive economic support) and for the confusion it may bring on several legal aspects: causation; non fulfillment of a contract; wrongful damage; actuality of damages. It can also be dangerously distorting when used to arbitrarily expand the area of recoverable (pure) economic losses straining rules and criteria set forth by the legislator. This straining is easily recognized in attempts to translate the conceiving of loss of chance within rights with weak and doubtful contents: for example, it was the case of 'the right to the integrity of the patrimony' sketched by the Supreme Court.[14] It is also useful to remember that most hypotheses labeled in the words of loss of chances are just non fulfillment cases aimed to solve problems of causation. A phrase from a recent Supreme court decision enlightens the point: 'several hypotheses of damages for loss of chances constitute application of the principle that flags the move from the singling out of the causal link throughout a criterion of certainty of the effects of a given behavior to that of probability and suitability of that behavior to produce those effects'.[15]

[28] (b) All other classifications singled out in the questionnaire have normative grounds in our legal system. Nevertheless, classifications do not pertain always to damages; sometimes a clear normative distinction is more shaded in actual cases or creates lively disagreements among scholars.

[29] B1) The distinction between direct and indirect damages is rooted in art. 1223 c.c. as recalled by art. 2056 c.c. *section* 1. However, the distinction has great relevance on the causation issue[16] because it is aimed to select direct consequences (or as courts say in their interpretation of the norm: regular consequences) of the harmful behavior itself appreciated for its suitability to produce those consequences.

[30] B2) The differentiation between *damnum emergens* and *lucrum cessans* describes and limits the whole area of recoverable (economic) damages according to the traditional conceiving contained in art. 1223 c.c. In actual cases that distinction is more in the shadow. In fact, the only certain distinction between them pertains to their evaluation under equitable criteria. Equitable criterion is the only one for *lucrum cessans* (see art. 2056 c.c. *section* 2), but it is only a residual one for *lucrum cessans*: 'when damage can not be proved in its exact amount' says art. 1226 c.c. recalled by art. 2056.

[31] B3) A distinction between contractual and non-contractual damages can be found in the joint reading of artt. 1225 and 2056 *section* 1 of the civil code regarding the foreseeability of the loss. In fact, art 1225 c.c., that limits damages for non fraudulent/willful non-fulfillment to those that could be predicted 'at the time the obligation arose', is not recalled by art,. 2056 c.c. when non-contractual damages evaluation is concerned. Therefore, the logic conclusion is that the latters can compensated regardless of their foreseeability. However this clear normative distinction tends to shade in day to day application. On one hand, courts tend to avail themselves of the foreseeability criterion in tort liability linking fault and foreseeability. On the other hand, scholars clarified that, in contract law, the rule given by art. 1225 c.c. concretely operates only when there is a considerable lack of time from the moment in which the obligation arose and the time of non-fulfillment, because only in those cases the foreseeability test leads to results different from those reached by causation as provided by art. 1223 c.c.

[32] B4) It has a well-grounded normative framework in the 'bipolar' system of art. 2043

14 C. Cass., 4 maggio 1982, n. 2765, [1982] *Giust. civ.* I, 1745.

15 Almost literally Cass. 6 febbraio 1998, n. 1286 *Foro it.*, 1998, I, 1917.

16 Please refer also to our report on causation.

c.c. and art. 2059 c.c. also the distinction between patrimonial and non patrimonial damages discussed in the foregoing *section*.

7. Monetary assessment of non-patrimonial damage

[33] In Italian law a general rule of liability (art. 2043 c.c.), without general limits to damages awards for pecuniary losses ('danni patrimoniali' as they can be defined *a contrario* from art. 2059 c.c.), lives together with a special rule of 'limited reparability' for non-pecuniary damages (art. 2059 c.c.). The former mainly aims at compensation goals, whereas the latter is mainly directed to satisfactory-punitive functions. However, the distinction we just noticed does not cover all kinds of losses that could go under the general understanding of non-pecuniary losses.

[34] The Italian system identifies non-economic losses as those that *cannot* be objectively evaluated economically (art. 2059 c.c.), while the general rule of art. 2043 c.c. covers all damages that *can* be evaluated economically, according to compensation goals. However, art. 2059 c.c. typifies too strictly non-economic damages – at least in the general scholar understanding of it – because it mainly links them to the existence of a crime (art. 185 criminal code).

[35] The distinction between patrimonial and non-patrimonial damages is a source of lively disagreements among scholars. The maximum of disagreement concerns the qualification (under this respect) of 'danno alla salute' (or 'danno biologico').

[36] In an old decision on the issue our Constitutional Court, accepting a broad conceiving of non-patrimonial damages (grounded the non-economic characteristic of the harmed interest) extended this notion to 'danno alla salute' regardless of the limits set forth by art. 2059 c.c. but confining its wording this way: 'in this actually examined case all requirements for protecting the right to health, acknowledged by the constitution as a fundamental rights, are found'.[17] However, the concern to not allow compensation limits in protecting the right to health, and its consequence of treating differently similar cases, led the Constitutional Court to come back on the argument bringing 'danno alla salute' under the general rule of art. 2043 c.c. The court expressly said that 'in the conceiving of non-patrimonial damages provided by art. 2059, only subjective *pretium doloris* characterized by a temporary, fundamentally transient, psychological upsetting must be contained'.[18]

[37] The distinction between damages to health – 'danni alla salute' – (always recoverable) and subjective *pretium doloris* (recoverable within the limits of art. 2059 c.c.) was confirmed by subsequent decision of the Constitutional Court[19] that – as confirmed by another recent decree[20] – did not go away from the precedent decision number 184/1986 'to which it added something on the peculiar case in which 'danno alla salute', linked to the death of a relative,

---

17 C. cost, 26 luglio 1979, n. 88, [1979] *Resp. civ. prev.* 698 with comments of G. Ponzanelli, *Danno non patrimoniale e danno alla salute: due sentenze della Corte Costituzionale*.

18 Corte Cost. 14 luglio 1986 n.184, quoted.

19 Corte Cost. 27 ottobre 1994, n. 372, [1994, I] *Giust. Civ.* 3035, with comment of F. D. Busnelli, *Tre 'punti esclamativi", tre 'punti interrogativi", un 'punto e a capo"*.

20 Corte Cost., 22 luglio 1996, ord. n. 293, [1997, II] *Giur. It.* 313ss with comment Comandé/ Ponzanelli.

is the final moment of a pathological process caused by the same psychological upsetting that constitutes subjective moral damage'.

[38] In the line of this trend of the Constitutional Court we can say that full compensation of 'danno alla salute' under the rule of art. 2043 c.c. is now a 'given data'.[21]

[39] We can also point out that a critical review of the thesis limiting non-patrimonial damages to subjective moral suffering has started. This process gains a relevant consensus by the most recent scholarly writings. Moreover, it was developed further on by a recent decision of our Corte di Cassazione tributing 'a new valency derived by the Constitution' that suggests to turn the idea of *pecunia doloris* in *pecunia lesae dignitatis*[22]. Moreover, the recent law on protection of individuals in the processing of personal data (law n. 675 of December 31st 1996, art. 29 *section* 9, in fulfillment of EC Directive 95/46/CE) confirmed this trend permitting non-patrimonial damages compensation as a safeguard for human being dignity ('dignità delle persone fisiche', *ex* art. 1 section 1 and art. 9 law 675/1996) with special reference to 'privacy and personal identity'.

[40] Hence, the distinction between damages (patrimonial or anyway) always recoverable under art. 2043 c.c. and non-patrimonial damages recoverable under art. 2059 c.c. can be summarized as follows: the formers are damages able to be objectively evaluated from an economic standpoint and they correspond to the general rule of full and unavoidable compensation; the latters, since they cannot be objectively evaluated economically, correspond to the selective rule of the seriousness of the harm, that art. 2059 c.c. – of which we urge a reform to make it more flexible – yet singles out in the possibility to find a crime in the actual case. Note that case law already started to read it in a more flexible way.[23]

8. Calculation of patrimonial damage

[41] The main problems in damages calculation concern 'danno alla salute'. Our Corte di Cassazione singled out for this peculiar fundamental item of damage the need of 'equitable evaluation that must be coherent with the kind of loss involved'.[24] This means for 'danno alla salute': a measurableness that finds its primary ground for uniformity in medico-legal evaluation of the psycho-physical disablement, evaluation that cannot be set aside and gives objective uniformity and measurableness; the possibility to grasp homogeneous grounds for evaluation of damages caused by the ascertained disablement from past case law on the merits; the safekeeping of the equitable power of each judge to adjust this objective measurement to the peculiarities of the case. The goal, expressly declared by the Constitutional Court, is to elaborate 'a criterion that fulfills, on one hand, the need of basic monetary uniformity (the same impairment can not be evaluated in a too different way from one individual to another)

21 This way among several Cass., 29 maggio 1995, n. 4991.

22 Cass., 10606/1996 (1997), *Resp. civ. prev.* 1997, 393.

23 A recent detailed analysis proposing an interpretation that moves toward the trend suggested in the text see E. Navarretta, *Diritti inviolabili e risarcimento del danno* (1996). For a discussion of actual cases that already moved the courts in the advised direction see also G. Comandé, *Danno non patrimoniale: giurisprudenza e dottrina a confronto, Contratto e Impresa* (1994), pp. 870 et seq.

24 Cass. civ., sez. III, 13 gennaio 1993 n. 357, [1993] *Corriere giur.* 303, with comment of V. Carbone, *I contrasti giurisprudenziali sui criteri di liquidazione*, *ibid.*, 305.

and, on the other hand, the need of elasticity and flexibility to adjust awards to actual effects of the ascertained disablements on activities of daily life'.[25]

[42] Courts of the merits tend to reach this goal, but they did not succeeded entirely. Tribunale of Pisa, inspired by the French experience of *calcul au point*, elaborated an equitative criterion of 'calcolo a punto' (evaluation by points) having as a starting point past decisions evaluating – on average – the point of infirmity. This criterion was pleased by our Corte di Cassazione that transparently refers to it talking about 'the results reached by the most sagacious courts of the merits'.[26] Nevertheless, developement of the system in each court created problems. Some Tribunals thought they could elaborate their own local tables of (monetary) values that, if compared among themselves, 'lead to extremely remarkable and disconcerting swingings' .[27]

[43] In order to face this risk that, after a first period of 'anarchical' jurisprudence when each judge was the arbiter to state his/her own equitable criterion, could open the field to a new era of uncertainty and not justifiable difference in evaluation from one court to another, the 'Gruppo pisano di ricerca sul danno alla salute' (the Research Group on Danno alla Salute of Pisa) under the auspices of the Italian National Research Council (CNR) elaborated a proposal for a national orientation schedule (Tabellazione Indicativa Nazionale-TIN)[28] that, since it was developed on relevant data coming from cases decided all over the country, is suitable to be a uniform national common ground for monetary assessments of 'danno alla salute'. The TIN was already welcomed from several courts and it might become an interesting reference point for the legislator when it will decide to answer to the increasing call for a statute regulating 'danno alla salute' (or 'biologico').

[44] It is worthwhile to remember that, on July 27th 1998, ISVAP (the Italian Institute for control on private and collective interest insurance companies) sent to the Ministry of Justice and to the Ministry of Industry a proposed statute arranged by a Commission of experts named by ISVAP itself. The proposed statute (proposta di legge) aims to adequately temper both ground uniformity and flexibility in adjusting evaluation to actual cases, according to the afore mentioned advises of the Constitutional Court. In order to pursue ground uniformity the p.d.l. gives to the Government the power to promulgate a national orientation schedule (Tabellazione Indicativa Nazionale)[29] bounding it to the principle that 'uniform monetary values to assess danno biologico must be elaborated on suggestions coming from courts decisions on a nationwide level' (art. 4). Flexibility should be insured by a twofold possibility to depart from uniform monetary values set forth by the TIN. The first case is the possibility each judge has in actual cases to increase those values up to one third of them (art. 3

25 Corte Cost. 14 luglio 1986 n.184, quoted.

26 Cass. Civ., sez. III, 14 aprile 1995, n. 4255, [1995] *Resp. civ. prev.* 519, with comment of G. Ponzanelli, *La Corte di Cassazione ed il criterio equitativo nella valutazione del danno alla salute*.

27 To use the words of decision: Pret. Lucca, 28 ottobre 1996. (1997) *Riv. giuc. circol. e trasp* 139.

28 On which see G. Turchetti, *Gli sviluppi dello studio sulla determinazione del valore monetario base del punto di invalidità*, in M. Bargagna/F. D. Busnelli (eds), *Rapporto sullo stato della giurisprudenza in materia di danno alla salute*, pp. 171 et seq. and G. Comandé, *La sperimentazione di una Tabella Indicativa Nazionale tra esigenze di prevedibilità ex ante del danno e di liquidazione equitativa ex post*, in *ibid.*, pp. 201 et seq.

29 Art. 3 section 1.

section 3). The second one gives more broad room for pure equitable assessment in cases of exceptionally serious losses: the judge can, with adequate written motivations, award damages according to his/her prudent judgement (art. 3 *section* 4). This proposal shares with the *Disposicion adicional VIII* in the Spanish law n. 30/1995 (*Ley de Ordenación y Supervisión de los Seguros Privados*) the idea of having a national scheduling for *las indemnisaciones basicas* that are contained in the Spanish *Tabla III* joined by the *Tabla IV* with *factores de correctiòn* left to the discretion of the judge. However, the Italian p.d.l. differs from the Spanish solution in several ways. First of all the Italian p.d.l. does not regulate only accidents linked to compulsory car *insurance*, but foster a regulation for 'danno alla salute' in the whole domain of tort law expressly modifying the civil code. Moreover, differently from the Spanish law that does not say a word on the source of data and criteria to elaborate the schedule, the Italian one makes express reference to case law. Finally, it sharply refuses any perspective of *globalisation* of personal injury damages. On the contrary, the idea of *globalisation* springs from the Spanish law that includes in the *indemnisaciones basicas* all together compensation for moral suffering and *lucrum cessan*: this insidiously changes – in Spain – the principle of full compensation of personal injury damages in a system of *limites indemnizatorios*. It is clearly suspicious under constitutional scrutiny.

[45] The p.d.l. articulates personal injury damages in three different kinds with their own required elements and their own evaluation criteria: danno alla salute (or biologico) regulated *ex novo*; non-patrimonial damages whose regulation (art. 2059 c.c.) is reformed in order to make them recoverable (always but only) 'when the illicit fact caused a serious harm to the person' (art. 2); patrimonial damages (in their strict meaning), specially *lucrum cessans*, whose regulation in the code is confirmed and enriched. In fact, *lucrum cessans* is a separate head of damages that must be separately proved according to the rules of evidence provided for by the civil code. However, when 'evidence does not offer more favorable elements to calculate it'[30] 'the income to be taken into account for compensation can not be lower than three times the annual revenue from social pension'. This rule was already provided for by the law regulating compulsory car insurance for traffic accidents.[31] Now it is proposed as a general rule by art. 7ff the p.d.l.

9. Compensation for particular kinds of losses

[46] On damages to the person, when there is no actual damage or there is not clear evidence of any other kind of damage, the injured party who suffered a psycho-physical disablement has still a right to compensation for his/her 'danno alla salute' (o biologico). Nowadays, decisions as outrageous as the one given on January 5th 1967[32] by Tribunale di Firenze can not be rendered again after 'judge made law' introduced the basic item of 'danno alla salute'. At that time the tuscanian court could 'rightly' – that is consistently with the law of that time – say that 'people without any value can exist, as it is the case of those who for old age are absolutely not fit to any earning producing activity'.

---

30 This way Corte Cost., 445/1995, that stress the residuary character of this criterion..

31 Art. 4 section 3 of the law n. 39 of Februay 26th 1977.

32 Trib. Firenze, 6 gennaio 1967, [1969] *Arch. resp. civ.* 130.

[47] On damages to the things, there is not analogous kind of 'presumed' damage as danno alla salute: damages must always be proved. Note, however that for 'presumed' in the case of danno alla salute we mean presumed in its extension (so far money evaluation is concerned) but not in its existence that must be shown with medical evidence. See, however answers to the cases for more details.
[48] On the issue of damages for loss of holiday or free time, since long ago well known to German courts and by now emerging also in Italy, the law n. 111 of March 17th 1995, in fulfillment of the EC Directive n. 90/314/CE on journeys, holidays and tours 'all included', recalls the International Convention on voyage contract (ratified by Italy with the law n. 1084 of December 27th 1977) that provides for tour operators' liability (art. 13) for 'whatever harm' caused to the traveler because of non-fulfillment. However it sets forth limits for personal injury damages. This last rule is not satisfactory an may be not even pass constitutional scrutiny. In a comparative fashion it may be useful to remember that in Germany, after the reform of 1994, par . 651 h BGB, introduced by the law of 1990 on contract for traveling, specifies that liability limits provided by the original formulation can be applied only to '*Schäden die nicht Körperschäden sind*'.

10. Compensation for emotional shock and loss of consortium

[49] (a) There is a considerable debate on borderline cases between damages to psychological health ('danno alla salute psichica') and simple emotions or discomfort: the case of a psychological shock to which refers the Constitutional Court in its decision n. 372/1994 is an exemplary model.
[50] There are two distinct interpretative trends on the issue.
[51]The first one, using those doctrines of psychiatry that deny the possibility to single out any distinguishing line between pathology and bare emotion (or discomfort), tends to group all psychological damages – understood as a *continuum* ranging from clear mental illness to bare psychological shock – under the general rule of art. 2043 c.c.
[52] The second explanatory trend, instead, thinks that medico-legal science, whose support cannot be set aside not only in evaluating 'danno alla salute' but also in defining this category, can fix a fundamental distinguishing line between clear pathology and physiological moral suffering, between illness and bare emotion or discomfort.[33]
[53] Both trends reveal difficulties. However, a clear choice between them must be done. The need to contain and circumscribe the floodgates of claims without lessening or eroding the protection for deeply deserving values – among which we certainly find physical and psychic health – enumerated by the constitution urge as to choose the trend that stresses, also on psychic damages, the not easily reached distinction between damages to (psychic) health, always recoverable under the general rule of art. 2043 c.c., and mere emotions (or discomforts), recoverable within the limits of art. 2059 c.c. This was the conclusion reached, for example, by Corte di Appello di Milano that, with consistent arguments, refused to identify

33 On the topic, for its relation with 'danno alla salute' and moral damages see the monographycal work of E. Navarretta, *Diritti inviolabili e risarcimento del danno* (1996), and in a comparative framework with the common law world see G. Comandé, *Le non pecuniary losses in common law*, [1993, I] *Rivista di diritto Civile* 453 et seq.

damages to psychic health in the deep and torturing pain that the wrongful loss of a nine years old daughter can provoke to her parents.[34]

[54] (b) As it will appear from our answers to hypos under case number 9 our system does not know a kind of damage as *loss of consortium*. Nevertheless, the concurring awards-usually admitted by courts – for lost (economic) support and compensation for non-patrimonial damages take well care of the problem. Moreover, in obviously exceptional cases, relatives could show they suffered damages to their psychic health (with evidence of a clear pathology). After the recent shift in the interpretative trend by our Corte di Cassazione, compensation to the non marital-partner is now permissible for his/her companion death if it is shown the existence of a 'fundamentally firm relationship that turns out in a communion of life'.[35]

[55] In the end, even without specific statutory provisions, the results reached by our judges are not too far from those suggested either by Swiss Code of Obligations, according to which 'if for the death other people are deprived of their support, this damage as well must be compensated' (art. 45 *section* 3) or by the Dutch civil code that provide for damages for 'loss of support' to relatives if 'wholly or partially supported' and to people cohabiting with the *victim* if 'wholly or largely supported' (art. 108, *section* 1, of Book VI).

11. Compensation of illegitimate losses

[56] Please refer to case 12 for some discussion on the point.

12. Compensation of collective damage

[57] There are not special rules dealing with mass tort litigation or small claims. However, small claims are under the jurisdiction of the Justices of peace that where created mainly to deal with them. Please refer to our report on causation for further details on mass tort litigation.

13. Special rules on compensation of ecological damage

[58] Please see above under n. 2 and refer also to our report on strict liability rules.

14. Harm causing also advantages

[59] The doctrine of *compensatio lucri cum damno* is acknowledged in our country. As we said, the general principle is to make the victim whole without wrongfully enriching him/her. However, courts often say that, in order to be set off, gain and losses should arise from the same title and the same causation. For further details please refer to our answer to case 19.

15. Certainty of damage

[60] Please refer to discussion above under nn. 6ff and to the answers to the cases.

---

34 App. Milano, 5 luglio 1994.
35 Cass. 28 marzo 1994, n. 2988.

16. Lump sum or rent

[61] Please refer to general discussion on art. 2057 c.c. above. Note, however, that there is not any specific rule on this point. Certainly both victims and wrongdoers (*rectius*: their insurers) actually prefer lump sums. A system such as structured settlements is not strongly developed in Italy yet.

Part II – Cases

1. Wrongful birth case

[62] Here the issue concerns damages for unwanted child (wrongful birth) due to a medical malpractice.[36]

[63] Clearly enough the existence of a contract (and its non fulfilment) makes it easier for the victim to go away with compensation. Indeed, several cases found contractual liability (for breach of contract) leading the hospital to pay all losses linked to the maintenance of the child.[37] Yet, the issue of liability could be dealt under tort law but wrongfulness of damages must be shown. However, wrogfulness cannot be found in the infringment of a 'right' to have an abortion that does not exist in our legal system. In fact, it is clear that our abortion law does not give any right to abort: the law n. 194/1978 only gives to the mother the faculty to abort under specific conditions and make it not a crime for doctors to perform it. Nevertheless, art. 4 of the law on abortion regards economic concerns, that could cause dangerousness for the mother's physical or psychological health,[38] as a reason for permitting abortion. In similar cases damages for the unwanted birth were confined to those moneys needed to the couple for overcoming discomforts linked to the birth,[39] but damages do not automatically correspond to costs of upbringing.[40] Therefore, it is clear that wrongful damages are linked to the infringment of the mother's right to health, even though linked to economic worries. She must show those economic concerns endangering her health that sustained the decision to abort (or that would have supported it) to obtain patrimonial damages.

[64] This reasoning explains how our Constitutional Court could say the law n. 194 of 1978 is not unconstitutional in denying any relevance to the father's will in the decision to abort:[41] it is the mother's health at stake, but there is not any 'right' to abort. Indeed, several cases acknowledge both contractual and tortious liability for damages in favor of the mother (damages to her health and costs of maintenance, education, and school), but deny any damage to the father because he has no say in the decision whether to abort or not and these damages cannot be wrongfully given since they do not come from a violation of any of his rights, but

36 Please refer to our reports on causation and wrongfulness for the general remarks on medical malpractice liability.

37 Trib. Cagliari, 23 febbraio 1995, [1995, I] *Nuova giur. civ. commen.* 1107 with comment of Orru'.

38 App. Venezia, 23 luglio 1990, [1991] *Riv. it. medicina legale* 1320.

39 Trib. Padova, 9 agosto 1985, [19986] *Riv. it. medicina legale* 870.

40 Note that in most of these cases judges found liability on the hospital together with that of the doctors.

41 C. Cost., 31 marzo 1988, n. 389, [1988, I] *Giust. civ.* 1381.

from the law (art. 146, 147, 148 c.c.).[42] Nevertheless, with hypocrisy, in some other cases of failed abortion, the father – not the husband of the mother – of the 'wrongfully' born child obtained compensation for his duty to maintain the child against doctors who mistaken the abortion procedure. The criterion to award damages was to endow the needed amount to reach economic stability. This shows an hypocritical contradiction of the Italian system: it consists in denying any power, even to the father/husband, while looking forward to stretch the law in order to give him compensation for the costs of upbringing. Note, however, that these decisions conflict with decisions of our Corte di Cassazione. The Court said that costs of upbringing cannot be recovered (under art 2236 c.c.) because this is not a wrongful damage since mother's economical concerns only justify abortion.[43]

[65] In summary under the proposed hypo: whether or not she is married, she can recover her 'danno alla salute' and her *pretium doloris* (if occurred). She will probably not need to claim for lost wages during the last 2 months of pregnancy and the first two after birth because social security takes care of them. She cannot recover the 7 more years of lost wages. It is her choice not to work. On the contrary she will recover the cost to undergo a second operation for sterilization, either under contract law or under tort. It is not entirely clear if lower courts would always award damages for upbringing in cases of medical malpractice, but in any event the afore mentioned conditions must be satisfied.

2. Wrongful life case

[66] The hypo looks for child's living costs. Nevertheless, under this hypo there are three main issues: damages for failed abortion (mother's claim), for wrongful life (child's claim), wrongful birth (mother's claim). For the first issue please refer to case 1. The mother will claim living costs on behalf of her child for the period after legal adult age (18 years) and on her name for upbringing him to majority.

[67] It is clear in some courts that a child can claim damages to health and *pretium doloris* linked to the infringement of his/her legitimate expectation to born healthy.[44] However, it is sometimes argued that the child has no expectation since his/her alternative to wrongful birth would have been no birth at all. Still both the mother and the father could claim compensation for their own *pretium doloris* and 'danno alla salute' (if occurred)[45] .

---

42 App. Bologna, 19 dicembre 1991, [1993] *Dir. famiglia* 1081.

43 *See* Cass. civ., sez. III, 8 luglio 1994, n. 6464, [1994] *Resp. civ. e prev.* 1029, and *Danno e Responsabilità* (1995), p. 91, applying art. 2336 c.c . In fact, this decision of our Corte di Cassazione overturned Trib. Padova, 9 agosto 1985, and the appeal decision of Corte appello Venezia 23 luglio 1990 both quoted above.

44 *See* Trib. Verona, 15 ottobre 1990, [1991, I] *Foro it.* 261

45 Even in decisions given under the 'old system' (see among several Trib. Treviso, 13 marzo 1986, [1987, I] *Foro it.* 962), judges awarded a sum naming it 'danno alla vita di relazione' (damages to social relations) because untill recent times courts denied pretium doloris to relatives of a personally injured person who survived the accident. For exceptions to this rule when extremely severe permanent injuries are at stake see Trib. Verona, 4 marzo 1991, [1992] *Giur. merito* 823. See also Trib. Milano 19 ottobre 1989, [1990] *Resp. civ. e prev.* 628, awarding danno alla salute, pretium doloris. cost for assistance both to the child and to his parents; Trib. Genova, 3 gennaio 1996, [1996] *Gius* 922 awarding danno biologico to the child according to the criterion of art. 4 law n. 39 1977 (so called system of three times the annual payments for the social pension).

3. Eye injury

[68] A special statute on product liability (Law n. 224 of May 4 1988 in fulfillment of the EC directive 85/374) rules the case on the liability issue. Under the special rule the injured party must prove only damages, defect and causal link between the former and the latter (art. 8). However, under these rules only damages for personal injury and death, destruction or deterioration of goods (other than defective product itself) normally destined to the private use of the injured party, can be awarded (art. 11). Therefore, V can certainly seek compensation for 'danno alla salute', lost wages (if any) and proved medical expenses. Of course most of the last named losses are covered by the social security system. However, this special strict liability rule does not exclude the application of other laws concerning liability (see art. 15). Note also that under this statute *pretium doloris* cannot be awarded. Hence, V will probably sue also under the general rules of tort law seeking to obtain this item of damages under the art. 2059 c.c. So far actual amount is concerned there is no difference in awarding 'danno alla salute' under the special law on product liability.
[69] Therefore, V may choose either to avail himself of the special law with an easement in the burden of proof, but foregoing moral damages, or to shoulder (also) the burden to show (at least) negligence to obtain also *pretium doloris*.

4. Costs for hospital visits and of adaptation of house

[70] Clearly enough A will recover reasonable costs for adapting his house. This is an actual loss. So far indirect losses are concerned, there were some cases dealing with those losses but usually courts say these are indirect consequences not recoverable under art. 1223 c.c..[46]

5. Scar case

[71] This is a tricky case. When scars are unavoidable incidents of personal injuries the amount for 'danno alla salute' takes care also of aesthetic damages. As a matter of fact, several cases award damages for future surgical operations (even cosmetic ones).[47] That is part of the caused loss. Courts say that when it is possible to face an aesthetic damage with a surgical operation, the tortfeasor must pay also for this costs.[48] Moreover, nobody can force someone else to undergo a (cosmetic) operation. Most probably, if A seek compensation for this costs together with the other losses he will receive them; it would happen the same after the operation even though he may be required to show actual costs. However, the mere fact he actually does not intend to undergo the operation do not prevent him to recover his actual loss, but the court will take into account that damages to health will be reduced by the operation thus awarding a corresponding (reduced) amount of damages. Aesthetic damages are 'danno alla salute', but if plaintiff can show it also impair specific abilities to work leading to economic damages such as *lucrum cessans* or *damnum emergens* they can be redressed as well.

---

46 Cass. civ., sez. III, 16 aprile 1996, n. 3564, [1996] *Riv. giur. circ. trasp.* 625, for example did not award damages for spouse's lost wages due to the assistance offered to the injured marital partner.

47 *See* Trib. Roma, 11 luglio 1995, [1996] *Riv. giur. circ. trasp.* 141.

48 Trib. Udine, 15 marzo 1990, [1990] *Dir. e prat. assicur.* 747.

6. Continued payment of wages

[72] So far lost earnings are concerned, there is not actual loss for P. He could seek his personal injury damages, but he cannot seek double recovery for lost wages just because he did not lose anything.[49]

[73] Note that under Italian law E could seek reimbursement from D. Note also that this principle was definitively settled with the case just cited. Before that courts reasoned in terms of *compensatio lucri cum damno* denying its application in order to give to the worker compensation for damages to health without expressly acknowledging 'danno alla salute'.[50] Still our Corte di Cassazione distinguished between permanent and temporary injuries: in the latter case if it allows the worker to work he could recover damages for difficulties in giving his services.[51] Note that this understanding must be enlightened by the theory of 'danno alla salute'.

7. Monk case

[74] The monk can certainly claim loss of earning capacity, but he can primarily claim 'danno alla salute' for, so called, temporary incapacity. Since an actual loss of wage cannot be claimed he cannot claim the equivalent of six weeks of lost wages. Nevertheless, courts made it clear that in awarding personal injury damages causing permanent impairments judges must look to all negative consequences both on for profit activities and on not for profit ones. In this case it should be taken in due account the impairment of those activities that, even though do not create earnings, nevertheless are something else than ordinary lifetime ('*cotidie agere*' in the word of the court),[52] because of their importance, requested time and social significance.

[75] In an actual nun case the court did not applied the general criterion provided for by a special law to deal with cases in which actual loss of earnings cannot be shown (art. 4 of the law n. 39/1977). Judges thought this is a bottom line that can be exceeded due to the special social value of the services provided by the damaged person. In fact, the injured nun was a professional nurse not earning from her highly specialized work[53] only because of her religious votes.

[76] A different issue may arise if we look to those who lost the monk's services. In a case

---

49 *See* expressely Cass. 2 aprile 1984, n. 2163, [1984] *Arch. giur. circ. strad.* 584.

50 For this reasoning see P. G. Monateri, *La responsabilità civile*, in: R. Sacco, *Trattato di diritto Civile* (1998), p. 346.

51 Cass. 15 aprile 1993, n. 4475, [1993] Foro it. Rep., voce Danni Civili, n. 30

52 *See* Trib. Roma, 14 aprile 1994, [1994] *Riv. giur. circol. trasp.* 656 with comment of Rossetti; Trib. Savona, 3 agosto 1995, [1996] *Riv. giur. circ. trasp.* 560. Courts take care of temporary impairments for non earning people, such as students, awarding damages for 'danno alla salute' a kind of damages that is not at all linked to earning capacity. See for example App. Milano, 18 settembre 1984, [1984] *Arch. giur. circol. e sinistri* 765. Note that under the old conventional understanding of personal injuries damages a child badly (but not permanently) injured could not recover anything, not even damages to health just because . . . since he did not work he did not suffer any economic loss (sic!): see Trib. Napoli, 8 novembre 1979, [1980] *Arch. giur. circol. e sinistri* 336.

53 Trib. Spoleto 3 aprile 1991, [1992] *Arch. giur. circol. e sinistri* 747.

the court gave to the monastery to which he belonged standing to claim damages suffered by the monk killed in an accident.[54] Indeed, they lost some economically valuable services they where expecting.

8. Lost earning capacity

[77] Please refer to the general part for the notion of 'danno alla salute' and proper ways of awarding it. See also under cases 3 and 7.
[78] Even though no actual lost wages can be shown the victim will always recover 'danno alla salute' in which the judge takes care of all effects of the impairment on the victim's life (on aesthetic, relational, standpoints).[55]
[79] In some occasions courts award students' damages taking into account together with damages to health also the ways in which the permanent impairment can reduce the victim's ability to work according to studies done and other experiences. When those parameters for equitable evaluation are missing – some courts say – the named criterion of art. 4 law December 23d 1976 n. 857 applies.[56]

9. Lost spouse / partner

[80] (a) Pecuniary (including funeral expenses[57]) and non pecuniary damages must be given to all people who suffered them because of the death (now also because of the severe impairment) of their relative both because of moral suffering[58] or for the loss of a presumably certain economic vantage for them coming from the deceased relative (a legitimate expectation to it).[59] They must prove that their relative's death deprived them of an economic utility they were enjoying before and that they would have continued to enjoy otherwise.[60] Among this economic utilities it can be included also economically valuable services concerning help and assistance (such those of an household).[61]

54 *See* Corte appello Torino 6 febbraio 1981, [1982] *Riv. giur. circol. trasp.* 338.

55 *See* amomg several decisions: Trib. Monza 7 maggio 1987, [1987] *Resp. civ. e prev.* 495.

56 *See* for example Trib. Palermo 26 gennaio 1991, [1991] *Arch. giur. circol. e sinistri* 588; Trib. Napoli 29 gennaio 1986, [1987, I] *Assicurazioni* 2, 32. For a sharp critique of using criteria such as shown inclinations and abilities or family and social conditions see Trib. Firenze, 5 marzo 1990, [1991] *Arch. giur. circol. e sinistri* 42.

57 *See* Cass. civ., sez. III, 29 maggio 1996, n. 4991, [1996] *Riv. giur. circol. trasp.* 936, for the principle according to which relatives must show the amount paid for funeral expenses.

58 Trib. Torino, 8 agosto 1995, [1996] *Resp. civ. e prev.* 282 with comment of ZIVIZ, qualifying as 'danno esistenziale' damages suffered by relatives of an injured person

59 Cass. civ., sez. III, 1 agosto 1987, n. 6672, [1987] *Giust. civ. Mass.* fasc. 8–9. Cass. civ., sez. III, 15 dicembre 1981, n. 6630, [1981] *Giust. civ. Mass.* fasc. 12., linking future economic losses for relatives to the ascertained probability of durable end continuous economic help from the deceased, taken away the fatal event, even though those benefits were not due to legal duties. See also Cass. civ., sez. III, 28 ottobre 1978, n. 4932, [1979] *Arch. giur. circol. e sinistri* 275.

60 Trib. Treviso, 27 dicembre 1994, [1995] *Resp. civ. e prev.* 617 with comment of Cassella presumed the father would have used at least a quarter of his income to mantein his children to the age of 21 and one third for his wife.

61 Cass. civ., sez. III, 3 novembre 1995, n. 11453, [1995] *Giust. civ. Mass.* fasc. 11; Cass. civ., sez. III, 17 settembre 1996, n. 8305, quoted, and more recently Cass. civ., sez. III, 6 novembre 1997,

[81] Earnings at the time of the death should be the basis to award future damages to relatives of a deceased.[62] Note however that court should make rough guesses on what would have been future income anyway, taking into account possible career or changes in life and work opportunities.[63]

[82] So far economic losses are concerned it might be raised also the issue of economic damages to parents / relatives of a dying student not producing any earnings. Sometimes courts say they should not get anything on the assumption that she/he would not have given anything to the parents even when gaining a salary in the future.[64] In other cases the court said parents can recover lost earnings only if they can show it;[65] sometimes courts said it can be inferred.[66]

[83] Therefore, under the previously stated conditions wife/husband can claim both *pretium doloris* and maintenance and (if occurred) their own 'danno alla salute.[67]

[84] It is different for non-marital partners:[68] the conventional wisdom in courts decisions looks for State acknowledgment of their link with the partner to obtain compensation. Hence, sometimes a religious marriage was deemed sufficient[69] to award damages sometimes it was not.[70]

[85] Italian scholars are bitterly divided on the issue,[71] but a fairly recent Corte di Cassazione decision clarified the issue, at least concerning moral damages to the non-marital partner. The Supreme Court made it clear that the proof of a firm and lasting relationship characterized by mutual moral and material assistance is the key issue to award both moral and economic damages to non-marital partners.[72] Accordingly the non marital partner must show stability of the relationship and the actual material assistance lost because of the death of his/her non-marital partner.

10923, [1998] *Danno e Responsabilità* with comment of Violante. See also Cass. civ., sez. III, 1 aprile 1980 n. 2112, [1980] *Giust. civ. Mass.* fasc. 4, establishing that loss of future income from the deceased to his/her relatives may be awarded only equitably.

62 Cass. civ., sez. III, 6 maggio 1988 n. 3351, [1988] *Giust. civ. Mass.* fasc.5; Cass. civ., sez. III, 25 giugno 1981 n. 4137, [1981] *Riv. giur. circol. trasp.* 1053

63 For a synthesis, in a case that took into account a new wedding after the spouse death, see Cass. civ., sez. III, 4 gennaio 1996, n. 25, [1996] *Danno e Responsabilità* 463 with comment of G.Ferrando.

64 Trib. Milano, 2 settembre 1993, [1994, I] *Nuova giur. civ. commen.* 680, with comment of De Matteis. Cass. civ., sez. III, 10 ottobre 1992 n. 11097, [1992] *Giust. civ. Mass.* fasc.10.

65 App. Bologna, 7 ottobre 1995, [1996] *Danno e Responsabilità* with comment of Ponzanelli.

66 Cass. civ., sez. III, 13 novembre 1997, n. 11236, [1998, I] *Foro it.* 54.

67 Cass. 17 settembre 1996, n. 8305, quoted.

68 *See*, for example, Trib. Trento, 19 maggio 1995, [1995, I] *Nuova giur. civ. commen.* 1017, with comment of De Giorgi, linking pretium doloris to a juridically relevant vinculus with the death person.

69 Trib. Firenze, 18 ottobre 1979, [1981] *Dir. Prat. Ass.* 170.

70 App. Firenze, 23 maggio 1980, [1981] *Dir. Prat. Ass.* 175.

71 In favor of tort compensation are, among others, Patti, *Famiglia e responsabilità civile*, p. 186; D. Angelo, *La famiglia di fatto* (1989), pp. 527 et seq.; Alpa, *Famiglia di fatto e risarcimento del danno*, [1976, IV] *Foro it.* 64; Bonilini, *Il danno non patrimoniale* (1983), p. 476. Contra Trabucchi, *Pas par cette voie s'il vous plaît*, [1981, I] *Riv. dir. civ.* 351.

72 Cass. civ., sez. III, 28 marzo 1994, n. 2988, [1995, I] *Giur. it.* 1,1366. Courts apply this doctrine: see App. Firenze, 29 aprile 1996, [1996] *Giur Tosc.* 59.

[86] Major problems were raised in cases of (severe) *personal injuries*. When a tort caused permanent injury it is possible – according to some courts – to award damages to the relatives (children's right to moral and material upbringing):[73] so called 'danni riflessi'. However, only recently the Corte di Cassazione overruled its previous state-ments that denied moral damages to the relatives in case of personal injury not leading to death.[74] Now they can be awarded if plaintiff clearly shows it.
[87] The previous understanding that denied moral damages in case of non fatal injuries created several inconsistencies. Courts inconsistently had to link losses such 'conjugal rights to have sexual intercourses'[75] and companionship to the concept of 'danno alla salute' in order to give compensation. The more consistent new trend started by Corte di Cassazione will make it easier to put losses under the right head of damages. Indeed a person does not suffer 'damages to his/her health' because his/her spouse can not have sexual intercourses.
[88] (b) Damages for pain and suffering (*pretium doloris*) provides compensation for loss of services. Please refer to Part I and to the previous case for more extensive discussion.[76]

10. Offending publication

[89] We assume the problem here is negligent defamation with untrue statements. In fact, willful defamation is a crime in Italy and it was never a problem to obtain compensation for it. In fact, there would not be any problem to claim compensation (mainly moral damages) even under a strict interpretation of art. 2059 c.c..[77]
[90] Nowadays, courts say that negligent defamation is an actionable tort on the basis of art. 2043 c.c..[78] They typified infringements of political,[79] economical or professional reputation[80]

73 Cass. civ., sez. III, 17 settembre 1996, n. 8305, [1997] *Resp. Civ. Prev.* 123; Cass. civ., 7 gennaio 1991, n. 60, [1991, I] *Foro it.* 459 with comment of Simone.

74 *See* Cass. civ., sez. III, 23 aprile 1998, n. 4186, [1996] *Danno e Responsabilità* 686 with comment of G. De Marzo. Untill recently our Corte di Cassazione affirmed the opposite principle: see, for example, Cass. civ., 17 novembre 1997, n. 11396, [1997] *Foro it.*, Rep. voce Danni Civili, n. 84. However, past decisions already fixed the required elements to award moral damages to relatives: see Cass. civ., sez. III, 23 giugno 1993, n. 6938, [1994] *Responsabilità Civile e Previdenza* 75 et seq., with comment of Comandè Risarcimento del danno morale ai congiunti: quando?

75 Trib. Genova, 5 luglio 1993, [1994, I] *Giur. it.* 2, 1048, with comment of Pinori expressely awarding pretium doloris because the partner permant imparirment reflected to him: damages to the husband of a woman that had lost the ability to have children. The first case on this issue decided by our Corte di Cassazione was Cass. civ., sez. III, 11 novembre 1986 n. 6607, [1987, I] *Giust. civ.* 572. This was confirmed by the Supreme Court: among several Cass. civ., sez. III, 21 maggio 1996, n. 4671, [1996] *Arch. giur. circ. strad.* 730.

76 However, see Trib. Napoli, 16 gennaio 1995, [1996, I] *Giust. civ.* 255 with comment of Giammaria; Trib. Trento, 19 maggio 1995, [1995] *Resp. civ. e prev.* 787, awarding to relatives psychological damages separated from pretium doloris if a patology can be showed

77 For a case study on damages for infringment of rights of personality see U. Scarselli/V. Zeno Zencovich, *Analisi di 170 sentenze sulla lesione della personalità rese dal Tribunale di Roma*, [1995] *Dir. inf. inf.* 701ff. One of the higher amount of damages awarded in Italy (600 milions) was given by Trib. Roma, 30 settembre 1995, [1996] *Danno e Responsabilità* 116 against a politician and his editor for untrue, statements in a TV transmission a newspaper director.

78 *See* among several Pret. Roma, 2 ottobre 1962, [1963] *Riv. dir. civ.* 72, but the first case is the so called Caruso case: Cass., 13 marzo 1958, n. 1563, [1958, I] *Giur. it.* 1, 1390.

79 *See*, for example, Trib. Roma, 27 marzo 1984, [1984, I] *Foro it.* 1687.

expanding the scope of this liability from individuals to political parties, to religious communities,[81] to national States.[82] The true problem here is that victims 'actual' losses almost always involve moral damages and some courts would not compensate them without a crime.[83] As already said, our Corte di Cassazione, criminal section, solved the problem affirming that the lack of the crime of defamation does not exclude a negligent tortious fact.[84]

[91] So far categories of individuals are concerned, it can be noted that politicians (that is political reputation) receive a generous protection with regard to damage awards because of statements ascribing facts that even though not defaming *per se* can infringe political credibility. Lawyers/magistrates are protected from statements that can impair their relationships with colleagues and the public at large.[85] Damages to the reputation (mainly moral damages) are awarded taking into account means used for the defamatory statements, discredit suffered, offended person's profession, spreading of the statements.[86]

[92] According to the hypothetical and since only damages are concerned, we disregard both different remedies (e.g. rectification) and defenses such as truth of the statement.

11. Rosenkavalier case

[93] The proposed case at first glance appears to deal with the so called 'damages for ruined holiday' searching for liability of professional tour operators or travel agents: when a travel agency was involved and tourists could not enjoy their holidays the Tribunale of Roma,[87] awarded moral damages for having holidays upset, without requiring any link to criminal provisions.

[94] However, here the issue is one of recoverable damages that must be faced according to the rule of art. 1223 c.c. which applies to liability for breach of contract, but also to liability for torts according to art. 2056. The rule allows compensation for those damages that are 'immediate and direct consequences' of the tort[88] in order to set a limit to 'remote or considerably indirect consequences'.[89] The damages A is claiming do not satisfy requirements provided for by the named article (please refer to our report on causation): not all consequences in his assets can be compensated. Moreover, there is not violation of a protected

80 On general terms see V. Zeno Zencovich, *Onore e reputazione nel sistema di diritto civile* (1985).

81 *See* Cass. pen, 16 gennaio 1986, [1986] *Dir. inf. inf.* 458.

82 Trib. Roma, 31 dicembre 1986, [1988, I*] Giur. it.* 2, 833.

83 *See* for example App. Firenze, 11 marzo 1960, [1960] *Giur. Toscana* 376.

84 Cass. pen., sez. VI, 20 giugno 1978, [1979] *Giust. pen.* 118, in which the court sustained that a civil judge can award damages for defamation even when in criminal trial there was no condemnation; and Trib. Roma, 27 marzo 1984, quoted

85 *See*, for judges and prosecutors, V. Zeno Zencovich, *La reputazione del magistrato*, [1986] *Dir. inf.* 138 et seq.

86 *See* Trib. Napoli, 22 marzo 1996, [1996] *Dir. inf. inf.* 583

87 Trib. Roma, 6 ottobre 1989, [1992] *Resp. civ. e prev.* 263. See also Tribunale Torino, 8 novembre 1996, [1997, I] *Giur. it.* 2, 58, espressely talking of damages from upset vacation ("da vacanza rovinata")

88 For the argument that art. 1223 c.c. presupposes other rules for causation see Gorla, *Sulla c.d. causalità giuridica: 'fatto dannoso e conseguenze"*, [1951, I] *Riv. Dir. Comm.* 450, 409; Visintini, *Trattato breve della responsabilità civile* (1996), p. 557.

89 This way Corte di Cassazione, 10 ottobre 1967, n. 2397, [1968, I] *Foro it.* 1311.

interest to make wrongful the damages claimed in the hypo according to art. 2043 c.c. (please refer to our report on wrongfulness for more details).

[95] Nevertheless, it seems useful to point out that there was an interference in a contractual relationship. It is clear that A could not claim moral damages for the missed concert, but still he cannot enjoy a – not repeatable – performance for which he paid. The breach of a right *in personam* by a third party does not imply, *per se*, obligatory damage compensation on the part of the third party to the creditor: to obtain compensation he must prove to have suffered a definite and irreparable loss. It may be the case (please refer to our answer on the cable case under the first report on hypotheticals).

12. Prostitute case

[96] Most probably she would not be able to demonstrate the amount of money she loses for not being able to 'work'.

[97] Nevertheless, Italian judges faced a very similar case to the suggested hypo.[90] They established that, even though not criminally prosecuted, prostitution is an activity against morality. Therefore, income springing from it has not legal protection because coming from relationship whose 'causa' is illicit. In the actual case damages awarded were those calculated on an average income of an household. The general principle is that whoever perform activities contrary to 'buon costume' has no right to *compensation* for loss of income springing from that activity.[91]

[98] Nowadays, she will recover all personal injury losses (permanent or temporary) linked to her damages to health.

13. Mercedes case

[99] Neither 23,000 nor 20,000 Euro were the actual value of the damaged Mercedes. Clearly enough courts will award 4,000 Euro. In fact, these are the cost for full (we assume) repair that should put P in the same position he would be the accident had not occurred.

14. Loss of use

(a) Immobilised car

[100] Courts constantly award what is called under Italian law 'danno da fermo tecnico': out of pocket expenses for renting a vehicle during the repair period. There are not fixed limits, but court will certainly award the amount of money to rent a car of the same level of the damaged one.

(b) Lost use of house

[101] A head of damages, such the one named in the hypo, does not exist in our legal system. We assume that it was not possible for B to live in his house during repairs just because it

90 Cass. civ., sez. III, 1 agosto 1986 n. 4927, [1987, I] *Foro it.* 493.

91 *See* A. De Cupis, *Il danno. Teoria generale della responsabilità civile* (1979, I), p. 298.

was damaged. Therefore, he decided to live for six months in a camper instead of renting a substitutive house. He may probably seek reimbursement for the cost (if any) of renting the camper. Clearly enough if he can prove that other damages occurred he could claim compensation. For example if he can show he suffered damages to his health or he lost some profits (say his office as medical doctor was as well in the house) they are recoverable.

15. Damaged, but unrepaired car

(a) Sale of unrepaired car

[102] What if A sells the car after suing B? Most probably A sold the car at a reduced cost. Therefore cost of repairs may compensate this different price.
[103] A need only to show actual damages: since he is claiming the money equivalent of the damages caused to the car, it is up to him the choice to sell at a reduced value (retaining repair damages) or to repair and receiving an higher amount from C.
[104] Cost of repair may often be higher than the final value of the damaged/repaired thing. This is the reason why often insurers insert a clause that allows them to pay for a new thing, suitable for the same use, instead of paying for repairs.
[105] In principle, A can recover the cost of repair. Nevertheless, applying art. 2058 c.c., a court stated that expenses for specific performance or compensation for damaged things cannot be higher than the value of the damaged thing itself.[92]
[106] It is noteworthy to remember also a decision[93] according to which, when costs of repair are higher than the market value of the car, compensation may cover market price for a suitable substitute with the same characteristics and efficiency of the undamaged car, including also the cost of searching it. Therefore, damages may be higher than the value of the car before the accident. But in other similar cases actual interest in continuing to use the damaged car lead to damages higher than pre-accident value.[94]
[107] In a case when repair costs exceeded actual value of the car (both in the pre and in the post-accident status) the judge denied specific performance (repair) allowing only the equivalent value of the undamaged car,[95] but a few recent ones went the other way round[96] because injured patrimony must be rebuilt regardless of the costs.[97]

(b) and (c) unworthy car repairs

[108] Still A can receive repair costs from B and selling the car without repairs. In the end he will 'gain' from the accident, but he can probably still recover (see above under case 15 (a).
[109] Recent cases under the same conditions (repairs higher than market value) opted for

---

92 Trib. Asti, 1 febbraio 1988, [1988] *Arch. giur. circol. e sinistri* 750.
93 Pretura Milano, 12 dicembre 1991, [1992] *Resp. civ. e prev.* 832.
94 Pretura Forlì, 19 dicembre 1990, [1991] *Riv. giur. circol. trasp.* 863. Contra see yet Trib. Asti 1 febbraio 1988, [1989] *Resp. civ. e prev.* 145; Corte appello L'Aquila, 3 gennaio 1978, [1979] *Dir. e prat. assicur.* 564.
95 Pretura Taranto, 9 marzo 1993, [1994, I] *Giur. it.* 2,1068 with comment of Marella.
96 *See* Pret. Catania, 2 gennaio 1997, [1997] *Arch. circol.* 169; Giud. Pace Catanzaro, 19 luglio 1996, [1997] *Giud. di pace* 43; Pret. Perugia, 3 gennaio 1997, [1997] *Rass. gur. umbra* 454.
97 Giud. Pace Milano, 25 maggio 1996, [1997] *Giud. di pace* 45.

compensation of the market value increased of the cost to demolish the car and registering a new one deducted the value of the relict.[98]

16. Additional car damage

(a) Accident car

[110] Our answer is definitively not. Certainly a repaired car has a lower value than a new/undamaged one. Nevertheless, the legal system assumes repairs puts the situation back to the pre accident status.

(b) New for old

[111] A will ask for what he spent. Nevertheless, in some cases the doctrine of *compensatio lucri cum damno* was applied in the same way the hypo is suggesting, thus reducing the amount of damages.[99]

(c) Rent of garage

[112] It is not an immediate and direct consequence according to the interpretation of art. 1223 c.c. (please refer to our report on causation for further details).

17. Damaged railway wagon

[113] Please refer to case 5 under our report on causation.

18. Detective case

[114] A cannot claim part of B' salary from the thief. B was employed just to catch thieves. Indeed this is both a problem of (legal) causation and of recoverable losses to be solved according to art. 1223 c.c.

19. Death of parents

[115] Judges apply the doctrine of *compensatio lucri cum damno*, according to which gains and losses to the victim of an illicit act should be set off, when gains and losses arise from the same source (the tort in our case) and with an immediate and direct causal link.[100] But the doctrine is a general one applying also to contracts.
[116] In a case of nuisances from a production site (cement factory) to a farming field the court denied application of *compensatio lucri cum damno* saying that the field was not made

98 Pretura Torino, 2 febbraio 1993, [1993, II] *Assicurazioni* 164.
99 *See* Pret. Roma, 10 aprile 1964, [1964] *Tmi Romana* 612; Pret. Pinerolo, 4 gennaio 1967, [1969] *Arch. resp. civ.* 486. For critiques to this decisions see P. G. Monateri, *La responsabilità civile*, quoted, 345.
100 *See* Cass. civ., sez. III, 19 giugno 1996, n. 5650, [1996] *Danno e Responsabilità* 693, with comment of Colonna, *Compensatio lucri cum damno*.

a building field – hence increasing its economic value – by the cement factory activity but by administrative laws.[101]

[117] The principle is also applied to personal injury cases: a seaman lost some fingers switching from his job to that of school-caretaker, but the court did not set off personal injury damages with 'gains' from the new employment.[102] In another decision the court did not set off damages linked to the death of the relatives and the pension the plaintiff received 'because' of that death.[103] The reasoning was based on a different title theory: the tortious death was only a condition for receiving the pension.[104] However, in an inverted case (parents claiming economic damages for the death of their 13 years old daughter) our Supreme Court held that those damages should be awarded taking as well into account that parents will have not to perform their own (economic) duties to maintain the child.[105] It is not entirely clear whether the reasoning (setting off expected costs with gains both springing from legal duties) would apply also to our hypo since neither of the two doctrine is prevalent yet.

[118] Therefore, probably A can claim loss of maintenance and a court would not set off 'gains' and losses according to the principle we recalled before.

101 Cass. 16 giugno 1987, n. 5287, [1989, I] *Giur. it.* 1,1, 380.

102 Cass., 30 luglio 1987, n. 6624, [1989, I] *Giur. it.* 1,1, 381 with comment of Petrelli.

103 Cass. 22 dicembre 1987, n. 9528, [1988] *Arch. giur. circ. strad.* 365. See recently Cass. civ., sez. III, 18 novembre 1997, n. 11440, [1997] *Mass.*

104 *See* also Cass., sez. lav., 1 luglio 1994, n. 6228, [1996] *Rass. giur. energia elettrica* 467.

105 Cass. civ., sez. III, 7 maggio 1996, n. 4242, [1996] *Danno e Responsabilità* 430 with comment of V. Carbone, *La compensatio lucri cum damno tra ambito del danno risarcibile e rapporto di causalità*, who makes a clear syntesis on the status of the doctrine of compensatio lucri cum damno in Italy.

The Netherlands

Damages under Dutch Law

Mark H. Wissink and Willem H. van Boom

Part I – General questions on the law of damages

General remarks

[1] 1. In drafting this country report we have not taken into account any influence of other areas of law (such as administrative law, social security law, tax law and EC-law) on obligations to pay damages. All references are to articles of the Civil Code, unless stated otherwise.
[2] 2. The Dutch Civil Code (*Burgerlijk Wetboek*) contains general rules pertaining to damages as part of the general law of obligations (Book 6, articles 95- 110). These rules deal with statutory obligations to pay damages, i.e. all cases in which statutory law (notably the Civil Code itself) states that an obligation to pay damages exists. Therefore, these general rules apply to obligations to pay damages arising from breach of contract (article 6: 74 *et seq.)*, tort and various forms of strict liability (article 6: 162 *et seq.)*, unjust enrichment (article 6: 212) and many others. Various other provisions in the Civil Code and other legislation deal with specific types of damages.
[3] The fact that articles 6: 95–110 contain general rules does not preclude the possibility that in certain cases these rules will be applied differently according to the basis for liability and/or the the types of damage involved. With one exception (the power of the court to mitigate the amount of damages; article 6: 109) the parties to a contract may deviate from these rules.
[4] 3. The above mentioned provisions of the Civil Code do not apply to contractual obligations to pay damages, such as those arising from insurance-contracts and (some) penalty-clauses. However, in these cases the general rules on damages will often be applied *per analogiam* unless the contract at hand requires otherwise.[1]
[5] The above mentioned rules on damages are to be applied by the regular courts (*burgerlijke rechter*) in cases governed by civil law. Claims for damages against governmental bodies may be entertained by the regular courts but in certain cases also by the administrative courts, applying administrative law. The administrative courts will generally refer to the provisions on damages of the Civil Code.[2]

---

1 *See Asser-Hartkamp III* (1998), nr. 404–407.
2 HR (Hoge Raad, the Dutch Supreme Court; hereinafter: HR) 24 October 1997, NJ (Nederlandse Jurisprudentie) 1998, 490.

U. Magnus (ed.), Unification of Tort Law: Damages, 143–158.

[6] 4. Generally, the courts have a wide margin of discretion with respect to the award of damages. Many provisions of substantive law leave much freedom to the court, e.g., with respect to the calculation of damages and the award of non-patrimonial damages. Furthermore, the court is not bound by the ordinary rules of evidence when establishing the types and amounts of damages to be awarded (though, of course, courts will generally require some proof). Damage does not have to be certain. Generally, it will suffice that the court is satisfied that damage is plausible (*aannemelijk*).

1. Aims of the law of damages

[7] (a) The aim of the law of damages is (full) compensation of the damage.
[8] Generally, the same is said of the general law of tort, though it would perhaps be more accurate to state that the law of tort aims at distinguishing between cases in which liability to compensate damages exists and cases in which no liability exists.
[9] Prevention of damage is not considered to be an aim of the law of damages. It is considered to be an aim of the law of torts.
[10] Penalizing the defendant for his behavior is not considered to be an aim of the law of tort nor of the law of damages.
[11] In legal writing other aims are mentioned as well with respect to specific cases, such as (i) taking away the enrichment of the defendant with respect to claims for damages in case of unjust enrichment or the application of article 6: 104 (*infra*, question 8), (ii) *restitutio in integrum* with respect to awards for damages not in the form of money and (iii) upholding of subjective rights (e.g. copyrights) in case of infringement thereof.[3] In the first and second cases no clear parallel with the aims of the law of tort exist. The third case may be said te refer back to the law of tort.
[12] (b) With respect to non-patrimonial damage the situation is somewhat different. The following aims are recognised:

- making good the non-patrimonial damage (though money-awards will never be able to compensate non-patrimonial loss);
- giving the injured person (financial) means to engage in activities which will distract his mind from the harmful event;
- allowing justice to be seen to be done, by obliging the liable person to pay money in order to make good non-patrimonial harm;
- prevention, though only as a subsidiary aim in cases of defamation and invasion of privacy.

[13] Generally it is not considered to be the aim of non-patrimonial damages (i) to give the claimant under this heading compensation for patrimonial damage which may have occured but could not be established (though in practice this may be the effect of an award for non-patrimonial damages) and (ii) to punish the liable person.[4]

---

3 *See Schadevergoeding* (looseleaf edition), Inleiding, aant. 4; *MON. NBW B-34* Bloembergen, nr. 2–3.

4 *See Schadevergoeding*, art. 106, aant. 6.

2. General principles of the law of damages

[14] The general principles of the law of damages include:
[15] – Full compensation (of patrimonial damage). This implies (i) that the real damage must be compensated, no more and no less; (ii) that the financial situation of the parties is not relevant to the amount of damages; and (iii) that all patrimonial damage must be compensated, including loss of profit, future damage and damages which must necessarily be estimated.[5] Several exceptions to this principle apply.
[16] – The defendant is liable only to the extent that the damage can be imputed to him (e.g., taking into account questions of causation and contributory negligence).
[17] – Advantages resulting from the damage causing event must be set off against the damage, as far as it is reasonable to do so.
[18] – The liable person and the person entitled to receive compensation must act vis-a-vis each other in accordance with the principle of good faith.[6]
[19] – Compensation in money. However, the court may, at the request of the injured party, award damages in any other form (article 6: 103).

3. Different forms of damages

[20] (a) Damages are compensatory damages. These include legal fees and judicial costs (*infra*, question 6).
[21] (b) Punitive or exemplary damages do not exist as a separate form of damages. However, factors such as the degree of fault on the part of the liable party may be taken into account to a certain extent within the framework of article 6: 98 (causation) or 6: 109 (mitigation) and thus affect the amount of damages due. Furthermore, a contractual penalty clause obliging a party to pay more than the amount of damage actually suffered, will in principle be enforceable.
[22] (c) Nominal damages do not exist as a separate form of damages.
[23] (d) Assessing non-patrimonial damages is in principle a matter of equity (*infra*, question 7). Generally, awards of non-patrimonial damages will also aim at being compensatory, in the sense that there should be some relation between the seriousness of the non-patrimonial loss suffered and the amount to be awarded, though it is recognised that this may be difficult to achieve. However, the court may take into account circumstances of the case at hand which may influence the award in such a way that the resulting amount may be said to be to a certain extent 'punitive' (i.e. in case of unlawful press publications the profits received may be taken into account).

4. Legislation on damages

[24] (a) The Civil Code contains general rules with respect to, *inter alia*: - patrimonial damage (articles 6: 95–96), including specific provisions for legal fees and judicial costs (article 6: 96), damages in case of personal injury/death (articles 6: 107–108), damages in

---

5 *See Schadevergoeding*, art. 95, aant. 14.
6 *See Schadevergoeding*, Inleiding, aant. 5; *MON. NBW B-34* (Bloembergen), nr. 4.

case of default of payments of sums of money (statutory interest, article 6: 119; damages as a result of changes in exchange-rates, article 6: 125) and damage to the environment (article 6: 184) (*infra*, questions 6, 7 and 12);
[25] – non-patrimonial damage (articles 6: 95, 6: 106, 7: 510) (*infra*, questions 6 and 7);
[26] – the assessment of damages (article 6: 97), including the assessment of future damages (article 105), the assessment by reference to profits made by the liable party (article 6: 104) and the assessment by reference to marketprices or coverpurchases (articles 7: 34–38) (*infra*, question 8);
[27] – advantages to be taken into account (article 6: 100) (*infra*, question 14);
[28] – the form of compensation (article 6: 103) (*supra*, question 2);
[29] – the power of the court to mitigate the amount of damages to be paid (article 6: 109) (*supra*, question 2);
[30] – the limitation of damages by statutory regulations (article 6: 110) (*supra*, question 2); limitations occur especially in the area of transport law.
[31] (b) Specific legislation with respect to damages is mentioned, *infra*, questions 7 and 13.

5. Definition of recoverable damage

[32] (a) The concept of damage is not defined in statute law. Patrimonial damage is generally understood to contain three elements: (i) a causal element, i.e. damage occurs as a result of a certain event; (ii) an element of comparison, i.e. comparison between the situations with and without the damage causing event; and (iii) a hypothetical element (see, *infra)*.
[33] (b) When comparing the present and hypothetical situations a distinction must be made between liability in case of breach of contract and other cases of liability.
[34] In the first case the present situation must be compared with the hypothetical situation in which the debtor executed faithfully all his contractual obligations. In this case the difference between the two situations refers to the so-called 'positive (contractual) interest' (*positief (contracts-) belang)*. This includes, *inter alia*, the loss of profit which would have arisen out of the contract.
[35] In the other cases (e.g. the case that a contract has been entered into by fraud and is avoided by the creditor) the present situation must be compared with the hypothetical situation in which the contract would not have been concluded. In this case the difference between the two situations refers to the so-called 'negative (contractual) interest' (*negatief (contracts)belang)*. This does not include the loss of profit which would have arisen out of the avoided contract, though may include the loss of profit which would have arisen out of another contract which the creditor would have entered into, had he not been induced by fraud to enter into the contract which he avoided later on.
[36] (c) The notion of damage is in legal doctrine somtimes understood as pertaining to the factual detriment arising from a certain occurrence (without prejudice, however, to its status as a legal concept which requires interpretation and clarification by law).[7] Other authors, however, maintain that the notion of damage is primarily a normative one.[8]

---

7 *See*, e.g., *Asser-Hartkamp III* (1998), nr. 409.
8 *See*, e.g., *MON. NIEUW BW B-34* Bloembergen, M. 24.

6. Different types of damages

[37] (a) Article 6: 95 distinguishes between patrimonial damage and non-patrimonial damage, the latter being recoverable only in the cases expressly mentioned in statutory law. Article 6: 95 describes non-patrimonial loss as 'other harm' (*ander nadeel*) than patrimonial loss. Therefore, the distinction between the two turns on the question whether or not the harm as such affects the present or future financial situation of the injured party. In certain cases the distinction between the two is not quite clear; generally, these cases will be treated as involving patrimonial damage rather than non-patrimonial damage (*infra*, question 9).
[38] (b) Patrimonial damage includes *damnum emergens* and loss of profit (article 6: 96).
[39] (c) Article 6: 96 expressly states that patrimonial damage also includes reasonable costs, incurred in order
[40] (a) to prevent or limit damage which may reasonably be expected to result from an occurrence for which another person is liable; article 6: 184 elaborates on this rule in cases of (a threat of) damage to the environment (*infra*, question 13);
[41] (b) to establish liability and the amount of damage;
[42] (c) to get voluntary payment by the liable party.
[43] It should be noted that both the incurring and the amounts of these costs must be reasonable. The costs mentioned under (b) and (c) may involve expenses for legal fees or expert opinions. In so far as these expenses are incurred in the course of legal proceedings, they may only be recovered if they are awarded as judicial costs (within the meaning of the Code of Civil Procedure) by the court. Judicial costs are generally awarded as fixed amounts on the basis of the nature and length of the proceedings (though costs for court appointed experts are fully recoverable). The costs are awarded to the prevailing party. The amounts involved do not cover the real expenses.
[44] d) Dutch law does not start out by making a distinction between damage to the person, damage to property and pure economic loss. They are treated as instances of patrimonial damage and as such fully recoverable. However, there are important exceptions to this principle.
[45] First: the distinction between these types of damages is relevant with respect to the application of certain general rules, such as those pertaining to causation and mitigation of damages – in both cases damage to the person is treated most favorable and pure economic loss the least favorable – and the calculation of damages (*infra*, question 8).
[46] Second: there are certain restrictions with respect to the recoverability of damage to the person. Damage to the person is fully recoverable by the victim (or his heirs), but only to a limited extent by third parties:
[47] – In case of personal injury article 6: 107 allows third parties to recover expenses incurred as a result of the injury (other than on the basis of an insurance-contract) and which would have been recoverable by the injured person himself if he would have made these expenses, e.g., the costs of visiting an injured husband at the hospital.
[48] – In case of personal injury article 6: 107a allows an employer, who is legally obliged to continue payment of wages to his injured employee (who is unable to work), to recover these payments as his own damage from the liable party.
[49] – In case of death article 6: 108 allows certain persons who were dependant on the deceased to claim the damage as a result of the loss of maintenance, viz. the (non-marital)

partner, the minor (illigimate) children, other members of the family of the deceased. This includes a claim for the compensation for loss of services by the deceased who maintained the common household.
[50] – In case of death article 6: 108 allows the recovery of burial-expenses by any person who incurred these expenses.
[51] Third: pure economic loss is not fully recoverable in certain cases of extra-contractual strict liability. The law limits the obligation to compensate this type of damage to losses suffered as a result of the damage to a person or to property. See articles 6: 173 (defective movable goods), 6: 174 (buildings and other structures) and 6: 175 (dangerous substances).
[52] (e) The distinction between direct and indirect loss has no fixed meaning in Dutch law. For instance, in contractual clauses limiting liability direct loss may cover damage to persons or property and indirect loss cover the economic loss resulting from direct loss. This distinction could also be understood as referring to the disctinction between damage in the first degree – i.e. damage suffered by the 'real' victim – and damage in the second (third, etc.) degree – i.e. damage suffered by others as a result of the damage suffered by the 'real' victim. This distinction is relevant in cases of personal injury: others than the injured party, can only claim their damage *'par ricochet'* within the limited scope set out by the articles 6: 107, 107a and 108. See *supra*, at d.
[53] The distinction may also come into consideration when the court must establish the causal chain and/or apply the *Schutznorm* principle (article 6: 163).
[54] (f) Both actual and future damage may be recovered. The distinction bears upon the assessement of the damages.
[55] (g) The same rules apply to contractual loss and tortious loss. However, the application of general rules with respect to damages may differ according to the basis of liability (*supra*, general remarks and question 5).

7. Monetary assessment of non-patrimonial damage

[56] (a) Non-pecuniary loss is assessed in accordance with the principles of equity (article 6: 106). See also, *supra*, question 3. Relevant factors include, *inter alia*: the nature, seriousness and permanency of the harm; the extent and duration of necessary medical treatment; the extent to which the claimant will be able to turn over a new leaf; and the ground for liability and the degree of fault on the part of the liable party. When determining the amount to be awarded the court will generally look at awards in similar cases by other Dutch courts and may take into account awards by foreign courts.[9] In practice a certain standardisation takes place, especially with respect to personal injury cases, on the basis of the systematic overview of case law published in the legal periodical *Verkeersrecht*.
[57] (b) Article 6: 106 – the core provision on non-patrimonial damages – allows awards of non-patrimonial damages:
[58] – if the liable party had the intention to inflict immaterial harm;
[59] – in case of physical personal injury (pain and suffering, loss of limbs, scars etc.);
[60] – in case of damage to the reputation of a person (*eer en goede naam*);
[61] – in case of harm to the person in any other way (*aantasting van de persoon op andere*

9 HR 8 July 1992, *NJ* 1992, 714.

wijze); the main categories deal with non-physical personal injury (psychiatric illness; excluding mere grief, distress or anxiety not resulting in non-physical personal injury) and rights of the person (such as invasion of privacy, freedom of movement, infringement of copyrights). The courts are quite restrictive in recognising harm to the person in any other way, though recent case law[10] may signal a somewhat more liberal approach. See also, *infra*, question 10.

[62] (c) Further legislation allows claims for non-patrimonial damage (restrictions apply):

[63] – in case of loss of enjoyment of a holiday (articles 7: 510 based on Directive 90/314/EEC);

[64] – in specific cases of unlawful detention (article 89 *et seq.* Code of Criminal Procedure, article 34j *Vreemdelingenwet*, article 59 *Uitleveringswet)*;

[65] – in case of unlawful seizure of a drivers licence by the police (article 164 *Wegenverkeerswet)*;

[66] – in case of invasion of privacy by unlawful registration of personal data (article 9 *Wet Persoonsregistraties)*;

[67] – in case of breach of a collective bargaining agreement (article 16 *Wet op de CAO*, article 3 *Wet op het algemeen verbindend en het onverbindend verklaren van bepalingen van CAO's*).

[68] (d) In case law a claim for non-patrimonial damages has been allowed on the basis of the European Convention on Human Rights.[11]

8. Calculation of patrimonial damage

[69] (a) As a general rule, article 6: 97 BW states that damages should be calculated in accordance with the nature of the damage. The courts therefore enjoy some freedom in choosing the method of assessing/calculating the damage which is the most appropriate in the case at hand. However, certain differences exist according to the type of damage. Generally, the calculation of damages takes place on the basis of objective factors. If an accurate calculation of the damage is not possible the court must estimate the damage.

[70] (b) Article 6: 97 gives the court the freedom to determine whether the damages must be calculated in a concrete or an abstract manner. In principle damages are calculated in a concrete way. Abstract calculation is the rule in case of breach of contract with respect to goods with a market value (articles 7: 36–38) and of damage to property, in which case the damage will be equal to loss of value of the property (which, in turn, will in principle equals to the normal costs of repair). See further on the subject, *inpa*, Part II, questions 13 *et seq.*

[71] Abstractly calculated damages are generally considered to be a minimum; the victim is entitled to a larger amount if it is shown that his damage (calculated in a concrete manner) exceeds the abstract damages.

[72] (c) Some special ways of calculating the damage include the following:

[73] – the damages to be paid in case of default in the payment of sums of money is fixed by law; the damages consist of the statutory interest (article 6: 119);

[74] – in case of contractual or tortious liability the court may assess the damage by

10 HR 2 May 1997, *NJ* 1997, 662.
11 HR 13 December 1996, *NJ* 1997, 682.

reference to the amount of profit the liable party gained by his behaviour (article 6: 104). According to HR 24 December 1993, NJ 1995, 421, this article must be understood as a case of abstract calculation of damages, it does not entitle the claimant to seize the profits of the defendant. By contrast, specific legislation in the area of intellectual property does entitle the claimant to claim the profits which the defendant derived from the infringement of the intellectual property right at hand, either in lieu of the damages or together with the damages.
[75] – in some cases of professional liability (lawyer, doctor) the courts have assessed the damage on the basis of the loss of a chance. Although these cases are as yet quite exceptional, in a recent landmark decision, the *Hoge Raad* has allowed for a calculation of the chance that a court verdict would have been overturned in appeal, had appeal been made.[12]
[76] – the court may either postpone the calculation of future damages or estimate them in advance (article 6: 105). See, *infra*, questions 15 and 16.
[77] (d) There is no formal standardisation of awards. However, in practice a certain measure of informal standardisation exists. In certain cases of termination of contracts of labour the county courts will generally calculate the amount of severance payment to be paid by the employer on the basis of a formula agreed upon by the county courts (*Kantongerechts-formule*). See with respect to awards for non-patrimonial damages, *supra*, question 7. Futhermore, organisations of insurance-companies may draft standards for the assessment of certain types of damage and promote the use thereof by insurance-companies.
[78] (e) Generally, factors of the type mentioned in the questionnaire are not involved in the calculation of damages as such.
[79] However, fault and social situation may be taken into account when determining the amount of non-patrimonial damages. The social situation of the victim (or his dependants) must also be taken into account when determining the amount of damages due in case of loss of income as a result of personal injury (or death) and when determining a reasonable amount for burial-expenses. In isolated cases, lower courts have taken the disposition of the award into account.[13]
[80] Generally, the claimaint is free to dispose of the damages in the way he chooses. This applies in particular to abstractly calculated damages and to non-patrimonial damages.

9. Compensation for particular kinds of losses

[81] (a) *Pure loss of use* will amount to patrimonial damage in case the object which cannot be used is temporarily replaced by a similar object (either rented from a third party or one held as reserve). Generally, it is held that the damage should be calculated in a concrete manner, taking into account the reasonableness of the (costs of) replacement and whether the claimant would have been using the replaced object during the relevant period. In case no replacement takes place, the courts have sometimes allowed a more abstract calculation of the damage, e.g. by referring to lost profits (ships) or a reasonable payment for the use (real property).[14]
[82] (b) *Pure loss of earning capacity* is recognised as patrimonial damage. However, as this

12 *See* HR 24 October 1997, *NJ* 1998, 257.
13 *See Schadevergoeding*, art. 106, aant. 60.21.
14 *See Schadevergoeding*, art. 96, aant. 41 et seq.

type of damage is in principle calculated in a concrete manner (though always involving estimates of future developments), loss of earning capacity will (generally) only result in a claim for damages if the injured persons has an income or is expected to have an income in the future. Nevertheless, a somewhat different approach prevails in practice in case of personal injury to a person who maintains a common houshold; often the damage is said to amount to the cost of hiring a help. In case of death article 6: 108 expressly allows compensation of these costs.[15]

[83] (c) *Pure loss of holiday* may amount (i) to patrimonial damage in so far as holiday-expenses appear to have been made (in part) in vain and (ii) to non-patrimonial damages (see, *supra*, question 7). *Pure loss of free time* does not constitute damage.

[84] (d) *Damage to things which remain unrepaired* consititutes patrimonial damage, because the damage is calculated in an abstract manner (*supra*, question 8).

[85] (e) *Expenses which become frustrated by the tortious act* are in principle recognised as patrimonial damage.

10. Compensation for emotional shock and loss of consortium

[86] As a rule compensation for emotional shock and loss of consortium is not awarded because (i) articles 6: 107–108 limit the possibility to claim damages as a result of the injury or death of another person and (ii) the courts interprete article 6: 106 restrictively as regards the possibilty to obtain damages for non-patrimonial damage in case of harm to the person in any other way.

[87] Therefore the claimant can only claim damages for, e.g., emotional shock if he can establish (i) that the defendant also committed an unlawful act vis-a-vis the claimant himself which resulted in the emotional shock (this is basically a problem of the *Schutznorm* principle contained in article 6: 163 and of causation) and (ii) that the emotional shock amounts to (non-) physical personal injury. If this is the case, in principle, the claimant should be able to recover patrimonial damages (such as costs for psychiatric treatment) and non-patrimonial damage on the basis of his personal injury.

[88] The law in this area is as yet unsettled. HR 8 April 1983, NJ 1984, 717, denied a claim of a mother whose child died in a car accident. However, in this case the cause of the damage was said to have been the death of the child and therefore the claim was excluded by (the predecessor of) article 6: 108. Although the parliamentary proceedings with regard to this subject are quite vague on the subject, they seem to allow (i.e., they seem not to bar) claims for non-patrimonial damage in case of severe shock resulting from witnessing or being confronted with a casualty.[16]

11. Compensation of illegitimate losses

[89] Illegal losses will generally not be compensated. Income from illegal activities will not be taken into account (e.g. those of a drugdealer; Dutch law will probably recognise the claim of the prostitute). The loss of income from legal activities which were not reported to

---

15 *See Schadevergoeding*, art. 95, aant. 20, art. 107, aant. 12 et seq. and art. 108, aant. 19.4.

16 *See Parlementaire Geschiedenis Nieuw BW* (Invoering Boeken 3,5 en 6), p. 1274,

the tax-authorities, is probably recoverable taking into account the taxes which should have been paid.[17]

12. Compensation of collective damage

[90] The statutory rules pertaining to collective action (articles 3: 305a-b, 6: 240–243) do not cover claims for damages. Similar actions have however been recognised in case law, prior to the enactment of the articles 3: 305a-b. The general rules regarding damages apply.

13. Special rules on compensation of ecological damage

[91] (a) In addition to the general rules on damages, certain specific rules exist with respect to ecological damage. The general rules provide for the compensation of personal injury, damage to property and pure economic loss as a result of pollution of the environment. Their application may pose specific problems as the damage will often accumulate slowly (*sluipende schade).*

[92] Damage to the environment involves specific expenses, such as costs of clean up, costs of prevention of (further) damage to the enivronment, costs of (maintenance of) installations isolating a source of pollution and costs of monitoring a source of pollution. Article 6: 184 expressly states that these costs are to be considered as patrimonial damages in case of, *inter alia*, liability to the environment by dangerous substances, land fills or oil and gas wells. Similar provisions apply to transportation of dangerous substances (articles 8: 620, 8: 1030 and 8: 1210). However, it should be noted that in the absence of these specific provisions the costs mentioned would in principle have been recoverable as patrimoninal damage on the basis of article 6: 96 (*supra*, question 6).

[93] (b) The Netherlands are party to several international treaties concerning liability to the enivironment, *inter alia*, the Council of Europe's Convention on civil liability for damage resulting from activities dangerous to the environment (this treaty has however not yet entered into force). Specific statutes deal with certain types of liability and damage with respect to the environment, such as nuclear accidents (*Wet aansprakelijkheid kern-ongevallen*, with a liability cap of NLG 625 million) and oil pollution caused by oil tankers (*Wet aansprakelijkheid olietankschepen*, allowing the liable party to limit his liability by creating a fund).

14. Harm causing also advantages

[94] (a)Article 6: 100 states that any advantage for the victim as a result of the event which caused the damage must be taken into account, if it is reasonable to do so. As far as the application of the reasonableness-test is concerned, much remains as yet unclear.

[95] (b) Generally, advantages will be of a financial nature and be set off against the amount of damages due. However, other solutions are possible as well, such as payment of the full value of damaged property by the defendant with the obligation of the claimaint to transfer the damaged property to the defendant.

17 *See Schadevergoeding*, art. 95, aant. 50; art. 107, aant. 16.

[96] (c) Generally, the setting off will concern similar types of damage and advantage, e.g. patrimonial damage and patrimonial advantage, non-patrimonial damage and non-patrimonial advantage,[18] damage and advantage in the tax area etc.
[97] (d) Sums paid by insurance companies will generally be taken into account if the payment is intended take away the damage suffered. Fixed sums payable under a contract of insurance in case of a harmful event will not always be taken into account. Payments by third parties to which the injured party is entitled by contract or law (e.g. continued payment of wages by his employer, social security payments) will be set off. Voluntary payments by third parties will generally not be taken into account. See also, *infra*, question 16.b (new for old).
[98] (e) In case of damage as a result of the death of a person, article 6: 108 precludes the normal operation of article 6: 100. The extent to which dependants of the deceased may claim damages for loss of maintenance depends, *inter alia*, on their need for further maintenance (*behoef- tigheid)*. In this respect the full financial position of the surviving dependants must be taken into account.

15. Certainty of damage

[99] Damage must be plausible (*aannemelijk*); see, *supra*, general remarks. Generally, courts will require some proof of data concerning the occurrence or extent of damage in order to be able to calculate the amount of damages. However, the court is free to estimate the damage if calculation is not feasible. The same applies to future damages (article 6: 105).

16. Lump sum or rent

[100] (a) Article 6: 105 allows the court to award damages either as a lump sum or as a periodic allowance; awards may be conditional and awards for rent may provide for a new award in case of material change of circumstances. The courts will generally choose the method proposed by the parties, though are not bound to do so. In practice in most cases (of damage to the person) a lump sum is claimed and awarded, though it is recognised that periodical payments would more accurately reflect the real damage. In part there are fiscal reasons to do so.
[101] (b) But also the parties often prefer settlement of the dispute by payment of a lump sum. The claimant will be able to invest the sum in a way which best suits him, has no need for further dealings with the (insurance company of the) defendant and can get on with his life without being reminded by periodical payments of the injuries he suffered. The (insurance company of the) defendant knows the exact amount of damages to be paid and has no further need of keeping an administration as in the case of periodical payments. Lump sums may be paid in different ways, e.g., in cash or be used to settle an interest bearing sum on behalf of the claimant.[19]

---

18 HR 21 February 1997, *NJ* 1999, 145.
19 *Schadevergoeding*, art. 105, aant. 3 et seq.

Part II – Cases

1. Wrongful birth case

[102] According to a recent and somewhat controversial decision of the *Hoge Raad*, claims for the cost of maintenance of a 'wrongfully' born child are permissible.[20]
[103] – Therefore, the woman can claim the average cost of maintenance; the court will apply the standards for child maintenance in family law. Any supplemental costs are most likely to be borne by the parents themselves.[21] The period of maintenance is probably limited to eighteen years (when the child comes of age).
[104] – The woman can indeed claim for lost earnings, if and insofar as her decision to abort her professional carreer is reasonable, all circumstances taken into consideration. The court will have to weigh the mother's freedom to make the choices she deems most compatible with her child's interests on the one hand, and her duty to avoid unnecessary accrual of damages on the other.
[105] – Although Dutch law is not quite clear on the subject, mere pregnancy does probably not suffice for a claim for pain and suffering, unless non-physical personal injury results from the pregnancy.[22] Actual pain and suffering as a consequence of the second operation will probably constitute a claim for non-patrimonial damages.

2. Wrongful life case

[106] Although it is not clear whether the child itself can claim, the mother certainly can.[23]

3. Eye injury

[107] Medical costs constitute patrimonial loss (art. 6: 95) and can be claimed in full. The partial loss of eyesight amounts to personal injury; this will support a claim for non-patrimonial loss (art. 6: 106). In similar cases, amounts for non-patrimonial loss in case of severe injuries to the human eye have been awarded ranging from NLG 20,000 to NLG 50,000.[24]

4. Costs for hospital visits and of adaptation of house

[108] All claims mentioned are in principle valid. They constitute patrimonial loss of the injured party, suffered as a result of the negligent act. See art. 6: 95.

5. Scar case

[109] In principle damages are calculated in a concrete manner. See supra, part I, question 8. The claim for the cost of cosmetic surgery will be denied unless they actually have been made or will be made.

---

20 *See* HR 21 February 1997, *NJ* 1999, 145.
21 HR 21 February 1997, *NJ* 1999, 145.
22 *See Schadevergoeding*, art. 106, aant. 23.
23 *See* supra, Question 1 (cf. HR 21 February 1997, *NJ* 1999, 145.
24 *See* Smartengeld-Gids, *Verkeersrecht* (1997).

6. Continued payment of wages

[110] P. is denied a claim for loss of wages. His employer is legally obliged to continue payment of wages. The employer is (more or less) subrogated in the rights of the employee *vis-a-vis* D, and as a result, employee P cannot claim damages (art. 6: 107a).

7. Monk case

[111] A cannot claim for loss of earning capacity; this loss is calculated in a concrete manner.[25] Although the law is not quite clear, it is most likely that the monastery cannot claim either, unless perhaps costs are made to replace the injured monk.

8. Lost earning capacity

[112] Art. 6: 105 provides that the court can either suspend calculation of future damages until more certainty exists on the amount of the damage (in this case, this method is not conclusive), or make an estimation of these damages on the basis of hypotheticals and plausibilities. In principle, the court will estimate future loss by deducting the actual future earnings from the amount of professional earnings of the average physicist. See generally: Part I, questions 15 and 16.
[113] – The *basis* of calculation would not be different, the outcome would however. The court will estimate future loss by estimating the amount of professional earnings of the average child of an average small income family. It must be said however, that no clear rules or indications exist on the question *how* a court can estimate these earnings. In practice, lower courts sometimes tend to wait for the uncertain future to unfold or to grant a sum in damages for the certain loss of opportunities (or: chances).[26]
[114] – No particular rules exist other than those mentioned *supra*. Therefore, A could indeed get compensation of patrimonial damage on the same basis as mentioned before. As far as non-patrimonial loss is concerned, Dutch law is unsettled on the issue whether a comatose patient as such can suffer non-patrimonial loss.

9. Lost spouse/partner

[115] (a) No claim is allowed for loss of consortium. Both spouses and non-marital partners can claim for loss of maintenance (art. 6: 108). Therefore, A can only claim for loss of maintenance.
[116] (b) Loss of services can support a claim, but, probably, only insofar as expenses have actually been made (art. 6: 108).

10. Offending publication

[117] B can claim for loss of income/earning capacity (art. 6: 95) and non-patrimonial loss (art. 6: 106).

---

25 HR 19 December 1975, *NJ* 1976, 305.
26 *See Schadevergoeding*, art. 107, aant. 23.

11. Rosenkavalier case

[118] Compensation for fees paid in vain is not barred (art. 6: 95 *et seq.)*, but it is open to debate whether this particular damage can reasonably be imputed to the owner as a foreseeable result of the tortious act (art. 6: 98). Compensation of the alleged non-patrimonial loss for having missed an opera performance is barred by the Civil Code: none of the categories mentioned in art. 6: 106 are at hand. See *supra*, Part I, question 7 b.

12. Prostitute case

[119] A is probably entitled to full compensation. See *supra*, Part I, Question 12.

13. Mercedes case

[120] Whenever repair is possible and reasonable, a claim for the cost of repair is permissible. In this case, repair is possible and reasonable. D has to compensate 4,000 Euro.[27] No special rules apply to the loss of profit that resulted from the accident. If the market value of the car, prior to the accident, was approximately 20,000 Euro, although X offered to buy it for 23,000 Euro, a claim for this loss of profit (3,000 Euro) will probably not hold up in court. According to the Dutch concept of causation, damage should only be repaired insofar it is reasonable, all circumstances taken into consideration, to consider the damage as caused by the accident (art. 6: 98). A central, although not decisive element in this so-called 'imputation test' is foreseeability. Especially when damage does not result from personal injury, a strict causal chain is used. The specific 'extra' loss of profit is not *a priori* foreseeable; as a result it can probably not be imputed to the liable person.

14. Loss of use

[121] (a) – the cost of a substitute vehicle can be filed under the cost concerned with mitigating a further increase of the damage. All *reasonable* expenses can be claimed (art. 6: 96), e.g., the rent of a similar vehicle.
[122] – a claim for loss of use *as such* is not permitted.[28] This does however not bar a claim for consequential damages, e.g., loss of income as a result of loss of use of a company vehicle. It must however be added that B has the duty to mitigate consequential damages by replacing the damaged vehicle.
[123] (b) The expenses paid for use of the caravan can be recovered; a claim for *temporary* loss of use of the house *as such* does not constitute a patrimonial loss and therefore cannot be awarded. However, lower courts have been known to grant damages for loss of use *per se*. See Part I, question 9a. It seems nevertheless to be most preferable to calculate such types of damages in a concrete manner rather than to grant fictituous amounts, especially when concrete expenses have been made.

---

27 *See* Barendrecht/Storm, *Berekening van Schadevergoeding* (1995), p. 91.
28 *See* Barendrecht/Storm (supra note 27) p. 112.

15. Damaged, but unrepaired car

[124] (a) The cost of repair is calculated in an 'abstract manner', so there is no need for actual repair. A can claim the fictituous costs.
[125] (b) According to Dutch law of damages, the repair of a motor vehicle is deemed inappropriate whenever the value of the damaged car *plus* the cost of repair exceed the market value of the repaired car.[29]
[126] Therefore, neither of the alternatives presented in this case bar a claim for damages.
[127] (c) In principle, A cannot claim the excess of costs of repair whenever these exceed the fall in market value. An exception to this rule has however been made in a disputed county court decision, allowing a senior citizen the excess costs of repair on the grounds that he could not be expected to accustom himself to another vehicle.[30]
[128] It must be noted that according to HR 1 July 1993, NJ 1995, 43, the aforementioned principle (*sc.* that the excess costs of repair cannot be claimed whenever these exceed the fall in market value) does not necessarily apply to real estate. This highly depends on the actual *use* of the premises.

16. Additional car damage

[129] (a)P can claim compensation for the fact that his car has decreased in value as a result of the accident, even though the damage itself was repaired.[31]
[130] (b) The patrimonial benefits from repair can indeed be set off against the loss (art. 6: 100). However, legal doctrine show much restraint (they rightly argue that the damaged party had no wish for new parts) and case law is not available.[32] Insurance practice is said to apply the 'new for old' dogma only to exhausts, batteries, tires and spare parts for 'ancient' vehicles.
[131] (c) P has paid rent in vain as a (remote) result of D's negligence. This constitutes a patrimonial damage and as such, it can be claimed. There is however the obstacle of causation. Although the 'but for' (*conditio sine qua non*) test is met, it is highly questionable whether this damage can be imputed to the negligence of D. Given the nature (pure economic loss) and remoteness of the damage, it is unlikely that P can claim from D.

17. Damaged railway wagon

[132] This type of damage is filed under costs concerned with mitigating further damage. All *reasonable* expenses can be claimed (art. 6: 96). According to HR 4 October 1957, *NJ* 1958, 12 and HR 31 October 1959, *NJ* 1959, 29, a proportionate share in the costs of maintaining reserve material can be claimed, if these costs were made wholly or partially in consideration of the possibility of damage caused by third parties.

---

29 *See Schadevergoeding*, art. 96, aant. 18 and Barendrecht/Storm (supra note 27) p. 94.
30 *See* Kantongerecht Heerlen 28 September 1973, *VR* 1975, 63; Barendrecht/Storm (supra note, 27) pp. 92–93.
31 *See* HR 3 December 1963, *NJ* 1964, 449; Barendrecht/Storm (supra note 27) p. 97.
32 *See* Barendrecht/Storm (supra note 27) pp. 55 et seq.

18. Detective case

[133] One could argue that the salary of a detective constitutes 'internal costs'. According to HR 16 June 1961, *NJ* 1961, 444,[33] the normal amount of salary that can be imputed to workmen repairing a damaged object, can be claimed instead of external cost of repair. It is unclear whether this principle can be applied in this particular case. Evidently, a major obstacle would be the assessment of the proportionate part of the salary to be imputed to the thief. **[134]** Apart from that, it remains to be seen to what extent the duty not to steal purports to protect against this type of damage (*Schutznorm*, art. 6: 163).

19. Death of parents

[135] Inheritance as such does not constitute grounds for set off; this would clearly be *unreasonable (cf.* art. 6: 100). A claim for loss of maintenance however, is limited by the scale of the financial *need* of the surviving relative (art. 6: 108). Therefore, the inheritance might indeed alleviate the needs of A and thus reduce his right to damages.

33 *Cf.* HR 1 July 1993, *NJ* 1995, 150.

South Africa

Damages under South African Law

Johann Neethling

Part I General questions on law of damages[1]

1. Aims of the law of damages

[1] The law of damages is that part of the law which indicates how the existence and extent of damage as well as the proper amount of damages or satisfaction (*solatium*) are to be determined in the case of *inter alia* delict and breach of contract.[2] Although the view is sometimes advanced that the object of the law of damages is the provision of the *fullest possible compensation of damage*, it would appear to be more accurate to see this as the object of a particular award of damages or satisfaction.[3] According to Visser and Potgieter[4] the object of the law of damages should rather be seen as the provision of just, logical and practical principles in solving problems regarding the determination of damage, damages and satisfaction.
[2] The primary aim of the law of delict (or delictual remedies) is to compensate the victim of delictual conduct by awarding damages for the damage he has suffered. Damages are the monetary equivalent of damage with the object of eliminating as fully as possible the victim's past as well as future damage.[5] However, if damage is incapable of being compensated because money cannot be a true equivalent of the impaired (personality) interest, satisfaction becomes relevant as an aim of the law of delict, that is, awarding an amount of money with the object of satisfying the victim's injured feelings (feelings of injustice and mental suffering sustained as a result of the perpetrator's conduct).[6]

---

1 *See* in general Visser/Potgieter, *Law of Damages* (*Damages*) (1993) *passim*; Visser/Potgieter, *Law of Damages Through the Cases* (1998) *passim*; Neethling/Potgieter/Visser, *Law of Delict* (1999), pp. 209–257; Van der Walt/Midgley, *Delict: Principles and Cases* (1997), pp. 183–205; Boberg, *The Law of Delict* (1984), pp. 475 et seq.; Erasmus/Gauntlett, 'Damages' 7 *LAWSA* 1 et seq.; Burchell, *Principles of Delict* (1993), pp. 123–145.
2 *See* Visser/Potgieter, *Damages*, p. 1.
3 *Idem* p. 4.
4 *Damages* p. 5.
5 *See* Neethling/Potgieter/Visser (supra note 1) p. 209; Visser/Potgieter, *Damages*, p. 147; *cf.* Van der Walt/Midgley, p. 183.
6 Neethling/Potgieter/Visser (supra note 1) pp. 209, 256.

U. Magnus (ed.), Unification of Tort Law: Damages, 159–173.

[3] In the law of contract, breach of contract is constituted by the non-fulfilment by a contractual party of a contractual personal right (claim) or an obligation to perform. Accordingly, the primary remedy for breach of contract is directed at enforcement, fulfilment or execution of the contract; a claim for damages as compensation for damage as a result of the breach only plays a secondary role.[7] Here the object of damages is, as far as possible, to play the role in the creditor's patrimony which performance by the debtor was supposed to do.[8]
[4] In conclusion, the aims of the law of damages may therefore coincide with those of the law of delict but are definitely wider than the latter.

2. General principles of the law of damages

[5] The general principles of the law of damages are the (i) awarding of damages or satisfaction (ii) which compensates or satisfies as fully as possible (iii) past as well as future damage (iv) in money.[9]

3. Different forms of damages

[6] In conformity with the aim of delictual remedies,[10] South African law accepts *compensation* as the main object and therefore main form of damages.[11] However, English principles of *aggravated*, *punitive*, *vindictive* or *exemplary* damages had a considerable influence on our law. Especially in older cases such damages were awarded to punish the defendant whenever his conduct was sufficiently outrageous.[12] Nowadays it is accepted that there is no room in the *actio legis Aquiliae* (action for patrimonial damages) and the action for pain and suffering (action for non-patrimonial damages for personal injuries) for punitive damages.[13]
[7] However, the *actio iniuriarum* (action for satisfaction for infringement of personality interests *animo iniuriandi*) is still to a certain extent considered to be an *actio vindictam spirans*, which obliges the wrongdoer to pay money as a private *penalty* in favour of the plaintiff to solace his injured feelings.[14] This viewpoint has, however, been subject to criticism.[15]

---

7 *See* Van Aswegen, *Die Sameloop van Eise om Skadevergoeding uit Kontrakbreuk en Delik* (*Sameloop van Eise*) (LLD-thesis University of South Africa 1991), pp. 300 et seq.
8 *See* Visser/Potgieter, *Damages*, p. 274.
9 *Cf* Neethling/Potgieter/Visser (supra note 1) pp. 235–236. Also compare the answer to question 1.
10 Supra question 1.
11 Visser/Potgieter, *Damages*, p. 156.
12 *Idem* p. 156 n 89.
13 *Idem* pp. 156–157, 174 et seq.; see also McKerron, *The Law of Delict* (1971), p. 7.
14 In *Masawi v Chabata* 1991 4 SA 764 (ZH) 772 the court stated: 'The primary object of an *actio iniuriarum* is to punish the defendant by the infliction of a pecuniary penalty, payable to the plaintiff as a *solatium*.' See also Visser/Potgieter, *Damages*, p. 171 n. 31; Neethling, *Persoonlikheidsreg* (1998), p. 72 n. 206.
15 *See* e.g. Van der Walt/Midgley (supra note 1) p. 5 who are of the opinion that this position is not justifiable in a modern legal system, where the basic function of a delictual action is to compensate the victim for actual harm done; it is for criminal law to punish and thereby discourage such conduct. This view was confirmed by the Constitutional Court in *Fose v Minister of Safety and Security* 1997 3 SA 786 (CC) 822–824, 826–828.

[8] *Nominal* damages were also awarded in many older decisions under the influence of English law[16] for the vindication or infringement of a right without proof of actual loss.[17] As with punitive damages, there is in the light of the compensatory function of delictual remedies, probably also no room for this type of damages in South African law.
[9] As a general rule a successful litigant in a delictual claim for damages is entitled to his *legal costs*,[18] but these costs, in so far as they were necessary to enforce the plaintiff's claim, do not qualify as damage.[19] However, under certain circumstances legal costs may constitute damage.[20]

4. Legislation on damages

[10] The following provisions are relevant: Assessment of Damages Act 9 of 1969 section 1 (when assessing damages for loss of support as a result of a person's death, no insurance money, pension or benefit from a friendly society or trade union, may be taken into account); Apportionment of Damages Act 34 of 1956 section 1(1)(a) (reduction of damages on account of the plaintiff's contributory fault); Apportionment of Damages Amendment Act 58 of 1971 section 1(a)(1B) and (b) (where a plaintiff suffers damage (loss of support) as a result of the death of the breadwinner caused by the deceased and a third party as joint wrongdoers, the court may, in assessing the amount of loss of support, deduct any benefit derived from the deceased estate (by succession) from the estimated value of the loss of support); Road Accident Fund Act 56 of 1996 section 18 (limitation of the maximum amount of damages that may be awarded to certain passengers injured in a motor-vehicle accident); Compensation for Occupational Injuries and Diseases Act 130 of 1993 section 47–53 (limitation on the maximum amount of damages that may be awarded for certain injuries or loss of earning capacity); Legal Succession to the South African Transport Services Act 9 of 1989 clause 2(2) schedule 1 (liability of the transport services is limited to a maximum amount of damages).[21]

5. Definition of recoverable damage

[11] The following definition is acceptable for South African law:[22] Damage is the diminution, as a result of a damage-causing event, in the utility or quality of a patrimonial or personality interest in satisfying the legally recognised needs of the person involved. In terms of this definition, damage is a broad or comprehensive concept which consists of patrimonial as well as non-patrimonial loss (injury to personality) as its two mutually exclusive

---

16 Visser/Potgieter, *Damages*, pp. 157–159.
17 *See* e.g. *Jansen v Pienaar* 1880 SC 276, 277; *Edwards v Hyde* 1903 TS 381.
18 *See* Visser/Potgieter, *Damages*, pp. 442–444.
19 *See* e.g. *Mediterranean Shipping Co Ltd v Speedwell Shipping Co Ltd* 1989 1 SA 164 (D) 170.
20 E.g., legal cocts wasted because of an attorney's negligence or an order as to costs in previous litigation (see Visser/Potgieter, *Damages*, pp. 324, 442 n. 114).
21 *See* in general Neethling/Potgieter/Visser (supra note 1) pp. 230, 155 et seq., 274.
22 *See idem* 210–213; Visser/Potgieter, *Damages*, pp. 22, 27 et seq. For other definitions see *idem* p. 22 n. 2.

components. There is no statutory or other generally accepted definition of recoverable damage.

6. Different types of damage

[12] The following types of damage are recognised in our law: *patrimonial loss* and *non-patrimonial loss* (the reasons for the distinction are that the nature of the damage is completely different – pecuniary versus non-pecuniary or injury to personality – and that different actions with different requirements are applicable to them: the Aquilian action for patrimonial loss and the action for pain and suffering and the *actio iniuriarum* for non-patrimonial loss);[23] *damnum emergens* (*actual* damage suffered up to the date of trial) and *lucrum cessans* (loss of profit and prospective or *future* loss) – the distinction is of analytical and practical importance, because of the speculative processes which are necessary to quantify prospective loss;[24] *damage to property* (physical thing) and *pure economic loss* (mere financial loss)[25] – this distinction is of importance since the requirements for liability differ: while damage to property is *prima facie* wrongful, this is not the case with pure economic loss;[26] *direct* (immediate or direct result of a damage-causing event) and *indirect* (consequential) loss (damage which flows from direct loss) – this distinction is made for the purposes of limitation of liability (remoteness of damage or legal causation).[27] [28]

[13] The following differences exist between the calculation and compensation of *contractual and delictual* loss: (i) Contractual damage (and damages) is calculated by comparing the plaintiff's present patrimonial position (after breach of contract) with the position he would have occupied if proper performance in terms of the contract had taken place (positive interesse); delictual damage is calculated by comparing the plaintiff's present position (after the delict)

---

23 *See* Neethling/Potgieter/Visser (supra note 1) pp. 5, 8 et seq., 210, 213; *Administrator, Natal v Edouard* 1990 3 SA 581 (A) 595; *Guardian National Insurance Co Ltd v Van Gool* 1992 4 SA 61 (A) 65; *Hoffa v SA Mutual Fire and General Insurance Co Ltd* 1965 2 SA 944 (C) 950–952; cf also supra question 3.

24 *See* Visser/Potgieter, *Damages*, pp. 54, 63; Neethling/Potgieter/Visser (supra note 1) pp. 220, 223.

25 Financial or economic loss refers to damage which does not result from damage to property or injury to personality (e.g. *Arthur E Abrahams and Cross v Cohen* 1991 2 SA 301 (C)), or where it does, it is either not the plaintiff's property or personality which has been harmed (e.g. *Coronation Brick (Pty) Ltd v Strachan Construction Co (Pty) Ltd* 1982 4 SA 371 (D)), or it is not the defendant who caused such damage or injury (e.g. *Joubert v Impala Platinum Ltd* 1998 1 SA 463 (BHC)). See also Neethling/Potgieter/Visser (supra note 1) pp. 293–294.

26 *See Knop v Johannesburg City Council* 1995 1 SA 1 (A) 26.

27 Neethling/Potgieter/Visser (supra note 1) p. 220; Visser/Potgieter, *Damages*, p. 55; see also as regards legal causation Neethling/Potgieter/Visser (supra note 1) pp. 181 et seq.

28 A distinction is also made between general and special damage. These terms are derived from English law and have various meanings. General damage often refers to damage which is presumed to flow from an unlawful act and which need only be pleaded generally, while special damage means loss in respect of which such a presumption does not apply and which has to be specially pleaded and proved. The term general damage is also used to describe non-patrimonial loss (see Neethling/Potgieter/Visser – supra note 1 – p. 221; Van der Walt/Midgley – supra note 1 – p. 185).

with the position he would have enjoyed had the delict not been committed (negative interesse);[29] (ii) the extent of damage recoverable can differ because different measures limiting liability apply;[30] (iii) the time for the computation of damage in the two instances differs.[31]

7. Monetary assessment of non-patrimonial damage

[14] Although both types of loss constitute damage, in essence patrimonial damage is pecuniary or financial loss while non-patrimonial damage concerns injury to personality which is non-pecuniary loss. The most important differences are the following:[32] (i) Patrimonial loss implies that the utility of a patrimonial interest is reduced while an interest of personality is the subject of reduction in non-pecuniary damage; (ii) patrimonial loss can be directly or naturally expressed in money while non-pecuniary loss is at most only indirectly measurable in this way; (iii) the extent of patrimonial loss can be ascertained with greater precision than the extent of non-patrimonial loss; (iv) unlike with damages for patrimonial loss, monetary compensation for non-patrimonial loss is not of the same nature as the impaired (personality) interest and can thus not be a genuine equivalent for such damage.[33]

[15] Theoretically non-patrimonial loss is determined by means of the comparative method. The utility or quality of the personality interest(s) involved before and after the delict are compared in order to establish the existence and extent of the loss. In this way information is obtained on the nature, seriousness, extent, intensity and duration of the *objective* part of the loss (that is, the generally recognisable manifestation of the impairment of personality) as well as the impairment of the victim's *subjective* feelings.[34]

[16] The different heads of non-pecuniary loss with regard to the physical-mental integrity (action for pain and suffering) are: pain and suffering,[35] emotional shock,[36] disfigurement,[37]

---

29 *See* Visser/Potgieter, *Damages*, pp. 60–61, 71–72, 275.

30 The extent of liability in the law of delict is not determined by a single yardstick (such as reasonable foreseeability), but a flexible approach is adopted (Neethling/Potgieter/Visser – supra note 1 – pp. 185–187). On the other hand, reasonable foreseeability is generally accepted as the only criterion for the limitation of contractual liability. The extent of the damage may thus differ if the law of delict should employ a different yardstick than the law of contract (see Van Aswegen – supra note 7 – pp. 328–330).

31 In the law of delict the extent of the damage is usually measured with reference to the date of the commission of the delict (Neethling/Potgieter/Visser – supra note 1 – p. 222). In the law of contract, on the other hand, the extent of the damage is usually measured with reference to the time of the conclusion of the contract (and not the breach thereof) (see Joubert, *General Principles of the Law of Contract* (1987), p. 253). Obviously these two calculations may differ (Van Aswegen – supra note 7 – pp. 330–332).

32 *See* Neethling/Potgieter/Visser (supra note 1) p. 214; Visser/Potgieter, *Damages*, pp. 30–31.

33 *See* however Neethling/Potgieter/Visser (supra note 1), p. 214 for criticism of these differences.

34 *Idem* p. 242.

35 E.g. *Blyth v Van den Heever* 1980 1 SA 191 (A) 227; Neethling/Potgieter/Visser (supra note 1), p. 245 n. 309.

36 *Bester v Commercial Union Versekeringsmaatskappy van SA Bpk* 1973 1 SA 769 (A); Neethling/Potgieter/Visser (supra note 1), pp. 245, 289 et seq.

37 E.g. *Eggeling v Law and Rock Insurance Co Ltd* 1958 3 SA 592 (D); *Solomon v De Waal* 1972 1 SA 575 (A); Neethling/Potgieter/Visser (supra note 1), p. 245.

loss of amenities of life[38] and shortened life expectancy.[39] As far as the *actio iniuriarum* is concerned, the infringement of the following personality interests constitutes non-patrimonial loss: body, physical freedom, good name, dignity, privacy, identity and feelings.[40]
[17] The relevant factors in assessing damages for non-pecuniary loss differ with reference to the interest of personality involved. The amount is estimated *ex aequo et bono* (what is just and good) and is completely *in arbitrio iudicis.*

8. Calculation of patrimonial damage

[18] There are different viewpoints as to how the existence and extent of damage may be determined in a given situation. It is, however, clear that a comparative method is necessary to determine damage, and here South African law applies the *sum-formula approach.* According to this approach delictual damage is calculated by comparing the plaintiff's present position (after the delict) with the position he would have enjoyed had the delict not been committed (hypothetical (potential) position).[41]
[19] The main principles for calculation are: (i) the date of commission of the delict is the proper time for the assessment of damage;[42] (ii) the plaintiff must claim damages for all damage already sustained or expected in future arising from a single cause of action ('once and for all' rule);[43] (iii) damages for prospective loss are discounted or capitalised[44] and provision is made for contingencies;[45] (iv) certain benefits that the plaintiff received as a

---

38 *Administrator-General v Kriel* 1988 3 SA 275 (A); Neethling/Potgieter/Visser (supra note 1) p. 246 n. 315.

39 *Goldie v City Council of Johannesburg* 1948 2 SA 913 (W); Neethling/Potgieter/Visser (supra note 1) p. 246 n. 316.

40 *See* Neethling (supra note 14) ch. 3–9.

41 *See* Visser/Potgieter, *Damages*, p. 59 et seq.; supra question 7 as to the application of this formula to non-patrimonial loss and the distinction between objective and subjective loss in this regard. As far as patrimonial loss is concerned, South African law favours an objective rather than a subjective approach (ie, having regard to the position of the particular plaintiff) to damage (see Van der Walt/Midgley – supra note 1 – p. 203; Visser/Potgieter, *Damages*, pp. 57–58). For criticism of the sum-formula approach, see *idem* pp. 64–65. It has been suggested that the sum-formula approach (an abstract theory of damage) should be replaced by a concrete concept of damage. Where the sum-formula compares someone's actual and hypothetical patrimonial positions, a concrete approach focusses on the withdrawal or deterioration of a particular part of a plaintiff's patrimony (see Neethling/Potgieter/Visser – supra note 1 – p. 222).

42 *Cf General Accident Insurance Co SA Ltd v Summers et al* 1987 3 SA 577 (A); Visser/Potgieter, *Damages*, pp. 75–76; Neethling/Potgieter/Visser (supra note 1) pp. 222–223.

43 E.g. *Evins v Shield Insurance Co Ltd* 1980 2 SA 814 (A); Visser/Potgieter, *Damages*, pp. 121–146; Neethling/Potgieter/Visser (supra note 1) pp. 225–228; Van der Walt/Midgley (supra note 1), pp. 193–194.

44 Ie, reduced by a certain percentage so that the plaintiff does not benefit from receiving the damages in advance (Visser/Potgieter, *Damages*, pp. 118–120).

45 *Idem* pp. 115–117; cf Neethling/Potgieter/Visser (supra note 1) pp. 223–225 as to prospective damage. In a wide sense contingencies were described as 'the hazards that normally beset the lives and circumstances of ordinary people' (*AA Mutual Ins Co v Van Jaarsveld* 1974 4 SA 729 (A)), and deductions are made for them (e.g. for the fact that the plaintiff could possibly earn income in the future despite his injuries). There may however also be favourable contingencies which may increase the amount of damages (e.g. the fact that a young child could have had an

result of the delict, may not be taken into account to reduce his damages (collateral source rule);[46](v) damages may be reduced in accordance with the plaintiff's contributory negligence;[47] (vi) damages cannot be calculated in respect of damage which is too remote;[48] (vii) damages may be disregarded in respect of loss of income or maintenance derived from illegal activities;[49] and (viii) the plaintiff has a duty to mitigate his loss, that is, to take reasonable steps to prevent his damage from accumulating.[50]

[20] Except for legislative provisions in a limited field (Compensation for Occupational Injuries and Diseases Act 130 of 1993 sections 47–53), no standardisation of awards exists in South African law.

9. Compensation for particular kinds of losses

[21] Loss of *use* is usually compensated on the basis of the reasonable rent for a substitute *res* for the relevant period;[51] loss of *earning capacity* is assessed by subtracting the present value of the plaintiff's estimated future income, if any, having regard to his injuries and disability, from the present value of his future income but for his injuries and disability, and then discounting and adjusting this figure in the light of contingencies;[52] loss of *holiday or free time* is not compensated except perhaps as part of loss of amenities of life;[53] *damage to unrepaired things* will be calculated by reference to the diminution in the market value of the thing – in this regard evidence of the reasonable cost of repairs may be *prima facie* proof of such diminution but the repairs need not actually have been undertaken, nor is it relevant whether the plaintiff intends to have the repairs done at all;[54] *frustrated expenses* constitute damage if reasonably incurred and compensation may be claimed for such expenses.[55]

---

exceptional career but for his injuries: *Southern Ins Ass Ltd v Bailey* 1984 1 SA 98 (A) 117).

46 *See* Visser/Potgieter, *Damages*, pp. 181–214; Neethling/Potgieter/Visser (supra note 1) pp. 228-234; Van der Walt/Midgley (supra note 1) pp. 199–200; Burchell (supra note 1) pp. 141 et seq.; see also *infra* question 14.

47 Apportionment of Damages Act 34 of 1956 s 1(1)(a); Neethling/Potgieter/Visser (supra note 1) p. 155 et seq.

48 I.e., where legal causation is absent (see supra note 27).

49 *See* Neethling/Potgieter/Visser (supra note 1) pp. 239–241; *infra* question 11.

50 E.g. *Da Silva v Coutinho* 1971 3 SA 123 (A); Visser/Potgieter, *Damages*, pp. 230–234; Neethling/Potgieter/Visser (supra note 1) pp. 234–235; Van der Walt/Midgley (supra note 1) p. 205.

51 *See* Neethling/Potgieter/Visser (supra note 1) p. 235; Visser and Potgieter, 'Skadevergoeding vir gebruiksverlies: 'n Welkome nuwe ontwikkeling', [1994] *THRHR* 312 et seq.; *Kellerman v South African Transport Services* 1993 4 SA 872 (C); *Shrog v Valentine* 1949 3 SA 1228 (T).

52 E.g. *Marine and Trade v Katz* 1979 4 SA 961 (A) 976–982; Visser/Potgieter, *Damages*, pp. 365 et seq., 368; Van der Walt/Midgley (supra note 1) p. 189; supra note 44, 45.

53 *Cf* Visser/Potgieter, *Damages*, pp. 91, 401; Neethling/Potgieter/Visser (supra note 1) p. 246.

54 E.g. *Erasmus v Davis* 1969 2 SA 1 (A); Visser/Potgieter, *Damages*, pp. 329–333; Neethling/Potgieter/Visser (supra note 1) pp. 237–238.

55 *See* Visser/Potgieter, *Damages*, p. 53.

10. Compensation for emotional shock and loss of consortium

[22] Compensation for *reasonably serious* emotional shock will in principle be awarded in the following circumstances: [56]where the shock resulted from *physical injury*;[57] where the plaintiff was in *personal danger* of being physically injured;[58] where the plaintiff was *informed* of the death or injury of a *close relative* in an incident;[59] and where the plaintiff *personally witnessed* the events causing the emotional shock.[60] Compensation for loss of *consortium* will be awarded where such loss was caused by adultery, abduction, enticement or harbouring.[61]

11. Compensation of illegitimate losses

[23] Patrimonial loss caused, in the case of bodily injury, by loss of income or earnings originating from *unlawful activities*, can in principle not form the basis of a delictual claim.[62] The question whether an activity is unlawful, must be answered with reference to *public policy*. It has accordingly been held that an activity which is *contrary to good morals*, or *criminal* or even only *statutorily prohibited* (but morally colourless) in circumstances where the income in question is unenforceable due to invalidity, is considered to be unlawful.[63] The principle that loss of income from an unlawful activity is not recoverable, has been extended to the action of dependants.[64]

---

56 *See* generally Neethling/Potgieter/Visser (supra note 1) p. 291.

57 E.g. *Gibson v Berkowitz* 1996 4 SA 1029 (W) 1048–1050.

58 *Masiba v Constantia Insurance Co Ltd* 1982 4 SA 333 (C) 343; *Bester v Commercial Union Versekeringsmaatskappy van SA Bpk* 1973 1 SA 769 (A) 781.

59 *Bester v Commercial Union Versekeringsmaatskappy van SA Bpk* 1973 1 SA 769 (A) 781; *N v T* 1994 1 SA 862 (C); *Boswell v Minister of Police* 1978 3 SA 268 (E); *Clinton-Parker and Dawkins v Administrator, Transvaal* 1996 2 SA 37 (W); *Barnard v Santam Bpk* 1999 1 SA 202 (SCA) 209.

60 *Cf Barnard v Santam Bank Ltd* 1997 4 SA 1032 (T) 1067.

61 *See* Neethling (supra note 14) pp. 253 et seq., 259–263; Neethling/Potgieter/Visser (supra note 1) pp. 359–360; *Bruwer v Joubert* 1966 3 SA 334 (A); *Smit v Arthur* 1976 3 SA 378 (A); *Peter v Minister of Law and Order* 1990 4 SA 6 (E).

62 This is also true for loss of the goodwill of a business which has been built up as a result of illegal or impermissible activities (Van Heerden/Neethling, *Unlawful Competition* (1995), p. 120 n. 17).

63 *Dhlamini v Protea Assurance Co Ltd* 1974 4 SA 906 (A); Van der Walt/Midgley (supra note 1) pp. 190–191. However, it is submitted that a distinction should be made in these cases between loss of income and loss of earning capacity. If a plaintiff bases his claim for damages on a loss (or impairment) of his earning capacity, the fact that he has previously earned income through an unlawful activity should not be a stumbling block and he should still be able to recover damages. This approach is evident in *Ferguson v Santam Insurance Ltd* 1985 1 SA 207 (C).

64 E.g. *Shield Insurance Co Ltd v Booysen* 1979 3 SA 953 (A). Here too, the dependant's claim should be based on the breadwinner's earning capacity and not on his illegal income (cf the previous fn). The rule was in any case qualified where the unlawful activity would not have continued for an indefinite period, or where the activity posed no danger to the public, or where the requirements of the legislation in question could have been challenged successfully, or where the unlawful activity (ANC) was legalised after the death of the breadwinner (see Neethling/Potgieter/Visser – supra note 1 – p. 240 n. 265).

12. Compensation of collective damage

[24] No.

13. Special rules on compensation of ecological damage

[25] No.

14. Harm causing also advantages

[26] The existence of the collateral source rule (ie that certain benefits which the plaintiff receives as a result of the delict are considered to be *res inter alios acta*) in South African law cannot be doubted. However, it is uncertain to which benefits it applies since its application is determined casuistically and without any logical foundation.[65] It is submitted that questions regarding collateral benefits are normative in nature: they have to be approached and solved in terms of policy principles and equity. The premise should be that a plaintiff cannot be allowed to recover damages in excess of his actual loss unless public policy, fairness and justice clearly dictate otherwise. Thus there should always be a weighing up of the interests of the plaintiff, the defendant, the source of the benefit as well as the community in establishing how benefits resulting from a damage-causing event should be treated.[66]

15. Certainty of damage

[27] As a general rule in South African law a plaintiff has to prove the fact as well as extent of his damage on a balance of probability (a possibility of more than 50%). However, because of the uncertainties about and therefore speculative nature of prospective loss, it is not required of a plaintiff to prove on this basis that he will in fact sustain damage in future. All that is required is that the plaintiff must prove on a balance of probability that there is a certain percentage (e.g. 40 %) chance that damage of a particular amount (e.g. R 1,000) may result. If so, the court will usually award 40% of the estimated damage, that is R 400.[67]

16. Lump sum or rent

[28] Because of the application of the 'once and for all' rule,[68] compensation is usually awarded as a lump sum. However, the Road Accident Fund Act 56 of 1996 section 17 makes provision for an undertaking by the Fund to pay future medical expences as they are incurred or to compensate loss of future support and income in instalments.[69]

---

65 Boberg (supra note 1) pp. 479 et seq. See Neethling/Potgieter/Visser (supra note 1) pp. 228–234 as to the practical guidelines on which benefits may not be taken into account in reducing the plaintiff's damages, and vice versa.

66 Neethling/Potgieter/Visser (supra note 1) p. 234.

67 E.g. *Burger v Union National South British Insurance Co Ltd* 1975 4 SA 72 (W); see Visser/Potgieter, *Damages*, pp. 112–115.

68 *See* supra question 8 n. 43.

69 *See* Visser/Potgieter, *Damages*, pp. 152, 363–364, 374 on s 43 of the MMF Act 93 of 1989, the predecessor of the present Act.

Part II – Cases

1. Wrongful birth case

[29] According to *Administrator, Natal v Edouard*[70] the woman will have an action based on breach of contract for the maintenance of the child. In principle there is however no reason why this loss, as well as loss of earnings, may not also be claimed with the Aquilian action if the requirements of this action are met.[71] However, the court was *obiter* not in favour (mainly because birth cannot simply be equated with inflicting bodily injury) of a delictual claim for pain and suffering.[72] The woman should therefore succeed with the claim for maintenance and lost earnings, but not with the claim for pain and suffering.

2. Wrongful life case

[30] According to *Friedman v Glicksman*[73] B's action (for *wrongful birth*) for the maintenance of the child as well for all future medical expenses, will succeed. However, the child's action (for *wrongful life*) for loss of future earnings will be unsuccessful.[74]

3. Eye injury

[31] In principle V may claim patrimonial damages for past and future medical expenses, as well as for loss of earning capacity, if any. She may also claim non-patrimonial damages for her pain and suffering, disfigurement (if any) and loss of amenities of life because of the reduction in her eyesight.[75]

4. Costs for hospital visits and of adaptation of house

[32] A may claim all medical expenses *reasonably* incurred by him in the treatment of his bodily injuries and its consequences.[76] This includes the travelling expenses of his wife to the hospital[77] and costs for modification of his house.[78]

5. Scar case

[33] Future medical expenses (such as operations) which are reasonable and attributable to the injury, may be claimed. If, however, it appears at the trial that A does not intend to un-

---

70 1990 3 SA 581 (A) 596–597.
71 *See* Neethling/Potgieter/Visser (supra note 1) pp. 265–267 on the concurrence of the *actio legis Aquiliae* and the contractual action.
72 *Edouard* p. 597.
73 1996 1 SA 1134 (W).
74 *See* Blackbeard 'Actions for wrongful birth and wrongful life' [1996] *THRHR* 711–715.
75 *Cf* supra question 7.
76 *See* Visser/Potgieter, *Damages*, pp. 359–361.
77 E.g. *Dickenson v Galante* 1949 3 SA 1043 (R).
78 Visser/Potgieter, *Damages*, p. 361 n. 44.

dergo the operation and that he will therefore not incur such expenses in future (that is, there is no chance of incurring them), his claim will probably be dismissed.[79]

6. Continued payment of wages

[34] Where an employer is legally bound to grant a plaintiff sick pay, such a payment will be taken into account to reduce the plaintiff's damages accordingly.[80] Therefore, the collateral source rule does not apply[81] and P's claim against D will be dismissed.

7. Monk case

[35] If a plaintiff claims loss of income as a result of injuries, it is incumbant upon him to prove what his income would have been had he not been injured.[82] Since A will not be able to prove any loss of income and thus damage, he does not have a delictual claim. However, the monastry may have a claim based on the loss of A's services for six weeks.[83] Damages may be assessed with reference to the reasonable cost of the employment of a substitute for the injured monk.[84]

8. Lost earning capacity

[36] Damages for loss of *earning capacity* and *pain and suffering* are relevant. There are two basic approaches to the calculation of loss of earning capacity in South African law: [85](i) a guesswork estimate by the court based on fairness and reasonableness; (ii) an actuarial mathematical calculation, on the basis of assumptions resting on the evidence. The second approach should as far as possible be used, but in some instances, such as in the case of a young child, the calculation of his/her earning capacity is to a great extent very speculative.[86] As said,[87] the present value of the plaintiff's future income before and after his injuries and disability must be estimated, the difference calculated, discounted and adjusted for contingencies. Where the plaintiff has been totally disabled by his injuries, the present value of the plaintiff's income after his disability will be nil.[88] On this basis the loss of B's earning capacity in each of the three situations should be calculated.

[37] As far as compensation for pain and suffering is concerned,[89] B will be compensated for his pain and suffering, emotional shock, disfigurement, loss of amenities of life and shortened

---

79 *Cf idem* p. 362; supra question 15.
80 E.g. *Serumela v SA Eagle Insurance Co* 1981 1 SA 391 (T).
81 *See* Neethling/Potgieter/Visser (supra note 1) pp. 229, 231.
82 *See* Visser/Potgieter, *Damages*, pp. 364–365.
83 *Cf idem* pp. 218, 385–386.
84 *Cf President Ins Co Ltd v Mathews* 1992 1 SA 1 (A) 5.
85 *Southern Ins Ass Ltd v Bailey* 1984 1 SA 98 (A) 113–114; Visser/Potgieter, *Damages*, pp. 366–367.
86 *See Roxa v Mtshayi* 1975 3 SA 761 (A) 769–770; see also Visser/Potgieter, *Damages*, p. 367.
87 Supra questions 8 (fn 44, 45) and 9 n. 52.
88 *See Marine and Trade Ins Co v Katz* 1979 4 SA 961 (A).
89 *See* supra question 7 as to the assessment of such damage.

life expectancy (whichever are present) in the first two instances, but not in the last (living dead). Since an unconscious person suffers no pain and experiences no anguish, and an award of money will not provide any consolation, non-pecuniary damages are not allowed.[90]

9. Lost spouse / partner

[38] (a). In South African law a *pretium doloris* or damages for mental suffering (grieve) because of a person's negligent death are not allowed.[91] Nor may a person who has a mere contractual right of support (non-marital partner), claim for loss of maintenance.[92] However, as wife, A has a claim for the loss of maintenance her husband had provided her since there is a reciprocal duty of support between spouses.[93]
[39] (b). A may claim for the loss of the services of her husband as part of her loss of maintenance.[94]

10. Offending publication

[40] A's publication undoutedly constitutes an actionable defamation against B in our law.[95] The amount of satisfaction (damages) is determined *ex aequo et bono*. Divergent factors may be taken into account in this assessment,[96] *inter alia* the position and status of the plaintiff.

---

90 *See Collins v Administrator*, Cape 1995 4 SA 73 (C) 92 (Van der Walt/Midgley – supra note 1 – p. 184). However, there are also cases supporting the opposite view, ie that an award should be made because the victim, objectively seen, has in fact been subjected to e.g. loss of amenities of life and shortened life expectancy (e.g. *Gerke v Parity Insurance Co Ltd* 1966 3 SA 484 (W) 494; see generally Neethling/Potgieter/Visser – supra note 1 – pp. 248–252).

91 E.g. *Union Government v Warneke* 1911 AD 657; *Hendricks v President Insurance Co Ltd* 1993 3 SA 158 (C) 159.

92 E.g. *Nkabinde v SA Motor and General Ins Co Ltd* 1961 1 SA 302 (D).

93 E.g. *Hendricks v President Insurance Co Ltd* 1993 3 SA 158 (C) 159–160; *Fourie v Santam Insurance Ltd* 1996 1 SA 63 (T) 65. See in general Neethling/Potgieter/Visser (supra note 1) pp. 279, 283 et seq. See also Visser/Potgieter, *Damages*, pp. 374 et seq. on the calculation of damages for loss of support caused by the death of a breadwinner.

94 *Cf Hendricks v President Insurance Co Ltd* 1993 3 SA 158 (C) 159. The damages for loss of a breadwinner's services are calculated on the same basis as that employed for his loss of support (see the previous note; Visser/Potgieter, *Damages*, p. 386).

95 *See* in general Neethling (supra note 14) pp. 158 et seq.; Neethling/Potgieter/Visser (supra note 1) p. 339 et seq.

96 E.g. *Skinner v Shapiro*(1) 1924 WLD 157 167: 'The amount of damages is entirely in the discretion of the Court. Such discretion, however, is exercised on reasonable and not arbitrary principles. One is entitled to have regard to the character of the defamatory words, their falseness and the malice displayed by the defendant; the rank and position of the parties in society, the special relationship which existed between them, the persons to whom the defamatory words were published and the place, time and mode of publication; the continuance of the circulation of the defamatory words; the tardiness, inadequacy or entire absence of any apology. The Court is also entitled to consider the general conduct of the defendant, from the date of the defamation; and the events leading up to it, down to and including his demeanour at the trial and the nature of his defence.' (See also *Iyman v Natal Witness Printing and Publishing Co (Pty) Ltd* 1991 4 SA 677 (N) 686–687; *Smith v Die Republikein (Edms) Bpk* 1989 3 SA 872 (SWA) 875–881; Neethling – supra note 14 – pp. 205–207; Neethling/Potgieter/Visser – supra note 1 – pp. 256–257.)

11. Rosenkavalier case

[41] As indicated,[97] frustrated expenses or expenses which have already been incurred but are rendered useless or worthless as a result of a delict, in principle constitute damage for which damages may be claimed. However, the wrongdoer will be liable only if the expenses were not too remote, that is legal causation must be established.[98] No compensation may be claimed for the negligent causing of injured feelings (here mainly feelings of disappointment) unless the injured feelings amount to actionable emotional shock[99] – and this does not seem to be the case *in casu*. It is also submitted that the expenses should not be attributed to the owner (driver) of the car since it will not be reasonable, fair or just[100] to hold him liable for damages which could quite easily have been avoided by the plaintiff through insurance (legal causation is therefore absent).

12. Prostitute case

[42] As said,[101] because her income was earned from illegal activities, the prostitute will not succeed in a claim based on loss of income. However, she may still recover damages if she bases her claim on loss of earning capacity, but this award may be very difficult to calculate if there are no other facts, except her illegal income, on which to base it.[102]

13. Mercedes case

[43] The general measure of damage to property is the diminution of its market value, and this is ascertained by a comparison of the market value before and after the damage-causing event. A more realistic approach, however, is to take the reasonable cost of necessary repairs as a measure of damage. But where the cost of repairs exceeds the diminution in the market value of the property, the latter is accepted as the plaintiff's damage.[103] A plaintiff may also claim loss of profit resulting from damage to property.[104] Because the cost of repairs (4 000 Euro) is more than the diminution in market value of the Mercedes (20 000–18 000 = 2 000 Euro), P may claim this diminution plus his loss of profit (3 000 Euro: 23 000 offer from X minus the previous market value of 20 000), that is 5 000 Euro in total.

14. Loss of use

(a) Immobilised car

[44] B may claim the *reasonable* cost of hiring a substitute motor car for the relevant

97 Supra question 9 n. 55.
98 *See* in this regard Neethling/Potgieter/Visser (supra note 1) pp. 181 et seq.
99 Supra question 10.
100 *See* Neethling/Potgieter/Visser (supra note 1) pp. 185–187 on the application of the flexible criterion for legal causation in our law.
101 Supra question 11.
102 *See Ntwetni v Allianz Ins Co Ltd* 1992 2 SA 173 (Ck) 716.
103 E.g. *Botha v Van Zyl* 1955 3 SA 310 (SWA); see also supra question 9 n. 54.
104 *See* in general Visser/Potgieter, *Damages*, pp. 329 et seq.

period.[105] However, there is merit in the argument that B's damage is really the difference between this cost and his usual running expenses of the damaged car.[106]

(b) Lost use of house

[45] Similarly, B may claim the reasonable cost of hiring a substitute house for six months.

15. Damaged, but unrepaired car

[46] (a) As indicated,[107] A is entitled to damages for his damaged car irrespective of whether repairs have actually been undertaken, or whether he intends to have the repairs done at all. The fact that he sold the car unrepaired should thus not make a difference as to the merit of his claim.

[47] (b) The worth of the *damaged car* plays no role in South African law to ascertain its recoverable damage. As said,[108] the diminution of the market value or the reasonable cost of repairs are the criteria for the measurement of such damage. So even if the cost of repairs would be higher than the value of the damaged car, this cost may be claimed if it is less than or the same as the diminution in the market value of the car. However, if the cost of repairs would be higher than the worth of the *repaired car* (presumably that is more or less the same as the pre-accident value of the car[109]), the cost of repairs is then more than what the plaintiff should reasonably obtain and the plaintiff is entitled only to the diminution in the market value.[110]

[48] (c) Compare the answer to case 13.

16. Additional car damage

(a) Accident car

[49] If after repair the car is restored to its pre-accident condition, but it is nevertheless not also restored to its pre-accident market value because of its proneness to accidents, the cost of repairs is too low to serve as criterion for full compensation. A should thus receive both the reasonable cost of repairs and damages for diminution in the value of the car not eliminated by the repairs.[111]

(b) New for old

[50] B may claim the reasonable cost of repairs (even if some parts are new – this will with regard to most cars damaged in accidents in any case almost be unavoidable), unless this cost exceeds the diminution in market value of the car.[112]

---

105 *See* supra question 9 n. 51.
106 *See* Visser/Potgieter, *Damages*, p. 335 n. 45; Boberg (supra note 1), p. 627.
107 Supra question 9 n. 54.
108 Supra question 9 and case 13.
109 This is however not necessarily the case (Visser/Potgieter, *Damages*, p. 330).
110 E.g. *Enslin v Meyer* 1960 4 SA 520 (T); Visser/Potgieter, *Damages*, p. 330.
111 *See Page v Malcomes* 1922 EDL 284; Visser/Potgieter, *Damages*, p. 330.
112 *Cf* supra question 9 and case 13.

(c) Rent of garage

[51] Since the rent of the garage is an expense frustrated for two weeks by D's negligence and thus constitutes damage, P should in principle be able also to claim the cost of two weeks rent.[113]

17. Damaged railway wagon

[52] If the amount for maintaining the wagon held in reserve does not exceed the reasonable rent for a substitute wagon for the relevant period, A should succeed.[114]

18. Detective case

[53] It does not seem that A suffered any financial loss caused specifically by B's attempt to steal. A would have had the expenses for the detective's salary whether or not any theft occurred at all. Therefore, if one compares A's patrimonial position before and after the attempted theft, his position did not worsen. A's action will therefore not succeed.

19. Death of parents

[54] According to South African law accelerated benefits from the estate of a deceased breadwinner (A's parents) are taken into account in reducing the dependants'(A) damages for loss of maintenance.[115] Therefore, the collateral source rule does not apply.

---

113 *See* supra question 9 and case 11.

114 *Cf* supra question 9 and case 14; cf however supra note 106.

115 E.g. *Legal Insurance Co Ltd v Botes* 1963 1 SA 608 (A) 620; Neethling/Potgieter/Visser (supra note 1), p. 232.

United States

Damages under US Law

Gary Schwartz

Part I – General questions

1. Aims of the law of damages

[1] The general goal of the law of damages in personal injury cases is to provide the plaintiff with full compensation for the injury he has suffered. For some harms, such as intense pain and suffering, the goal of full compensation seems impractical; in such cases, tort law aims for the goal of fair compensation. As to the ultimate objectives of tort damage rules, much may depend on the views of the particular judge or scholar. Those who see corrective justice as the principal objective of tort law will see compensatory damages as a way of remedying the wrong that the defendant has inflicted on the plaintiff. Those who understand tort law as a deterrence measure will see damage rules as involving a threat of liability which, it is hoped, will deter potential defendants from behaving negligently in the first place. For the first group of judges and scholars, full compensation is needed to fully remedy a past wrong. For the second group, fully compensatory damages are needed in order to fully deter defendants from engaging in negligence.

2. General principles of the law of damages

[2] See above.

3. Different forms of damages

[3] In tort cases, it is generally understood that there are several forms of damages: compensatory damages for out-of-pocket or monetary losses (mainly health-care expenses and income losses); compensatory damages for non-monetary losses such as pain and suffering; and punitive damages, which are available in a limited number of cases. The right to recover for nominal damages is an issue that arises only in a limited number of cases: the plaintiff who has not suffered a significant injury is unlikely to bring suit in the first place. The general American rule is that a party's legal fees are not recoverable as part of the damage

U. Magnus (ed.), Unification of Tort Law: Damages, 175–182.

award. While there are statutory exceptions to this general rule, few of these exceptions pertain to ordinary injury cases.

4. Legislation on damages

[4] The general rules on damages have been developed by courts pursuant to the common law process. Statutes in some states then qualify or modify those general common law rules. Statutes in several states have placed 'caps' on the size of awards for pain and suffering, at least in certain categories of cases. In California, for example, there is a $250,000 cap on pain and suffering awards in medical malpractice cases. Also, statutes in many states place caps or other limits on the amount of awards for punitive damages.

5/6. Definition of recoverable damage/different types of damages

[5] These questions blur the line between the rules of damages and the rules concerning liability. The concept, for example, of 'pure economic loss' is well enough understood by American courts. The relevant question is the extent to which the rules of liability do in fact permit recovery for pure economic loss caused by a defendant's negligence. In general, American courts reject the idea of liability in negligence for pure economic loss. But there are particular cases in which liability is endorsed (for example, attorney malpractice and negligent misrepresentation.) Tort damage rules and contract damage rules tend to be quite different. The breach-of-contract plaintiff can more easily recover for the loss of future profits. But that plaintiff can in general not recover for pain and suffering, nor can he seek punitive damages.

7. Monetary assessment of non-patrimonial damage

[6] American law does not use the language of 'patrimonial' damages. Pain and suffering damages are referred to as 'non-monetary' damages, or 'non-pecuniary' damages.
[7] The traditional common-law practice of assessing damages for non-pecuniary loss is that the jury determines pain and suffering damages without much by way of guidance from the court. However, if the court regards the jury's award as 'excessive', the court can reduce that award. The more dramatic the award is, the more vulnerable it is to a reduction by the trial court or by the appellate court. But all of this is a largely intuitive practice.
[8] In recent decades, a number of states have adopted caps on pain and suffering damages. In some states, these caps apply to all personal injury cases. In other states, they apply to certain categories of cases – for example, medical malpractice cases or suits against public agencies. In a jurisdiction with a cap, the jury typically makes up its own mind as to the proper award for pain-and-suffering damages; but if the jury's award turns out to exceed the cap, that award is then reduced to the cap by the trial judge.
[9] As for pain and suffering, some states, but not others, allow plaintiffs to make a 'per-diem' argument – that the plaintiff's suffering can be calculated in terms of a certain dollar amount per day. It is generally believed that a per-diem argument leads to a higher overall pain and suffering award. One interesting question that has emerged in the last twenty years concerns the status of damages for the lost enjoyments of life. Some states allow plaintiffs

to recover separately for (1) pain and suffering, and (2) lost enjoyments. Other states, however, say that lost enjoyments are a subset of what should be a single award for pain and suffering. Almost all American states now provide for liability in invasion of privacy cases. But what the components of damages are in a privacy case is a question that has not been dealt with extensively. Defamation is a tort with deep roots in the common law and ecclesiastical law. There is a wide variety of highly technical damage rules that pertain to the defamation tort.

8. Calculation of patrimonial damage

[10] The calculation of damages is initially done by the jury, under instructions from the judge that express the relevant legal principles. The wide discretion enjoyed by the jury in rendering damage awards means that much of American damage practices is informal and ad hoc. One clear legal rule is that future damages should be discounted to present value. That is the case, at least, for monetary damages such as lost income. Whether future pain and suffering should be discounted to present value is a question that has divided American courts. Once the jury's verdict is in, the jury's award – if deemed to be excessively large – can in effect be reduced by the trial judge, or by an appellate court. Similarly, if the award is deemed to be excessively low, the award can in effect be increased by the trial judge or appellate court. The jury makes its original award in a kind of vacuum: the jury is given no information as to what awards other juries have given in previous cases. Those previous awards, however, are generally considered by the trial judge and the appellate court in considering whether the jury's damage award should be allowed to stand. The more dramatic is the award that the jury returns, the more likely it is to be reduced by the judiciary. This, by the way, creates a kind of bias in the public awareness of tort verdicts. A dramatically high award handed down by the jury is likely to be a page-one story in the newspaper. A judge's later reduction in that award tends to be reported on page ten (if at all). There are not many complaints about inaccuracies or unevenness in the jury's calculation of economic losses. But many scholars allege there is an excessive degree of variability in jury awards for pain and suffering. Based on this belief, many scholars have recently proposed procedural reforms that could do a better job in standardizing awards for pain and suffering.

[11] In general, in personal injury cases the rules relating to damages remain the same, regardless of the nature of the defendant's tort – whether that tort is intentional, negligent, or covered by a particular rule of strict liability. To be sure, when employees sue employers for on-the-job injuries, a rule of strict liability is applied and is combined with damage practices that limit recovery to economic losses and deny recovery for pain-and-suffering. But these are workers' compensation cases, which are covered by special statutes, handled by administrative agencies, and generally regarded as *not* part of tort law as such. Rather, workers' compensation is deemed to be a clear 'alternative' to tort.

9. Compensation for particular kinds of losses

[12] American courts would allow for the loss of use – the fair rental value of property which has been destroyed or damaged by the defendant's negligence. American courts in tort cases allow for recovery for the loss of earning capacity, even in the absence of a loss of actual income. Thus, a religious person who has taken a vow of poverty can recover for lost earning capacity; and the homemaker who is disabled can recover for either the cost of replacement services – or (if this is higher) for the value of the work she could have done outside the home. If property is damaged but not repaired, the owner can recover for the cost of repairs, or the decreased value of the property in its unrepaired condition – whichever number is less. American judicial opinions have not dealt explicitly with the question of loss of holiday time. This may well be the kind of question that is dealt with in an informal and ad hoc way by individual juries.

10. Compensation for emotional shock and loss of consortium

[13] This emotional shock question primarily concerns rules of liability rather than rules of damages as such. If the defendant's negligence produces an accident that injures X, and if a close family member of X witnesses the accident, many American courts would allow the family member to recover for emotional shock. Those states would generally not allow recovery, however, if the observer were not a close family member, or if the close family member did not observe the accident itself, but only learned of it shortly afterwards. As far as loss of consortium is concerned, a consortium award concerns the three S's: services, sociability, and sexuality. The traditional common law rule allowed the husband to recover for the loss of consortium of his wife, but did not allow the wife to recover for loss of consortium when her husband was injured. This unjustified discrimination has now been eliminated by granting to the wife a loss of consortium action for injury to her husband. Courts are divided as to whether parents can recover for the loss of consortium of their injured children, or whether a child can recover for the loss of his parent's consortium. Of course, when recovery is allowed, it is for services and sociability only, not sexuality.

11. Compensation of illegitimate losses

[14] American courts, perceiving the illegitimacy of the lost income incurred, would in all likelihood deem it not compensable.

12/13. Compensation of collective damage

Special Rules on Compensation of Ecological Damage

[15] These questions cannot be answered in the abstract. Question 12 largely concerns what happens in so-called 'class actions.' Much depends on what practices are accepted for the distribution of a class action award, and the procedural rules that are developed concerning settlement of class action claims. There are many different kinds of ecological damages. There are no special rules that apply to ecological damages as such.

14. Harm causing also advantages

[16] When the tort committed by the defendant against the plaintiff injures the plaintiff but also provides him with some benefits, then the general rule is that the recovery the plaintiff receives is reduced by the amount of the benefits. But: to justify an offset, the benefit must concern the same 'interest' of the plaintiff which the defendant's tort has damaged; and offset can be denied if permitting it would be 'inequitable'.

15. Certainty of damage

[17] Some American courts would say that the plaintiff has to prove reasonable future income loses to a 'reasonable certainty.' Other American courts would be satisfied by a showing that those future income loses are 'more-likely-than-not.' The issue has not received much attention.

16. Lump sum or rent

[18] American courts would not use the term 'rent,' but would rather would speak of 'periodic payments.' But the general rule in tort is that the plaintiff recovers a 'lump sum' rather than receiving periodic payments. That rule has been modified by statute, however, in particular states for particular categories of cases. Of course, even when a lump sum is legally available, the plaintiff and the defendant can before trial agree to a 'structured settlement,' pursuant to which the defendant makes monthly payments to the plaintiff.

Part II – Cases

1. Wrongful birth case

[19] A problem here is that American tort law is state law, and states have taken different positions in cases of this sort. The majority rule is to deny recovery for child-rearing expenses when the baby is born healthy. But a minority rule would allow recovery. In explaining the majority rule, courts tend to reason that child-rearing costs are more than offset by the benefits of parenthood.

2. Wrongful life case

[20] Given the child's handicap, the mother can recover at least for the extra costs of raising a child with a handicap of this sort. When the child reaches the age of majority, he himself bears the burden of the costs of his disability. Whether he can recover from the defendant for those costs is an uncertain question. After all, had his mother aborted, the child would not even exist.

3. Eye injury

[21] The medical costs are of course recoverable. It is unclear what sorts of losses V incurs because of the reduction in sight in her one eye. There may be enjoyments of life which are lost or at least diminished because of this injury. If because of her imperfect vision she may be unable to secure a job she otherwise could have won, then her lost income or reduced earning capacity may be recoverable.

4. Costs for hospital visits and of adaptation of house

[22] This is an interesting question that American opinions have not explicitly addressed. Because the wife can in most states recover for the loss of her husband's consortium and sociability, it is likely she can recover for the time she spends seeking to minimize her own sociability losses. Adapting the home to wheel-chair use would be recoverable as a form of medical expenses.

5. Scar case

[23] A can recover under the heading of pain and suffering for the embarrassment associated with the scar that remains. If cosmetic surgery is available that would eliminate that scar, the availability of this would suggest A's failure to mitigate damages.

6. Continued payment of wages

[24] Under the collateral source rule, he can recover for his wage loses, even though those losses have been dealt with by the employer's sick leave. However, the collateral source rule has been modified by statute in several jurisdictions.

7. Monk case

[25] This is a prime case for allowing recovery for loss of earning capacity.

8. Lost earning capacity

[26] The job of the jury would be to make its best estimate as to A's future earnings. At the age of 20, A presumably has a considerable record in terms of his education and abilities that the jury can take into account. In assessing A's claim, however, much would depend on how the court resolves the choice between 'reasonable certainty' and 'more-likely-than-not' as the relevant standards of proof. If A is only six years old, a court would probably rely on information concerning the average income of Americans generally over a lifetime. It is unlikely that courts would be willing to consider the income situation of the particular family. This would raise an excessive risk of class or racial bias.

9. Lost spouse/partner

[27] These questions raise issues as to damages for wrongful death. Wrongful death is governed by statute in every state. Wrongful death statutes generally limit recoveries to spouses, and deny recovery to non-marital partners. In general, there are substantial variations among wrongful death statutes. Still, the primary measure of recovery in wrongful death is the economic support that the victim would otherwise have provided to his family. Bereavement is generally not compensable. Whether loss of household services is compensable is a matter that varies from state to state.

10. Offending publication

[28] This is a defamation claim. Defamation damage rules are quite elaborate. A can recover for lost income due to the defamation. A can also recover for the emotional distress caused by defamation (especially defamation that is in writing rather than oral.) Previously, the jury, under the heading of 'general damages,' simply made an educated guess about the extent of the plaintiff's emotional distress. Currently, as a result of the Supreme Court's interpretation of the Constitutional guarantee of free speech, A must prove his emotional distress with actual evidence. In extreme circumstances, A can also recover punitive damages.

11. Rosenkavalier case

[29] It is likely that A can recover, under the heading of 'special damages,' for the cost of the tour he is no longer able to take. However, having allowed recovery for this cost, a court would probably find it excessive to allow a specific recovery for the inability to attend 'Rosenkavalier'.

12. Prostitute case

[30] See I.11 above. The illegitimate loss is probably non-compensable. A can recover, however, for her more general loss of earning capacity.

13. Mercedes case

[31] P can certainly recover the 2,000 he has lost in terms of the reduction in the offer by Y. But P can probably recover the additional 3,000 as well. The offer of 23,000 from X would probably be regarded as the fair market value of the car – which has been depreciated by the collision caused by D.

14. Loss of use

[32] (a) It is doubtful that B can recover for the cost of renting a substitute car. But: he can recover for the lost rental value of his own car during the time it is in for repairs. And this value should be about equal to the rental value of a substitute car of equal quality.
[33] (b) B can recover for the lost rental value of his own house.

15. Damaged, but unrepaired car

[34] A can recover for the reduced value of his car due to the accident. If the car is totaled, and if repair costs are less than the fair market value of the car at the time of the accident, fair market value is all that A can recover. Likewise, if the reduced value is less than the cost of repairs, then reduced value sets the ceiling for A's recovery. As a practical matter, however, B's insurance company might be willing to pay for repair costs in (c).

16. Additional car damage

[35] (a) Older cases deny liability for the reduced value of the 'accident car,' but more recent cases tend to affirm compensation for this.
[36] (b) As a practical matter, in a simple auto case, the extra value of the new parts would probably be ignored. But when the stakes are larger the result might well be different. For example, if the defendant's negligence requires the plaintiff to replace the furnace in his home, and if the plaintiff ends up with a new furnace, the extra value of the new furnace would offset the damages the plaintiff gets for having to purchase the new furnace.
[37] (c) There would be no damages as such for the garage rental, but the plaintiff can recover for the lost rental value of his own car, which might be about equal to the value of renting a substitute car.

17. Damaged railway wagon

[38] The ongoing costs of maintaining a wagon in reserve would not be compensable. But any special costs incurred in actually using that wagon while the damaged wagon is being repaired would be compensable.

18. Detective case

[39] There are no damages for this. Similarly, a store owner cannot recover from a burglar for the cost of locks on doors that in general help keep burglars out of the store.

19. Death of parents

[40] A is suing for wrongful death. I am aware of no cases, but in all likelihood courts not allow the setoff. Note that the parents would eventually die anyway, and that the child would inherit at that time.

Comparative Report

Comparative Report on the Law of Damages

Ulrich Magnus

Part I – General questions on the law of damages

1. Aims of the law of damages

[1] The answer to the question of the aims served by the law of damages is not of theoretical interest only but has consequences in practice, for the extent of damages depends on the goals pursued by the law of damages.

(a) Compensation

[2] The national reports on the law of damages unanimously agree that the primary aim of damages is to compensate the injured person for the loss it suffered.[1]
[3] By that principle we mean restoring the victim to the status before the injury as far as this can be achieved by means of damages.[2]
[4] There is much less unanimity whether compensation is the only aim or whether the law of damages does or should serve further aims also and which these aims are. The variety ranges from laws which explicitly accept further functions of the law of damages to those legal systems which strictly deny such extension.
[5] On the extensive side English law ranks first. By the instruments of aggravated, exemplary, nominal and – although disputed – restitutionary damages it acknowledges a number of additional functions of the law of damages.[3]
[6] On the other end of the scale there stands the example of Greek law where damages 'can only be compensatory'.[4] The Italian law seems to have adopted this position as well.[5]
[7] But the picture differs further when we look closer at the possible additional functions attributed to the law of damages.

(b) Prevention

[8] Prevention is understood here in the sense that the threat of damages can force potential wrongdoers to behave more cautiously so that future damage is prevented. This preventive function of the law of damages is acknowledged in Austria,[6] in France,[7] to some extent by the English Common Law,[8] Belgian Law[9] and the South-African law[10] and it is at least

---

1 Koziol 1 (all notes refer to the numbers at the text of the country reports); Cousy/Vanderspikken 1; Galand-Carval 1, Rogers 1, Magnus 1, Kerameus 1, Busnelli/Comandé 1, Wissink/van Boom 7, Neethling 1s, Schwartz 1.
2 *See* especially Kerameus 2; Rogers 1.
3 *See* Rogers 1ss.
4 Kerameus 3.
5 Busnelli/Comandé 1ss.
6 Koziol 2.
7 Galand-Carval 6.
8 Rogers 3ss.

U. Magnus (ed.), Unification of Tort Law: Damages, 185–217.

welcomed 'as a desirable side effect' in Germany.[11] Greek,[12] Italian[13] and Dutch law[14] are reluctant to attribute a separate preventive function to the law of damages, although Italian and Dutch law know of preventive elements in the general law of torts.[15] In the U.S.A., prevention as an aim of the law of damages is only partly recognized by the courts.[16]

[9] If a preventive function of damages is recognized, this may lead to higher awards than would be given when strictly compensating the actual loss. But apparently no national law grants damages merely based on the purpose of prevention. Some actual loss must always be present. A good example is found in the mass media cases[17] where it is one consideration for the assessment of damages that by increased damages the wrongdoer should be deterred from repeating his wrong.[18]

[10] The underlying philosophy is that in the interest of preventing damage it should not be cheaper to cause damage than to avoid it. The comparison shows that it is rather widely accepted that the law of damages has and should have some preventive effect. It is therefore proposed here that the principles should adopt prevention of damage as an aim of the law of damages.

(c) **Sanction/punishment**

[11] English,[19] French,[20] Austrian[21] and especially U.S. law[22] rather frankly recognise a punitive function – that the tortfeasor must be taught that tort does not pay – of the law of damages although these laws restrict it to specific situations of outrageous misbehaviour, grave fault or the like. The same is true for the South African law.[23] A similar line is followed by the German and seemingly by the Italian law in cases where non-pecuniary damages have to be assessed.[24] Here also the gravity of fault influences the measure of damages.

[12] Dutch and Greek law on the other hand do not consider punitive purposes in any way an aim of the law of damages even as far as non-pecuniary damage is concerned.[25] The same is true for Belgian and U.S. law.[26]

[13] Taken together there is rather wide support that at least on some occasions the law of

---

9 Cousy/Vanderspikken 1.
10 Neethling 2s.
11 Magnus 2.
12 Kerameus 1s.
13 Busnelli/Comandé 2.
14 Wissink/van Boom 9.
15 Busnelli/Comandé, Wissink/van Boom *ibid.*
16 Schwartz 1.
17 For England see: John v. Mirror Group Newspapers [1997] Q.B. 586 and Rogers 5; for Germany see: BGHZ 128, 1; BGHZ 132, 13, see Magnus 2; for the Netherlands see Wissink/van Boom 11.
18 *See* the cited cases.
19 Rogers 3.
20 Galand-Carval 3ss.
21 Koziol 3.
22 Schwartz 3.
23 Neethling 2.
24 Magnus 3; Busnelli/Comandé 3, 9.
25 Kerameus 1; Wissink/van Boom 11, 13.
26 Cousy/Vanderspikken 17.

damages has (and should have) a punitive function insofar as the measure of damages should correspond to the kind and degree of misbehaviour. The most common occasion for that punitive effect is the assessment of non-pecuniary damages in case of intentional or quasi-intentional injury to the corporeal integrity or to the privacy of the person.

(d) Declaration of right/'Rechtsfortsetzungsfunktion'

[14] A number of European legal systems know of nominal or symbolic damages which funtion as a means to state that a right has been infringed although no specific damage has been suffered.[27] A similar idea is adopted by the Austrian 'Rechtsfortsetzungsfunktion' which leads to abstract and objective compensation irrespective whether any actual loss ensued.[28] The other European laws do not provide for nominal damages.[29] Under German law, the aim of ascertaining a right is served by procedural means.[30]

[15] To sum up: there is a clear need for a judicial declaration that states that a right is infringed. But only few legal systems use a judgement for nominal damages for that purpose.

(e) Restitutionary damages/gain avoidance

[16] The calculation of damages is only rarely influenced by the possible gain the wrongdoer made or had. It seems to be common understanding that, apart from special situations like infringement of intellectual property rights, the law of damages does not aim at the skimming off of the wrongdoer's profits.[31] It is only within the context of prevention that the law of damages is accorded the function to secure that wrongdoing is not more profitable than law abiding behaviour.

(f) Summing up

[17] The main goal of the law of damages is compensation. But prevention is widely recognised as an additional, though not independent aim. Damages cannot be based on preventive purposes only. They presuppose some actual loss.

[18] There is also a commonly accepted need for the possibility of a declaration that a right is infringed irrespective whether any actual loss accrued or could be proved. But it is not shown that the need must be met by the means of nominal or symbolic damages. A pure declaration stating the illegal infringement would suffice.

[19] Other aims like sanction/punishment or avoidance of illegal gains are partly accepted as additional considerations. But nowhere can those considerations solely found an award of damages. At least for assessing non-pecuniary damage in personal injury cases the degree of fault has to be taken into account.

---

27 For England see Rogers 11; for Belgium see Cousy/Vanderspikken 19 concerning damages for pain and suffering; for France Galand-Carval 15. For South Africa Neethling 8 doubts whether nominal damages are still a valid remedy.

28 *See* Koziol 4.

29 Expressly for the Netherlands: Wissink/van Boom 22; implicitly for Greece: Kerameus 2 and for Italy: Busnelli/Comandé 1ss.

30 Magnus 4.

31 *See* Rogers 7; Magnus 5; Kerameus 1.

2. General Principles of the law of damages

[20] General Principles on the law of damages may be divided into two categories: Principles concerning the quantum of damages and those concerning the mode of compensation.[32]

(a) Full or limited compensation

[21] Almost all European countries follow the principle of restitutio ad integrum: The wrongdoer has to make good the entire damage he caused, leaving apart, however, contributory negligence and mitigation. And he has to compensate the damage as fully as possible.[33] Therefore the principle of full compensation is the unanimously accepted starting point.

[22] The measure of full compensation depends in general on nothing else but on the loss of the injured party. An exception to this rule is Austrian law. Under Austrian law the extent of compensation depends in general on the degree of fault (§ 1324 ABGB). In case of slight negligence compensation of the mere actual loss is granted whereas lost profits and immaterial losses are compensated only in case of gross negligence or intent.[34] But it must be stated that the cited rule of Austrian law is qualified by statutory and judge-made exceptions.[35]

[23] Moreover, all European legal systems provide for greater or lesser exceptions to the principle of full compensation: partly international conventions, especially in the field of transport law, set limits to the amount of compensation.[36] So do national statutes on strict liability in Austria and Germany.[37] Furthermore, in the field of contract law immaterial losses are compensated in some countries with great reluctance only.[38]

[24] To sum up: The common starting point is full redress for the entire damage both in contract and tort situations and both for pecuniary and non-pecuniary losses. But this principle is subject to different restrictions: maximum limits as to the amount of compensation apply (contracts of transportation, some strict liability statutes) or recoverability is restricted (immaterial contract losses).

(b) Restitution in kind v. compensation in money

[25] The majority of European laws adopt the view that damages are primarily owed in money,[39] wheras a minority favours restitution in kind as the general principle.[40] But both views must provide for exceptions.[41]

---

32 *See* also Galand-Carval 7ss.

33 Galand-Carval 7; Cousy/Vanderspikken 11ss; Rogers 1; Magnus 7; Kerameus 1; Busnelli/Comandé 5; Wissink/ van Boom 15; Also for South Africa Neethling 5 and for the U.S.A. Schwartz 1s.

34 Koziol 5.

35 Koziol 5.

36 *See* Warsaw Convention, CMR, COTIF and the Maritime Conventions; as to the constitutionality of the limits of the Warsaw Convention under Italian law compare Busnelli/Comandé 6.

37 Compare Koziol 7s; Magnus 8.

38 *See* Koziol 6; German BGB § 253; Kerameus 11.

39 England: Rogers 9; France: Galand-Carval 12s; Greece: Kerameus 2; Italy: Busnelli/Comandé 7; Netherlands: Wissink/van Boom 19. Also South Africa: Neethling 5.

40 Austria: Koziol 9; Belgium: Cousy/Vanderspikken 13s; Germany: Magnus 9.

41 *See* the cited authors.

[26] It is evident that money cannot always grant adequate compensation: e.g., in case of defamation a correcting notice may better restore the injured party's reputation than money can do.[42] On the other hand it is nearly self-evident that in most cases wrongdoers are neither able nor apt nor willing to restitute the damage in kind, e.g. to heal the injured party or to repair themselves the damaged things. Thus, under a practical point of view money should be the normal mode of damages. But the injured party should be permitted to claim restitution in kind when this is possible and not too burdensome for the wrongdoer.[43] However, the different ways of redress – either by money or by restitution in kind – should not lead to differing levels of compensation so that it becomes an object of speculation whether the injured party in the end gets more by one way or the other.[44]

3. Different forms of damages

[27] As already seen under I.1., the European law family knows of a certain variety of forms of damages depending on the general aims of the law of damages. But it is only the English and Irish law that recognises explicitly the specific remedy of exemplary or aggravated damages. And even there this remedy is of limited application. Moreover, it may be doubted whether exemplary damages are available in cases where no damage at all had ensued.

[28] With regard to nominal or symbolic damages there is a need for declaration that a right has been infringed, but as mentioned above it does not seem necessary that the declaration has to be in terms of damages.

[29] As far as legal fees and judicial costs are dealt with in the national reports, it is stated that these expenditures are mainly regulated by special rules of procedural law and are therefore generally no part of the law of damages.[45] Only in exceptional situations, e.g. where legal costs towards third parties result from the tortfeasor's wrong, the injured party can claim these costs as damages.[46] Only the Dutch law provides otherwise. The Nieuw Burgerlijk Wetboek contains specific provisions on legal fees and judicial costs under the head of damages (art. 6: 96 BW).[47]

[30] The situation can be summed up by saying that there is no great necessity for different modes of damages. It speaks for itself that the 'mixed jurisdiction' of South African law has more or less abolished special modes of damages like exemplary, aggravated and nominal damages which it originally had inherited from English law.

4. Legislation on damages

[31] The national reports show that the legislators are reluctant to regulate the general law

42 Further examples are given by Galand-Carval 12 and Rogers 9.

43 *See* the Italian solution in art. 2058 Codice Civile and the Greek solution in art. 297 Civil Code; the Dutch regulation in art. 6: 103 Burgerljik Wetboek is similar, but even more liberal.

44 *See* the example of Germany where there is a difference of up to 30% between both ways of calculation.

45 Austria: Koziol 12; Germany: Magnus 12. Even for England: Rogers 12 and South Africa: Neethling 9; for the U.S.A.: Schwartz 3.

46 *See* Rogers 12; compare also Neethling 9; Magnus 12.

47 Wissink/van Boom 24.

of damages in detail, if at all. But it must be pointed out that the New Dutch Civil Code contrasts with this general picture insofar that it contains a more elaborated set of rules on damages than other codes.

[32] Where we find provisions on damages, they tend to be either wide and vague in application and formulation or very special and limited to a narrow field of law.[48] Again, the new Dutch Code provides otherwise with its rather comprehensive system of provisions on damages.[49] When comparing the codified provisions on the law of damages in general, they rule partly on the question whether restitution in kind or compensation in money ranks first,[50] or whether the loss suffered (damnum emergens) and lost profits (lucrum cessans) are recoverable heads of damage;[51] they distinguish between pecuniary and non-pecuniary damage, the latter often being recoverable under certain restrictions only.[52] Clear rules on how to assess damages in general are rather the exception. Modern Dutch law contains specific provisions on the assessment of damages in general.[53] But in special fields of law, in particular in the field of environmental law, other European countries have also promulgated provisions which contain more specific rules on damages; partly these rules limit damages to maximum amounts especially where strict liability is provided for.[54]

5. Definition of recoverable damage

[33] With the exception of Austria, no statutory definition of the term damage is to be found in the European law family. Even the new Dutch Code has refrained from defining what recoverable damage is.[55]

[34] It is, however, rather clear from the national reports that the concept of damage – in Austria as well as in the other countries – is a legal concept, although it may start from a 'natural' meaning of damage.[56] Only that damage can be recovered which is damage in the eyes of the law.

[35] The singular statutory definition of damage, contained in § 1293 of the Austrian Code,

---

48 *See* Koziol 13s; Galand-Carval 16ss; Magnus 13ss; Rogers 13; Kerameus 4; Busnelli/Comandé 14ss.

49 Compare Wissink/van Boom 24ss.

50 For Austria; Koziol 13; for Germany, Magnus 13s.

51 Austria: Koziol 13; France: Galand-Carval 17 (art. 1149 Cc for contractual damages); Germany: Magnus 14; Greece: Kerameus 4; Italy: Busnelli/Commandé 14; Netherlands: Wissink/van Boom 24ss. The same rule is also true for the Common Law, see Rogers 13; in the same sense for the South African law Neethling 12.

52 Austria: Koziol 13; Germany: Magnus 14; Greece: Kerameus 7; Italy: Busnelli/Comandé 3, 15s; Netherlands: Wissink/van Boom 25. For English law compare Rogers 26ss. French law provides for the most farreaching compensation of non-pecuniary loss ("dommage moral"), compare Galand-Carval 31.

53 Wissink/van Boom 26.

54 *See* for Austria: Koziol 14; the same is true for Germany: Magnus 16; for England see Rogers 13; for the U.S.A. see Schwartz 4. As to the environmental law see under I. 13.

55 Wissink/van Boom 32.

56 *See* for Austria: Koziol 16, 18; Belgium: Cousy/Vanderspikken 21, 16; France: Galand-Carval 21ss; Germany: Magnus 17s; England: Rogers 14; Greece: implicitly Kerameus 5; Italy: Busnelli/Comandé 17ss; Netherlands: Wissink/van Boom 36; very clear also for the South African law: Neethling 11.

runs as follows: 'Damage is called every detriment which was inflicted on someone's property, rights or person. This is distinguished from the loss of profit which someone has to expect in the usual course of events'.[57] The distinction between damage and lost profits is a technical one and today in Austria the term 'damage' is normally understood in the broad sense as the whole harm including lost profit'.[58]

[36] Despite the lack of statutory definitions, the courts and scholarly writings in other countries use or advance definitions rather similar to the Austrian one: e.g., 'any loss that somebody sufferred with respect to his legally protected rights, goods and interests',[59] 'a detriment capable to be evaluated from an economic standpoint',[60] 'factual detriment arising from a certain occurrence'[61] or 'the diminution, as result of a damage-causing event, in the utility or quality of a pecuniary or personality interest in satisfying the legally recognized needs of the person involved'.[62] But it is also clear that such a broad formula can only be a guiding principle, the application of which depends on further considerations fitting to the case at hand.[63] On the basis of the national reports it may be doubted whether a more detailed definition of damage would be desirable and even feasible. There is a strong need for flexibility in order to secure that the rules on the law of damages would fit even for the most uncommon case and that the rules could also easily be adapted to changing conditions.

[37] As far as they go, all attempts to define the term damage agree in that they presuppose that a negative variation (attributable to the wrongdoer) in the legally protected sphere of the injured party must have taken place. And in order to judge whether a change is negative, a comparison between two states of affairs is necessary – the 'Differenzyhpothese'.[64] The outcome of the comparison, however, evidently depends on the positions which are included in the comparison and from the respective worth which is attributed to them. Thus, the comparing of different positions is an inherent method of assessing damages, but does not in itself necessarily decide what constitutes recoverable damage.

[38] Taking all the above together, the notion of damage can be defined. But it must be in very broad and nearly meaningless terms if the definition is to suit all situations: damage is any negative modification in the injured party's legally protected sphere. It must be questioned whether such a general definition of damage is necessary or helpful. It is clear from the reports that for different groups of cases more specific considerations apply.

6. Different types of damage

[39] All legal systems under review distinguish between different categories of damage.

---

57 *See* thereto Koziol 17.
58 Koziol 17.
59 Germany: Magnus 18.
60 Italy: Busnelli/Comandé 17.
61 Netherlands: Wissink/van Boom 36.
62 South Africa: Neethling 11; similarly Belgium: Cousy/Vanderspikken 16.
63 *See* Busnelli/Comandé 17ss; Magnus 18; Rogers 14: ''Damage' seems to me to be a legal concept, the meaning of which will vary from one category of liability to another".
64 *See* for Austria: Koziol 17, 43; Belgium: Cousy/Vanderspikken 16; Germany: Magnus 22, 30; Greece: implicitly Kerameus 4; Italy: Busnelli/Comandé 18; Netherlands: Wissink/van Boom 34; South Africa: Neethling 13.

(a) Pecuniary and non-pecuniary loss

[40] The most common distinction is the one between pecuniary and non-pecuniary damage (see thereto also I.7.). The assessment in terms of money is different for both kinds of damage: while for the former the objective market price is the usual yardstick, non-pecuniary damage must and can only be subjectively estimated.[65] Moreover, compensation for non-pecuniary loss is subjected to different restrictions: in the field of contract law some legal systems generally exclude its compensation in money;[66] in the field of tort law most European laws confine compensation for non-pecuniary damage to cases of injury to the person, e.g. to the body, to privacy or to reputation. Only Austria and in particular France recognize the possibility of compensating non-pecuniary damage concerning things.[67] Furthermore, in some countries statutes on strict tort liability exclude compensation of non-material harm.[68]

(b) Contractual and tortious damage

[41] The distinction between pecuniary and non-pecuniary damage overlaps to some extent with the distinction between contractual and tortious damage. To the differences just cited – in particular that contract law is reluctant to compensate immaterial loss – a further variant must be added: in some systems pure economic loss is regularly compensated under contract law but only in exceptional situations under tort law.[69] The mentioned differences may be viewed as those concerning the basis of liability instead of the measurement of damage. But the assessment of damage in tort and contract is also concerned insofar as in contract, the loss is usually measured by what the creditor would have had, had the contract been properly performed (the expectation interest or 'positives Interesse'), while in tort the normal measure is the difference to the situation which would have existed had the tort not been committed (the integrity interest or 'negatives Interesse').[70] The point of reference – the hypothetical situation with which the actual situation is compared in order to assess whether there is a negative difference – therefore varies between tort and contract damage. Besides that, however, compensation of both kinds of damage follows identical principles in most European countries.[71]

[42] Only few laws provide for further distinctions between contractual and tortious damage: thus, French and Belgian law – and to a lesser extent Italian law – require for contracts the previsibility of damage which is no requirement in tort.[72]

---

65 For Austria: Koziol 26, 40; France: Galand-Carval 33; Germany: Magnus 19; England: Rogers 22; Greece: Kerameus 9s; Italy: Busnelli/Comandé 6, 7; Netherlands: Wissink/van Boom 23, 70; South Africa: Neethling 14s.

66 For Germany: Magnus 20; Greece: Kerameus 5; Netherlands: Wissink/van Boom 37.

67 For Austria: Koziol 29 (special intent is required); France: Galand-Carval 9 (no such restriction).

68 For Austria: Koziol 26s; Germany: Magnus 8.

69 *See* in particular Rogers 23ss, also Magnus 23; Wissink/van Boom 51.

70 *See* Rogers 24; Neethling 4; Wissink/van Boom 15, 35.

71 *See* for Austria: Koziol 1, 19; Germany: Magnus 23; England: Rogers 23ss; Greece: Kerameus 1; Netherlands: Wissink/van Boom 4ss. For the case of South Africa: Neethling 13.

72 Galand-Carval 29; Cousy/Vanderspikken 8; Busnelli/Comandé 31.

(c) Direct and indirect damage

[43] Further distinctions between different types of damage have a limited impact on the assessment of damages, if at all. The distinction between direct and indirect damage has some bearing on causation – and in Austria on limitation of liability[73] – but not on the calculation of damages.[74] Moreover, in tort it seems to be the preferred rule that only the directly injured party can claim damages, but again, this is no matter of damages but of the grounds of liability. On the contrary, Belgian law limits contractual damages to immediate and direct consequences of the non-compliance with contractual obligations.[75]

(d) Actual and future damage; damnum emergens and lucrum cessans

[44] The distinction between damnum emergens and lucrum cessans is familiar to most European legal systems.[76] It has some similarity to the distinction between actual and future loss. Consequences from this distinction follow primarily for purposes of evidence. Since future losses (of actual injuries) are less certain, the standard of proof is usually reduced: regularly mere probability suffices.[77] But Dutch law as well as Belgian law does not seem to make that distinction for evidentiary purposes.[78] Austrian law, on the other hand, attributes greater importance to the distinction between damnum emergens and lucrum cessans in that the latter is regularly recoverable only if the wrongdoer acted with intent or gross negligence.[79]

(e) Damage to person and property and pure economic loss

[45] The categories of damage to person and property and pure economic loss add no further conceptual or other aspects. It has already been mentioned that in some systems pure economic loss is only rarely recoverable in tort situations. But whether it is a loss is judged according to the ordinary principles.[80]

(f) Summary

[46] In summary, it can be said that for the assessment of damage different types of damage have to be distinguished. Most important is the distinction between pecuniary and non-pecuniary damage, since the method of computing damages – either objective calculation or subjective estimation – varies for both according to the nature of the damage.
[47] The distinction between contractual and tortious damage appears also to be a necessary one since it reflects the different objects of contract and tort law: protection of legitimate

---

73 Koziol 23; the same is true for South Africa: Neethling 12.
74 Austria: Koziol ibid; France: Galand-Carval 25; England: Rogers 18; Greece: implicitly Kerameus 5s; Italy; Busnelli/Comandé 29; Netherlands: Wissink/van Boom 52s; also in South Africa: Neethling 12.
75 Cousy/Vanderspikken 9.
76 But it is completely unknown to the Common Law: Rogers 19.
77 *See* for France: Galand-Carval 56; Germany: Magnus 32; England: Rogers 17; Greece: Kerameus 6; Italy: Busnelli/Comandé 26s.
78 *See* Wissink/van Boom 6, 54; Cousy/Vanderspikken 68ss.
79 Koziol 22.
80 *See* Koziol 22, Magnus 24, Rogers 16, 14s.

expectations through contract law and protection of the integrity of one's own sphere through tort law.

[48] Finally, at least under aspects of evidence, actual and future loss must be separated from each other since the latter cannot be proven with the same certainty as the former. Further distinctions, on the other hand, seem not to constitute necessary integral parts of a law of damages.

7. Monetary assessment of non-pecuniary damage

(a) Distinction

[49/50] The distinction between pecuniary and non-pecuniary damage is not always clear.

[51] In general, pecuniary damage is given if the injured party's patrimony is diminished.[81] But the term patrimony – or like expressions – is ambiguous. Thus, non-pecuniary damage is often concluded from the fact that a loss cannot be measured by easy reference to some objective standard like the market price.[82] In addition, non-pecuniary damage regularly follows from the infringement of immaterial positions such as personal feelings (pain and suffering, reputation etc.) the worth of which depends to a large extent on the injured party's subjective conditions.[83]

[52] All European laws under review recognise that non-pecuniary damage must be compensated in case of tortious injuries to the body, health and personality of the injured party. But as already mentioned, the majority of the reviewed laws are reluctant to compensate non-pecuniary losses outside the province of tort.[84] French law, however, and to some extent also Austrian law allows compensation of 'dommage moral' beyond these limits.[85]

(b) Assessment

[53] Even for the assessment of non-pecuniary damage the comparative method (*Differenz-hypothese*) has its merits and is the theoretical starting point.[86] The impaired state must be compared with the state that would exist without the impairment. But since immaterial harm is not exactly measurable in money, the extent of the loss must be estimated and translated into terms of money.

As far as non-pecuniary damage in case of bodily harm is concerned, some legal systems split the assessment into different heads of damage or 'chefs de préjudice'. Each head must be separately evaluated; added together they constitute the damages for the non-pecuniary

---

81 Koziol 32; Kerameus 9; Magnus 19; Wissink/van Boom 37; Neethling 14.

82 Busnelli/Comandé 34; Rogers 21: 'pecuniary loss . . . covers those losses which are concerned with a person's wealth, whether money, intangible property . . . or tangible property such as land and goods"; Neethling 14.

83 *See* e.g. the Belgian Cour de Cassation, according to which the pain, the grief and other moral sufferings are to be compensated, see Cousy/Vanderspikken 24.

84 *See* Austria: Koziol 29 (with extensions to further cases); Germany: Magnus 20; England: Rogers 23ss; Greece: Kerameus 5; Italy: Busnelli/Comandé 33; Netherlands: Wissink/van Boom 56ss (with extensions to further cases); South Africa: Neethling 13.

85 Galand-Carval 32ss; Koziol 29 and above I 6.a.

86 *See* especially Neethling 15.

harm. The most prominent example is French law, where the actual pretium doloris for pain and suffering is regularly accompanied by compensation for loss of comfort (préjudice d'agrément) and for harm to appearance (préjudice esthétique). Even further losses (préjudice sexuel etc.) may be claimed as the case may be.[87] Equally, English law provides in the case of injury to the person for compensation of pain and suffering on the one hand and loss of amenity on the other. Both together constitute the non-pecuniary loss and in nearly all cases there is a single, global award for this.[88] U.S. law is broadly similar, though there are different opinions on whether the two categories should be separated.[89] Other European laws do not distinguish between different heads of non-pecuniary damage; they award one single sum for all immaterial loss which is connected with bodily harm. And the measurement of the sum must take into account all relevant factors such as 'the significance of the injury, the consequences for the state of health and duration as well as the intensity of physical pain' or 'emotional strain'.[90] Among the latter system, views differ as the impact of fault and other subjective factors (age, financial situation) on the assessment of the non-pecuniary damage is concerned: Under Austrian law these factors do not matter[91] while under Dutch and German law they do.[92]

(c) Summary

[54] The overall comparison shows that both pecuniary and non-pecuniary damage should be fully compensated. The distinction between these categories of damage relates to the fact that pecuniary damage can rather easily be measured by market-oriented objective standards while non-pecuniary damage is related to the non-economic sphere and includes a necessary subjective element of estimation.

[55] The assessment of non-pecuniary loss could be achieved in two ways: either in splitting off the different heads of immaterial loss or in awarding one general sum for the whole immaterial harm. In the interest of greater objectivity the former mode might be preferable. While assessing the single heads or the general sum all relevant factors, also the degree of fault and the personal situation especially of the victim, should be taken into consideration.

8. Calculation of pecuniary damage

(a) General method

[56] The starting point seems to be more or less everywhere a comparison in the kind of the 'Differenzmethode': two different states of the injured party's pecuniary situation must be

---

87 *See* Galand-Carval 32; very similar in Belgium: Cousy/Vanderspikken 24.

88 *See* Rogers 28. Very similar are the different heads of non-pecuniary loss under South African law; compare Neethling 16.

89 Schwartz 9.

90 For Austria: Koziol 35; for Germany: Magnus 27s; Italy: Busnelli/Comandé 40 ("seriousness of the harm"); Netherlands: Wissink/van Boom 56; in Greece the assessment of non-pecuniary damage is left to the discretion of the court: Kerameus 9.

91 *See* Koziol 36 (although disputing the correctness of this decision).

92 *See* Wissink/van Boom 56ss; Magnus 27s.

compared in order to assess whether there is a diminution and hence a recoverable damage.[93] As already mentioned, the outcome of the comparison depends on the factors included in the calculation. For pecuniary loss, generally every position is recognized which concerns the economic sphere and is measurable in money.[94]

(b) Abstract v. concrete calculation

[57] Whether there is a negative change in the pecuniary situation of the injured party is in general determined according to a concrete-subjective standard. This is the position of the clear majority of legal systems here under review: Only if the present claimant suffered a concrete loss concerning his patrimony, is he entitled to redress.[95]

[58] But there are important exceptions to the approach of concrete calculation: Austria allows objective-abstract calculation of pecuniary damage whenever the tortfeasor has acted with slight negligence.[96] Here objective-abstract calculation is the rule and a concrete-subjective approach the exception. Certain objective-abstract elements, too, creep in where methods of standardization are used. In particular, English law follows a rather strict standardization in cases of future economic consequences of personal injuries: a multiplicand, the injured party's annual net loss is multiplied by the probable number of years (the multiplier) the loss is likely to last. The multiplier reflects the probable general development in abstracto although it can also be adjusted to special features of the case at hand.[97] Also, in France abstract tables ('barèmes') are used in cases of this kind, although with caution since they are not binding.[98] And most clearly the Italian report shows the difficulties to achieve some uniformity by abstract standardization in personal injury cases.[99] The other legal systems seem to refrain from attempts to standardize the assessment of economic loss in personal injury cases.[100]

[59] But there are further fields where abstract calculation of damages is permitted: e.g.,

---

93 *See* for Austria: Koziol 43 (but with farreaching exceptions); Belgium: Cousy/Vanderspikken 27s.; France: (implicitly) Galand-Carval 10, 36; Germany: Magnus 30; Greece: Kerameus 4; Italy: Busnelli/Comandé 18ss (with some qualifications); Netherlands: Wissink/van Boom 34s; South Africa: Neethling 18.

94 Austria: Koziol 32: 'patrimony which is measurable in money'; France: Galand-Carval 31: 'dommage économique'; Germany: Magnus 19: 'all positions of economic or financial worth'; England: Rogers 21: 'losses which are concerned with a person's wealth, whether money. . ., intangible . . . or tangible property'; Greece: Kerameus 9: loss of 'the plaintiff's assets in the broad sense of the word'; Italy: Busnelli/Comandé 36: economic characteristic of the harmed interest; Netherlands: Wissink/van Boom 37: 'harm (that) affects the present or future financial situation of the injured party', in case of doubt it is assumed that a pecuniary damage is given; South Africa: Neethling 14: 'pecuniary or financial loss'.

95 For Austria (but only in case of gross negligance or intent of the wrongdoer): Koziol 43; Belgium: Cousy/Vanderspikken 28; France: Galand-Carval 36; Germany: Magnus 32, England (but for damage to persons only to a limited extent): Rogers 31ss; Greece: Kerameus 12; Netherlands: Wissink/van Boom 70. In South Africa the question is disputed: Neethling 18 n. 41.

96 Koziol 40.

97 *See* Rogers 31; for recent developments concerning the multiplier *see* Rogers 32.

98 Galand-Carval 33, 36; in Belgium, various tables with fixed annuities are used for standardization, Cousy/ Vanderspikken 32.

99 Busnelli/Comandé 41ss.

100 Germany: Magnus 34; Greece: Kerameus 10; Netherlands: Wissink/van Boom 77ss; South Africa: Neethling 20.

under commercial contract law where the plaintiff often can claim the difference between the contract-price and the market-price when the defendant has not fulfilled his obligations.[101] In the Netherlands, abstract calculation is the rule even in case of any 'breach of contract with respect to goods with a market value'.[102] As far as abstract calculation is admitted, it regularly fixes the minimum damage: the injured party may claim a higher concrete damage.[103]

(c) Assessing the value of the damaged position

[60] In the field of pecuniary damage it is the economic value of the damaged position which has to be made good by the money sanction. This value is regularly represented by the market value of the position or by the costs of restoring the prior state: in case of personal injuries, e.g., expenses for healing and lost income, in case of damaged things the costs of repair or what the undamaged thing would have cost on the market.[104] But different solutions exist as to the correct date of the calculation: partly it is the time when the wrong was committed, partly the date when the damage has to be assessed. Austrian law even differentiates: the 'damage-day' counts for abstractly calculated damages and the 'judgement day' for concretely calculated damages.[105] English law seems to prefer a more actual date than the 'damage day'.[106] South African law, on the other hand, favours the date of the commission of the delict,[107] whereas Belgian law takes the time of judgement as decisive.[108]

(d) Standardization

[61] Some attempts to standardize money awards for pecuniary loss in the field of personal injury claims have already been dealt with supra I.8.b). Another rather unique example of standardization of damages is the immobilization table for motorvehicles in Germany that fixes the amount of the daily loss of use for each kind of motorvehicle.[109]

(e) Free disposal of awarded damages?

[62] Once the victim is entitled to damages, it is generally his free choice to spend any awarded sum for purposes even entirely unrelated to the damaging event. Generally, the victim is under no obligation to spend any damages for repair, restoration or the like of the original damage. Moreover, the amount of compensation does not depend on how the victim uses – or will use – the sum of damages.[110]

---

101 For England: sec. Sale of Goods Act; Germany: Magnus 32; Greece: Kerameus 6.
102 Wissink/van Boom 70.
103 *See* Germany: Magnus 31; Netherlands: Wissink/van Boom 71.
104 For Austria: Koziol 40; Germany: Magnus 32s; England: Rogers 33ss; Greece: Kerameus 8 (for personal injuries); Netherlands: Wissink/van Boom 70 (for damage to property).
105 Koziol 43.
106 Rogers 35.
107 Neethling 19.
108 Cousy/Vanderspikken 7.
109 Magnus 34.
110 For Belgium: Cousy/Vanderspikken 139 (explicitly only for cars); France: Galand-Carval 38; England: Rogers 43; Germany: Magnus 33 (but with the exception that expenses for hypothetical medical operations cannot be claimed); Netherlands: Wissink/van Boom 80.

(f) Further factors governing the assessment

[63] With the exception of Austrian law,[111] the gravity of fault is generally not considered decisive for the assessment of pecuniary loss. Fault plays its role as far as the basis of liability is concerned; also contributory fault (negligence) of the victim may reduce his damages. But apart from that, fault generally does not influence the assessment of pecuniary loss.[112] The same is true for the question whether the social situation of the parties has some bearing on assessing the amount of damages for pecuniary loss.[113]

9. Losses on the borderline between pecuniary and non-pecuniary damage

(a) Pure loss of use

[64/65]Concerning compensation for pure loss of use, the European solutions vary widely.
[66] French, Greek, South African and U.S. law provides for compensation of loss of use irrespective whether a substitute had been hired or profits were lost or not.[114] Under English law, damages for mere loss of use are recoverable in principle. But there is 'some reluctance to apply this nowadays in the case of 'private' property'.[115] In Belgium, case law seems to move towards a more permissive solution on pure loss of use.[116] German law has adopted a split solution: lost use of essentially needed things as house, flat, car or ship is indemnified, whereas lost use of other things is not.[117] Austrian law, on the other hand, considers pure loss of use to be non-pecuniary damage which the injured party cannot claim from the wrongdoer.[118] Also Italian law seems to follow that line.[119]
[67] The different solutions mirror the fact that things evidently have some objective useable value but that their concrete value for the user also depends on the use he makes of them. This combination of objective and subjective elements seems to militate rather in favour than against compensation for mere loss of use. But in order to avoid misuse it could be advocated to exclude damages in cases where the lost use has no substantial importance for the average user.

(b) Pure loss of earning capacity

[68] Concerning pure loss of earning capacity without any actual or probable future loss of income, the solutions are less divergent than in case of pure loss of use.
[69] Most of the countries under review recognise pure loss of earning capacity as recover-

111 *See* Koziol 39ss.
112 France: Galand-Carval 37; Germany: Magnus 7, 33; England: Rogers 37s (with the exception of exemplary damages); Greece: Kerameus 12; Netherlands: Wissink/van Boom 78s; South Africa: Neethling 18ss (implicitly).
113 *See* preceeding reference.
114 France: Galand-Carval 39; Greece: Kerameus 13; South Africa: Neethling 21; U.S.A.: Schwartz 12.
115 Rogers 40.
116 Cousy/Vanderspikken 124ss.
117 Magnus 35s.
118 Koziol 46.
119 Busnelli/Comandé 47.

able damage and allow damages on an objectively calculated basis.[120] Only French, German and South African law denies indemnification for any reduction in earning capacity which is unaccompanied by some concrete financial loss of actual or future income.[121] But German law allows an exception in case of injuries to the housekeeping spouse who can claim the costs of a comparable housekeeper.[122] Again, earning capacity as such has clearly some objective value. But its concrete worth for the injured party depends also on that party's situation and whether or not he or she exploits it. Nonetheless, the majority of the reviewed laws regards pure loss of earning capacity as a pecuniary damage.

(c) Pure loss of holiday or free time

[70] Compensation for loss of holiday or free time is treated in a rather uniform way. The prevailing solution is that in general no separate compensation of that item is provided for.[123] But two qualifications apply: under travel contract law due to the European directive (No. 90/314/EEC) loss of enjoyment of holiday may be indemnified.[124] Besides that the holiday factor may lead to increased sums for pain and suffering, especially under the head of loss of amenities of life.[125] Even more favorable towards compensation of lost holiday or free time is Belgian law.[126] There the injured party can claim compensation for any loss of holiday or free time. At least in theory (although not in practice) Greek law follows the same solution.[127] In American legal practice, this decision is left to the ad hoc discretion of court juries.[128]

(d) Damage to things which remain unrepaired

[71] With one exception the countries under review accept that the injured party can claim costs for repair of damaged property irrespective whether or not the property is in fact repaired.[129] The presumptive costs of repair are regarded as a practical measure for or even as prima facie evidence of the diminution in value of the damaged property.[130] The mentioned exception to this general rule is the Austrian law, which does not allow calculation of dam-

---

120 Austria: Koziol 47; England: Rogers 41, although expressing some doubts; Greece: Kerameus 13; Italy: Busnelli/Comandé 46; in principle also Netherlands: Wissink/van Boom 82, but with restrictions when assessing the damage; U.S.A.: Schwartz 12.

121 France: Galand-Carval 43; Germany: Magnus 37; South Africa: Neethling 21; for Belgium explicitly only in cases of invalidity: Cousy/Vanderspikken 92s, 96ss.

122 Magnus *ibid.*

123 Austria: Koziol 48; England: Rogers 42; Germany: Magnus 38; Italy: Busnelli/Comandé 10; Netherlands: Wissink/van Boom 83; South Africa: Neethling 21.

124 *See* for Germany: Magnus 38; Italy: Busnelli/Comandé 48; Netherlands: Wissink/van Boom 63.

125 For England: Rogers 42; Germany: Magnus 38; South Africa: Neethling 21.

126 Cousy/Vanderspikken 38.

127 Kerameus 13.

128 Schwartz 12.

129 Belgium: Cousy/Vanderspikken 39, 139; England: Rogers 43; France: Galand-Carval 46s, 83s (with the qualification that the injured party must still own the damaged property; after sale costs for fictitious repair cannot be claimed any more); Germany: Magnus 39; Greece Kerameus 13; Italy: probably the same solution applies; Busnelli/Comandé 102ss; Netherlands: Wissink/van Boom 84; South Africa: Neethling 21.

130 *See* especially Rogers 43; Neethling 21. For this reason, U.S. law grants the costs of (fictitious) repair only if they are lower than the decreased value of the unrepaired property; Schwartz 12.

ages on the basis of the costs of a fictitious repair if repair is neither intended nor done, but then only compensates the difference to the market price of the undamaged thing.[131] This appears to be in line with the general attitude of Austrian law to calculate damages rather on an objective-abstract basis.[132]

(e) Frustrated expenses

[72] Compensation for expenditures rendered futile by a tortious act is an unsafe field. On the one hand the injured party generally has not incurred expenditures in reliance on the tortfeasor's act – in contrast to similar contract situations.[133] Nor has the tortfeasor in the strict sense caused the injured party's expenditures since they had ensued anyhow.[134] Nevertheless most countries under review feel some necessity to allow for compensation of frustrated expenses – not only in the area of contracts, where this head of damages is a familiar one, but also in the area of tort.[135] However, it is only with farreaching restrictions that the injured party can expect redress for futile expenditures: either typically or reasonably incurred costs[136] or costs spent in the expectation to avoid or mitigate damage of the kind that occurred must be rendered useless.[137]

[73] On the contrary, Greek and Italian law are reported to deny damages for frustrated expenses at all.[138] They mainly doubt whether causation is established.[139]

[74] Expenditures are of a clear pecuniary nature. But it is evident that the injured party cannot claim compensation for all and every expenditure which became useless by the tortfeasor's conduct. There must be a specific relationship between the expenditure and the tortious act so that they can be connected to each other despite the fact that a strict causal link is missing, since the expenditure is no consequence of the tortious act. Whether and how far the typicality or reasonableness of any expenditure suffices must be doubted.

10. Compensation for emotional shock and loss of consortium

(a) Compensation for emotional shock

[75] The prevailing view is that emotional shock in itself does not justify compensation. Only if the shock causes some manifest physical or psychic injury is indemnification for the injured party's own loss awarded. This view is taken by Austrian, English, Belgian, German, Greek, Italian and probably by Dutch law.[140] Moreover, in the Common Law jurisdictsions

---

131 Koziol 50.
132 *See* thereto Koziol 40.
133 *See* especially Rogers 69.
134 *See* Rogers *ibid.*
135 *See* for Austria: Koziol 51s; Belgium: Cousy/Vanderspikken 40; England: Rogers 69; Germany: Magnus 40; Netherlands: Wissink/van Boom 85; South Africa: Neethling 21.
136 For Austria: Koziol 52; South Africa: Neethling 21.
137 Germany: Magnus 40.
138 Kerameus 7; Busnelli/Comandé 112.
139 Keraumeus, Busnelli/Comandé *ibid.*
140 *See* for Austria: Koziol 53; England: Rogers 44s; Germany: Magnus 41; Greek: Kerameus 14; Italy: Busnelli/Comandé 49ss; Netherlands: Wissink/van Boom 86ss.

additional requirements may have to be met – some close relationship between the claimant and the person actually injured; and/or, some proximity in time and place and particular gravity of the event.[141] In this area France appears to have the most extensive liability.[142]

[76] Except where family members are involved, the mere watching of normal daily horror scenes – of traffic accidents and the like – does not justify claims for compensation of pain and suffering.

(b) Loss of consortium

[77] Loss of consortium concerns the case that a person loses the society of some near person by the latter's death or severe injury. The law has to decide whether the harm which is connected with such loss, and which is purely immaterial and does not include any eventual loss of services, should be indemnified in money. Some of the reviewed countries do not consider the death or severe injury of a near person as a case demanding separate compensation of the immaterial harm thereby done to the remaining person(s). Neither Austrian nor German law recognises such a claim.[143] Probably Greek and Dutch law deny it as well.[144] On the contrary, under French law spouses, non-marital partners, other family members and under English law spouses and minor children can claim their immaterial damage of being bereaved of the society of some near person.[145] U.S. law grants damages for the loss of consortium of the spouse, but is divided as far as the relationship between parents and children is concerned.[146] In England, the sum for 'bereavement' is fixed by statute[147] whereas in France it depends on the circumstances[148] but can be relatively high. Italian law knows of a similar remedy in case of criminal acts of the tortfeasor.[149] And South African law allows for damages because of loss of consortium where the tortfeasor intentionally broke into the family relationship either between spouses or parents and child.[150]

[78] Taken together it cannot be denied that the death of a near relative due to the conduct of a tortfeasor belongs to the most harmful experiences of human life. Thus more often than not legal systems award damages for this immaterial harm.

11. Compensation of illegitimate losses

[79] It is a generally accepted rule that nobody can claim damages for the loss of positions he is not entitled to by the law.[151] Illegitimate losses in that sense deserve no protection.[152]

---

141 For England: Rogers 44s; South Africa: Neethling 22; U.S.A.: Schwartz 13.
142 Galand-Carval 48.
143 For Austria: Koziol 53; Germany: Magnus 42.
144 For Greece: Kerameus 14; Netherlands: Wissink/van Boom 86ss.
145 For England: Rogers 44; France: Galand-Carval 48.
146 Schwartz 13.
147 £ 7.500, *see* Fatal Accidents Act 1976 s. 1 A.
148 Galand-Carval 48.
149 *See* art. 185 Codice penale; Rescigno, Codice civile (1992) Art. 2059 n. 1 f.
150 Neethling 22.
151 *See* for Austria: Koziol 54; Belgium: Cousy/Vanderspikken 42; England: Rogers 46; France: Galand-Carval 26, 79; Germany: Magnus 43; Greece: Kerameus 15; Italy: Busnelli/Comandé 96ss; Netherlands: Wissink/van Boom 89; South Africa: Neethling 23; U.S.A.: Schwartz 14.

[80] The same rule is extended by some countries to the loss of immoral profits or earnings like in the case of an injured prostitute.[153] But even in that case the laws under review tend to indemnify at least part of the damage.[154] It must also be stressed that somebody engaged in illegal activities may nevertheless claim compensation for any loss or reduction of his earning capacity.[155]

12. Compensation of collective damage

[81] So far this is a speciality of French law. It terms as collective those kinds of damage where either minimal damage is done to very many people or where a collectivity – an unspecified group of persons – is damaged. For these situations procedural means are provided to claim damages in the interest of others or in the common interest.[156] And considerable sums can be awarded,[157] e.g. to a community which claims that the open sea before its coast is polluted by a tortfeasor.
[82] But none of the other countries under review knows so far of comparable regulations.[158]

13. Special rules on compensation of ecological damage

[83] Damage to the environment involves some specific problems also for the law of damages: costs for the restoration of the environment can be extremely high; it is often difficult and therefore costly to detect the source of pollution; costs of protection against environmental damage may also be considerable. It is doubtful whether all these costs can be claimed under the traditional rules on damages.[159] In particular fields – nuclear energy, oil pollution through tankers – international conventions exist which provide for compensation of damage caused by these sources. However, by and large they leave it to the applicable national law to define which damage can be recovered.[160] The majority of the countries under review (Austria, Belgium, England, France, Greece, South Africa, U.S.A.) do not prescribe specific rules for environmental damage.[161] But even so at least some measures are available or under

---

152 Koziol 54.
153 For France: Galand-Carval 79; Germany: Magnus 43; South Africa: Neethling 23, 42.
154 *See* for Germany: Magnus 43; as to the difficulties under South African law to assess damages in this case: Neethling 8 n. 63 and 64; in France a more liberal attitude may be expected only in future: Galand-Carval 79.
155 *See* especially Koziol 56; Neethling 23 n. 63, 64.
156 Garland-Carval 50ss.
157 Galand-Carval 52.
158 For Austria: Koziol 57; Belgium: Cousy/Vanderspikken 44; England: Rogers 47; Germany: Magnus 44; Greece: Kerameus 16; Italy: Busnelli/Comandé 57; Netherlands: Wissink/van Boom 90; South Africa: Neethling 24; not generally impossible in U.S. law: Schwartz 15.
159 For Dutch law Wissink/van Boom 91 answer that question in the affirmative.
160 *See* Art. 11 Paris Convention on Third Party Liability in the Field of Nuclear Energy; Art. I (k) and Art. VIII Vienna Convention on Civil Liability for Nuclear Energy; more specific is Art. I (6) and (7) of the International Convention on Civil Liability for Oil Pollution Damage where pollution damage is defined as including preventive measures (which are also defined).
161 For Austria: Koziol 58; Belgium: Cousy/Vanderspikken 46; England: Rogers 48; France: Galand-Carval 53; Greece: Kerameus 17; South Africa: Neethling 25; U.S.A.: Schwartz 15.

discussion: Austria considers legislative steps;[162] in France it is in particular the field of environmental damage that the above cited possibility of compensation of collective damage is used;[163] moreover, French law allows damages for 'troubles anormaux du voisinage': no owner must tolerate unusual immissions onto his property.[164] Greek law provides for special rules on environmental damage caused by maritime accidents.[165] The other countries under review know of special rules on environmental damage.[166] The core of these rules is to ensure that – even disproportionately high – costs for restitution and costs of preventive measures can be claimed as damages.[167]

14. Collateral benefits

[84] There is no clear cut rule in the countries under review whether any advantages the victim of a wrong gathered by that wrong should always or never be taken into account when calculating the amount of damages. The tendency is to start out by a rule that advantages should be set off against the loss which the injured party suffered.[168] This corresponds to the general principle that damages should not enrich the injured party.[169] Austrian law, however, follows that guiding line only when damages are calculated in a subjective-concrete manner, which is the exception under Austrian law.[170] Where compensatio lucri cum damno is recognised, the further requirements under which any advantage can be set off against the damage are rather vague. One first requirement is that advantage and damage must be causally linked together.[171] But in addition it must be reasonable and equitable under the circumstances to set off any advantages against the actual amount of damages. In particular such set off must not contradict the purposes of the collateral benefits.[172] Social security or insurance payments as well as continuing wages usually do not have the final effect and purpose to relieve the wrongdoer from liability.[173] There are, however, considerable variations among the systems on the questions of how far receipts of social security and insurance payments go to reduce the plaintiff's loss in his claim against the tortfeasor and whether and

162 Koziol 58.
163 Galand-Carval 53.
164 *See* Galand-Carval 12; similarly Belgium: Cousy/Vanderspikken 46ss.
165 Kerameus 17.
166 For Germany: Magnus 45; Italy: Busnelli/Comandé 7; Netherlands: Wissink/van Boom 90ss.
167 For Germany: Magnus 45; Italy: Busnelli/Comandé 7; Netherlands: Wissink/van Boom 90ss.
168 *See* for England: Rogers 49; France: not quite clear Galand-Carval 54; Germany: Magnus 46; Greece: Kerameus 18; Italy: Busnelli/Comandé 59, 115; Netherlands: Wissink/van Boom 93; South Africa: Neethling 26; U.S.A.: Schwartz 16.
169 *See* especially Busnelli/Comandé 59 and Neethling 26.
170 Compare Koziol 59ss.
171 For Austria: Koziol 61 (as far as set off of collateral benefits is recognised); Belgium: Cousy/Vanderspikken 56, 58; England: Rogers 49; Germany: Magnus 47; Grecce: Kerameus 18; Italy: Busnelli/Comandé 59, 115; Netherlands: Wissink/van Boom 93.
172 *See* for Austria: Koziol 61; Germany: Magnus 47; Greece: Kerameus 18; Netherlands: Wissink/van Boom 95ss; also South Africa: Neethling 26 (weighing of all relevant factors).
173 *See* for Austria: Koziol 61, Belgium: Cousy/Vanderspikken 65, England: Rogers 50, Germany: Magnus 47; but contrary in the Netherlands , as far as continued wages and social security payments are concerned: Wissink/van Boom 96.

when a claim passes by legal assignment (subrogation) to the provider of the benefit.[174]
[85] As far as benevolent payments of third parties are concerned, there seems to be wide agreement that they have to be ignored for the calculation of damages since it is equally not their purpose to benefit the wrongdoer.[175]

15. Certainty of damage

[86] Certainty of damage is concerned with the standard of proof required for any adjudication in damages.
[87] The general starting point seems to be that strict proof of the existence and extent of damage is necessary. Strict proof means that the judge verifies a fact so that no reasonable doubts remain.[176] The degree of required probability, however, varies. While under English law probability of the kind 'more likely than not' suffices,[177] German as well as Belgian law in general demand probability next to certainty.[178] But there are widely accepted exceptions to the strict proof rule. It is commonly agreed that a lower standard of proof, namely mere probability, applies for the assessment of lost profits and especially for future income losses.[179]
[88] In England, this lower standard is already reflected by the multiplier adopted in personal injury cases. This multiplier tries to take notice of the normal contingencies of life.[180] Another wide spread exception concerns cases where it is certain that some damage occured but where the precise amount is too difficult or too costly to prove. Then the courts are regularly allowed to estimate the amount of damage.[181] Even more liberal in this respect is Dutch law. Damage must be plausible. The judge then has a wide discretion and possibility to estimate the damage where exact calculation is not feasible.[182]

16. Lump sum or rent

[89] The general rule is that damages are awarded as lump sum so that the entire damage is compensated at one time.[183] In most countries a rent can be claimed only for permanent damage in personal injury cases[184] or – as in France and the Netherlands – where the choice between lump sum or rent is left to the court's discretion.[185] But even in the latter countries

174 These questions will be dealt with in greater detail in a separate project of the European Centre of Tort and Insurance Law, Vienna.
175 For Belgium: Cousy/Vanderspikken 66; England: Rogers 50; Netherlands: Wissink/van Boom 96.
176 *See* for France: Galand-Carval 55s; Germany: Magnus 48.
177 Rogers 51; partly also in the U.S.A.: Schwartz 18 (but partly 'reasonable certainty' demanded).
178 Magnus 48; Cousy/Vanderspikken 68.
179 For Austria: Koziol 62; Belgium: Cousy/Vanderspikken 70ss; France: Galand-Carval 56; Germany: Magnus 48; Greece: Kerameus 6; Italy: Busnelli/Comandé 14; South Africa: Neethling 27.
180 Rogers 52.
181 For Austria: Koziol 62; France: Galand-Carval 56; Germany: Magnus 48.
182 Wissink/van Boom 98.
183 England: Rogers 53; Germany: Magnus 49; Italy: Busnelli/Comandé 61; South Africa: Neethling 19, 28 ('once and for all rule'); U.S.A.: Schwartz 18.
184 Austria: Koziol 63; Germany: Magnus 49; Greece: Kerameus 20; Italy: Busnelli/Comandé 61; partly in South Africa: Neethling 28.
185 *See* for France: Galand-Carval 57; Netherlands: Wissink/van Boom 99s.

a lump sum is the rule in practice.[186] Only English law requires both parties' consent for a rent payment.[187]

Part II – Cases

Damage to the person

1. Wrongful birth case

(a) Maintenance

[90] The majority of the countries under review favours the solution that the mother is to be compensated for the costs of maintaining the unwanted child.[188] Not the child but the costs of maintenance is considered to be the pecuniary damage. On the contrary, Austrian and French law take the view that costs and advantages of having a child cannot be strictly separated. These laws therefore deny any claim for maintenance for wrongful birth. English law has recently moved to this position from the other.[189] The American majority rule holds that maintenance as well as lost earnings and pain and suffering be only indemnified when the child is born not healthy.[190]

[91] Since liability in wrongful birth cases can regularly be based on breach of a contract the very purpose of which is the avoidance of further pregnancies and of the economic burden associated with them, much speaks in favour of compensation for the undesired maintenance obligation.

[92] As far as the reports have answered the question of the amount of damages, the latter is usually oriented at the average cost of maintenance generally applied in family law.[191]

(b) Lost earnings

[93] Again, no uniform solution exists. The majority of the reviewed laws favours compensation of lost earnings in the case of a failed sterilisation.[192]

[94] Belgian, French and German law, however, disallow compensation for that position.[193] It is argued here that the scope of protection either of the contract on which a claim primarily has to be based but also of tort law does not extend to these consequences.[194]

---

186 Wissink/van Boom 99.

187 Rogers 53.

188 For Belgium: Cousy/Vanderspikken 75ss; Germany: Magnus 50; Greece: Kerameus 21; probably also Italy: Busnelli/Comandé 62ss; Netherlands: Wissink/van Boom 101ss; South Africa: Neethling 29.

189 For Austria: Koziol 66; France: Galand-Carval 58ss; England: Rogers 54.

190 Schwartz 19.

191 For Germany: Magnus 51; Netherlands: Wissink/van Boom 102.

192 Austria: Koziol 67; Greece: Kerameus 21; Italy: Busnelli/Comandé 65 (probably in favour); Netherlands: Wissink/van Boom 103 (when it is reasonable to give up professional career); South Africa: Neethling 29.

193 For Belgium: Cousy/Vanderspikken 77; France: Galand-Carval 58ss; Germany: Magnus 52.

194 Magnus *ibid.*

(c) Pain and suffering

[95] All countries under review but one grant damages for pain and suffering caused by the second operation.[195] The reasoning is not always easy especially for those countries which generally do not admit damages for pain and suffering in contract law.[196] It is argued here that the first ineffective sterilisation is also a tort because consent was given to an effective sterilisation only. The first operation being a tort, the wrongdoer, then, must bear all consequences connected with it, even the pain and suffering of the second operation.[197] Some countries permit additional damages also for pain and suffering of the first operation.[198] But since the woman would have suffered pain and suffering of one operation in any case it seems logical and reasonable that she can claim compensation for her operation pains only once.
[96] As far as pain and suffering of the undesired pregnancy is concerned, this does in the view of the majority of the reviewed countries not justify compensation 'mainly because birth cannot simply be equated with inflicting bodily injury'.[199] This view may be doubted on the ground that pregnancy and birth which are necessarily related with pain and suffering are not in themselves equated with bodily injury but are consequences of the wrong lying in the ineffective first sterilisation.

2. Wrongful life case

[97] There is a majority of views that in wrongful life cases the mother should be entitled to compensation for the full maintenance including additional extra costs for raising a handicapped child.[200] Austrian law is the only one so far having entirely denied compensation here;[201] Greek and U.S. law restrict compensation to the extra expenses caused by the handicap of the child and this may now be the position of English law.[202] Since the contract with the medical expert aims at avoiding to have an unhealthy child and consequently to have the burden to raise it it is submitted here that full maintenance should be paid.
[98] From the reports it is also rather clear that the child's own action for damages must fail.[203] In France, Italy and the Netherlands the question is, however, open to debate.[204] The

---

195 For Austria: Koziol 68s; England: Rogers 54; Germany: Magnus 54; Italy: Busnelli/Comandé 65; Netherlands: Wissink/van Boom 104. Only Belgium denies 'moral damages' in this case (Cousy/Vanderspikken 77).

196 Therefore Greek law denies damages for pain and suffering here: Kerameus 21.

197 *See* especially German law: Magnus 54.

198 Austria: Koziol 68s; Germany: Magnus 53.

199 Neethling 29; see also for Austrian law: Koziol 68; France: Galand-Carval 58; Netherlands: Wissink/van Boom 104. But contrary is English law: Rogers 54 and German law: Magnus 53.

200 Belgium: Cousy/Vanderspikken 82 (at least for cases of pregnancy due to illegal behaviour of a man); France: Galand-Carval 61; Germany: Magnus 55s; Italy: Busnelli/Comandé 66; Netherlands: Wissink/van Boom 105; South Africa: Neethling 30.

201 Koziol 70s, but with reference to a recent decision of the Supreme Court awarding compensation for the additional costs caused by the handicap of the child.

202 Kerameus 9; Schwartz 20; Rogers 55.

203 For Austria: Koziol 72; Belgium: Cousy/Vanderspikken 80s; England: Rogers 55; Germany: Magnus 57; South Africa: Neethling 30; U.S.A.: Schwartz 20 (at least until the child is of age). Probably also Greece.

204 France: Galand-Carval 61 (the child may claim); Italy: Busnelli/Comandé 67 (views are devided);

main argument of the prevailing view is that the child cannot base its claim for damages on the ground that it would not have existed had the doctor acted carefully. That is the only possible argument for the child. For, the doctor did not cause the handicap but only did not advise to end the child's prenatal existence.

3. Eye injury

[99] The solution of this case is relatively uniform. All laws under review grant full compensation of medical expenses. Also compensation for reduced earning capacity and thereby eventually reduced income is awarded. And it is quite clear that damages for pain and suffering are owed.[205] However, the latter vary considerably between the reviewed countries. They range from about 2,500 Euro on Germany[206] to 10,000–25,000 Euro in the Netherlands[207] or 15,000–30,000 Euro in England.[208]

4. Costs for hospital visits and of adaptation of house

[100] It is widely agreed that the cost of hospital visits of a near relative is regularly recoverable from the person liable to the injured hospitalized person[209] because such visits normally 'serve a therapeutic purpose'.[210] The Greek report on the contrary considers them as caused by the relationship and not by the injury.[211]

[101] There is a unanimous answer to the question whether the injured party can claim necessary adaptation costs: all countries answer in the affirmative[212] at least when these costs are reasonable.[213]

5. Cost of operation for scar

[102] Most of the countries under review disallow compensation for the abstract costs of an operation that is neither executed nor intended.[214] Partly the reasoning for this solution is

---

Netherlands: Wissink/van Boom 105 (not clear under Dutch law).

205 *See* for Austria: Koziol 73ss; Belgium: Cousy/Vanderspikken 84s; England: Rogers 56; France: Galand-Carval 62; Germany: Magnus 58; Greece: Kerameus 23; Italy: Busnelli/Comandé 68; Netherlands: Wissink/van Boom 106; South Africa: Neethling 31; U.S.A.: Schwartz 21.

206 Magnus 58.

207 Wissink/van Boom 106.

208 Rogers 56.

209 For Austria: Koziol 77; Belgium: Cousy/Vanderspikken 87 (disputed whether to be claimed by the visiting relative); England: Rogers 57; France: Galand-Carval 63; Germany: Magnus 59; Netherlands: Wissink/van Boom 107; South Africa: Neethling 32; U.S.A.: Schwartz 22 (only for spouse).

210 Rogers 57; also Koziol 77.

211 Kerameus 9. The Italian report is silent on that question.

212 For Austria: Koziol 78; Belgium: Cousy/Vanderspikken 86; England: Rogers 58; France: Galand-Carval 64; Germany: Magnus 59; Greece: Kerameus 24; probably also Italy: Busnelli/Comandé 70; Netherlands: Wissink/van Boom 107; South Africa: Neethling 32; U.S.A.: Schwartz 22.

213 For England: Rogers ibid; South Africa: Neethling *ibid.*

214 *See* for Austria: Koziol 79; Belgium: Cousy/Vanderspikken 88; England: Rogers 59; Germany: Magnus 60; Greece: Kerameus 25; Netherlands: Wissink/van Boom 108; probably also South Africa: Neethling 33; U.S.A.: Schwartz 23.

based on the generally concrete calculation of damages,[215] partly on the fact that there is no actual financial loss,[216] partly on the circumstance that the remaining scar is already taken account of when damages for pain and suffering are assessed.[217] French law and probably also Italian law hold that the intention of the injured party does not matter so that the party can claim the cost of a possible operation which could remove the scar even if the operation is in fact never executed.[218]

6. Continued payment of wages

[103] The unanimous solution of the case is that the employee's action for two weeks of wages from the tortfeasor must fail.[219] The employee is deemed to have suffered no economic damage any more due to the continuing payments of his employer.[220] Only U.S. law acknowledges the employee's claim.[221] But it is also clear that the employer's payment does not aim at relieving the tortfeasor. Thus, the employer generally acquires the employee's claim through assignment by virtue of law so that he can sue in subrogation of the injured employee.[222]

7. Monk case

[104] The prevailing view is that neither the monk nor the monastery can claim damages. According to that view the monk cannot show any actual financial loss because he does not exploit his earning capacity in an economically relevant way.[223] The monastery equally faces no financial loss unless money must be paid for a substitute.[224] Another reasoning stresses that the monastery's loss of the monk's services would be a pure economic loss, in consequence of a third party's bodily injury. As such it would not be actionable.[225] On the other side, Austrian and U.S. law grant the monk damages because his loss of earning capacity would be calculated in an objective-abstract manner.[226] This solution avoids any underesti-

215 Germany: Magnus 60; Netherlands: Wissink/van Boom 108.

216 Austria: Koziol 79 (in Austria the injured party must even refund any awarded costs if the party later does not undergo the operation); Greece: Kerameus 25.

217 England: Rogers 59; U.S.A.: Schwartz 23.

218 For France: Galand-Carval 65s; Italy: Busnelli/Comandé 71.

219 For Austria: Koziol 80; England: Rogers 60ss; France: Galand-Carval 67; Germany: Magnus 61; Greece: Kerameus 26; Italy: Busnelli/Comandé 72s; Netherlands: Wissink/van Boom 109; South Africa: Neethling 34.

220 *See* especially Rogers 60; Kerameus 26; Busnelli/Comandé 72; Neethling 34.

221 'Collateral source rule', *see* Schwartz 24.

222 *See* for Austria: Koziol 80; Belgium: Cousy/Vanderspikken 89; England: France: Galand-Carval 67; Germany: Magnus 61; Italy: Busnelli/Comandé 73; Netherlands: Wissink/van Boom 109. Contrast England: Rogers 60.

223 *See* for England: Rogers 63; France: Galand-Carval 68; Germany: Magnus 62; Greece: Kerameus 27; Netherlands: Wissink/van Boom 110; South Africa: Neethling 35.

224 *See* especially for France: Galand-Carval 69; Greece: Kerameus 27; Netherlands: Wissink/van Boom 110.

225 For England: Rogers 63; Germany: Magnus 62.

226 Koziol 81s; Schwartz 25.

mation of social, cultural or else gratuitous labour the loss of which would be otherwise left without remedy.

[105] Likewise, Italian law accords the monastery a claim for compensation of the loss of 'some economically valuable services'.[227] The same line is followed by South African law[228] and by Belgian law, if the monastery's gain was sufficiently continuous.[229]

[106] In weighing the different arguments it probably cannot be denied that the labour of the monk has some objective worth which can also easily be measured by the costs of a substitute. Moreover, it seems to be contradictory if the owner of a destroyed thing can claim its worth no matter whether or not he earned money by it while the 'owner' of an injured personal capacity can claim damages only if he exploited his capacity financially.

8. Future income losses; living dead

(a) The injured chemistry student

[107] The first alternative of the case – severe injuries to the 20 year old chemistry student – is answered in a rather uniform way: The loss of income has to be compensated. Its amount is calculated from the difference between the future earnings which the injured party will probably in fact earn and those future earnings which the injured party probably would have earned as a chemist.[230] Both the prospective real income and the prospective would be-income must be estimated as accurately as possible. But there always remains an element of speculation.[231] Nevertheless, the estimation can follow a more subjective or more objective approach in that either average figures of income and life expectancy are used[232] or the very personal prospects of the injured party are investigated, for, e.g., to become a brilliant or low qualified chemist etc. Excessively differing solutions of both approaches can be avoided, however, if damages for loss of future earnings are awarded as rent which can always be adapted to changing conditions and if the injured party is placed under a duty to disclose any relevant increase in actual income.

[108] Any damages for lost future income in a particular profession presupposes that there was a serious chance to finish the relevant studies and to be employed in that profession. Probability in both respects suffices.[233] Furthermore, any rent for lost future income starts to run no earlier than from the time education and studies would probably have ended.[234] Dutch courts can for that reason postpone adjudication of damages to that date or until more certainty on the amount of damage otherwise exists.[235]

---

227 Busnelli/Comandé 74ss.
228 Neethling 35.
229 Cousy/Vanderspikken 90s.
230 For Austria: Koziol 83; Belgium: Cousy/Vanderspikken 100ss; England: Rogers 64; Germany: Magnus 63s; Greece: Kerameus 28; Italy: Busnelli/Comandé 78; Netherlands: Wissink/van Boom 111; South Africa: Neethling 36; U.S.A.: Schwartz 26; probably also France.
231 *See* Magnus 63s; Neethling 36; Cousy/Vanderspikken 100ss.
232 In particular in England: Rogers 64.
233 *See* for Austria: Koziol 83s; England: Rogers 64; France: Galand-Carval 71; Germany: Magnus 63s; U.S.A.: Schwartz 26.
234 For Austria: Koziol 83; Germany: Magnus 64.
235 Wissink/van Boom 111.

(b) Child of six years

[109] In such cases the prospective future income of the child in most countries under review is assessed having regard to the parents' earning situation.[236] American law would calculate the compensation according to the average income of Americans in general.[237] In all other respects the method of calculation indicated under (a) seems to be followed.

[110] Only French law decides otherwise. The report shows that the chance of a child to earn a better living than without the injury is regularly too vague to found a claim.[238]

(c) Living dead

[111] A person who is reduced to the state of a living dead (e.g., coma over years) by the injury can nevertheless claim any loss of income calculated in the normal way. Only Belgian law takes the living costs of the victim as the basis of calculation.[239]

[112] Most of the countries under review apply, moreover, the normal measure of damages for non-pecuniary loss. That leads regularly to sums which belong to the highest awards for pain and suffering.[240] Coma or other impossibility to feel the impairment is deemed to be no reason to reduce damages for immaterial harm.[241] South African law, however, denies damages for pain and suffering to a person in a state of living death because he cannot suffer pain or experience anguish in his state.[242] Under Dutch law the question is still unsettled.[243]

9. Lost spouse or partner

(a) Pretium doloris for death of spouse or partner

[113] Whether a spouse or non-marital partner can claim a pretium doloris for the death of his/her spouse or partner is quite differently answered. A number of countries refuse any damages for such immaterial loss.[244] Others award a fixed sum to the spouse who has lost his or her spouse (in England £7,500 for bereavement).[245]

[114] Finally, we find the solution that spouses or non-marital partners are compensated for their immaterial harm when loosing the spouse or partner.[246] The partner is entitled to compensation of that kind if he or she can prove that the relationship was a stable and lasting

---

236 *See* for Austria: Koziol 84; England: Rogers 64; Germany: Magnus 65; probably also Greece: Kerameus 28; Netherlands: Wissink/van Boom 112.

237 Schwartz 26.

238 Garland-Carval 71.

239 Cousy/Vanderspikken 104.

240 For Austria: Koziol 85; England: Rogers 65; France: Galand-Carval 72; Germany: Magnus 66; Greece: Kerameus 28.

241 In particular for France: Galand-Carval 72; Germany: Magnus 66.

242 Neethling 37.

243 Wissink/van Boom 113.

244 For Austria: Koziol 86; Germany: Magnus 67s; Netherlands: Wissink/van Boom 114; South Africa: Neethling 38; U.S.A.: Schwartz 27.

245 England: Rogers 66; Belgium: average award of 250,000 Bef. (Cousy/Vanderspikken 107).

246 For France: Galand-Carval 73ss; Italy: Busnelli/Comandé 80ss.

one.[247] In principle it is submitted that the last mentioned solution should prevail because the measure of harm caused by the death of a living partner does not depend on the bond of marriage.

(b) Maintenance

[115] There is unanimity as to the solution that the surviving spouse should be entitled to the maintenance he or she loses by the other spouse's death. All countries under review recognise this right to damages.[248] The majority also allows the surviving partner of a stable and lasting[249] relationship such a claim.[250] With the increase of non-marital relationships this solution will gain further support.

(c) Loss of services

[116] The clearly prevailing view is that the surviving spouse may claim damages for loss of services.[251] Generally – with the exception of Dutch law – no actual expenses for a substitute seem to be required to found the claim.[252]

10. Offending publication

[117] Negligent or wilful publication of untrue and defamatory statements is uniformly considered to be an actionable tort which obliges to compensate for any pecuniary loss.[253] Moreover, the injured party can claim compensation for immaterial harm but under differing conditions. Most countries require nothing else than negligence on the part of the wrongdoer.[254] Others restrict compensation of immaterial loss to cases of grave fault[255] or to cases where the defamation is published by mass media.[256] Under Greek law, non-pecuniary loss is not indemnified.[257] The amount of compensation depends regularly on various factors,

---

247 Busnelli/Comandé 85.

248 For Austria: Koziol 87s; Belgium: Cousy/Vanderspikken 105 (implicitly); England: Rogers 66s; France: Galand-Carval 75; Germany: Magnus 67; Greece: Kerameus 30; Italy: Busnelli/Comandé 80; Netherlands: Wissink/van Boom 114; South Africa: Neethling 38; U.S.A.: Schwartz 27.

249 In England two years are required: Rogers 66.

250 For England: Rogers ibid; France: Galand-Carval 75; probably also Greece: Kerameus 29; Italy: Busnelli/Comandé 85; Netherlands: Wissink/van Boom 114. In Belgium, the situation is unclear, see Cousy/ Vanderspikken 111s.

251 For Austria: Koziol 88; Belgium: Cousy/Vanderspikken 113; England: Rogers 67 (although included in the general claim for support); France: Galand-Carval 73; Germany: Magnus 69; Greece: Kerameus 29s; Italy: Busnelli/Comandé 88 (although included in damages for pain and suffering); South Africa: Neethling 39; U.S.A.: varying from state to state, *see* Schwartz 27.

252 For Dutch law: Wissink/van Boom 115.

253 For Austria: Koziol 89; Belgium: Cousy/Vanderspikken 114s; England: Rogers 68; France: Galand-Carval 76; Germany: Magnus 70; Greece: Kerameus 31; Italy: Busnelli/Comandé 89ss; Netherlands: Wissink/van Boom 116; U.S.A.: Schwartz 28.

254 For France: Galand-Carval 76; Italy: Busnelli/Comandé 89s; Netherlands: Wissink/van Boom 116; South Africa: Neethling 40.

255 Germany: Magnus 70.

256 Austria: Koziol 89.

257 Kerameus 31.

among which the position of the injured party also matters.[258] Reported amounts of comparable cases are in the range of £25,000[259] and 100,000 DM.[260]

11. Rosenkavalier case

(a) Compensation for paid fee

[118] A considerable number of the reviewed countries grant compensation for the costs of the concert-and-opera-tour[261] while the other countries deny[262] or doubt it.[263] The principle question of redress for futile expenses has been already discussed. In addition, it may be argued here that there is no difference in principle between the case that the tour ticket is stolen or destroyed – a claim against the wrongdoer seems to be undeniable – and the case that someone cannot use the tour ticket because of being hurt by the wrongdoer.[264] In both cases the injured party is deprived of the possibility to use the worth of the tour ticket.

[119] On the other hand it can be argued that it makes a difference whether it is the usable object which is destroyed or the using subject who is hindered. In the end a policy choice seems necessary. It is submitted that policy weighing here militates rather in favour than against compensation.

(b) 'Tort moral'

[120] The majority of the countries under review refuses either any[265] or at least any separate compensation for the non-pecuniary loss claimed here.[266] Under the latter solution the element of lost opera enjoyment modestly increase the normal measure of damages for pain and suffering for the slight injury in the present case.[267] Only under French law the present préjudice moral would be separately assessed under the head of 'préjudice d'agrément'; but probably a lower amount than claimed would be awarded.[268] Belgian law would probably grant symbolic damages.[269]

---

258 *See* for England: Rogers 68; France: Galand-Carval 76; Germany: Magnus 70; Italy: Busnelli/Comandé 90s; South Africa: Neethling 40.
259 England: Rogers 68.
260 Germany: Magnus 70.
261 For Belgium: Cousy/Vanderspikken 117; England: Rogers 69; France: Galand-Carval 78; Germany: Magnus 71s; Greece: Kerameus 32; U.S.A: Schwartz 29.
262 Austria: Koziol 93.
263 Italy: Busnelli/Comandé 94s (probably no compensation); Netherlands: Wissink/van Boom 117 (questionable whether loss imputable); South Africa: Neethling 41 (in principle compensation possible but contrary solution preferable).
264 *See* for Germany: Magnus 72.
265 For Greece: Kerameus 32 (probably no compensation); Italy: Busnelli/Comandé 19 s (probably also no compensation); Netherlands: Wissink/van Boom 117; South Africa: Neethling 41; U.S.A.: Schwartz 29.
266 For Austria: Koziol 92; England: Rogers 70; Germany: Magnus 73.
267 Koziol, Rogers, Magnus *ibid.* But in case of a very slight injuries the prevailing view of German courts denies any 'Schmerzensgeld'.
268 *See* Galand-Carval 78.
269 Cousy/Vanderspikken 117.

12. Injured prostitute

[121] It is commonly agreed that an injured prostitute can at least recover some basic compensation for lost earnings[270] or lost earning capacity.[271] Full compensation for any lost earnings, however, is allowed by some of the reported countries, namely by Austria[272] and probably England,[273] Greece[274] and the Netherlands.[275] Belgian law, on the contrary, does not acknowledge damages for lost earnings, since they are deemed illegitimate.[276]

Damage to things

13. Mercedes case

[122] It is commonly accepted that the cost of a possible and reasonable repair is a suitable yardstick to measure the injured party's damage.[277] Thus in the present case at least 4,000 Euro can be recovered.[278] Only Austrian law requires in addition that repair must have been in fact undertaken.[279] And only German and Dutch law appear to provide the requirement that repair must still be possible.[280] According to some laws also diminution in value (2,000 Euro) plus lost profits (3,000 Euro) can be claimed instead of the costs of repair.[281] Again, the outcome depends on some policy weighing. It is submitted here that the injured party in general should choose the cheaper way of compensation if several ways exist on which entire compensation can be achieved.

14. Loss of use

(a) Lost use of car

[123] The laws under review agree on the point that the injured party can generally recover the cost of hiring a comparable vehicle.[282] Partly it is stressed that only reasonable costs may

---

270 For Germany: Magnus 74 (standard minimum income); probably also Italy: Busnelli/Comandé 97 (standard average income).

271 South Africa: Neethling 42; probably also France for 'incapacité temporaire'; U.S.A.: Schwartz 30.

272 Koziol 94.

273 Rogers 72s.

274 Kerameus 33.

275 Wissink/van Boom 118.

276 Cousy/Vanderspikken 118.

277 For Austria: Koziol 95ss; Belgium: Cousy/Vanderspikken 119ss; England: Rogers 74; France: Galand-Carval 80; Germany: Magnus 75; Greece: Kerameus 34; Italy: Busnelli/Comandé 99; Netherlands: Wissink/van Boom 119; South Africa: Neethling 43; U.S.A.: Schwartz 31.

278 *See* the precited authors.

279 Koziol 95.

280 For Germany: Magnus 75; Netherlands: Wissink/van Boom 119.

281 For Austria: Koziol 97 (but in case of gross negligence only); Germany: Magnus 75 (but only where repair is impossible); South Africa: Neethling 43; U.S.A.: Schwartz 31.

282 For Austria: Koziol 98; Belgium: Cousy/Vanderspikken 137; England: Rogers 75; France: Galand-Carval 81; Germany: Magnus 76; Greece: Kerameus 35; Italy: Busnelli/Comandé 100; Netherlands: Wissink/van Boom 120; South Africa: Neethling 44; doubted for the U.S.A.: Schwartz 32.

be incurred.[283] Austrian law exempts substitute costs for luxury models from compensation since that would contradict the injured party's duty to mitigate the damage.[284] German law disallows for the same reason the hiring of a substitute if the use of taxi would be cheaper. Moreover, regularly the injured party must deduct about 15 % from the hiring costs because of own savings.[285] If no substitute is hired French,[286] German,[287] Greek,[288] Italian[289] and South African[290] law award damages for the lost use while Austrian,[291] Dutch[292] and probably English[293] law refuse such a solution. As far as damages are granted, their amount corresponds either to the full rental costs of a substitute[294] or to a part of it.[295]

(b) Lost use of house

[124] By and large the lost use of the house is treated on the same footing as the lost use of a car.[296] Only Italian law seems to differentiate between them.[297] In Belgium, there are differing views.[298] Whether pure loss of use should be compensated has been already discussed (I. 9. (a)). The solution depends on which principle decision is adopted there.

15. Damaged, but unrepaired car

(a) Cost of fictitious repair

[125] The prevailing view is that the injured party can claim the 'fictitious' cost of repairs even if the damaged thing (car) has already been sold meanwhile. It is followed by Dutch, English, German, Italian and South African law.[299] It is argued by these laws that in most cases the cost of repairs represents correctly the loss of the injured party suffered;[300] furthermore the injured party is entitled to dispose of the awarded damages as he pleases and is

---

283 For Netherlands: Wissink/van Boom 120; South Africa: Neethling 13.
284 Koziol 98.
285 Magnus 76; Cousy/Vanderspikken 138 ('usually a lump sum').
286 Galand-Carval 81.
287 Magnus 77.
288 Kerameus 35.
289 Busnelli/Comandé 100.
290 Neethling 44.
291 Koziol 99.
292 Wissink/van Boom 121.
293 Rogers 75.
294 So does French; Greek and Italian law: Galand-Carval 81; Kerameus 35; Busnelli/Comandé 100.
295 So in Germany (30–40 % of rental costs): Magnus 77.
296 *See* for Austria: Koziol 99; England: Rogers 76; France: Galand-Carval 82; Germany: Magnus 78; Greece: Kerameus 35; Netherlands: Wissink/van Boom 122; South Africa: Neethling 45; U.S.A.: Schwartz 33.
297 Busnelli/Comandé 101.
298 Cousy/Vanderspikken 127.
299 For Belgium: Cousy/Vanderspikken 139 (not answered for sold car); England: Rogers 77; Germany: Magnus 79; Italy: Busnelli/Comandé 102ss; Netherlands: Wissink/van Boom 123; South Africa: Neethling 46.
300 *See* for England: Rogers 77.

therefore not obliged to repair.[301] On the other hand, Austrian, French and Greek law allow no damages for fictitious cost of repairs after sale of the damaged thing.[302] There, it is thought that under these circumstances the damage is the diminution in value only.

(b) Cost of repairs exceeding value of car

[126] It is commonly felt that cost of repairs (although in general a proper yardstick of damage) cannot be awarded in full if they considerably exceed the value of the damaged or of the repaired thing. According to the most favoured solution there is no claim for cost of repairs when it exceeds the value of the damaged thing. This solution is followed by Austria, Belgium, France, Greece, the U.S.A. and probably also by Italy.[303] Dutch and South African law regard the market value of the repaired car as the upper limit for compensation of cost of repair,[304] English law that of the undamaged car before the accident.[305] German law sets the limit even at 130 % of the value of the undamaged thing.[306]

[127] When the limit is exceeded, the diminution in value – the difference of the market value before and after the damaging event – seems to be the preferred measure of damage.[307]

(c) Cost of repairs exceeding diminution in value

[128] If the cost of repairs exceeds the diminution in value, many of the countries under review restrict compensation to the amount of the diminution.[308] Others do not regard diminution in value as decisive.[309]

(d) Summary

[129] In general cost of repairs is a suitable and practical standard to measure the extent of damage. However, cost of repair must not be out of proportion to the value of the damaged thing. It is therefore suggested that cost of repairs can only be recovered if it does not exceed the amount of diminution in value.

16. Additional car damages

(a) Accident car

[130] With the exception of Italian law[310] all reviewed laws agree that any remaining

301 *See* for Germany: Magnus 79.

302 For Austria: Koziol 101; France: Galand-Carval 83 (the claim depends on ownership); Greece: Kerameus 36.

303 *See* for Austria: Koziol 101ss; Belgium: Cousy/Vanderspikken 140; France: Galand-Carval 84; Greece: Kerameus 36; U.S.A.: Schwartz 11; Italy: Busnelli/Comandé 108s.

304 For the Netherlands: Wissink/van Boom 124s; South Africa: Neethling 47.

305 Rogers 78.

306 Magnus 80.

307 *See* expressly for Austria: Koziol 102; Greece: Kerameus 36.

308 For Austria: Koziol 103; Greece: Kerameus 36; Netherlands: Wissink/van Boom 126; South Africa: Neethling 48; U.S.A.: Schwartz 34.

309 For German law: Magnus 81; for Belgium: Cousy/Vanderspikken 140.

310 Busnelli/Comandé 110; disputed in Belgian jurisdiction: Cousy/Vanderspikken 141.

'diminution in value of the car not eliminated by the repairs' should be compensated.[311] A certain percentage of the cost of repairs could be taken to measure the reduced market value ('merkantiler Minderwert').[312]

(b) New for old

[131/132] Differing views are held whether deductions for new for old must be made.
[133] Some of our countries – Austria, Belgium, Germany, the Netherlands, sometimes Italy – prescribe deductions for those new parts which the injured party otherwise would have had to replace in future.[313] The main reason is that the injured party should not be enriched through damages. The other countries – England, France, Greece, South Africa and the U.S.A. – refuse any deduction.[314] The argument advanced here is that the injured party otherwise would be forced to spent money he would not have spent at that time.[315] Moreover, the amount of deduction is difficult to assess.[316]

(c) Useless rent for garage

[134] Whether the rent for the garage can be recovered is denied by the prevailing view. Austrian, Dutch, French, German, Greek, Italian and U.S. law do not recognise such a claim, although the solution is partly doubted in these countries.[317] Belgian, English and South African law allow, however, compensation for the futile expenses in principle.[318]
[135] The solution depends on, and should be in line with, the general principle which is adopted for the compensation of frustrated expenses.

17. Damaged railway wagon

[136] There is common agreement that the railway line should succeed in this case.[319] One

---

311 For Austria: Koziol 104; England: Rogers 79; France: Galand-Carval 85; Germany: Magnus 82; Greece: Kerameus 37; Netherlands: Wissink/van Boom 128; South Africa: Neethling 49 from whom the citation in the text is borrowed; U.S.A.: Schwartz 35.

312 German law knows of this method using figures of 10–30 %; Magnus 82.

313 For Austria: Koziol 105s; Belgium: Cousy/Vanderspikken 142; Germany: Magnus 83; Netherlands: Wissink/von Boom 129 (but disputed): In Italy the courts sometimes order deductions: Busnelli/Comandé 22.

314 For England: Rogers 80; France: Galand-Carval 86; Greece: Kerameus 37; South Africa: Neethling 50; U.S.A.: Schwartz 36.

315 *See* for France: Galand-Carval 46 (implicitly).

316 *See* for Greece: Kerameus 37.

317 For France: Galand-Carval 87; Germany: Magnus 84 (disputed); Greece: Kerameus 37; Italy: Busnelli/ Comandé 112; Netherlands: Wissink/van Boom 130 (because of missing causation); U.S.A.: Schwartz 37.

318 For Belgium: Cousy/Vanderspikken 143; England: Rogers 81; South Africa: Neethling 51.

319 For Austria: Koziol 107 (although the claim had to based on negotiorum gestio); England: Rogers 82; France: Galand-Carval 88; Germany: Magnus 85; probably also Greece: Kerameus 38; Netherlands: Wissink/van Boom 131; South Africa: Neethling 52; U.S.A.: Schwartz 38.

reason is that the injured party could have rented a substitute anyhow,[320] probably at higher cost. The preventive measure could also mitigate the damage.[321]

Pure economic loss

18. Detective case

[137] With the exception of German law[322] the answer of all other laws under review is negative on whether part of the detective's salary can be claimed.[323] Mainly, causation is denied. It is thought that the thief did not cause the payment of the detective's salary.[324] Under German law, the thief has to pay a modest contribution (regularly 50,- DM) to the cost of preventing thefts.[325] Mainly policy reasons found this solution.

Compensation of advantages and disadvantages; collateral benefits

19. Death of parents

[138] English, Belgian, French and U.S. law refuse to take account of any benefits which a child has from the estate of a parent killed by a third party when assessing the child's damages for loss of maintenance.[326] Greece and Italy probably follow the same solution.[327] Austria, Germany, the Netherlands and South Africa take the contrary view.[328]

[139] Under Austrian and German law, the inherited property has to be set off in full when the child would not have inherited under normal circumstances. If the child would have inherited anyhow, only the prior use of the property can be regarded as a benefit which must be set off.[329] Under Dutch law the need for maintenance is reduced by the inherited estate.[330] South African law takes into account any benefits from the estate without further restrictions.[331] It is suggested to follow the Dutch solution.

---

320 Neethling 52.

321 Wissink/van Boom 131; probably also Kerameus 38.

322 Magnus 86.

323 For Austria: Koziol 108; Belgium: Cousy/Vanderspikken 145; England: Rogers 83; France: Galand-Carval 89 (but doubting); Greece: Kerameus 39 (also doubting); Italy: Busnelli/Comandé 114; Netherlands: Wissink/van Boom 132s (doubting); South Africa: Neethling 53; U.S.A.: Schwartz 39.

324 So especially Koziol 108; Cousy/Vanderspikken 145, and Neethling 53; also Galand-Carval 89.

325 Magnus 86.

326 For Belgium: Cousy/Vanderspikken 146, 56ss; England: Rogers 84; France: Galand-Carval 90; U.S.A.: Schwartz 40.

327 For Greece: Kerameus 40; Italy: Busnelli/Comandé 115ss.

328 For Austria: Koziol 109s; Germany: Magnus 87s; Netherlands: Wissink/van Boom 134; South Africa: Neethling 54.

329 Koziol ibid; Magnus *ibid.*

330 Wissink/van Boom 18.

331 Neethling 54.

Index

Abortion 26, 117, 148, 149, 202
Actio legis Aquiliae 182, 184, 190
Actio iniuriarum 182, 184, 185
Actio vindictam spirans 182
Action civile 98
Adaptation of houses 52, 82, 100, 118, 131, 150, 175, 190, 202, 232
Abduction 188
Adultery 57, 188
Advantage 23, 25, 37, 46, 51, 78, 99, 116, 123, 130, 134, 147, 163, 164, 172, 189, 200, 227, 230, 242
Affektionsinteresse 112
Amenities, loss of 101, 185, 187, 190, 192, 219, 223
Assault 69, 73
Assessment, overall 18
Ausgleichsprinzip 105
Australia 86
Austria 11–33
Austrian
  Commercial Code 12
  Criminal Code 26
  Environmental Liability Act 23
  General Civil Code 11
  General Social Insurance Act 28
  Insurance Act 28
  Media Act 16, 29, 30
  Railway and Motorcar Liability Act 24
  Supreme Court 12, 15, 17, 18, 22, 23, 25, 26, 27, 29, 30, 31

Barèmes d'indemnisation 95, 220
Bargaining agreement 168
Belgian
  Act on Claims/Environment 44
  Act on Commercial Practices 43
  Act on Consumer Credit 43
  Act on Employment Contracts 53
  Act on Legal Actions/Environment 43
  Act on Misleading Publicity 43
  Cour de Cassation 36, 37, 38, 39, 40, 45, 48, 51, 57, 58, 60, 62, 63
  Financial Services Act 43
  Product Liability Act 39, 51
Belgium 35–64
Benefits 89, 92, 183, 186, 201, 202, 243
  collateral 68, 79, 83, 99, 188, 227, 228, 242
  patrimonial 178
Bereavement 225

Calcolo a punto 143
Calculation 40, 168, 169
  objective-abstract ~ 19, 20, 23, 26, 28, 31, 220
  subjective-concrete ~ 19, 23, 220, 227
Capitalisation 39–41, 48, 54, 57, 186
Case law 68, 91, 139, 140, 143, 171
Causation 67, 125, 130, 131, 133, 134, 140, 141, 158, 163, 164, 166, 171, 177, 179, 184, 193, 217, 224, 242
Cessio legis 118
Chefs de préjudice 219
Class action 43, 98, 201
Clause pénal 36
Coincidence 49
Collateral source rule 186, 188, 203
Comatose 29, 76, 82, 101, 235
Commercial transactions 12, 14
Common law 70, 85, 198, 200, 225
  strict liability at ~ 75
  system 66
  principles 68
Compensatio lucri cum damno 158
Compensation 11, 12, 13, 15, 20, 21, 22, 29, 35, 91, 113, 126, 135, 136, 137, 164, 182, 209
  claim for ~ 12
  complete (full) ~ 12, 13, 37, 40, 46, 52, 63, 92, 106, 107, 111, 126, 132, 144, 162, 163, 181, 182, 195, 197, 212, 219
  extent of ~ 19
  in kind 15, 17
  in money (monetary ~) 13, 14, 15, 16, 17, 30, 35, 36, 37, 45, 59, 107, 108, 110, 113, 125, 136, 163, 185, 213, 214, 216
  in natura 93, 125
  limited ~ 12, 212
  principle 105
  symbolic ~ 38, 45
Competition, unfair 92
Consortium, loss of 22, 42, 77, 97, 114, 115, 129, 145, 171, 187, 188, 200, 202, 225
Consumer
  organisations 43
  protection 129
Contract 66, 70, 75, 114, 140
  breach of ~ 17, 21, 35, 36, 68, 69, 71, 73, 85, 91, 93, 94, 135, 146, 148, 155, 161, 165, 181, 190, 198, 221, 230
  validity of ~ 22

Contracts
  employment ~ 110
  insurance ~ 161, 166, 173
  medical ~ 25, 149
  sales ~ 116
  tourist travel ~ 21, 114, 145, 223
  transportation ~ 212
Contractual
  liability 11, 12, 105, 125, 126, 135, 148, 169
  warranty 72
Copyright 70, 71, 162, 167
Cosmetic surgery 175, 203
Costs
  fictual ~ 62
  judicial ~ 14, 68, 108, 163, 164, 166, 183, 213
  living ~ 26, 49, 56, 57, 58, 131, 149
  medical ~ 26, 27, 50, 51, 81, 82, 85, 92, 100, 113, 118, 120, 127, 149, 174, 189, 190, 191, 197, 202, 221, 231, 232

Damage
  actual ~ 16, 37, 38, 41, 75, 127,131, 133, 140, 145, 167, 217
  by non-performance 15
  certainty of ~ 47, 79, 99, 102, 116, 130, 147, 173, 189, 201, 228
  contractual ~ 111, 142, 167, 184, 216, 217, 218
  direct ~ 217
  ecological ~ 23, 43, 44, 78, 98, 108, 109, 115, 129, 136, 147, 164, 166, 172, 188, 201, 226, 227
  economic ~ 140, 141, 159
  future ~ 40, 44, 48, 139, 140, 163, 164, 167, 175, 181, 182, 199, 217
  hypothetical ~ 49, 59
  immaterial ~ 11, 12, 13, 14, 16, 27, 109
  indirect ~ 217
  in reality (real ~) 15
  legal definition of ~ 14, 69, 94, 109, 126, 138, 164, 183, 198, 214, 215
  moral ~ 39, 42, 50, 55, 56, 58, 73, 91, 95, 96, 97, 98, 100, 102, 128, 135, 137, 142, 150, 154, 155, 218
  non-contractual ~ 139, 141
  non-economic 141
  non-monetary ~ 198
  non-patrimonial ~ 14, 15, 16, 17, 21, 39, 44, 72, 95, 110, 111, 126, 128, 141, 142, 144, 162, 163, 164, 165, 167, 168, 170, 171, 173, 182, 185, 190, 198
  non-pecuniary ~ 12, 29, 95, 107, 109, 110, 131, 136, 152, 192, 198, 210, 211, 212, 214, 218, 219, 222
  notion of ~ 14
  patrimonial ~ 14, 15, 16, 17, 19, 20, 21, 39, 73, 110, 112, 113, 128, 141, 142, 143, 144, 145, 148, 163, 164, 165, 166, 170, 171, 172, 175, 179, 185, 190, 199
  pecuniary ~ 110, 152, 214, 218, 220, 221, 223, 230
  primary (direct) ~ 16
  psychological ~ 100, 146
  tortious ~ 111, 167
  types of ~ 15, 39, 110, 126, 127, 136, 139, 163, 165, 182, 184, 197, 198, 213, 216
  wanton ~ 12, 17
Damages
  aggravated ~ 108, 182, 209, 213, 214
  avoided ~ 37
  collective ~ 23, 43, 78, 98, 115, 129, 146, 171, 188, 201, 226, 227
  compensatory ~ 67, 76, 126, 163, 197
  exemplary ~ 38, 66, 67, 73, 76, 91, 93, 108, 163, 182, 209, 213, 214
  measurement of ~ 14
  nominal ~ 13, 38, 67, 93, 106, 108, 163, 183, 197, 209, 211, 213, 214
  personal ~ 39, 44
  punitive ~ 13, 38, 58, 91, 93, 98, 106, 108, 163, 164, 182, 197, 198, 204, 210
  restitutionary ~ 66, 67, 209, 211
  symbolic ~ 211, 213
  vindictive ~ 182
Damnum emergens 70, 93, 94, 111, 127, 137, 138, 141, 150, 165, 184, 214, 217
Dangerousness 13
Danno alla salute 142, 143, 144, 145, 149, 150, 151, 152, 153
Danno biologico 142
Danno da fermo tecnico 156
Danno futuro 140
Data 168
Death 48, 56, 58, 64, 69, 73, 84, 88, 103, 119, 123, 132, 134, 137, 146, 152, 158, 166, 170, 171, 173, 181, 183, 196, 203, 206, 225, 226, 235, 236, 242
Debt, monetary 19
Declaration of right 211
Dédommagement symbolique 93
Defamation 29, 65, 68, 132, 154, 162, 204, 213, 236
Detention 73, 168
Deterrence 35, 66, 197
Deutscher Juristentag 115

Differenz ~
hypothese 110, 112, 215, 219
methode 19, 23, 220
theorie 138
Dignity 142
Discretion, judicial 162
Discrimination 110, 200
Disfigurement 190, 192
Disposicion adicional 144
Domestic services 77
Drittschäden 118
Due care 35
Dutch
Code of Civil Procedure 166
Code of Criminal Procedure 168
Hoge Raad 169, 174
Uitleveringswet 168
Vreemdelingenwet 168
Wegenverkeerswet 168
Wet op de CAO 168
Wet Persoonsregistraties 168
Duty of care 26, 36, 70

Earning capacity 20, 22, 25, 26, 40, 42, 53, 73, 76, 84, 97, 101, 114, 118, 119, 120, 132, 139, 151, 170, 175, 176, 183, 187, 190, 191, 193, 200, 202, 204, 223, 226, 232, 233, 234, 238
Earnings 73, 118
expected ~ 40
future ~ 71, 73, 97, 127, 170, 187, 190, 203, 223, 234, 235
illegal ~ 133, 236
lost ~ 21, 24, 25, 26, 28, 29, 43, 53, 81, 82, 83, 86, 100, 101, 117, 132, 149, 150, 174, 175, 188, 190, 203, 230, 233, 238
EC
Directive on Product Liability 39, 51, 137
Economic analysis of law 105
Eisenbahn- und KraftfahrzeughaftpflichtG 16
Emotional
pain (suffering) 27, 28, 42
trauma 77
Employer 23, 28, 166, 233
Employment, future 56
England 65–89
English
Administration of Justice Act 89
Animals Act 75
Court of Appeal 65, 66, 73, 78, 85, 87, 89
Damages Act 68
Fatal Accidents Act 77, 85, 88
Social Security Act 83

Enjoyments, lost 199, 202
Environmental tort cases 38, 44
European Convention on Human Rights 168
Evidence 217, 218
Expectation, loss of 70, 111
Expenses 15, 21, 22, 30, 32, 42, 73, 74, 85, 96, 114, 119, 127, 131, 166, 169, 170, 175, 187, 193, 194, 224, 237, 242
Eyesight 27, 51, 81, 100, 118, 131, 149, 174, 190, 202, 232

Fault 11, 36, 125, 141
degree (gravity) of ~ 11, 12, 18, 107, 111, 126, 130, 163, 167, 212, 219, 220, 222, 236
victim's own ~ 39, 183, 222
Fees, legal 14, 68, 108, 163, 164, 166, 197, 213
Feststellungsklage 106
Floodgates 146
Forseeability of loss 141, 177
France 91–103
Franc symbolique 98
Fraud 69, 165
Free time 21, 42, 77, 114, 145, 170, 187, 223
French
Code de procédure civile 94
Conseil d'Etat 100
Cour de cassation 91, 93, 94, 95, 99, 100, 101, 103
Nouveau code de procédure civile 94
Frustrationslehre 114
Funeral expenses 152

Genugtuungsfunktion 106
German
Civil Procedure Code 108
Commercial Code 112
Entgeltfortzahlungsgesetz 118
Federal Court 115, 117, 120, 123
Gentechnikgesetz 108
RegelunterhaltsVO 117
Straßenverkehrsgesetz 120
Umwelthaftungsgesetz 108, 115
Germany 105–123
Globalisation 137, 144
Good faith 163
Governmental bodies 161
Greece 125–134
Greek
Code of Civil Procedure 129
Court of Cassation 128
Supreme Court 125, 127

Handicap 26, 27, 50, 52, 81, 100, 117, 118, 202, 231, 232
Holiday 21, 42, 77, 85, 86, 110, 114, 145, 155, 168, 170, 187, 200, 223
Honour 44, 126
Hospital visits 27, 52, 82, 100, 118, 131, 150, 166, 175, 190, 202, 232
House of Lords 74, 75
Housekeeping 48, 57, 58, 97, 109, 114, 115, 132, 152

Imprisonment 65, 69
Imputation test 177
Incapacity 54, 55, 56
Income
- annual ~ 96
- loss of ~ 22, 53, 54, 56, 57, 59, 70, 99, 113, 119, 176, 177, 187, 189, 191, 193, 197, 199, 200, 202, 204, 221, 223, 234

Indemnités 95
Index Linked Government Stocks 74
Industrial accidents 55
Inflation 49, 74, 75, 92
Injured
- party 12
- person 11, 12

Injurer 12, 16
Injury
- bodily ~ 16, 18, 21, 22, 30, 65, 69, 70, 73, 74, 75, 91, 95, 110, 111, 137, 139, 153, 164, 167, 169, 170, 172, 174, 177, 182, 187, 188, 199, 216, 221

Insurance 22, 23, 28, 63, 79, 83, 85, 92, 96, 111, 135, 144, 169, 173, 178, 183, 193, 205, 228
Integritätsinteresse 20
Intellectual property 112
Intent 12, 15, 16, 17, 18, 21, 217
Interest rate 63, 74, 75, 93, 164, 169
Invalidity 39, 48, 51, 53, 54, 55, 188
Italian
- Constitutional Court 136, 137, 138, 139, 142, 143, 144, 145, 148
- Corte di Cassazione 137, 138, 139, 140, 142, 143, 146, 148, 151, 153, 154
- National Research Council 143
- product liability law 149
- Workers' Compensation Act 137

Italy 135–159

Judge, role of 66

Kantongerechtsformule 169

Law
- administrative ~ 161
- contract ~ 11, 35, 67, 181, 212, 216, 221, 231
- criminal ~ 12, 17
- environmental ~ 214
- of damages, aims of ~ 11, 12, 35, 36, 65, 91, 105, 125, 135, 162, 197, 209
- of damages, general principles 12, 37, 67, 91, 107, 125, 135, 163, 181, 197, 212
- of obligations 161
- procedural ~ 14
- tort ~ 11, 12, 91, 162
- transport ~ 164, 212

Law Commission 66, 73
Legislation on damages 14, 39, 68, 93, 108, 126, 137, 164, 183, 197, 214
Liability 69, 79, 83, 105, 111, 125, 136, 137, 161, 162, 164, 166, 167, 184, 197, 198, 199, 200, 216, 230
- contractual ~ 11, 12, 36, 148, 169
- delictual ~ 126, 127, 129
- fault ~ 11, 12, 75
- limitation of ~ 93, 136, 172, 217
- pre-contractual ~ 126
- professional ~ 169
- strict ~ 11–14, 16, 27, 35, 75, 95, 107, 147, 150, 161, 166, 199, 212, 214
- tortious ~ 11, 135, 141, 169

Libel 69, 71, 73
Liberty 66, 73
Licence 45, 112
Life expectancy 57, 96, 185, 192, 234
Limit of liability 39, 184, 185
Limits 117, 164, 183, 198, 212, 214
Locus standi 98
Loss
- abstract ~ 112
- actual ~ 13, 14, 15, 19, 30, 106, 112, 150, 154, 182, 210, 212, 217, 218
- consequential ~ 70, 74, 76, 86
- contractual ~ 15, 39, 184
- delictual ~ 184
- direct ~ 70, 167, 184
- ecological ~ 98
- economic ~ 16, 69, 70, 84, 91, 92, 95, 98, 103, 111, 134, 137, 138, 139, 140, 152, 166, 167, 172, 184, 198, 199, 216, 217, 221, 233, 242
- future ~ 70, 99, 113, 184, 217, 218
- illegitimate ~ 22, 43, 77, 98, 115, 129, 146, 171, 188, 200, 226
- immaterial ~ 17, 22, 29, 30, 66, 70, 110, 212, 216, 219, 235, 236

indirect ~ 184
legitimate ~ 102
material ~ 71
moral ~ 127, 131
non-pecuniary ~ 18, 29, 39, 71, 72, 81, 82, 85, 95, 96, 101, 141, 185, 212, 216, 219, 235, 237
non-patrimonial ~ 71, 127, 162, 165, 174, 176, 183, 184, 186
patrimonial ~ 71, 175, 177, 183, 184, 185, 186, 188
pecuniary ~ 69, 71, 72, 84, 95, 96, 136, 212, 216, 220, 221, 222, 236
prospective ~ 15
psychological ~ 101
of affection 39
of chance 140, 169
of opportunity 71
of services 29, 236
of use 20, 31, 42, 59–61, 63, 76, 87, 88, 96, 97, 102, 110, 113, 121, 133, 156, 170, 177, 187, 194, 204, 222, 223, 239
tortious ~ 15, 39
transferred ~ 19
Lucrum cessans 70, 93, 94, 111, 127, 137, 140, 141, 144, 150, 184, 214, 217
Lugano Convention 129
Lump sum 24, 36, 49, 56, 58, 62, 68, 73, 80, 99, 109, 116, 117, 130, 147, 173, 189, 201, 229

Maintenance 24, 25, 29, 50, 51, 117, 118, 119, 123, 132, 148, 153, 159, 166, 173, 174, 176, 181, 187, 190, 192, 196, 230, 231, 236, 243
Malpractice, medical 148, 149, 198
Market value (price) 12, 14, 17, 19, 20, 21, 30, 31, 71, 74, 112, 127, 157, 164, 177, 178, 187, 194, 195, 204, 216, 218, 221, 240, 241
Maximum amounts 13, 14
Media 29, 30, 112, 164, 210, 236
Mental distress 69, 71
Merkantiler Minderwert 31, 122, 133, 241
Mitigation 70, 163, 166, 212, 239, 242

Naturalrestitution 107
Negatives Interesse 184, 216
Negligence 12, 13, 14, 15, 16, 17, 18, 19, 27, 30, 31, 56, 63, 67, 69, 75, 79, 95, 103, 107, 119, 120, 163, 178, 186, 193, 195, 197, 198, 200, 205, 212, 217, 236
Netherlands 161–179
New Zealand 86
Nichtvermögensschaden 110
Non-marital partner 57, 94, 119, 132, 153, 166, 176, 192, 203, 225, 235, 236
Normzweck 22
Nuisance 95

Obligation 15, 36, 161, 164, 181
Ommission, wrongful 36

Pain and suffering 12, 16, 17, 19, 22, 25, 27, 30, 38, 39, 48, 51, 57, 69, 71, 73, 95, 105, 107, 110, 111, 112, 114, 117, 118, 119, 120, 154, 167, 174, 182, 185, 190, 191, 192, 197, 198, 199, 203, 218, 219, 223, 224, 230, 231, 232, 233, 235, 237
Patent 70
Patrimony 218
Pecunia doloris 142
Pecunia lesae dignitatis 142
Penalty 106, 126, 161, 162, 163, 182
Pension 83, 92, 144, 158, 183
Per-diem argument 198
Periodic payments 201
Personality
damage to ~ 16, 29, 185, 218
right of ~ 18, 112, 128, 168
rights 38, 96, 105, 110
Perte de jouissance 102
Plaintiff 12, 13, 16, 19, 20, 22, 23, 24, 30, 38, 44, 45, 60, 62, 65, 66, 67, 68, 69, 71, 72, 74, 75, 76, 77, 78, 79, 81, 82, 83, 84, 85, 86, 87, 92, 94, 96, 126, 133, 150, 158, 182, 186, 187, 188, 189, 191, 193, 194, 197, 198, 201, 205, 221
Pollution 44, 98, 172, 226
Positives Interesse 184, 216
Pregnancy 25, 50, 81, 117, 149, 174, 230, 231
Préjudice d'affection 101
Préjudice d'agrément 39, 100, 219, 237
Préjudice esthétique 217
Préjudice particulier 100
Préjudice physiologique 95
Préjudice sexuel 219
Pretium doloris 39, 100, 101, 115, 119, 120, 142, 149, 150, 153, 154, 192, 219, 235
Pretium voluptatis 39
Prevention 11, 35, 92, 98, 105, 108, 162, 209, 210, 211
Profit 38, 58, 72, 76, 164, 169, 198, 211
lost ~ 12, 14, 15, 16, 17, 20, 21, 24, 97, 109, 115, 121, 127, 131, 135, 137, 156, 163, 165, 177, 184, 194, 212, 215
illegitimate ~ 22, 66, 106, 224

Property 22, 32, 33, 70, 75
damage of ~ 12, 14, 16, 17, 18, 19, 20, 21, 44, 60, 69, 74, 92, 95, 96, 97, 98, 101, 109, 111, 139, 166, 168, 172, 184, 194, 200, 217, 224
intellectual ~ 211
use of ~ 66, 170
Prostitution 22, 30, 59, 86, 94, 102, 115, 120, 133, 155, 171, 176, 193, 204, 226, 238
Protection
legal ~ 12, 126
Protective purpose 26
Psychiatric illness 69, 77, 168
Public decency 39, 59
Public health service 81
Publicity, harmful 38, 58, 85, 102, 120, 132, 154, 176, 193, 204, 236
Public policy 188, 189
Punishment 38, 92, 105, 106, 126, 210, 211

Quadriplegia 84, 112

Reasonableness 115, 128, 136, 166, 170, 172, 174, 177, 178, 181, 190, 191, 224, 227
Rechtsfortsetzungs ~
funktion 12, 19, 209
gedanke 106
Rechtsfortwirkungsgedanke 23
Remoteness 67, 70, 71
Rent 24, 26, 41, 54, 80, 99, 116, 117, 119, 130, 147, 173, 189, 201, 229, 234
Repair 20–22, 30–32, 37, 42, 59–61, 70, 74, 75, 77, 85, 86, 87, 93, 96, 97, 101, 102, 103, 113, 114, 121, 122, 133, 134, 156, 157, 169, 170, 177, 178, 181, 187, 194, 195, 200, 204, 205, 213, 221, 222, 224, 238, 239, 240, 241
Reputation
infringement of ~ 16, 44, 66, 69, 71, 73, 102, 154, 155, 167, 213, 216, 218
Restitutio in integrum 162, 212
Restitution
costs 108
infeasible ~ 108, 109
in kind 13, 14, 20, 32, 107, 110, 213, 214
of benefits 38
of damage 125
principle 121
Restoration 20, 31
Right
value of an existing ~ 15
Rules of evidence 162

Sanction 11, 108, 135, 210, 211
Satisfaction 106, 108, 136, 141, 181, 182
Schaden
erlittener ~ 14
ideeller ~ 16
realer ~ 15
wirklicher (positiver) ~ 14
Schadensminderungspflicht 31
Schadloshaltung, eigentliche 12
Schutznorm 167, 171, 181
Schmerzensgeld 30, 109, 111, 112, 114
Schmerzensgeldtabellen 112
Selbstbindung ohne Vertrag 139
Sexual intercourse 153
Shares 71
Shock, emotional 22, 42, 77, 97, 114, 115, 129, 145, 171, 185, 187, 188, 192, 193, 200, 225
Social security 53, 83, 92, 101, 119, 133, 135, 137, 149, 150, 161, 228
South Africa 181–196
South African
Apportionment of Damages Act 183
Apportionment of Damages Amendment Act 183
Assessment of Damages Act 183
Compensation for Occupational Injuries and Diseases Act 183, 187
Legal Succession to the South African Transport Services Act 183
Road Accident Fund Act 183, 189
Specific performance 37, 45
Splitsingsmethode 39, 48
Spouse, lost 56, 84, 101, 119, 132, 152, 176, 192, 203, 235
Standardisation 41, 73, 96, 113, 128, 167, 169, 187, 199, 220, 221
Sterilisation 25, 50, 149, 230, 231
Structured settlement 201
Subjective right 44
Sums, fixed statutory 18
Support, loss of 183
Swiss Code of Obligations 146

Tabellazione Indicativa Nazionale 143, 144
Tables 41, 49, 143
Tariffs, judicial 18, 41, 60, 69, 72, 73, 74, 82, 95
Tax 22, 86, 89, 171, 172
Theft 63, 158, 181, 195, 242
Tortfeasor 12, 14, 15, 16, 17, 19, 20, 21, 22, 23, 27, 28, 29, 32, 35, 37, 45, 47, 53, 128, 136, 150, 210, 226, 233
Totalreparation 107, 109
Trade union 94, 181

Trade value 12
Transactions, legal 15
Transportation 63, 172
Troubles du voisinage 93

United States 197–206
  Supreme Court 204

Value
  decrease of ~ 31, 86, 88, 103, 107, 108, 109, 156, 178, 205, 238, 240, 241
  economic ~ 56, 57, 58, 110, 221
  mercantile ~ 19
  monetary ~ 71
  sentimental (affection) ~ 12, 17, 19, 20, 21, 74
Vasectomy 50
VAT 60
Vermögensschaden 110
Vorteilsausgleichung 116, 123

Wages *see earnings*
Warsaw Convention 136
Wertersatz 108
Wert, gemeiner 14
Workers' compensation 137, 151, 197
Working capacity 97
Worth, objective 113
Wrongful
  birth 50, 51, 81, 100, 117, 131, 148, 174, 190, 202, 230
  life 50, 51, 81, 100, 117, 131, 149, 174, 190, 202, 231
Wrongfulness 140

www.ingramcontent.com/pod-product-compliance
Lightning Source LLC
Chambersburg PA
CBHW071243230926
51849CB00001B/214
9789041114815